ISBN: 9781313876728

Published by:
HardPress Publishing
8345 NW 66TH ST #2561
MIAMI FL 33166-2626

Email: info@hardpress.net
Web: http://www.hardpress.net

EZEKIEL'S STATUE OF RELIGIOUS LIBERTY
IN FAIRMOUNT PARK, PHILADELPHIA.

HISTORY OF THE JEWS IN AMERICA

FROM THE PERIOD OF THE DISCOVERY OF THE NEW WORLD TO THE PRESENT TIME

BY

PETER WIERNIK

NEW YORK

THE JEWISH PRESS PUBLISHING COMPANY

1912

PREFACE.

There were less than ten thousand Jews in the New World three centuries after its discovery, and about two-thirds of them lived in the West Indies and in Surinam or Dutch Guiana in South America. While the communities in those far-away places are now larger in membership than they were at the beginning of the Nineteenth Century, their comparative importance is much diminished. The two or three thousand Jews who lived in North America or in the United States one hundred years ago have, on the other hand, increased to nearly as many millions, the bulk of them having come in the last three or four decades. On this account neither our conditions nor our problems can be thoroughly understood without the consideration of the actual present. The plan of other works of this kind, to devote only a short concluding chapter to the present time, or to leave it altogether for the future historian, could therefore not be followed in this work. The story would be less than half told, if attention were not paid to contemporary history.

The chief aim of the work—the first of its kind in this complete form—being to reach the ordinary reader who is interested in Jewish matters in a general way, original investigations and learned disquisitions were avoided, and it was not deemed advisable to overburden the book with too many notes or to provide a bibliographical apparatus. The plan and scope of the work are self evident; it was inevitable that a disproportionately large part should be devoted to the United States. The continuity of Jewish history is made possible only by the preservation of our identity as a religious community; local history really begins with the formation of a congregation. Each of the successive strata of immigration was originally represented by its own synagogues and when the struggle to gain a foothold or to remove disabilities was over, communal activity was the only one which could properly be described as Jewish. Economic growth could have been entirely neglected, despite the present day tendency to consider every possible problem from the standpoint of economics. But the material well-being of the Jews of the earlier periods was an important factor in the preparation for the reception and easy absorption of the larger masses which came later, and this gives wealth a meaning which, in the hands of people who are less responsible for one another than Jews, it does not possess. The Marrano of the Seventeenth or the Eighteenth Century who brought here riches far in excess of what he found among the inhabitants in the places where he settled, would probably not have been admitted if he came as a poor immigrant, and his merit as a pioneer of trade and industry interests us because he assisted to make this country a place where hosts of men can come and find work to do. Without this only a small number could enjoy the liberty and equality which an enlightened republic vouchsafes to every newcomer without distinction of race or creed.

Still these absorbingly interesting early periods had to be passed over briefly, despite the wealth of available material to keep within the bounds of a single volume, and to be able to carry out the plan of including in the narrative a comprehensive view of the near past and the present. While no excuse is necessary for making the latter part of the work longer than the earlier, though in most works the inequality is the other way, the author regrets the scarcity of available sources for the history of the Jewish immigration from Slavic countries other than Russia. There were times when German Jewish historians were reproached with neglecting the Jews of Russia. In those times there was a scarcity of necessary *"Vorarbeiten"* or preparation of material for the history of the Jews of that Empire. To-day as far as the history of the Jewish immigrant in America is concerned, the scarcity is still greater as far as it concerns the Jews who came from Austria and Roumania.

The principal sources which were utilized in the preparation of this work are: *The Publications of the American Jewish Historical Society* (20 vols., 1893-1911), which are referred to as "Publications"; *The Jewish Encyclopedia* (Funk and Wagnalls, 12 vols., 1901-6); *The Settlement of the Jews in North America*, by Judge Charles P. Daly, edited by Max J. Kohler (New York, 1893), often referred to as "Daly"; *The Hebrews in America*, by Isaac Markens (New York, 1888); *The American Jew as Patriot, Soldier and Citizen*, by the Hon. Simon Wolf, edited by Louis Edward Levy (Philadelphia, 1895). Other works, like Dr. Kayserling's *Christopher Columbus*, Mr. Pierce Butler's *Judah P. Benjamin* (of the American Crisis Biographies, Philadelphia, 1906) and the Rev. Henry S. Morais' *Jews of Philadelphia*, were also drawn upon for much valuable material which they made accessible. All of these works were used to a larger extent than is indicated by the references or foot-notes, and my indebtedness to them is herewith gratefully acknowledged.

Where biographical dates are given after the name of a person born in a foreign country, the date of arrival in the New World is often fully as important as that of birth or death. This date is indicated in the text by an *a.*, which stands for *arrived*, as *b.* stands for *born* and *d.* for *died*.

In conclusion I gladly record my obligation to Mr. Abraham S. Freidus of the New York Public Library for aid in the gathering of material; to Mr. Isaiah Gamble for re-reading of the proofs; to Mr. Samuel Vaisberg for seeing the work through the press, and to my sister, Bertha Wiernik, for assistance in the preparation of the index.

P. W., New York, July, 1912.

CONTENTS.

PART I.

THE SPANISH AND PORTUGUESE PERIOD.

CHAPTER I.

THE PARTICIPATION OF JEWS IN THE DISCOVERY OF THE NEW WORLD.

CHAPTER II.

EARLY JEWISH MARTYRS UNDER SPANISH RULE IN THE NEW WORLD.

CHAPTER III.

VICTIMS OF THE INQUISITION IN MEXICO AND IN PERU.

CHAPTER IV.

MARRANOS IN THE PORTUGUESE COLONIES.

PART II.

THE DUTCH AND ENGLISH COLONIAL PERIOD.

CHAPTER V.

THE SHORT-LIVED DOMINION OF THE DUTCH OVER BRAZIL.

CHAPTER VI.

RECIFE: THE FIRST JEWISH COMMUNITY IN THE NEW WORLD.

CHAPTER VII.

THE JEWS IN SURINAM OR DUTCH GUIANA.

CHAPTER VIII.

THE DUTCH AND ENGLISH WEST INDIES.

CHAPTER IX.

NEW AMSTERDAM AND NEW YORK.

CHAPTER X.

NEW ENGLAND AND THE OTHER ENGLISH COLONIES.

PART III.

THE REVOLUTION AND THE PERIOD OF EXPANSION.

CHAPTER XI.

THE RELIGIOUS ASPECT OF THE WAR OF INDEPENDENCE.

in North Carolina that the Pope might be elected President of the United States—None of the liberties won were lost by post-revolutionary reaction, as happened elsewhere. . . . . Page 80

CHAPTER XII.

HE PARTICIPATION OF JEWS IN THE WAR OF THE REVOLUTION.

aptain Isaac Meyers of the French and Indian War of 1754—David S. Franks and Isaac Franks—David Franks, the loyalist—Solomon and Lewis Bush—Major Benjamin Nones—Other Jewish Soldiers, of whom one was exempted from duty on Friday nights—The Pinto brothers—Commissary General Mordecai Sheftal of Georgia—Haym Salomon, the Polish Jew, and his financial assistance to the Revolution. . . . . Page 87

CHAPTER XIII.

THE DECLINE OF NEWPORT; WASHINGTON AND THE JEWS.

England's special enmity to Newport caused the dispersion of its Jewish congregation—The General Assembly of Rhode Island meets in the historic Newport Synagogue—Moses Seixas' address to Washington on behalf of the Jews of Newport and the latter's reply—Washington's letters to the Hebrew Congregations of Savannah, Ga., and to the congregations of Philadelphia, New York, Richmond and Charleston. . . . . Page 98

CHAPTER XIV.

OTHER COMMUNITIES IN THE FIRST PERIODS OF INDEPENDENCE.

Rabbi Gershom Mendez Seixas—Growth of the Jewish community of Philadelphia on account of the War—Protest against the religious test clause in the Constitution of Pennsylvania—Benjamin Franklin contributes five pounds to Mickweh Israel—Secession of the German-Polish element—New Societies—Jewish lawyers; Judge Moses Levy—Congressman H. M. Phillips—The Bush family of Delaware—New Jersey and New Hampshire—North Carolina: the Mordecai family and other early settlers. . . . . Page 104

CHAPTER XV.

THE QUESTION OF RELIGIOUS LIBERTY IN VIRGINIA AND I] NORTH CAROLINA.

CHAPTER XVI.

THE WAR OF 1812 AND THE REMOVAL OF JEWISH DISABILITIE IN MARYLAND.

CHAPTER XVII.

MORDECAI MANUEL NOAH AND HIS TERRITORIALIST-ZIONISTI PLANS.

pressive ceremonies in Buffalo which were the beginning and the end of "Ararat"—His "Discourse on the Restoration of the Jews"—Short career on the bench—Jewish activities. .... Page 128

PART IV.

THE SECOND OR GERMAN PERIOD OF IMMIGRATION.

CHAPTER XVIII.

THE FIRST COMMUNITIES IN THE MISSISSIPPI VALLEY.

npetus given to immigration to America by the reaction after the fall of Napoleon—The second period of Jewish immigration—First legislation about immigration (1819)—The first Jew in Cincinnati—Its first congregation, Bene Israel—Appeals to outside communities for funds to build a synagogue—The first Talmud Torah—Rabbis Gutheim, Wise and Lilienthal—Cleveland—St. Louis—Louisville—Mobile—Montgomery and its alleged Jewish founder, Abraham Mordecai—Savannah and Augusta—New Orleans—Judah Touro .... Page 135

CHAPTER XIX.

EW SETTLEMENTS IN THE MIDDLE WEST AND ON THE PACIFIC COAST.

ıcrease in general immigration—Estimated increase in the number of Jews—The natural dispersion of small traders over the country—Chicago—First congregations and other communal institutions—Indiana—Iowa: Polish Jews settle in Keokuk and German Jews in Davenport—Minnesota—Wisconsin—Congregation "Bet El" of Detroit, Mich.—The first "minyan of gold seekers in San Francisco—"Mining congregations"—Solomon Heydenfeldt—Portland, Oregon .... Page 149

CHAPTER XX

THE JEWS IN THE EARLY HISTORY OF TEXAS. THE MEXICA WAR.

CHAPTER XXI.

THE RELIGIOUS REFORM MOVEMENT.

CHAPTER XXII.

CONSERVATIVE JUDAISM AND ITS STAND AGAINST REFORM.

CHAPTER XXIII.

INTERVENTION IN DAMASCUS. THE STRUGGLE AGAINST SWISS DISCRIMINATION.

PART V.

THE CIVIL WAR AND THE FORMATIVE PERIOD.

CHAPTER XXIV.

THE DISCUSSION ABOUT SLAVERY. LINCOLN AND THE JEWS.

CHAPTER XXV.

PARTICIPATION OF JEWS IN THE CIVIL WAR. JUDAH P. BENJAMIN.

CHAPTER XXVIII.

NEW SYNAGOGUES AND TEMPLES. IMMIGRATION FROM RUSSIA PRIOR TO 1880.

PART VI.

THE THIRD OR RUSSIAN PERIOD OF IMMIGRATION.

CHAPTER XXIX.

THE INFLUX AFTER THE ANTI-JEWISH RIOTS IN RUSSIA IN 1881.

CHAPTER XXX.

COMMUNAL AND RELIGIOUS ACTIVITIES AMONG THE NEW COMERS.

PART VII.

THE TWENTIETH CENTURY. PRESENT CONDITIONS.

CHAPTER XXXVI.

SYNAGOGUES AND INSTITUTIONS. THE ENCYCLOPEDIA. ROUMANIA AND THE ROUMANIAN NOTE.

CHAPTER XXXVII.

HELP FOR THE VICTIMS OF THE RUSSIAN MASSACRES IN 1903 AND 1905. OTHER PROOFS OF SYMPATHY.

CHAPTER XXXVIII.

THE AMERICAN-JEWISH COMMITTEE. EDUCATIONAL INSTITUTIONS AND FEDERATIONS.

CHAPTER XXXIX.

THE JEWS IN THE DOMINION OF CANADA.

CHAPTER XL.

JEWS IN SOUTH AMERICA, MEXICO AND CUBA.

CHAPTER XLI.

MEN OF EMINENCE IN THE ARTS, SCIENCES AND THE PROFESSIONS.

CHAPTER XLII.

LITERATURE: HEBREW AND ENGLISH. PERIODICALS.

CHAPTER XLIII.

YIDDISH LITERATURE, DRAMA AND THE PRESS.

CHAPTER XLIV

LIST OF ILLUSTRATIONS.

PAGE

INTRODUCTION.

THE JEWS AS EARLY INTERNATIONAL TRADERS.

The ten centuries which passed between the fall of the Western Roman Empire and the discovery of the New World are commonly known as the Middle Ages or the Dark Ages. They were, on the whole, very dark indeed for most of the inhabitants of Europe, as well as for the Jews who were scattered among them. It was a time of the fermentation of religious and national ideas, a formative period for the mind and the body politic of the races from which the great nations of the present civilized world were evolved. It was a period of violent hatreds, of cruel persecutions, of that terrible earnestness which prompts and justifies the extermination of enemies and even of opponents; there was almost constant war between nations, between classes, between creeds and sects. The ordinary man had no rights even in theory, the truths "that all men are created equal, that they are endowed by their Creator with certain unalienable rights, that among these are life, liberty and the pursuit of happiness" were not self-evident then; they were not even thought of until a much later era.

The treatment accorded to the Jews in our own times in the countries where the general conditions are nearest to those prevailing in the dark ages, gives a clear idea of what the Jew had to undergo when the average degree of culture was so much lower than it is in the least developed of the Christian countries at present. The records of the times are so filled with pillage, expulsions and massacres, that they impress us as having been common occurrences, though they happened further apart to those who lived through the peaceful intervals which distance of time makes to appear short to us. There were, of course, some bright spots, the most shining of which was the Iberian peninsula during the earlier part of the Moorish domination. Sometimes a kind-hearted king would afford his Jews protection and even grant them valuable privileges; a clear-headed prince often found it to his own interest to utilize them for the advancement of the commerce of his dominion, and in a rare period of peace and prosperity there also happened a general relaxation of the severity which characterized the time. But if we view the entire thousand years as a single historical period, we find the condition of the Jews slowly deteriorating; with the result that while the modern nations were welded together and came out of the medieval furnace strengthened and developed, the Jews were pushed back, segregated and degraded, ready for the numerous expulsions and various sufferings which continued for more than two centuries in Western Europe and are not yet over in other parts of the Old World.

The favorable position of the Jews at the beginning of the Middle Ages is less familiar to the reading public, even to the Jewish reader, than the troublesome times which came later. As a matter of fact the Jews were, except for the lack of national unity and of the possession of an independent home, better situated materially four centuries after the destruction of the Second Temple than before the last dissolution of the Kingdom of Judah. The instinct for commerce which is latent in the "Semitic" race was awakened in the Diaspora and, after an interruption of more than a thousand years, we find, at the end of the classical times, international trade again almost exclusively in the hands of members of that race. The Sumero-Accadians or original Babylonians who were the earliest known international traders on land, and the Phoenicians, who first dared to trade over seas, were of Semitic origin. As foreign commerce is the highest form of activity in regard to the utilization of human productivity, so it is also the forerunner of mental activity and of the spread of an ennobling and instructive culture. The beginnings of both Egyptian and Greek civilization, according to the latest discoveries, point unmistakably to Mesopotamian or Phoenician origin, with a strong probability that the latter received it from the former in times which we usually describe as pre-historic, but about which we now possess considerable exact information. Culture followed the great route of the caravans to Syria and Egypt on one side, to Iran, India and as far as China in an opposite direction. And if we accept the wholly incorrect and un-scientific division of the white race into Aryans and Semites, then this original and most fertile of the cultures of humanity was undoubtedly Semitic. A more modern and more nearly correct division would place these ancient inhabitants of the plateau of Asia as a part of the great Mediterranean or brunette race, which includes, besides all the so-called Semites, a number of European nations which are classed as Aryans. Greece succeeded Phœnicia and was in turn succeeded by Rome in the hegemony of international trade as well as in that of general culture. Both commerce and culture declined when the ancient civilization was all but destroyed by the invasion of the blond barbarians of the northern forests, who were themselves destined to attain in a far-away future the highest form of civilization of which mankind has hitherto proven itself capable. (See *Zollschan* "Das Rassenproblem," Vienna, 1910, pp. 206 ff.)

It so happened that at the time of the downfall of the Roman Empire, or, as it is usually called, the beginning of the Middle Ages, another people of Semitic origin, the Jews, were for the most part engaged in international trade. There are records of Jewish merchants of that period shipping or exporting wine, oil, honey, fish, cattle, woolens, etc., from Spain to Rome and other Latin provinces, from Media to Brittannia, from the Persian Gulf and Ethiopia to Macedonia and Italy; there was no important seaport or commercial center in which the Jews did not occupy a commanding position. Their prominence as importers and exporters rather increased than diminished by the downfall of the great Empire. The new nations of the Germanic kingdoms which were founded on the ruins of Rome, knew nothing of international trade, and the position of the Jews as merchants was accepted by them as a matter of course. Hence the first traces of Jewish settlements in modern European countries are almost exclusively to be found in the earliest records of commerce and of trading privileges. They are then known as traders with distant countries, as sea-going men, as owners of vessels and as slave-traders. The commercial note or written obligation to pay, which is accepted in lieu of payment and is itself negotiable as a substitute for money, is a Jewish invention of those times. They developed industries and improved the material conditions of every place in which they were found in large numbers. As late as 1084, when their position had been already much weakened and the coming Crusades were casting their shadows, Bishop Rudiger of Speyer began his edict of privileges granted to the Jews with the statement: "As I wish to turn the village of Speyer into a city . . . I call the Jews to settle there." (See ibid p. 351.)[1]

THE SPANISH JEWS AS LAND OWNERS.

Canon Law on one side and the rise of cities on the other shattered the position of the Jews until they were reduced to sore straits at the end of the Middle Ages. The church labored persistently and relentlessly through the centuries in which Europe was thoroughly Christianized, to separate the Jews as far as possible from their Gentile neighbors. The ties which united the two parts of the population by a thousand threads of mutual interest, friendship, co-operation and beneficial intercourse, were slowly loosened and, where possible, all but severed. At the various Church Councils, from Nicea to the last Lateran, there was laid down the theory of the necessity to force the Jews out of

[1] A remarkable work by Werner Sombart, *Die Juden und das Wirtschaftsleben* (Leipsic 1911), which appeared after the above was written, deals exhaustively with the important part which the Jews played in the development of business and finance in medieval as well as in modern times. While it is avowedly a partisan work written for a special purpose, it is a notable contribution to social-economic Jewish history which no student of the subject can afford to neglect.

the national life of the countries in which they dwelt, and to segregate them as a distinct, inferior and outlawed class. The principles enunciated by the higher clergy were disseminated by the priests and the demagogues among the masses. Special laws and restrictions were often followed by attacks, sacking of the Jewish quarters and degradations of various kinds. In the twelfth and the following three centuries the ill-treatment was often followed by expulsions and cancellation of debts, while heavy fines on individual Jews or on entire communities were accepted on both sides as a lesser evil or as easy terms for escaping greater hardships. The climax of this method of dealing with the Jews, the greatest blow administered to the unhappy Children of Israel by Christian princes, was the expulsion from Spain in 1492, and its concomitant, the expulsion from Portugal five years afterwards.

But the Church alone could never have accomplished the ruin of the Jews if the changing economic conditions and the rise of a large and powerful class of Christian merchants did not help to undermine the position of the erstwhile solitary trading class. The burgher classes were the chief opponents and persecutors of their Jewish competitors: they seconded, and in many cases instigated, the efforts of the clergy to exclude the Jews from many occupations. So when the city overpowered the land owner and began to exert a preponderant influence on the government, the cause of the Jew was lost, or at least postponed until a more humane and liberal time, when the ordinary claims of the brotherhood of man were to overcome the narrow-minded mercantile and ecclesiastical policies of a ruder age. The great historian Ranke pointed out that the struggle between the cities and the nobility in Castille was decided in favor of the former by the marriage of Queen Isabella to Ferdinand of Aragon. It was also this marriage which sealed the doom of the Spanish Jews, as well as that of their former friends and protectors, the Moors, who had by that time sunk so low, that it was impossible for them to keep their last stronghold in Europe much longer.

Though the outlook in Spain was very dark, it was much worse in all other known countries, which accounts for the fact that there was hardly any emigration from the Christian parts of Spain in the time immediately preceding the expulsion. The Spanish Jew was then, and has to some extent remained even unto this day, the aristocrat among the Jews of the world. His intense love for that country is still smouldering in the hearts of his descendants, and not without reason. In other European countries the Jew could, during the middle ages, only enjoy the sympathy and sometimes be accorded the protection of the nobility. In Spain and Portugal he actually belonged to that class. For, as Selig (Dr. Paulus) Cassel has justly remarked (in his splendid article *Juden* in Ersch and Gruber's Encyclopædia) sufficient attention has not been paid by Jewish historians to the important fact that Spain and Portugal were the only considerable countries during the Middle Ages in which the Jews were permitted to own land. The statement, for which there is an apparent Jewish authority, that they owned about a third of Spain at the time of their exile, is doubtless an exaggeration, but there can be no question of their being extensive holders of land-properties.

This largely explains why the Jew in Spain has not sunk in public estimation as much as he did in other countries, why his fate was different, and, in the end, worse than that of his more humiliated and degraded brother elsewhere. When the German or French Jew was forced out of commerce he could only become a money-lender at the usurious rates prevailing in those times. This vocation drew on him the contempt and hatred of all classes, as was always the case and as is the case in many places even to-day. But while the usurer was despised he was very useful, often even indispensable, especially in those times when there was a great scarcity of the precious metals and of convertible capital. This may explain why the exiled Jews were in other countries usually called back to the places from which they were exiled. The prejudice of the age may render their work disreputable, but it was none the less necessary; they were missed as soon as they left, and on many occasions negotiations for their return were begun as soon as the popular fury cooled down, or when the object of spoliation was attained.

Not so in Spain. The Jewish merchant who could no longer hold his own against his stronger non-Jewish competitor, could do what is often done by others who voluntarily retire from such pursuits, i. e., invest his capital in landed estates. We can imagine that the transition did not at all seem to be forced, that those who caused it, and even its victims, might have considered it as the natural course of events. After the great massacres of 1391, a century before the expulsion, many Jews emigrated to Moorish North Africa, where there still remained some degree of tolerance and friendliness for them, mingled perhaps with some hope of re-conquering the lost parts of the Iberian peninsula. But later there was less thought of migration, least of all of emigrating to the parts of Spain which still remained in the possession of the Moors. The race which was, seven centuries before, assisted by the Jews to become masters of Iberia, and which together with them rose to a height of culture and mental achievement which is not yet properly appreciated in modern history, has now become degenerate and almost savage in its fanaticism. The Jew of Spain was still proud, despite his sufferings. He could not see his fate as clearly as we can now from the perspective of five hundred years. He was rooted in the country in which he lived for many centuries. He was, like most men of wealth and position, inclined to be optimistic, and he could not miss his only possible protection against expropriation or exile—the possession of full rights of citizenship—because the Jews nowhere had it in those times and had not had it since the days of ancient Rome.

The catastrophe of the great expulsion, which came more unexpectedly than we can now perceive, was possibly facilitated by the position which the Jews held as land owners. It certainly contributed to make the decree of exile irrevocable. The holder of real property is more easily and more thoroughly despoiled, because he cannot hide his most valuable possessions or escape with them. He is not missed when he is gone; his absence is hardly felt after the title to his lands has been transferred to the Crown or to favorites of the government. When the robbery is once committed only compunction or an awakened sense of justice could induce the restitution which re-admission or recall would imply. And as abstract moral forces had very little influence in those cruel days, it is no wonder that the expulsion was final—the only one of that nature in Christian Europe.

This peculiar position of the Jews in Spain and Portugal was also the cause of the immense number of conversions which gave these anti-Jewish nations a very large mixture of Jewish blood in their veins. The temptation to cling to the land and to the high social position which could not be enjoyed elsewhere was too strong for all but the strongest. Thus we find Marranos or secret Jews in all the higher walks of life in the times of the discovery of America. The more steadfast of their brethren who were equally prominent in the preceding period assisted in various ways earlier voyages of discovery, and even contributed indirectly to the success of the one great voyage, which did not begin until they were exiled from Spain forever.

But we must constantly bear in mind, when speaking of the Middle Ages and of the two centuries succeeding it, the sixteenth and the seventeenth, that the Jews did not possess the right of citizenship and were not, even when they were treated very well, considered as an integral part of the population. This was the chief weakness of their position and the ultimate cause of all the persecutions, massacres and expulsions. Still they had many opportunities and made the most of them to advance their own interests and those of the countries in which they dwelt. We find them in the thirteenth and fourteenth centuries in close touch with the current of national life in the countries which were most absorbed in enterprises of navigation and discovery. Many of them were still great merchants, numerous others were scholars, mathematicians and astronomers or astrologers; some had influence in political life as advisers or fiscal officials at the royal courts. They accomplished much, as Jews and as Marranos, even when the danger of persecution must have been ever-present, or later, when in constant terror of the Inquisition. Many of them could therefore participate in the work which led to the discovery of a New World, where their descendants were destined to find a home safer and more free than was ever dreamt of in medieval Jewish philosophy.

PART I.

THE SPANISH AND PORTUGUESE PERIOD.

CHAPTER I.

THE PARTICIPATION OF JEWS IN THE DISCOVERY OF THE NEW WORLD.

The Jew of Barcelona who has navigated the whole known world—Judah Cresques, "the Map Jew," as director of the Academy of Navigation which was founded by Prince Henry the Navigator—One Jewish astronomer advises the King of Portugal to reject the plans of Columbus—Zacuto as one of the first influential men in Spain to encourage the discoverer of the New World—Abravanel, Senior and the Marranos Santangel and Sanchez who assisted Columbus—The voyage of discovery begun a day after the expulsion of the Jews from Spain—Luis de Torres and other Jews who went with Columbus—America discovered on "Hosannah Rabbah"—The Indians as the Lost Ten Tribes of Israel—Money taken from the Jews to defray the expenditure of the second voyage of Columbus—Vasco da Gama and the Jew Gaspar—Scrolls of the Thorah from Portugal sold in Cochin—Alphonse d'Albuquerque's interpreter who returned to Judaism.

In the days when Church and State were one and indissoluble, and when all large national enterprises, such as wars or the search for new dominions by means of discovery, were undertaken avowedly in the name and for the glory of the Catholic religion, it could not have been expected that governments will make an effort to protect international trade as long as it was in Jewish hands. We must therefore go as far back as to the first half of the 14th century to find a record of Jews who went to sea on their own account in an independent way. According to the great authority on the subject of this chapter (Dr. M. Kayserling, "Christopher Columbus and the participation of the Jews in the Spanish and Portuguese Discoveries," English translation by the late Prof. Charles Gross of Harvard University) Jaime III., the last king of Mallorca, testified in 1334 that Juceff Faquin, a Jew of Barcelona, "has navigated the whole then known world." About a century later we find again a Jew prominently identified with navigation; but in this instance he is a scientific teacher, in the employ of an energetic prince who considered navigation as a national project of the greatest moment. Prince Henry the Navigator of Portugal (1394-1460), who helped his father to capture Ceuta, in North Africa, and there "obtained information from Jewish travellers concerning the south coast of Guinea and the interior of Africa", established a naval academy or school of navigation at the Villa do Iffante or Sagres, a seaport town which he caused to be built. He appointed as its director Mestre Jaime of Mallorca whose real name was Jafuda (Judah) Cresques, the son of Abraham Cresques of Palma, the capital of Mallorca. Jafuda was known as "the Map Jew," and a map which he prepared for King Juan I. of Aragon and was presented by the latter to the King of France, is preserved in the National Library of Paris.[1] He became the teacher of the Portuguese in the art of navigation as well as in the manufacture of nautical instruments and maps. In this work he had no superior in his day.

While this Jewish scholar helped the Portuguese to many notable achievements in their daring voyages, another one, at a later period, was almost the direct cause of their being overtaken by the Spaniards in the race for new discoveries. For it was Joseph Vecinho, physician to King João, of Portugal, considered by the high court functionaries to be the greatest authority in nautical

[1] A fac-simile of this map is found in the "Jewish Encyclopedia," vol. III., opp. p. 678.

matters, who influenced the King to reject the plan submitted by Christopher Columbus (1446?-1506), and thereby caused the latter to leave Portugal for Spain in 1484.

Columbus came to Spain when Ferdinand and Isabella, with the aid of the newly introduced Inquisition, were despoiling the wealthy Marranos, who were burned at the stake in large numbers. The last war with the Moors had already begun.

Another and more famous Jewish scholar was to make amends for whatever suffering was caused to the great discoverer by Vecincho's fatal advice. Abraham Ben Samuel Zacuto, who was born in Salamanca, Spain, about the middle of the 15th century and died an exile in Turkey after 1510, was famous as an astronomer and mathematician, and in his capacity as one of the leading professors in the university of his native city was formerly the teacher of the above named Vecinho. He was more discerning than his pupil, and when he learned to know Columbus, soon after the latter's arrival in Spain, he encouraged him personally and also gave him his almanacs and astronomical tables, which were a great help in the voyage of discovery. Zacuto was among the first influential men in Spain to favor the plans of Columbus, and his favorable report caused Ferdinand and Isabella to take him into their service in 1487. The explorer was then ordered to proceed to Malaga, which was captured several weeks before, and there made the acquaintance of the two most prominent Jews of Spain in that time—the chief farmer of taxes, Abraham Senior, and Don Isaac Abravanel. These two men were provisioning the Spanish armies which operated against the Moors, and were in high favor at Court. Abravanel was one of the first to render financial assistance to Columbus.

Louis de Santangel and other Marranos interposed in favor of Columbus when he was about to go to France in January, 1492, because Ferdinand refused to make him Viceroy and Life-Governor of all the lands which he might discover. Santangel's pleadings with Isabella were especially effective, and when the question of funds remained the only obstacle to be overcome, he who was saved from the stake by the King's grace at the time when several other members of the Santangel family perished, advanced a loan of seventeen thousand florins—nearly five million maravedis—to finance the entire project. Account books in which the transfer of money from Santangel to Columbus, through the Bishop of Avila, who afterwards became the Archbishop of Granada, were recorded, are still preserved in the *Archive de India* of Seville, Spain.

"After the Spanish monarchs had expelled all the Jews from all their Kingdoms and lands in April, in the same month they commissioned me to undertake the voyage to India"—writes Christopher Columbus. This refers to the Decree of Expulsion, but the coincidence of the actual happening was still more remarkable. The expulsion took place on the second day of August, 1492, which occurred on the ninth day of the Jewish month of Ab, the day on which, according to the Jewish tradition, is the anniversary of the destruction of both the first Holy Temple of Jerusalem in the year 586 B. C. and also of the second Temple at the hands of the Romans in the year 70 C. E. The day, known as "Tishah be'Ab," was observed as a day of mourning and lamentation among the Jews of the Diaspora in all countries and is still so observed by the Orthodox everywhere to this day. Columbus sailed on his momentous voyage on the day after—the third of August. The boats which were carrying away throngs of the expatriated and despairing Jews from the country which they loved so well and in which their ancestors dwelt for more than eight centuries, sighted that little fleet of three sailing craft which was destined to open up a new world for the oppressed of many races, where at a later age millions of Jews were to find a free home under the protection of laws which were unthought of in those times.

Neither all the names nor even the number of men who accompanied Columbus on his first voyage are known to posterity. Some authorities place the number at 120, others as low as 90. But among the names which came down to us are those of several Jews, the best known among them being Louis de Torres, who was baptized shortly before he joined Columbus. Torres knew Hebrew, Chaldaic and some Arabic, and was taken along to be employed as an interpreter between the travellers and the natives of the parts of India which Columbus expected to reach by crossing the Ocean. Others of Jewish stock whose names were preserved are: Alfonso de Calle, Rodrigo Sanchez of Segovia, the physician Maestro Bernal and the surgeon Marco.

Land was sighted October 12, 1492, on "Hosannah Rabbah" (the seventh day of the Jewish Feast of the Booths), and Louis de Torres, who was sent ashore with one companion to parley with the inhabitants, was thus the first white man to step on the ground of the New World. As the place proved to be not the Kingdom of the Great Khan which Columbus had set out to reach, but an island of the West Indies, with a strange hitherto unknown race of copper-colored men, it is needless to say that the linguistic attainments of the Jewish interpreter availed him very little. After he managed to make himself somewhat understood, he was favorably impressed with the new country and finally settled for the remainder of his life in Cuba. He was the first discoverer of tobacco, which was through him introduced into the Old World. It is also believed that in describing in a Hebrew letter to a Marrano in Spain the odd gallinaceous bird which he first saw in his new abode, he gave it the name "Tukki" (the word in Kings I, 10 v. 22, which is commonly translated peacock) and that this was later corrupted into "turkey," by which name it is known to the English-speaking world.

It may also be remarked, in passing, that the belief identifying the red race which was surnamed Indian with the lost ten tribes of Israel, began to be entertained by many people, especially scholars and divines, soon after the discovery of America. It attained the dignity of a theory in the middle of the 17th century when Thorowgood published his work: "The Jews in America; or, Probabilities that the Americans are of that Race." (London, 1650.) This view was supported among our own scholars by no less an authority than Manasse Ben Israel, who wrote on the same subject in his "Esperança de Israel" which was published in Amsterdam in the same year.

Columbus wrote the first reports of his wonderful discovery to Louis de Santangel and to Gabriel Sanchez. The letter to the first is dated February 15, 1493, and was written on the return voyage, near the Azores or the Canaries.

It was decreed by a royal order of November 23, 1492, that the authorities were to confiscate for the State Treasury all property which had belonged to the Jews, including that which Christians had taken from them or had appropriated unlawfully or by violence. This gave Ferdinand sufficient means to provide for the second voyage of Columbus (March 23, 1493). The King and the Queen signed a large number of injunctions to royal officers in Soria, Zamora, Burgos and many other cities, directing them to secure immediate possession of all the precious metals, gold and silver utensils, jewels, gems and other objects of value that had been taken from the Jews who were expelled from Spain or had migrated to Portugal, and everything that these Jews had entrusted for safe keeping to Marrano, relatives or friends, and all Jewish possession which Christians had found or had unlawfully appropriated. The royal officers were later ordered to convert this property into ready money and to give the proceeds to the treasurer, Francisco Pinelo, in Seville, to meet the expenditure of Columbus' second expedition.

One of the specific instances of these confiscations which deserves to be mentioned, is the order to Bernardino de Lerma to transfer to Pinelo all the gold, silver and various other things which Rabbi Ephraim (who is sometimes referred to in contemporary documents as Rabi Frayn, also as Rubifrayn, and who was perhaps the father of the great Rabbi Joseph Caro, author of the Shulhan Aruk, etc.), the richest Jew in Burgos, had before emigrating left with Isabel Osoria, the wife of Louis Nunez Coronel of Zamora. Not merely the clothing, ornaments and valuables which had been taken from the Jews were converted into money, but also the debts which they had been unable to recover were declared by order of the Crown to be forfeited to the state treasury, and stringent measures were adopted to collect them. A moderate estimate places the sum thus obtained at six million maravedis, to which ought to be added the two millions contributed by the Inquisition of Seville as a part of the enormous sums which it wrested from Jews and Moors. According to another order, issued in the above-named date, it was from this Jewish money that Columbus was paid the ten thousand maravedis which the Spanish monarchs had promised as a reward to him who should first sight land.[1]

In the days of suffering and disgrace which came to Columbus after his discoveries, Santangel and Sanchez remained faithful to him and often interceded in his behalf with Ferdinand and Isabella. They both died in 1505, about one year before the great discoverer whose success they made possible. Their immediate descendants occupied high positions in the royal service.

* * * * *

Columbus was not the only renowned discoverer of that time who was directly and indirectly assisted by Jews. The great and cruel Vasco da Gama, who did for Portugal almost as much as Columbus did for Spain, could hardly have carried out his important undertakings without the help of at least two Jews. One of them was the above-mentioned Abraham Zacuto, who, like many of his unfortunate brethren, went from Spain to Portugal after the calamity of 1492. He was highly favored by King João and by his successor, Dom Manuel, and the latter consulted him on the advisability of sending out under Vasco da Gama's command the flotilla of four boats which was to reach India by the way of Cape of Good Hope. Zacuto pointed out the dangers which would have to be encountered, but gave it as his opinion that the plan was feasible and predicted that it would result in the subjection of a large part of India to the Portu-

[1] There is a record that it was not Columbus himself but a sailor from Lepe who first saw a distant light and cried "land!" and who, when he found that he had been defrauded of the gratuity, obtained his discharge, went to Africa and there discarded Christianity for his old faith. But the chronicler does not inform us whether the sailor's old faith was Judaism or Islam.

guese crown. Zacuto's works and the instruments which he invented and made available materially facilitated the execution of the enterprises of Vasco da Gama and other explorers. As in the case of Columbus and Spain, da Gama sailed in the year of the expulsion of the Jews from the country which fitted out his expedition (1497). When he returned Zacuto was an exile in Tunis, though he probably could have remained in Portugal, just as Abravanel could have remained in Spain.

It was during his return voyage to Europe, while staying at the little island of Anchevide, sixty miles from Goa (off the Indian coast of Malabar) that Vasco da Gama met the second Jew who became very useful to him and to Portugal. A tall European with a long white beard approached his ship in a boat with a small crew. He had been sent by his master, Sabayo, the Moorish ruler of Goa, to negotiate with the foreign navigator. He was a Jew who, according to some chronicles, came from Posen, according to others from Granada, whose parents had emigrated to Turkey and Palestine. From Alexandria, which some give as his birthplace, he proceeded across the Red Sea to Mecca and thence to India. Here he was a long time in captivity, and later was made admiral (capitao mór) by Sabayo.

The Portuguese were overjoyed "to hear so far from home a language closely related to their native speech." But he was soon suspected of being a spy and was forced by torture to join the expedition and—as a matter of course—to embrace Christianity. The admiral acted as his godfather and his name came down to us as Gaspar da Gama or Gaspar de las Indias. He was brought to Portugal, where he was favored by King Manuel and "rendered inestimable service to Vasco da Gama and several later commanders." He accompanied Pedro Alvarez Cobral on the expedition in 1500 which led to the independent discovery of Brazil, which became a Portuguese possession. On the return voyage Gaspar met Amerigo Vespucci, who received much information from him and mentions him as a linguist and traveller who is trustworthy and knows much about the interior of India.

On another expedition in which he accompanied his godfather

in 1502, Gaspar found his wife in Cochin. She had remained true to him and to Judaism since he was carried away by the Portuguese, but probably both of them considered it unsafe for her to join him. He again journeyed to Cochin in 1505 in the retinue of the first Viceroy of India, which also included the son of Dr. Martin Pinheiro, the Judge of the Supreme Court of Lisbon. The young Pinheiro carried along a chest filled with "Torah" scrolls which were taken from the recently destroyed synagogues of Portugal. Gaspar's wife negotiated the sale in Cochin, "where there were many Jews and synagogues," obtaining four thousand parados for thirteen scrolls. The viceroy later confiscated the proceeds for the state treasury and sent an account of the whole affair to Lisbon.

Another Portuguese commander and governor of India, Alphonse d'Albuquerque, obtained much information and valuable assistance from his interpreter, a Jew from Castille whom he induced to embrace Christianity and to assume the name Francisco d'Albuquerque. His companion Cufo or Hucefe underwent the same change of religion and visited Lisbon, but soon found himself in danger and escaped to Cairo, where he again openly professed Judaism.

CHAPTER II.

EARLY JEWISH MARTYRS UNDER SPANISH RULE IN THE NEW WORLD.

Children torn from their parents were the first Jewish immigrants—Jewish history in the New World begins, as Jewish history in Spain ends, with the Inquisition—Emperor Charles V., Philip II. and Philip III.—Lutherans persecuted together with Jews and Mohamedans—Codification of the laws of the Inquisition, and its special edicts for the New World.

We have seen in the preceding chapter that the Jews were expelled forever from Spain and Portugal at the time when these two nations, with considerable assistance from professing and converted Jews, discovered the New World and took possession of it. Nothing could therefore have been farther from the thoughts and the hopes of the Jews of those dark days than the idea that America was to be, in a far-away future, the first Christian country to grant its Jewish inhabitants full citizenship and absolute equality before the law. For nearly a century and a half no professing Jew dared to tread upon American soil, and even the secret Jews or Marranos were as much in danger in the newly-planted colonies as in the mother countries under whose rule they remained for a long time.

The first Jewish immigrants in the New World were children who were torn away from the arms of their parents at the time of the expulsions, and even they were persecuted as soon as they grew up. The Marranos who sought a refuge in America in these early days were soon followed by the same agencies of persecution which made life a burden to them in their old home. We meet in America for more than a century after its discovery almost the same conditions as in Spain and Portugal after the Jews were exiled. Where the history of the Jews in Spain ends —says Dr. Kayserling—the history of the Jews in America begins. The Inquisition is the last chapter in the record of the confessors of Judaism on the Pyrenean peninsula and its first chapter in the western hemisphere. The Nuevos Christianos concealed their faith, or were able to conceal it, as little in the New World as in the mother country. With astonishing tenacity, nay, with admirable obstinacy, they clung to the religion of their fathers; it was not a rare occurrence that the grandchildren and great-grandchildren of the martyred Jews sanctified the Sabbath in a most conscientious manner, by refraining from work as far as possible and by wearing their best clothing. They also celebrated the Jewish Festivals, observed the Day of Atonement by fasting, and married according to the Jewish customs. They clung to their faith and suffered for it even as late as the eighteenth century, which means that the Jewish religion was handed down secretly and preserved in the seventh and eighth generation after the exile. Many went to the stake or died in the prisons of the Inquisition in the New World; many others were transported in groups to Spain and Portugal and gave up their lives as martyrs in Seville, Toledo, Evora or Lisbon. Their religious heroism will be apparent in all its magnitude when the immense documentary material which is heaped up in the archives of Spain and Portugal, and other places on this side of the ocean, will have been sifted and worked up. ("Publications," II, p. 73.)

Intolerance reigned supreme in America almost immediately after its colonization, and the secret Jews who settled there were not permitted to enjoy peace or prosperity. Juan Sanchez of Saragossa, whose father was burnt at the stake, was the first to obtain permission of the Spanish government to trade with the newly-discovered lands. In 1502 Isabella permitted him to take five caravels loaded with wheat, barley, horses and other wares to Española (Little Spain, the large West Indian Island containing Haiti and Santo Domingo), without paying duty. In 150' e was again permitted to export merchandise to that country. ther secret Jews went to the new places and settled there, some ven obtaining positions in the public service. As early as 1511 e hear already of measures taken by Isabella's daughter, Queen anna of Castille, against "the sons and grandsons of the urned" who held public office. The Inquisition was introduced iere by a decree of that year, and one of its first victims was iego Caballera of Barrameda, whose parents, according to two itnesses, had been prosecuted and condemned by the same ibunal in Spain.

The Inquisitor-General of Spain, Cardinal Ximenes de Cis-eros, on May 7, 1516, appointed Fray Juan Quevedo, Bishop f Cuba, his delegate for the Kingdom of *Terra Firma*, as the nainland of Spanish America was then called, and authorized im to select personally such officials as he needed to hunt down nd exterminate the Marranos. Emperor Charles V. (1500-558), with the permission of his former teacher, Cardinal Had-an (1459-1523), the Dutch Grand-Inquisitor of Aragon who ter became Pope (Hadrian or Adrian VI. 1522-23), issued an lict on May 25, 1520, whereby he ordained Alfonso Manso, ishop of Porto Rico, and Pedro de Cordova, Vice Provincial f the Dominicans, as Inquisitors for the Indies and the islands f the ocean.

At first the secret Jews were not the only victims of the perse-utions and not even the most numerous among them. "There ere many heathenish natives who were forcibly converted by e mighty clerical arm of the Spanish conqueror, but who never-ieless remained at heart loyal to their hereditary belief and ractised their idolatrous customs with as much zeal as the fear f discovery and consequent punishment would allow." Fiend-h atrocities were committed in the name of religion against iose Indian Marranos, and the fearful persecutions depopulated ie country to such an extent that the tyrants themselves per-eived that they must desist.

The Inquisition in Spain itself had, however, fallen more or ss into desuetude during the reign of the above-mentioned Emperor Charles V., who was the grandson of Ferdinand and Isabella, and had inherited their Spanish and American possessions. It was revived and invigorated under the more bigoted rule of his son, King Philip II. (1527-1598), who ascended the Spanish throne in 1556, after his father's abdication. Under the new reign the laws of the Inquisition were codified and promulgated at Madrid on September 2, 1561. A printed copy of the new code was sent to America in 1569. Another document, dated February 5, 1569, issued by Cardinal Diego de Spinosa, General Apostolic Inquisitor against Heresy, Immorality and Apostasy, addressed "to the Reverend Inquisitors Apostolic . . . in his Majesty's Dominions and Seignories of the Provinces of Piru (Peru), New Spain and the new Kingdom of Granada and the other provinces and Bishoprics of the Indies of the Ocean" consists of forty sections prescribing the rules of procedure. (See Elkan Nathan Adler, *The Inquisition in Peru,* Publications XII, pp. 5-37.)

A later document containing the general edicts to be read on the third Sunday of Lent and the fourth Sunday of Anathema in every third year in the Cathedral of Lima and all the towns of the districts, was printed in Peru itself shortly after 1641, and records the names of the places which were included in the jurisdiction of those issuing it. It reads: "We, the Inquisitors against Heresy, Immorality and Apostasy in this city and Archbishopric of Los Reyes (Lima) with the Archbishopric of Los Charcas and Bishoprics of Quito, Cuzco, Rio de la Plata, Paraguay, Tucuman, Santiago and Concepcion of the Dominions of Chile, la Paz (Bolivia), Santa Cruz de la Sierra. Guamanga, Areguipa, and Truxillo, and in all the Dominions, Estates and Seignories of the Provinces of Peru, and its Viceroyalty Government and district of the Royal Audiencias thereto appertaining." In this document we find the name of a new Christian sect which is to be punished for heresy together with the unbelievers who were known to the Inquisition of the earlier period. Lutherans are now enumerated among heretics after the Jews and the Mohamedans. Among the books and engravings which are considered as heretical and indecent are mentioned the books of Martin Luther and other heretics, the Alcoran or other Mohamedan books, "Biblias en romance" (Bibles in the vernacular) and others prohibited by the censorships and catalogues of the Holy Office, etc. Then follow lengthy descriptions of how to detect Jews, Mohamedans and Lutherans; and in the case of the first even the drinking of Kosher wine and the making of a "berakah" or pronouncing a blessing before tasting it are not omitted from the practices which characterized the secret Jew whom the Inquisition was to discover and punish.

But it seems that the Marranos came to America in large numbers despite all the severity of Philip II. His son Philip III. (1578-1621), who succeeded him in 1598, endeavored to prevent their emigrating to the New World and issued in the beginning of the seventeenth century, the following edict:

> "We command and decree that no one recently converted to our holy faith, be he Jew or Moor, or the offspring of these, should settle in our Indies without our distinct permission. Furthermore we forbid most emphatically the immigration into New Spain of any one [who is at the expiration of some prescribed penance] newly reconciled with the Church; of the child or grandchild of any person who has ever worn the 'san benito' publicly; of the child or grandchild of any person who was either burnt as a heretic or otherwise punished for the crime of heresy, through either male or female descent. Should any one [falling under this category] presume to violate this law, his goods will be confiscated for the benefit of the royal treasury, and upon him the full measure of our grace or disgrace shall fall, so that under any circumstances and for all time he shall be banished from our Indies. Whosoever does not possess personal effects, however, should atone for his transgression by the public infliction of one hundred lashes."

This characteristic specimen of anti-immigration legislation of three centuries ago, including what would in the colloquialism of to-day be called a "grandfather clause," was the cause of much suffering; but it is not possible to state with any degree of certainty how far it was effective. It is probable that the number of Marranos in the "Indies" which belonged to the King of Spain went on increasing until about the middle of the seventeenth century, when certain territories were for the first time opened for them in the New World where they could practise Judaism openly.

CHAPTER III.

VICTIMS OF THE INQUISITION IN MEXICO AND IN PERU.

Impossibility of obtaining even approximately correct figures about the Inquisition—A few typical cases—The Carabajal family—Relaxation for several decades—The notable case of Francisco Maldonado de Silva.

The Inquisition, or, as it styled itself, the Holy Office, was an institution of tremendous power and influence which during its existence of more than three centuries deeply impressed the character of the Spanish and Portuguese peoples. A great number of books were written about it, but the material to be dealt with is so vast that none of the works purporting to be histories of the Inquisition really deserve that name. It has been mentioned already in the preceding chapter that an immense mass of documentary material which is heaped up in various archives awaits to be sifted and worked up. An idea of the actual quantity of this material can be obtained from the statement made by Mr. E. N. Adler, in the monogram on the Inquisition in Peru quoted above, that thirty-three million documents, relating to the Inquisition, are preserved in 80,000 "legajos" or bundles in the *castille* of Simancas, a small town, seven miles from Valladolid, in Spain.

It is therefore next to impossible to attempt to give a general review of the work of that awful tribunal in the old world or the new; it is even unsafe to quote figures as to the total number of trials, Autos da Fé or of victims, because most of the authorities contradict one another or disagree in vital points. Many facts which are given at one time as reasonably certain, are soon disproved by the discovery of more authentic records, which necessitates a constant changing of the time, the place and the identity of persons spoken of in such descriptions. It is therefore considered best to mention here only a few typical cases of victims about whose identity and Jewish extraction there can be no doubt. From these the reader may form his own opinion as to what was constantly happening in the various places since the Inquisition's firm establishment in the New World in the second half of the sixteenth century, until its final disappearance at the end of the eighteenth and in some instances as late as the beginning of the nineteenth centuries.

Several members of the Carabajal (Carvalho?) family suffered martyrdom in Mexico at the end of the sixteenth century and at the beginning of the seventeenth. Francisca Nunez de Carabajal, born in Portugal about 1540, was among the members of the family seized by the Inquisition in 1590. She was tortured until she implicated her husband and her children, and the entire family was forced to confess and abjure Judaism at a public Auto da Fé which was celebrated on Saturday, February 24, 1590. Later, after more than five years' imprisonment, they were convicted of relapsing into Judaism, and Francisca, her son Luis and her four daughters were burned at the stake in Mexico City, December 8, 1596. She was the sister of Don Luis de Carabajal y Cueva (born in Portugal, 1539), who was appointed Governor of New Leon, Mexico, in 1579 and is said to have died in 1595. He arrived in Mexico in 1580, where, in consideration of his appointment as governor of a somewhat ill-defined district, he undertook to colonize a certain territory at his own expense, being allowed the privilege of reimbursing himself out of the revenue. There were many Spanish Jews among his colonists, and within a decade after their settlement more than a score were denounced and more or less severely punished for Judaizing. He is the subject of a work, half romantic and half historical, by Mr. C. K. Landis, entitled *Carabalja the Jew, a Legend of Monterey* (Vineland, 1894).

Another heroic martyr of Mexico was Don Tomas de Sobremonte, a Judaizer, who died at the stake April 11, 1649, without uttering a groan, mocking "the Pope and his hirelings" and taunting his tormentors with his last breath.

The Inquisition in Lima, Peru, is known to have solemnized thirty-four Autos da Fé at that place between 1573 (November 15) and 1806 (July 17) and at ten or eleven of them there were Jewish victims, their numbers ranging from one or two to as high as fifty-six (January 23, 1639). From the earliest day ot its establishment it looked with suspicion upon the Portuguese who settled there. In this case as in many others, Portuguese was only another name for Marranos, and they were treated with great severity. There is a record of one David Ebron, who in 1597 sent a memorial to Philip II. relating to his discoveries and services in South America, but it is not known how far his claims were recognized. About 1604 or 1605 a number of those who were accused in Peru of Judaizing sent memorials to the King of Spain in which they pleaded that life under such conditions had become unbearable. Relief was obtained in the form of an Apostolic Brief from Pope Clement VIII., commanding the Inquisitors to release, without delay, all Judaizing Portuguese in Peru. When this order arrived in Lima, only two prisoners were still detained in the dungeons of the Tribunal, Gonzolo de Luna and Juan Vicente. The others had either become reconciled or had suffered death at the stake.

The liberal decree, which arrived too late for most of the complainants who were to benefit by it, still seems to have had the effect of securing the Marranos against molestation for several decades. But as soon as they had increased in wealth and influence the establishment of a new Tribunal was ordered in the Province of Tucuman, it having been ascertained that quite a colony of Jews were domiciled in the Rio de la Plata. In consequence of this order, dated May 18, 1636, the Portuguese were again hounded and many of them lost life and fortune. The Inquisition succeeded in ferreting out the fact that in Chili alone, at that time, there were no less than twenty-eight (secret) Jews, most of them enjoying the rights of citizenship and living securely and at peace with their neighbors. It has now been practically ascertained that a considerable number of Jews or Marranos lived in Peru, Chili, Argentine, Cartagena and La Plata towards the end of the sixteenth century, that their number and wealth increased in the first half of the seventeenth, when the new era of persecutions was ushered in by attacks and denunciations.

A notable instance, typical of the times, was the case of Francisco Maldonado de Silva. His sister Doña Isabel Maldonado, forty years old, on the 8th day of July, 1626, testified before the Commissioner of the City of Santiago de Chile that her brother had, to her horror and indignation, confessed to being a Jew, imploring her not to betray him and using all endeavors to convert her too. He was arrested in Concepcion, Chili, April 29, 1627, and was transported to Lima in July of the same year, where he was imprisoned in a cell of the convent of San Domingo. He is described in the records of the Tribunal as a bachelor, thirty-three years old, an American by birth, having been born of new-Christian parents in the city of San Miguel, Province of Tucuman, Peru. His father, the Licentiate Diego Nunez de Silva, and his brother, Diego de Silva, were both reconciled by the Inquisition at an auto held in Lima March 13, 1605. He confessed that he was brought up as a Catholic and that up to his eighteenth year he rigidly observed the tenets of the Christian faith. According to a circumstantial description of his case (Publications, XI, pp. 163 ff.), he remained in prison for nearly twelve years, during which time he had many hearings and disputed with many priests who undertook to convert him. He also wrote much in defence of his views and at one time made a nearly successful effort to escape. In the last years of his confinement he fasted very much, thereby becoming so feeble that he could not turn in his bed, "being nothing but skin and bones." He was, with ten others, burnt at the stake in Lima, on January 23, 1639, at a splendid and gruesome Auto da Fé, for which the preparations were costly and elaborate, involving fifty days of uninterrupted labor, holidays included.

CHAPTER IV

MARRANOS IN THE PORTUGUESE COLONIES.

Less persecution in Portugal itself and also in its colonies—Marranos buy right to emigrate—They dare to profess Judaism in Brazil, and the Inquisition is introduced in Goa—Alleged help given to Holland in its struggle against Spain.

While the expulsion of the Jews from Portugal, which took place five years after the great expulsion from Spain, was in many respects more cruel and accompanied by greater atrocities, notable among which were the forced conversions and the robbing of children from their Jewish parents to be brought up as Christians, the conditions in the Portuguese colonies, including Brazil, were somewhat more favorable for the reception of Jewish refugees than in the Spanish possessions of the New World. This happened because the conditions in Portugal itself were much more favorable to the Jews prior to the era of expulsions, and the sudden severity against the Jews in 1497, which was almost unexpected, was due to the influence of the Spanish rulers. It was Queen Isabella of Spain who prevailed on King Manuel of Portugal (reigned 1495-1521), her future son-in-law, to exile the Jews of his dominion, vowing she would never set foot on Portuguese soil until the country was clear of them.

In the preceding centuries the Jews, though they were recognized and treated as a separate nation in Portugal even more than in Spain, their condition when judged by the standards of the dark ages was much more favorable and well nigh secure. There are no records of systematic persecutions in Portugal before the exile from Spain. The influence of the Church grew much more slowly in the former country, and its kings followed the old Spanish policy of protecting the Jews and Moors against the encroachments of the clergy long after it was abandoned by Spain. Marranos and other Jews who escaped from the Inquisition to Portugal before the Spanish expulsion were—because the King did not want or did not dare to harbor them—permitted to go to the Orient but not to Africa, because in the latter place they could become dangerous to him as allies of the Moors. So it came to pass that while in the more extensive Spanish domains across the Atlantic we hear only of individual crypto-Jewish settlers and more of their misfortunes and the Autos da Fé of which they were the victims, than of their successes, we learn of considerable settlements of Marranos in Brazil early in the sixteenth century.

But even the better conditions in the Portuguese territories must not be taken in the sense which such a term would imply to-day or even a hundred years ago. The Portuguese policy was cruel and vaccillating, only a little less so than that of its larger and more consistent neighbor. King Manuel forbade the neo-Christians, in 1499, to leave Portugal, the prohibition was removed in 1507 and again put into effect in 1521. His successor John III. (reigned 1521-57) was even less favorably disposed towards the secret Jews who remained in his Kingdom, and in 1531 the Inquisition was introduced there by the authorization of Pope Clement VII. The Marranos bought from John's successor King Sebastian (reigned 1557-78) the right of free departure for the sum of 250,000 ducats. But there were other involuntary departures in the periods when the emigration of those suspected converts was prohibited. For a considerable time in the 16th century Portugal sent annually two shiploads of Jews and criminals to Brazil, and also deported persons who had been condemned by the Inquisition. The banishment of large numbers to Brazil in 1548 is especially mentioned.

Jews or Marranos were soon settled in all the Portuguese colonies, and they carried on an extensive trade with various countries. "As early as 1548 (according to some, 1531) Portuguese Jews, it is asserted, transplanted the sugar-cane from Madeira to Brazil." Some of them began to feel so secure that they dared to profess Judaism openly. The result was the introduction of the Inquisition into Goa, the metropolis of the Portuguese dominions in India, with jurisdiction over all the possessions of that country in Asia and Africa, as far as the Cape of Good Hope. It was therefore but natural for the hunted and despairing new-Christians to sympathize with the Dutch who were at that time (beginning at 1567) fighting for their freedom, and to help them later against Portugal itself in the New World and in the Far East. The charge that the Marranos of the Indies sent considerable supplies to the Spanish and Portuguese Jews in Hamburg and Aleppo, who in turn forwarded them to Holland and Zeeland, is probably not true. But the act would have certainly been justified in times when the Marranos were legally burned alive when convicted of adhesion to the religion of their forefathers. The charge also proves that the Jews and Marranos of various and distant countries were then believed to be in communication, and to render assistance to one another or to their friends when the occasion required it. We may recognize in such charges the false accusations which were circulated about Jews from times immemorial to our present day; but it nevertheless tends to prove that the Jews retained some recognizable importance as international traders even in times when their fortunes were at the lowest ebb.

Except for the brief period in the 17th century (which is dealt with more extensively in a subsequent chapter), in which Brazil came under the domination of the Dutch, it remained almost entirely free of Jews until the present time. The time was approaching when liberal and enterprising nations, pursuing a more enlightened and more profitable policy, were beginning to grant the Jewish refugee not only shelter and security, but also the religious liberty and broad human tolerance which were almost unknown in the Catholic countries in the Middle Ages. The dawn of a new era began for the Jews in Europe with the ascendency, first of Holland and then of England, and the Children of Israel were soon to share openly in the invaluable benefits which the discovery of the New World brought to mankind in general.

PART II.

THE DUTCH AND ENGLISH COLONIAL PERIOD.

CHAPTER V.

THE SHORT-LIVED DOMINION OF THE DUTCH OVER BRAZIL.

The friendship between the Dutch and the Jews—Restrictions and privileges in Holland—Dutch-Jewish distributors of Indian spices—Preparations to introduce the Inquisition in Brazil—Jews help the Dutch to conquer it—Southey's description of Recife—Vieyra's description.

The United Provinces of Netherland, or, as it is commonly called, Holland, became a safe place for Jews as soon as the Union of Utrecht (1579) made its independence reasonably secure. When the liberator of these provinces, William of Orange ("The Silent," 1533-84), was installed as Stadtholder in 1581 he declared that "he should not suffer any man to be called to account, molested or injured for his faith or conscience." This implied, and actually resulted in, better treatment of the Jews, which led to their enjoying a larger degree of prosperity and security in Holland in the following century than anywhere else. The friendship between the Jews and the Dutch which commenced at that period has never, unto this day, been marred by systematic persecution or any retrogressive step. It proved mutually beneficial in various parts of the world, and has cost Spain and Portugal much more than is ordinarily known even to students of History.[1]

But while the treatment was immeasurably better, the vicious principle of separation remained. The Jews in Holland were as much a nation apart, in theory at least, as in Spain and Portugal before the expulsion. They did not enjoy the full rights of citizenship (until they received it, somewhat against their will, during the French invasion at the end of the eighteenth century) and were not even free from other restrictions. They were not permitted to serve in the train bands or militia of the cities, but paid a compensation for their exemption therefrom. The prohibition of intermarriage with Christians could hardly be considered a hardship for Jews of the seventeenth century; but the fact that they were not allowed any mechanical pursuit or to engage in retail trade has a much deeper significance. It explains, at least partly, why the Dutch succeeded where the Portuguese failed, notably in that Indian trade, whose interruption by the Turkish conquest of Constantinople was the cause of searching new water routes to the East and of the discovery of the New World.

Having exiled their best international traders and kept those remaining as Marranos in constant terror, the Portuguese could not derive the full benefit from that lucrative trade in spices which was to be the reward of their great discoveries. When the sixty years' captivity—as the domination of Spain over Portugal, from 1580 to 1640, is called—brought, among other disasters, the capture of the Portuguese Indian possessions by the Dutch, the superiority of the latter's methods were soon apparent. They succeeded with more ease "since, with true commercial spirit, they not only imported merchandise from the East to

[1] This subject is treated extensively in the chapter headed "Services rendered by the Jews to the Dutch, 1623-44," in Mr. Simon Wolf's valuable work "*The American Jew as Patriot, Soldier and Citizen*," p. 443 ff., and in the monogram "Damage done to Spanish Interests in America by Jews of Holland," which is incorporated in the "Publications," vol. XVII.

Holland, but also distributed it through Dutch merchants to every country in Europe; whereas the Portuguese in the days of their commercial monopoly were satisfied with bringing over the commodities to Lisbon and letting foreign nations come to fetch them." It is not difficult to surmise who were those Dutch merchants who distributed the spices to every country in Europe, when we think of that class of wealthy Marrano immigrants in Holland who were not permitted to follow mechanical pursuits or to engage in retail trade. Holland's tendency was clearly apparent. The Jews, mostly Portuguese, were permitted to use their wealth, their abilities and their foreign connections to carry on and extend that trade which languished in the hands of those who banished them. The Jews were exceedingly grateful for the opportunity which Holland afforded them to be useful to themselves and to her, and the very effective results of the friendship between the Jews and the Dutch were soon apparent in the ensuing struggle between the latter and the Portuguese over the possession of Brazil.

The Dutch commenced the realization of their ambitious scheme for the conquest of Brazil in the second decade of the seventeenth century, at a time when the large number of Marranos who lived there were terrorized by rumors of the introduction of the inquisition. These rumors became current as early as 1610, when it was reported that the physicians of Bahia, who were mainly new-Christians, prescribed pork to their patients in order to lessen the suspicion that they were still adhering to Judaism. In connection with some of the earliest Brazilian intrigues in favor of the Dutch, mention is made of one Francisco Ribiero, a Portuguese captain, who is described as having many Jewish relatives in Holland. About 1618 the Inquisition in Oporto, Portugal, had arrested all merchants of Jewish extraction. Many of the victims were engaged in Brazilian trade, and the Inquisitor-General applied to the government to assist the Holy Office to recover such parts of their effects as might be in the hands of their agents in Brazil. Accordingly, Don Luis de Sousa was charged to send home a list of all the new-Christians in Brazil "with the most precise information that can be obtained of their property and place of abode." It seems highly probable that it was the Dutch war alone which prevented the introduction of the dreaded Tribunal in Brazil.

The Dutch West India Company, which was formed in 1622 in furtherance of the project of conquering Brazil, had Jews of Amsterdam among its large stockholders, and several of them in its Board of Directors. One of the arguments in favor of its organization was "that the Portuguese themselves—some from their hatred of Castille, others because of their intermarriage with new-Christians and their consequent fear of the Inquisition—would either willingly join or feebly oppose an invasion, and all that was needful was to treat them well and give them liberty of conscience."

When the Dutch fleet was sent to Bahia all the necessary information was obtained from Jews. The city was taken in 1624 and Willeken, the Dutch commander, at once issued a proclamation offering liberty, free possession of their property and free enjoyment of religion to all who would submit. This brought over about two hundred Jews, who exerted themselves to induce others to follow their example. Bahia was re-captured by the Portuguese in 1625, and though the treaty for its deliverance provided for the safety of the other inhabitants, the new-Christians were abandoned and five of them were put to death. Many others, however, seemed to have remained there for several years.

Another foothold was gained by the Dutch when the city of Recife or Pernambuco, which had a large Crypto-Jewish population, was captured in 1631. Most of the Jews and new-Christians from Bahia and other Brazilian towns soon removed to that city. The conquerors appealed to Holland for colonists and craftsmen of all kinds, and many Portuguese Jews came over in response to that call. Robert Southey, the historian of Brazil, asserts that the Jews there made excellent subjects of Holland. "Some of the Portuguese Brazilians gladly threw off the mask which they had so long been compelled to wear, and joined their brethren in the Synagogue. The open joy with which they celebrated their ceremonies attracted too much notice. It excited the horror of the Catholics; and even the Dutch themselves, less liberal than their own laws, pretended that the toleration of Holland did not extend to Brazil." The result was an edict by which the Jews were ordered to perform their rites more privately.

When in 1645 Vieyra was inciting the Portuguese to re-conquer Brazil, he pointed particularly to Recife, calling attention to the fact that "that city is chiefly inhabited by Jews, most of whom were originally fugitives from Portugal. They have their open Synagogues there, to the scandal of Christianity. For the honor of the faith, therefore, the Portuguese ought to risk their lives and property in putting down such an abomination." The Portuguese, who had shortly before thrown off the Spanish yoke and regained their independence at home, responded to that call and redoubled their effort to reconquer their gigantic South American colony. But although the history of that first really Jewish settlement in the New World was brief, extending over less than two decades, it was so brilliant in itself and had such far-reaching consequences in the settlement of Jews in other parts of America that another chapter must be devoted to its description.

CHAPTER VI.

RECIFE: THE FIRST JEWISH COMMUNITY IN THE NEW WORLD.

The "Kahal Kodesh" of Recife or Pernambuco in Brazil—Manasseh ben Israel's expectation to make it his home—Large immigration from Amsterdam—Isaac Aboab da Fonseca and his colleagues—First rabbis and Jewish authors of the New World—The siege and the surrender—The return, and the nucleus of other communities in various parts of America.

The rebuke to the joyful demonstrations of the Jews in Recife did not prevent the establishment there of the first real Jewish community in the New World. The Dutch Stadtholder of Brazil, John Maurice, of Nassau, was a just and honorable official who encouraged the development of the community and its steady increase by immigration. The Jews of Recife, who were soon numbered by thousands, called themselves "Kahal Kodesh" (The Holy Congregation) and had a governing body consisting of David Senior Coronel, Abraham de Mercado, Jacob Mucate and Isaac Casthunho. One of the earliest settlers there was Ephraim Sueiro, a step-brother (or brother-in-law) of the famous Rabbi of Amsterdam, Manasseh Ben Israel (1604-57). Don Francisco Fernandez de Mora, who had a grandchild in Amsterdam, held important offices; while another member of the community, Gaspar Diaz Ferrena, was considered one of the wealthiest men in the country. Dr. Kayserling, in his paper on "The Earliest Rabbis and Jewish writers in America" ("Publications" III, p. 13 ff.) quotes from the correspondence between the old Vossius and Hugo Grotius, in which they speak of the intention of their mutual friend, the above-named Rabbi Manasseh, to emigrate to Brazil in order to improve his material condition, which was unsatisfactory in Amsterdam, notwithstanding the high communal position which he held there. He dedicated the second part of his "Conciliador" to the prominent men of the congregation of Recife, probably in anticipation of the expected journey, which, however, was never made.

But though the man who was later to induce Oliver Cromwell to admit Jews into England did not come, other reputable Hebrew scholars soon arrived to lend lustre to the new congregation. In 1642 about six hundred Spanish-Portuguese Jews from Amsterdam embarked for Brazil, accompanied by two men of learning, Isaac Aboab da Fonseca (1605-93) and Moses Raphael de Aguilar (d. 1679). Aboab became the Chacham or Rabbi—the first in America. Aguilar, who was also a grammarian, became the reader or cantor. A congregation was also organized at Tamarica, which had its own Chacham, Jacob Lagarto, the first Talmudical author in the Western Hemisphere. A certain Jacob de Aguilar is also mentioned as a Brazilian rabbi of that time. Considerable numbers of Jews also resided at other places in Brazil, particularly at Itamarica, Rio de Janeiro and Parahibo. But Recife was the great center, and its fame soon spread even into the Old World. Nieuhoff, the historian, writes that the Jews there had built stately homes, that they had a vast traffic and purchased sugar mills. Several years later they raised large sums to assist the Dutch in defending the coast.

The last and most important immigrants were barely settled when the sanguinary struggle between the Portuguese and the Dutch for the possession of the colony began in 1645. A conspiracy into which native Portuguese entered for the purpose of assassinating the Dutch authorities at a banquet in the capital was discovered and exposed by a Jew, and a possible sudden termination of Dutch rule was averted. Open war broke out in 1646 and Recife had to endure a long and costly siege. Jews vied with Dutch in suffering and in bravery, and there is a record of the fact that Marranos in Portugal used their influence to call the attention of the government of the Netherlands to the gravity of the situation in South America. But the resources of the West India Company were exhausted by the possession of Brazil, and as the home government would not or could not give it proper support, the heroism and the self-sacrifice of both Dutch and Jews served only to prolong the struggle. It probably also served to cement the friendship between the defenders, who were later to dwell together for longer periods in other parts of America.

Aboab commemorated the thrilling experience of this war in the introductory chapter of his Hebrew version of Abraham Cohen Herrera's *Porta Coeli* (Sha'ar ha-Shomayim). He also wrote a poetical account of the siege in a work entitled "*Zeker Rab*: Prayers, Confessions and Supplications which were composed for the purpose of appealing to God in the trouble and the distress of the congregation when the troops of Portugal overwhelmed them during their sojourn in Brazil in 5406 (1646)." The Rabbi ordered fasts and prayers, while wealthy members of the community, like Abraham Coen, contributed material support. "Many of the Jewish immigrants were killed by the enemy, many died of starvation; the remainder were exposed to death from various causes. Those who were accustomed to delicacies were glad to be able to satisfy their hunger with dry bread; soon they could not obtain even this. They were in want of everything, and were preserved alive as if by a miracle."

Among the instances of individual heroism which deserve to be recorded is that of one of the Pintos, who is said to have manned the fort Dos Affrogades single-handed, until, overwhelmed by superior force, he was compelled to surrender.

On the 23d of January, 1654, Recife, together with the neighboring cities of Mauritsstad, Parahiba, Itamarica, Seara and other Hollandish possessions, was ceded to the Portuguese conquerors, with the condition that a general amnesty should be granted. The Jews, as loyal supporters of the Dutch, were promised every consideration; nevertheless the new Portuguese Governor ordered them to quit Brazil at once. Sixteen vessels were placed at their disposal to carry them and their property wherever they chose to go, and they were also furnished with passports and safeguards.

Aboab, Aguilar, the Nassys, Perreires, the Mezas, Abraham de Castro and Joshua Zarfati, both surnamed *el Brasil*, and many others returned to Amsterdam. Jacob de Velosino, (b. in Pernambuco, 1639, d. in Holland, 1712), the first Hebrew author born on American soil, settled at The Hague. Others went to Surinam, Cayenne and Curaçao, and it is generally assumed that the first Jewish settlers who in that year arrived in New Amsterdam (the future New York) came directly—or at least indirectly—from Pernambuco. The community of Recife formed thus, by its dissolution, the nucleus of several of the oldest and most important Jewish communities in the New World.

CHAPTER VII.

THE JEWS IN SURINAM OR DUTCH GUIANA.

Jews in Brazil after the expulsion of the Dutch—The community of Paramaraibo, Surinam, was founded when Recife was still flourishing—First contact with the English, whom the Jews preferred—David Nasi and the colony of Cayenne—Privileges granted by Lord Willoughby—"de Jooden Savane"—Trouble with slaves and bush negroes—Plantations with Hebrew names—German Jews—Legal status and banishments—Jewish theaters—Literature and history.

The history of the Jews in Brazil practically ends with the termination of the Dutch rule, and there is a gap which extends until the new settlements at the beginning of the twentieth century. There was the usual aftermath of Marranos and persecutions which was almost a repetition of the happenings under Portuguese dominion prior to the short, liberal era under Holland's sway. Some new-Christians continued to reside in Brazil after the capitulation of 1654. Their number was largely increased towards the end of the seventeenth century, when Portugal again banished to Brazil the Marranos who had become reconciled. These transportations continued from 1682 to 1707; and the Jews again became to be known as a distinct class. They were closely watched, however, and many were sent back to Lisbon from time to time, to be tried by the Inquisitior Many Jews from Rio were burned at an Auto da Fé at Lisbon in 1723. Several of these martyrs were men of great repute, the most prominent being the famous Portuguese poet and dramatist, Antonio José da Silva, a native of Rio de Janeiro, who was burned as a Jew at Lisbon in 1739. In 1734 Jews appear to have been influential in controlling the price of diamonds in Brazil.

The transportations to Lisbon of those accused of Judaizing had become so common at the middle of the eighteenth century, that "a wide ruin was produced and many sugar mills at the Rio stopped in consequence." The influential Marquis de Pombal, with all his power, did not venture to proclaim toleration for the Jews; but he succeeded in having laws enacted making it penal for any person to reproach another for his Jewish origin, and removing all disabilities of Jewish blood, even from the descendants of those who had suffered under the Inquisition. He prohibited public Autos da Fé, and required all lists of families of Jewish extraction to be delivered up. These statutes deprived the Inquisition of its most important means of accusation; and as a result the Marranos were ultimately absorbed in the Catholic population of Brazil.

The Jewish community which was founded in Surinam or Dutch Guiana, near Brazil, in the days when the community of Recife was still in a flourishing condition, and which soon rose to prominence after the dispersion of the latter, has enjoyed an almost uninterrupted existence until the present day. According to the latest researches, the oldest indication in the archives of the Dutch-Portuguese Jews shows that the Jews had already settled in Surinam in the year 1639.[1] As far as can be traced, the first Jewish marriage was celebrated there between Haham Isaac Mehatob and Judith Mehatob in 1643. The text of the "Ketubah," which has been preserved, proves that Surinam, or rather the city of Paramaribo, had already in that year a sufficient number of Jews to require the services of a Haham or Rabbi.

Though the Dutch had claims on it, Guiana was at that time

[1] Rabbi P. A. Hilfman of Paramaribo, Surinam, in "Publications" XVI, p. 7 ff., supplementing the chronology made by Prof. Richard Gottheil in the same Publications at the beginning of Vol. IV. See also Rev. J. S. Roos of the Dutch Congreg. in Paramaribo, Ibid Vol. XIII, pp. 126 ff.

practically British territory, and it was there that the Jew came first in contact with the Englishman in the New World, many years before they began to dwell together in North America. And while it was recognized that of all European nations the Dutch were then the most friendly to the Jews, many of the latter who had experience with both nationalities in that part of the world soon learned to prefer the English. Lord Willoughby, who arrived for the second time in Surinam in 1652, brought with him several Jewish families, and the community was thus increasing even before the influx of refugees from Brazil two years later.

On September 12, 1659, the Jews were permitted, under the patronage of David Nassi, to found a colony on the island of Cayenne (French Guiana). According to the tenor of the eighteen articles contained in the letters patent of that date, all the land over which they exercised the rights of possession within four years from that date, would become their property; and they would be allowed to administer justice according to the Jewish usages and customs. The colony was further increased by the arrival, in 1660, of one hundred and fifty-two Jews from Leghorn, Italy. But the four years' limit was barely passed when the French took Cayenne in 1664, and all the Jews left the island for Surinam under the leadership of the above-mentioned David Nassi. The French of the time of "the Grand Monarch" Louis XIV would not suffer Jews to be settled in their colonies; a century and a quarter had to pass before France, shaken to its very foundations by the great revolution which began in 1789, was the first of modern European nations to grant its Jews the absolute equality which is implied in full citizenship.

Even while the Portuguese Jews were still in Cayenne, they were given by Lord Willoughby, in 1662, the same privileges in Surinam as the English colonists. A year after their return, on August 17, 1665, was issued the famous grant of privileges by the Governor, Council and Assembly of Surinam, of which the preamble reads as follows:

"Whereas, it is good and sound policy to encourage as much

as possible whatever may tend to the increase of a new colony, and to invite persons of whatsoever country and religion to come and reside here and to traffic with us; and whereas, we found that the Hebrew nation, now already resident here, have, with their persons and property, proved themselves useful and beneficial to this colony; and being desirous further to encourage them to continue their residence and trade here, we have with the authority of the Governor, his Council and Assembly passed the following act:

The provisions of the act (the full text of which is reproduced in "Publications, vol. III, pp. 145-46; vol. IX, pp. 144-45, and vol. XVI, pp. 179-80) is extremely favorable to the Jews. The British Government of Surinam therein ratified all former privileges of the Jews, guaranteed them full enjoyment and free exercise of their religious rites and usages, and made void any summons served upon them on their Sabbaths and holidays. They were not to be called for any public duties on those days, except in urgent cases. Civil suits of less value than ten thousand pounds of sugar were to be decided by their Elders, and the magistrates were obliged to enforce their judgments. They were also permitted to bequeath their property according to their own laws of inheritance. They were given ten acres of land for the erection of a Synagogue and such buildings as the congregation might need; and in order to induce Jews to settle there, it was decided that all who came for that purpose should be considered as British-born subjects, in return for obeying all the decrees of the King of England which did not infringe on their privileges.

For Portuguese Jews of the seventeenth century, i. e., for extremely conservative Jews whose relatives were at that very time tortured and burned at the stake for adherence to their religion, these privileges were probably much more acceptable than an outright admission to full citizenship could have been. There was no desire or striving for assimilation on either side in those times. No especially organized movement was necessary to emphasize the fact, which was then self-evident, of the existence of a separate Hebrew nation. Nobody thought otherwise before the philosophers of the eighteenth century instilled in the minds of the civilized nations the idea of the modern assimilationist. The frank selfishness of the preamble was, therefore, a better guarantee of good faith and more convincing than phrases about humanity and inherent rights could possibly be in those illiberal times. The English were thus less sentimental and more business-like in their dealings with the Jews than the Dutch, and were probably on that account more trusted. When Surinam became a Dutch province, July 13, 1667, the Jews were allowed all rights of citizenship. Still a number of them left with the English and went to Jamaica. Another declaration by the home government of Holland, made two years later, to the Jews of Surinam, that they would be allowed free exercise of their religion, tends to prove that there must have been cases, or at least fears, of restraint in that respect. Even if the "Documents relating to the attempted departure of the Jews from Surinam in 1675" (edited by Dr. J. H. Hollander, in "Publications" VI, pp. 9-29) in which the anxiety of many Jews to leave Surinam for British territory is described, should be considered as somewhat exaggerated, it could not have been entirely an invention. The Jews' preference for the British rule was therewith clearly established, and so was their acknowledged usefulness in the newly founded colonies.

The Jews of Surinam were then chiefly engaged in agriculture, the wealthy among them being large planters and slave holders. The chief men of the congregation were David Nassi, Isaac Perreira, Isaac Aries, Henriques de Caseras, Raphael Aboab, Samuel Nassi, Isaac R. de Pardo, Aaron de Silva, Alaus de Fonseca, Isaac Mera, Daniel Mesia, Jacob Nunez, Israel Calaby Cid, Isaac da Costa, Isaac Drago, Bento da Costa. The first Synagogue was built in 1672, on an elevated spot in Thorarica belonging to the Jews, da Costa and Solis. There are still some tombstones with illegible Hebrew inscriptions. We hear about that time of Rabbi Isaac Neto who was called from England as minister of the congregation of Paramaribo (1674 or 1680), and later we find recorded the name of another rabbi, David Pardo, who also came from London and died in 1713 (or 1717). The last named wrote, while still in Europe, "Sefer Shulhan Tahor" (Amsterdam, 1686), extracts from the "Shulhan Aruk," and is considered the most distinguished rabbi of Surinam.

In 1682 the above-named Samuel Nassi, who has been described as capitein and as the richest planter in Surinam, gave to the Jews an island on the river Surinam, about seventy miles from the sea, where most of them settled and which was henceforth known as "de Jooden Savane" (Savannah of the Jews, the name originally meaning: a treeless region) and was the principal seat of the Jewish community of Surinam. It was there that the Congregation Berakah-we-Shalom (Blessing and Peace) built its splendid Synagogue in 1685. One hundred years later the centennial of the dedication of that Synagogue was appropriately celebrated on Wednesday, Heshwan 8, 5546 (October 12, 1785), of which a record was printed in Amsterdam the following year, partly in Hebrew and partly in Dutch. (See Roest, *Catalog . . der Rosenthalschen Bibliothek* I, p. 738.)

When a French squadron attacked Surinam in 1689, the Jews under the leadership of Samuel Nassi did good service in beating them off. Similar valuable service was rendered in 1712, this time under Capitein Isaac Pinto, against another French attack under Cassard. The unfriendliness of the French was demonstrated again in that year, when they took the Jewish Savannah and desecrated the Synagogue by slaughtering a pig on the "Teibah" or Ammud. The Jews, on the other hand, did not always get the protection to which they were entitled. When the slaves on the plantation of M. Machado revolted and killed their master in 1690, Governor Van Scherpenhuitzen refused to assist the Jews. At a later period (in 1718), when there was continual trouble with bush negroes, who destroyed the plantation of David Nassi, they were chastised by Jews under the leadership of Capitein Jacob d'Avilar. David Nassi (1672-1743) himself served under him with distinction, and his praises were sung by the Judeo-Spanish poetess Benvenide Belmonte. We also find traces of legal restrictions in such instances as the decree of 1703, by which all Jewish marriages contracted in Surinam up to that year are confirmed, but henceforth they must be made in conformity with the Dutch marriage law of 1580. Sunday-closing laws were also brought into force against them, but they were later repealed.

A list of the names of about sixty-five plantations belonging to Jews at that period and the names of the owners has been preserved. ("Publications," IX, p. 129 ff.) Some of the plantations bear Hebrew names like Carmel, Hebron, Succoth and Beer-Sheba. The number of Jews in Surinam was then (about 1694) 570, consisting of ninety-two Dutch or Portuguese families, about fifty unmarried persons and ten or twelve German families. They possessed about nine thousand slaves.

Difficulties between the earlier settlers and the Germans, who arrived later, soon arose, and in 1734 the latter requested permission to form a separate community, which was granted. They were, however, prohibited to own any possession on the Jewish Savannah, nor were they allowed to have their own jurisdiction. The act of the separation of the "Hoogduytsche" (High-German) Jews, who founded the congregation Neweh Shalom, is dated January 5, 1735. It is signed by A. Henry de Scheusses (Governor) and Samuel Uz. Davilar, Ishac Carrilho, Abraham Pinto Junior, Jehoshuah C. Nassi, for the Portuguese; Solomon Joseph Levie, I. Meyer Wolff, Gerrit Jacobs, Jakob Arons Polak for the German Jews. The Portuguese thereupon built a new Synagogue, "Zedek we-Shalom," which was dedicated in 1737. But the Germans also stuck to the Portuguese Minhag or prayer-book, and we have it on the authority of Rabbi Roos of Paramaribo (1905) that there never existed a Synagogue with the Minhag Ashkenaz in Surinam.

Bloody conflicts with negroes continued for about forty years longer, and many valiant deeds of Jewish military leaders and their followers embellish the records of that period. David Nassi was killed in battle at the age of 71 (in 1743), after being successful in more than thirty skirmishes, and was succeeded as capitein by Isaac Carvalho. In 1749 another Jewish capitein, Naär, won a victory against the Auka negroes; while in 1750 young Isaac Nassi and three hundred of his men were killed by an overwhelming force of bush negroes. At last, in 1774, forts were erected and a military line drawn from the Savannah of the Jews along the river Commoimber to the sea; and we hear no more of negro wars.

The legal status of the Jews was undergoing some changes, as is almost unavoidable so long as there is not the same law for Jew and Gentile alike. Some measures could be considered as improvements, like the law of 1749, which granted the Jews of Surinam their own judiciary in matters affecting less than 600 gulden. On the other hand we hear of an unsuccessful attempt in 1768 to institute a Ghetto in Paramaribo, and in 1775 Jews were forbidden to visit a certain amateur theatre of that town. At that time the two communities also began to make use of the right which was bestowed on them by the English Charter of Privilege (and later confirmed by the Dutch authorities), of "banishing troublesome people and persons of bad demeanour." The "Deputies of the Jewish Nation" had only to declare to the Governor the reasons why they wished to have these persons banished, and they were expelled. The above named Rabbi J. S. Roos has noted five cases of such banishments:

Solomon Montel was banished in 1761 on the request of the Portuguese deputies, because he refused to restitute rents or usury "which is contrary to the Mosaic law." In 1772 Noach Isaaks was banished on the request of the German deputies, and in the following year Abraham Isaac Moses Michael Fernandes Henriques, alias Escarabajos, was, on the request of the Portuguese deputies, made to quit the place. Elias Levin was banished in 1781 by the Germans and Abraham de Mesquita, the last of those exiled, belonged to the Portuguese part of the community.

The German Jews kept on increasing in numbers, and in 1780

their Synagogue in Paramaribo was enlarged and two burial grounds were procured. In 1784 the Jewish theatre of that city, probably the first in modern history, was enlarged and embellished. The Savannah, of which only ruins remain now, was on its decline, and had only about forty houses in 1792; while the community in Paramaribo was growing and two Jewish play houses are mentioned in that year. The Portuguese were still the majority, numbering 834, but the Germans were gaining fast, and from the ten families at the end of the seventeenth century they rose now to the number of 477. There were also about 100 Jewish mulattoes in Paramaribo in that time.

The Jews of Surinam in that period also commenced to display considerable literary activity. J. C. Nassi and others wrote the *Essai historique sur la Colonie de Surinam avec l'histoire de la nation juive y etablie* (Paramaribo, 1788), which is one of the principal sources of the history of the Jews of Surinam. A highly interesting correspondence between representative Jews of that community and Christian Wilhelm v. Dohm (1751-1820) relating to the latter's work favoring the Jews, is printed at the end of that Essay. (Reproduced in "Publications," XIII, pp. 133-35). Various other works of historical, religious and poetical nature were written and published there in the following half century.

The history of the community of Paramaribo in the nineteenth century is uneventful. In 1836, when the German congregation, which now numbered 719 souls, already exceeded the Portuguese portion, which had declined to 684, a new "Hoogduitsche of Nederlandsche" Synagogue was erected. In 1838 Rabbi B. C. Carrilon became the spiritual head of the Dutch-Portuguese congregation. Twenty years later M. J. Lewenstein (1829-64) was inaugurated as the Chief Rabbi of the congregation of Paramaribo and held the position for six years, until his death. In 1900 the city contained about 1,500 Jews, who occupied an honorable position and controlled the principal property of the colony. Even modern Antisemitism has not failed to invade this distant Jewish settlement, the oldest in the New World.

At present (1911.) there are about 4,000 Jews in Surinam, mostly in Paramaribo, which has now about 50,000 inhabitants. The two communities, both strongly orthodox, are still in existence, and each has its rabbi. The most prominent Jewish citizen in the colony is Mr. David De Costa, a former President of the Provincial Parliament, who was lately appointed by the Dutch Government to be the presiding judge of the Supreme Court of the colony. Mr. da Costa was for many years Parnass or President of the Portuguese congregation. Another member of the Jewish community, M. Benjamin, is at the head of the educational system of the province. Several families trace their descent from the original settlers who came there in 1639, and all of them, now fully enfranchised for several generations, have no other mother-tongue than the Dutch. Their staunch orthodoxy has saved them from being absorbed in the non-Jewish population, as happened with most of the early settlers in the British colonies in North America.

CHAPTER VIII.

THE DUTCH AND ENGLISH WEST INDIES.

The community of Curaçao—Encouragement to settle is followed by restrictions—Plans of Jewish colonization—Trade communication with New Amsterdam—Stuyvesant's slur—The first congregation—Departures to North America and to Venezuela—Barbadoes—Taxation and legal status—Decay after the hurricane of 1831—Jamaica under Spain and under England—Hebrew taught in the Parish of St. Andrews in 1693—Harsh measures and excessive taxation—Naturalizations.

Another early settlement on Dutch territory which is still in a flourishing condition is on the island of Curaçao, Dutch West Indies. It is probable that Jews from Holland were among the first settlers in the island under the Dutch Government, which captured it from Spain in 1634; but there is no definite record until 1650, when twelve Jewish families—De Meza, Aboab, Perreire, De Leon, La Parra, Touro, Cardoze, Jesurum, Marchena, Chaviz, Oliveira and Henriques Coutinho—were granted permission by Prince Maurice of Orange to settle there. Mathias Bock, Governor of the island, was directed to grant them land and supply them with slaves, horses, cattle and agricultural implements, in order to further the cultivation and develop the natural resources of the island. The land assigned to them was situated at the northern outskirts of the present district of Willemstad, which is still known as the "Jodenwyk" (Jewish quarter). But despite the favorable conditions under which they settled there, severe restrictions were put on their movements, and they were even prohibited in 1653 from purchasing additional negro slaves which they needed for their farms.

By a special grant of privilege, dated February 22, 1652, Joseph Nunez de Fonseca (known also as David Nassi), who undertook to emigrate and take with him a large number of people under a Jewish patron named Jan de Illan, two leagues of land along the coast were to be given him for every fifty families, and four leagues for every hundred families which he should bring over. The colonists were exempted from taxes for ten years, and could select the land on which they desired to settle. They were also accorded religious liberty, though they were restrained from compelling Christians to work for them on Sunday, "nor were any others to labor on that day." The project was, however, not carried out on any extensive scale.

It was only after the re-conquest of Brazil by the Portuguese in 1654, and the consequent expulsion and dispersion of the Jews from the territory which was now again forbidden to them, that their effective settlement in Curaçao began. The Brazilian Jews who came there in that period brought with them considerable wealth, and they laid the foundation of that prominence in the commerce of the island which they have since retained.

Shortly afterwards (1657) regular communications for the purposes of trade were established between New Amsterdam and Curaçao, and it was principally in the hands of Jews. An original bill of lading (in Spanish) and an invoice of goods shipped from Curaçao to New Netherland in 1658 and addressed to Joshua Mordecai En-Riquez, includes Venetian pearls and pendants, thimbles, scissors, knives, bells, etc. An illicit trade was also carried on with Isaac de Fonseca of Barbadoes, which tended to undermine the trade monopoly enjoyed by the Dutch West Indies Company. But Fonseca's threat to abandon Curaçoa and turn his trade towards Jamaica, kept the authorities from interfering.

Peter Stuyvesant (1592-1672), the Governor of New Netherlands, complained to the directors of the West India Company in the following year, that the Jews in Curaçao were allowed to hold negro slaves and were granted other privileges not enjoyed by the colonies of New Netherlands; and he demanded for his own people, if not more, at least the same privileges as were enjoyed by "the usurious and covetous Jews."

The Congregation Mickweh Israel was founded in 1656 under the direction of the Spanish and Portuguese community of Amsterdam, and regular daily services were held in a small wooden building which was rented for the purpose. The Rev. Abraham Haim Lopez de Fonseca, who, according to one of the oldest tombstones on the Jewish burial ground in Curaçao, died Ab. 22, 5432 (1672), was the earliest hazzan or rabbi whose name has come down to us. The first regularly appointed Hakam was Joshua Pardo, who arrived from Amsterdam in 1674 and remained until 1683, when he left for Jamaica. A new Synagogue was erected in 1692 and consecrated on the eve of Passover of that year, the services being read by the Hazzan David Raphael Lopez da Fonseca (d. 1707). The building, which was enlarged in 1731, still stands.

In the last decade of the seventeenth century a considerable number of Jews left the island for the continent of America, many of them, including the Touro family, going to Newport. A number of Italian settlers who originally came from the Jewish colony of Cayenne, which was dispersed in 1664, went to Tucacas, Venezuela, where they established a congregation called "Santa Irmandade."

The prosperity of those who remained in Curaçao went on increasing in the eighteenth century. A benevolent society was established in 1715; five years later they responded liberally to an appeal for aid from the Congregation Shearith Israel of New York, and in 1756 met with an equal generosity a similar appeal from the Jews of Newport. By 1750 their numbers had increased to about two thousand. They were prosperous merchants and traders, and held positions of prominence in the commercial and political affairs of the island. By the end of the century they owned a considerable part of the property in the district of Willemsted; and as many as fifty-three vessels are said to have left in one day for Holland, laden with goods which for the most part belonged to Jewish merchants.

A new congregation, which called itself "Neweh Shalom" and occupied a tract across the harbor from Willemsted, was organized about 1740, and its Synagogue in the "Otrabanda" was consecrated on Ellul 12, 5505 (1745). It was established chiefly in order to save those who lived there from crossing the water on the Sabbath to attend divine services, and for a time it was regarded as merely a branch of the older congregation and as under its direction. This led to a series of disputes which culminated, in 1749, in an open breach. It was settled by the intervention of Prince William Charles of Orange-Nassau, in a decree dated April 30, 1750, in which the original jurisdiction of the older congregation, subject to the regulations of the Portuguese community of Amsterdam, was sustained. The arrangement lasted for the following one hundred and twenty years, when the younger congregation became independent (1870).

The increase in numbers and material well-being continued during the nineteenth century, but the community was not without internal dissensions. It was due to one of these controversies between the Parnassim and the ministers that a society called the "Porvenir" was founded in 1862. In the following year it developed into a Reform Congregation under the name "Emanuel," whose new Synagogue, in the quarter "Scharlo," was dedicated in 1866. About three years before a moderate change in the direction of reform was introduced into the liturgy of the oldest congregation.

The congregations of Curaçao now have more than one thousand members, nearly four-fifths of it belonging to Mickweh Israel. The Jews are among the leading citizens of the island, in business, as well as in the professions; they occupy executive and judicial positions, and are well represented among the officers of the militia. Almost all of them, like in Holland itself, are true to their religion, and there are probably less apostasies and intermarriages than in any other free community in which the emancipation of the Jews has been fully carried out in theory as well as in practice.

* * * * *

The Jewish settlements in the British West Indies also enjoyed long periods of increase and prosperity; but they declined when the English colonies of the North American continent, and later, the United States, offered a wider field of activities and better opportunities under conditions which were so similar to those prevailing in the older places as to make the change of residence a matter of very little inconvenience. The oldest settlement under the English flag in the West Indies was probably on the island of Barbadoes, where, it is believed, Jews came first in 1628. On April 27, 1655, Oliver Cromwell issued passes to Abraham de Mercado, M. D., Hebrew, and his son, Raphael, to go to Barbadoes to exercise his profession. In 1656 the Jews were granted, upon petition, the enjoyment of the privileges of the laws and statutes of the Commonwealth of England and of the Island relating to foreigners and strangers.

In April, 1661, Benjamin de Caseres, Henry de Caseres and Jacob Fraso petitioned the King of England to permit them to live and trade in Barbadoes and Surinam. Their petition was supported by the King of Denmark, which tends to prove that they must have been men of considerable importance. In the report made by the Commissioners of Foreign Plantations, to whom it was referred, it is stated that the whole question of the advisability of allowing Jews to reside in and trade with his majesty's colonies "hath been long and often debated." The merchants of England were opposed to the admission of Jews, because of their ability to control trade wherever they entered, and because they would divert it from England to foreign countries. The planters, on the contrary, favored their admission and accused the merchants of aiming to appropriate the whole trade to themselves. The commissioners refrained from deciding the general question, but advised that these three highly recommended Jews, who had behaved themselves well and with general satisfaction in Barbadoes, should be granted a special license to reside there or in any other plantations.

The Jewish community was soon increased to a considerable extent, partly by the arrival of former members of the dissolved colony of Cayenne (1664). It is recorded in the minutes of the vestry of St. Michael's Parish (July 9, 1666) "that the Jews inhabiting this Parish do pay the quantity of 35,000 pounds Muscovado sugar, to be levied by themselves and paid to Senior Lewis Dias and Senior Jeronimo Roderigos, who are hereby ordered to pay it to the present church wardens." The order is repeated in October, 1666, and again in 1667; and in that year another order making the levy for the year 20,000 pounds was issued. In 1669 the order in January was for 14,000 pounds, and in March for 16,000. In 1670 it was again for 16,000, but the Jews sent in a petition declaring the amount to be excessive. This had the effect of reducing the amount of the tax to 7,000 pounds in 1671 and to "half of what was levied last year" in 1672. For the following five years it was mostly 7,000 pounds a year, "levied for their trade." In 1680 it is 8,500 pounds, apportioned among forty-five Jews, some being made to contribute only twelve pounds, several others as high as 792 each, with David Raphael de Mercado heading the list with 1,075 pounds. (See list of names in "Publications," XIX, pp. 174-75.)

Antonio Rodrigo Rigio, Abraham Levi Regio, Lewis Dias, Isaac Jerajo Coutinho, Abraham Pereira, David Baruch Louzada and other Hebrews who were made free denizens by His Majesty's letters patent, petitioned in 1669 about the refusal to accept the testimony of Jews in the courts of the colony. The governor, in forwarding the petition, says, that "they had not been exposed to any other injuries in their trade or otherwise." But the privilege granted was only for cases "relating to trade and dealing." Special taxes continued to be imposed at various times until 1761, when all additional burdens were lifted, and afterward the Jews were rated and paid taxes on the some scale as other inhabitants. All political disabilities were removed by act of the local government in 1802, and by act of Parliament in 1820.

The number of Jews in Barbadoes was never as large as that of Surinam. In 1681 the total Jewish population of the island was 260. They went on increasing slowly, the great majority living in Bridgetown (where the first Synagogue was erected, probably prior to 1679) and a small number in Speightstown. In 1792, at the beginning of the period of the greatest prosperity of the community, the congregation of Bridgetown had 147 members, and 17 pensioners were supported. The name of the congregation was "Kehol Kodesh Nidhe Israel," and its ministers were all selected by the vestry of the Spanish and Portuguese Synagogue in London.

The decline of the Jewish community of Barbadoes dates from the great hurricane in 1831 which devastated the island, and also destroyed the Synagogue. Though a new edifice was erected and dedicated in 1833, and even a religious school was established several years later, the members kept on leaving the island for the United States, most of them going to Philadelphia. In 1848 there were only 71 Jews left. In 1873, those remaining petitioned for relief from taxation of property held by the congregation. The census of 1882 showed 21 Jews, and the number was still smaller at the end of the nineteenth century.

* * * * *

When England conquered the largest of its West Indian possessions, the island of Jamaica, in 1655, a considerable number of Jews, known as "Portugals," were living there. They dared not profess Judaism openly, or organize themselves into a congregation; but they were less in danger on account of their faith than in any other Spanish colony. The proprietary rights of the island was vested in the family of Columbus until about 1576, when it passed to the female Braganza line, and these exclusive rights exempted the island from the jurisdiction of the Inquisition, and prevented it from being included in the bishopric of Cuba. The British were careful to distinguish between the Portuguese Jews and the Spaniards, with the result that the Jews at once began to establish and develop the commercial prosperity of the colony. Sir Thomas Lynch, governor of Jamaica, writing in March, 1672, to the Council for Trade and Transportation, mentions, as points in favor of the Jews that "they have great stocks, no people, and aversions to the French and Spaniards."

Several years before that time Jacob Joshua Bueno Enriques, a resident of Jamaica for two years, petitioned the King for permission to work a copper mine, and that he and his brothers, Josef and Moise, "may use their own laws and hold Synagogues." In 1668 Solomon Gabay Faro and David Gomes Henriques were recommended by the King to the governor to remain and trade in Jamaica as long as they behaved well and fairly. There were considerable increases by arrivals from Brazil, later from the withdrawal of the British from Surinam, by direct immigration from England and even from Germany. But there must have been also considerable emigration of Jews, for at the end of the seventeenth century the number of Jews in Jamaica is figured at eighty. While the inclusion of Hebrew in the curriculum of the free school which was established in the Parish of St. Andrews in 1693—the earliest known instance of the teaching of Hebrew in an English settlement in the New World—may be taken as a concession to the Jewish inhabitants, there was no lack of harsh and galling measures. In 1703 the Jews were prohibited, under penalty of five hundred pounds, from holding Christian servants. In 1711 they were prohibited, along with mulattoes, Indians and negroes, from being employed as clerks in any of the judicial or other offices.

The struggle of the Jews of Jamaica against heavy taxation forms an interesting chapter in their history at the beginning of the eighteenth century. (See "Publications" II, p. 165 ff.) In 1700 a memorial was presented to Sir William Beeston, Governor-in-Chief of the Island of Jamaica, against the excessive special taxation of four assemblies, and against "being forced to bear arms on our Sabbath and holy days . . . without any necessity or urgent occasion (which is quite contrary to our religion, unless in case of necessity, when an enemy is in sight or apprehension of being near us)." The reply by the governor and council begins with the admission of the truth of the statement about taxation; but a counter-claim is advanced that "their first introduction into this island was on the condition that they should settle and plant, which they do not, there being but one considerable and two or three small settlements of the Jews in all the island. But their employment is generally keeping of shops and merchandise, by the first of which they have engrossed that employment, and by their parsimonious living (which I do not charge as a fault in them) they have thereby means of underselling the English; that they cannot, many in them, follow that employment, nor can they in reason put their children to the Jews to be trained up in that profession, by which the English nation think they suffer much, both in their own advantages and what may be made to their children hereafter."

The governor then proceeds to explain that the Jews themselves requested that "they might on any occasion be taxed by the lump," and that because of their controlling of trade, especially of the retail trade, the Assembly have thought it but just that they should pay something in proportion more than the English. He continues: "As for their bearing of arms, it must be owned that when any public occasion has happened or an enemy appeared they have been ready and behaved themselves very well; but for their being called into arms on private times and that have happened upon their Sabbath or festivals, they have been generally excused by their officers, unless by their obstinacy or ill-language they have provoked them to the contrary."

Traces of retrogression are also discernible in a document which was presented in 1721 to the Jamaica House of Representatives, entitled: "A petition of Jacob Henriques, Moses Mendes Quixano and David Gabai on behalf of themselves and the rest of the Jews now resident in this island . praying that the House will take into consideration the great disparity there is between the numbers, trade and substance of the Jews now resident in this island in this and former times, and to mitigate the assessment of tax to be laid upon them." But it seems that there was an improvement and an increase of the community about the middle of that century; for not less than 151 of the 189 Jews in the British-American Colonies whose names have been handed down as naturalized between 1740 (under the act of Parliament of that year) and 1755 resided in Jamaica.

Among the leading Jewish families which contributed most signally to the development of Jamaica's trade are: de Silva, Soarez, Cardozo, Belisario, Belinfante, Nuñez, Fonseca, Guttereet, de Cordova, Bernal, Gomez, Vaz and Bravo.

Kingston was from the time of its foundation (1693) the principal seat of the Jewish community; an earlier Synagogue which is mentioned in 1684 and 1687 was probably situated in Port Royal. There were also settlements in Spanish Town, Montego Bay, Falmouth and Lacovia.

Here also, like in most other Dutch and English colonies, the local authorities were less liberal than the home governments, especially in matters of taxation. The assistance of the crown was necessary to abolish all special taxation, and also to check such attempts as were made during the reign of William III. to expel the Jews from the island. There is a record (see "Publications" XIX, p. 179-80) of a Mr. Montefiore who made an application to be admitted as an attorney in Jamaica in 1787, and produced a certificate of his admission in the Court of King's Bench, in London, in 1784; but the above-mentioned anti-Jewish law of 1711 was cited to disqualify him from acting as attorney in Jamaica. It is believed that the man who met with this refusal was Joshua Montefiore (1762-1843), an uncle of Sir Moses Montefiore (1784-1885).

The community was in a flourishing condition in 1831, when all civil disabilities were finally removed, and the Jews immediately began to take a leading part in the affairs of the colony. In 1838 Sir Francis H. Goldsmid (1808-78) was able to compile a long list of Jews who were chosen to civil and military offices in Jamaica since the act of 1831, which was used by him as an argument in favor of removing the Jewish disabilities at home.

Alexander Bravo was the first Jew to be chosen as a member of the Jamaica Assembly, being elected for the district of Kingston in 1835. He later became a member of the council and afterward receiver-general. In 1849 eight of the forty-seven members of the colonial assembly were Jews, and Dr. C. M. Morales was elected Speaker in that year. Phinchas Abraham (d. 1887) was one of the last survivors of the body of merchants who contributed to the prosperity of the West Indies (see *Jew. Encyclopedia* s. v.).

The Spanish and Portuguese Synagogue of Kingston, situated on Princess street until the time of its destruction by the great fire of 1882, was consecrated in 1750. It was replaced by a new edifice on East street in 1884. The English and German Synagogue was consecrated in 1789, a third (German) was merged with the first in 1850. The Synagogue of the "Amalgamated Congregation of Israelites," which was consecrated in 1888, was destroyed by the earthquake of January, 1907. The United Congregation now worships at the East street Synagogue, which was enlarged for the purpose. The English-German Congregation consecrated a new Synagogue in 1894. There is also a Hebrew Benevolent Society and a Gemilut Hasodim Association which is more than a century old.

Among the rabbis of Jamaica were: Joshua Pardo who came there from Curaçao in 1683; his contemporary, the Spanish poet, Daniel Israel Lopez Laguna; Hakam de Cordoza (d. in Spanish Town, 1798); Rev. Abraham Pereire Mendes (b. Kingston, 1825; d. New York, 1893); Rev. George Jacobs; Rev. J. M. Corcos, and the present rabbi of the English-German Synagogue on Orange street, Rev. M. H. Solomon. The two Synagogues in Kingston are the only ones in the colony, which has about two thousand Jews, or nearly ten per cent. of the white population of Jamaica.

CHAPTER IX.

NEW AMSTERDAM AND NEW YORK.

Poverty of the first Jewish immigrants to New Amsterdam—Stuyvesant's opposition overruled by the Dutch West India Company—Privileges and restrictions—Contributions to build the wall from which Wall street takes its name—The first cemetery—Exemption from military duty—Little change at the beginning of the English rule—The first synagogue after a liberal decree by the Duke of York—Marranos brought back in boats which carried grain to Portugal—Hebrew learning—Question about the Jews as voters and as witnesses—Peter Kalm's description of the Jews of New York about 1745—Hyman Levy, the employer of the original Astor.

The wealth which made the Spanish and Portuguese Jew welcome, or at least insured him sufferance, in the other Dutch and English colonies of the New World, was absent in the case of those who first settled in what is now New York. In September, 1654, the year in which the Dutch lost control of Brazil and the great Jewish community of Recife was scattered, there arrived in the port of New Amsterdam (as New York was called by its Dutch founders) the barque St. Catarina, of which Jacques de la Motthe was master, from Cape St. Anthony (Cuba?), carrying twenty-seven Jews, men, women and children. These passengers, the first Jews to arrive in what is now the United States, were so poor that their goods had to be sold by the master of the vessel by public auction for the payment of their passage. The amount realized by the sale being insufficient, he applied to the Court of Burgomaster and the Schoepens that one or two of them, as principals, be held as security for the payment of the balance in accordance with the contract made with him by which each person signing it had bound himself for the payment of the whole amount, and under which he had taken two of them, David Israel and Moses Ambrosius, as principal debtors.

The court accordingly ordered that they should be placed under civil arrest, in the custody of the provost marshal, until they should have made satisfaction; that the captain should be answerable for their support while in custody, as security for which a certain proportion of the proceeds of the sale was directed to be left in the hands of the secretary of the colony. But as no further proceedings appear upon the records, the matter was doubtless arranged and was probably nothing more than a dispute or misunderstanding between them and the captain as to whether they were bound to make good the deficiency, which was probably enhanced by the forced sale of their effects by auction.[1] It is more likely that their embarrassment was only temporary and was due to their being robbed shortly before or after they left their last stopping place or residence, which was probably Jamaica. (See Leon Hühner, *Whence came the First Jewish Settlers of New York?* "Publications," IX, p. 75 ff.) It is mentioned that some of them were awaiting remittances, which must have come in time to enable the refugees to hold their own until the question of permitting them to remain in the colony was settled in their favor through correspondence with Holland.

Peter Stuyvesant, the governor of the colony, a man of strong will and strong prejudices, was hostile to the new arrivals, and he soon wrote to the Directors of the Dutch West India Company in Amsterdam requesting that "none of the Jewish nation be permitted to infest New Netherland." He received a reply that

[1] Daly, "The Settlement of the Jews in North America," p. 7 ff. The names of those early immigrants (some of them coming from Holland about the same time) as far as can be gathered from the records, are as follows: Abraham d'Lucena, David Israel, Moses Ambrosius, Abraham de la Simon, Salvatore d'Andrade, Joseph da Costa, David Frera, Jacob Barsimson, Jacob C. Henrique (or Jacob Cohen), Isaac Mesa and Asser Levy.

such a course "would be unreasonable and unfair, especially because of the considerable loss sustained by the Jews in the taking of Brazil, and also because of the large amount of capital which they have invested in the shares of this company. After many consultations we have decided and resolved upon a certain petition made by said Portuguese Jews, that they shall have permission to sail to and trade in New Netherland and to live and remain there, provided that the poor among them shall not become a burden to the company or to the community, but be supported by their own nation." This is the end of the reply, dated, April 26, 1655, which began with the ominous sentence: "We would have liked to agree to your wishes and request, that the new territories should not be further invaded by people of the Jewish race, for we forsee from such immigration the same difficulties which you fear." But the influence of the Jews in Amsterdam overcame the predilections and the fears of the company, and a special act was issued July 15, 1655, expressly giving Jews in New Netherlands the privileges contained in the above letter to the governor.

Before the favorable decision could arrive from Holland, the position of the Jews was precarious. On the 1st of March, 1655, Abraham de la Simon was brought before the Court of Burgomaster and the Schoepens upon the complaint of the Schout or Sheriff for keeping open his store on Sunday during the sermon, and selling at retail. The Sheriff on that occasion informed the court that the Governor and Council had resolved that the Jews who had come in the preceding autumn, as well as those that had recently arrived from Holland, must prepare to depart forthwith. The Court, which was also a council for the municipal government of the city, was asked by the Sheriff whether it had any objection to make; whereupon, says the record, it was decided that the Governor's resolution should take its course.

There is reason to believe that some Jews left on account of that resolution before the orders from Holland arrived. They presumably went to Rhode Island. Those who remained were still objects of the Governor's aversion, and even the more friendly Company was not too liberal. A letter from the directors to Stuyvesant, dated, March 13, 1556, contains the following: "The permission given to the Jews to go to New Netherlands and enjoy the same privileges as they have here (in Amsterdam), has been granted only as far as civil and political rights are concerned, without giving the said Jews a claim to the privilege of exercising their religion in a synagogue or a gathering."

But it must be said to the credit of the directors that they insisted on what they granted to the Jews, and in another letter, dated, June 14, 1556, they write to the self-willed governor: "We have seen and heard with displeasure, that against our orders of the 15th of February, 1655, issued at the request of the Jewish or Portuguese nation, you have forbidden them to trade to Fort Orange (Albany) and the South River (Delaware), also the purchase of real estate, which is granted to them without difficulty here in this country, and we wish it had not been done, and you have obeyed your orders which you must always execute punctually and with more respect. Jews or Portuguese people, however, shall not be employed in any public service (to which they are neither admitted in this city) nor allowed to have open retail shops; but they may quietly and peacefully carry on their business as beforesaid and exercise in all quietness their religion within their houses, for which end they must without doubt endeavor to build their houses close together in a convenient place on one or the other side of New Amsterdam—at their choice—as they do here."

These instructions came as the result of a petition sent to the directors by Abraham d'Lucena, Salvatore d'Andrade and Jacob Cohen, for themselves and in the name of others of the Jewish nation, asking for a confirmation of the privileges, which was thus granted. These three and two other Jews, Joseph da Costa and David Frera, were in the preceding year, 1655, assessed each 1,000 florins to defray the cost of erecting the outer fence or city wall, from which Wall street takes its name. It was the same amount as was imposed upon the wealthiest of the citizens, and the five adduced it as a reason for their being entitled to the rights to trade and to hold real property.

Abraham d'Lucena, who appears to have been the most prominent of the early Jewish immigrants, and several others, applied in July, 1655, for a burying ground; but the request was refused with the reply "that there was no need for it yet." There was need for it, however, about a year later, and on July 14, 1656, a lot was granted to them outside of the city for a place of interment. This is the old cemetery on Oliver street and New Bowery, which was augmented by further purchases in the following century.

The city was at that time exposed to attacks from Spanish cruisers and pirates, and to assaults from hostile Indians. The encroachments of the English on Long Island and Westchester was a subject of constant anxiety, England never having conceded the rights of the Dutch to settle New Netherlands. This caused all the male inhabitants capable of bearing arms to enroll in the Burgher Guard, and a watch was kept up night and day with the steadiness and vigilance of a beleaguered town. A few months after the arrival of the Jewish immigrants the question arose whether the adult males among them should be incorporated in the Burgher Guard; the officers of the guard submitting the question to the Governor and Council. It was duly deliberated upon and an ordinance was passed (August 28, 1655), which, after reciting "the unwillingness of the mass of the citizens to be fellow-soldiers of the aforesaid nation" or watch in the same guard-house, and the fact that the Jews in Holland did not serve in the train bands of the cities, but paid a compensation for their exemption therefrom, declared that they should be exempt from that military service, and for such exemption each male person between the ages of sixteen and sixty shall pay a monthly contribution of sixty-five stivers.

Jacob Barsimson and Asser Levy (d. 1682) petitioned to be allowed to stand guard like other burghers, or to be relieved from the tax, which was refused by the Governor and Council with the remark that "they might go elsewhere if they liked."

But after the last order from Amsterdam favorable to the claims of the Jews was received, Asser Levy applied to be admitted to the right of citizenship, and exhibited his certificate to the court to show that he had been a burgher in Amsterdam. His request, as well as the one made for the same purpose by Salvatore d'Andrade and others, was not complied with. The matter was brought before the Governor and Council, and as the directions from Holland were controlling, an order was made April 21, 1657, that the Burgomaster should admit them to that privilege. Here the struggle virtually ended, and they were no longer troubled during the Dutch rule.

When the British captured the city in 1664 and renamed it New York, the condition of the Jews remained practically unchanged. There is a record of at least one Jew who removed from Newport to New York in that period, and had difficulties with the local authorities because they enforced against him the regulation which did not permit a Jew to engage in retail trade. The Charter of Liberties and Privileges which was adopted in 1683 by the colonial legislature declared that "no one should be molested, punished, disquieted or called in question for his religious opinion, who professed faith in God by Jesus Christ," which meant that the Jews and unbelievers were excluded from the privileges of religious freedom. A petition by the Jews to Governor Dongan, in 1686, for liberty to exercise their religion, i. e., to have public worship, was consequently decided in the negative. But James, Duke of York (afterwards King James II., 1633-1701), to whom New York was granted by his brother, had previously sent out instructions, which arrived about that time, "to permit all persons of what religion soever, quietly to inhabit within the government, and to give no disturbance or disquiet whatsoever for or by reason of their differing in matters of religion."

The exact date when the Jews took advantage of that liberal decree is not known, but it is presumed that the religious services, which had been heretofore conducted semi-privately, were soon performed in a house devoted to that purpose. It is certain that there was a Jewish Synagogue in New York in 1695, probably as early as 1691, while the restrictions as to trade were removed a few years before. The Synagogue, the first on the North American continent, was situated on the south side of the present Beaver street, between Broadway and Broad street. When it became too small for the community which was increasing in wealth and in numbers, a new edifice was erected in 1728 on Mill street (about the present site of South William street), where the congregation, which now assumed the name of "Shearith Israel" (Remnant of Israel), continued to worship for more than a century.

A profitable commerce was carried on between New York and the West Indies at the beginning of the eighteenth century in which numerous Jewish merchants participated. There was also carried on, though for a short period, a considerable business of exporting wheat to Portugal, on account of the scarcity in Europe about the close of the French war. Abraham d'Lucena and Louis Moses Gomez, who engaged in that traffic to Portugal, not only became two of the most affluent of the Jewish residents of New York, but they also incidentally caused an increase of the number of their co-religionists in the community. It is presumed that the vessels which carried grain to the Iberian peninsula brought Jewish or Marrano passengers on the return voyage. Most of the new Jewish names which began to appear here about that time are of undoubted Spanish and Portuguese origin. But there were also in the city Jews from other countries. When the Rev. John Sharpe proposed the erection of a school-library and chapel in New York, in 1712-13, he points out among the advantages which the city afforded for that purpose that: "It is possible also to learn Hebrew here as well as in Europe, there being a Synagogue of Jews, and many ingenious men of that nation from Poland, Hungary, Germany, etc."

The above-mentioned Louis Moses Gomez (b. Madrid, 1654; d. New York, 1740) who arrived in America about 1700, was until the time of his death one of the principal merchants of

New York. He had five sons, and his descendants have intermarried with most of the old-time American-Jewish families.

While the community was increasing in number and wealth, something occurred which sharply reminded the Jews that the time of complete emancipation had not yet come. In 1737 the election of Col. Frederick Phillips as representative of the General Assembly for the County of Westchester was contested by Captain Cornelius Van Horne. Colonel Phillips called several Jews to give evidence on his behalf, when an objection was made to their competency as witnesses. After arguments on both sides were heard, they were informed by the speaker that it was the opinion of the House that "none of the Jewish profession could be admitted as evidence." It seems that Jews had voted at the election, for after again hearing arguments from the counsel of both parties, the House resolved that, as it did not appear that persons of the Jewish religion had a right to vote for members of Parliament in Great Britain, it was the unanimous opinion of the House that they could not be admitted to vote for Representatives in the colony. This decision has been described by a later historian as remarkable, and in explanation of it he says: "That Catholics and Jews had long been peculiarly obnoxious to the colonists," that "the first settlers being Dutch and mostly of the Reformed Protestant religion, and the migration from England, since the colony belonged to the Crown, being principally Episcopal, both united in their aversion to the Catholics and the Jews." (Quoted by Daly, *The Settlement of the Jews in North America,* p. 46.)[1]

[1] Judge Daly himself, however, sees no ground for inferring that the decision proceeded from aversion. He thinks it was simply a question of law. The law of New York colony was especially modeled upon that of the mother country. New York was a conquered province, and when it was taken from the Dutch, the English mode of procedure in all matters of law and government was introduced bodily; and from this circumstance English forms, precedents and modes of proceeding came into use to an extent that did not prevail in other colonies where the people themselves had been left to originate and frame such a system of government and laws as was suggested by their wants and most conducive to their interests. The Legislative Assembly was therefore simply declaring the law as it existed in England at that time. (l. c.)

The general condition of the Jews of New York was, nevertheless, highly favorable, as is attested by Peter Kalm (1715-79), the Swedish botanist and traveler, who spent a considerable time in the colony in the following decade. He says: "There are many Jews settled in New York who possess great privileges. They have a Synagogue and houses, great country-seats of their own property, and are allowed to keep shops in the town. They have likewise several ships which they freight and send out with their goods; in fine, the Jews enjoy all the privileges in common to the other inhabitants of this town and province."

The increase of the community between that time and the American Revolution was very slow in comparison with the fast growth of the general population of the city, which was less than 5,000 in 1700, about 9,000 in 1750, and nearly 23,000 in 1776. The natural increase and the additions which the Jewish community received by immigration, chiefly from England, was barely sufficient to counteract the loss of others who went to Newport, Charleston and Philadelphia. But, though small, it continued to be a highly respectable and influential body, having among its members some of the principal merchants of the city. Of this number was Hayman Levy (d. 1790) who carried on an extensive business chiefly with the Indians, and by winning their respect and confidence became the largest fur trader in the colonies. Upon his books are entries of moneys paid to John Jacob Astor (1763-1848), the founder of the Astor family, for beating furs at the rate of one dollar a day. Miss Zeporah Levy (d. 1833), a daughter of Hayman, was married in 1779 to Benjamin Hendricks, a native of New York, the founder of a well-known and long-maintained Jewish commercial house.

CHAPTER X.

NEW ENGLAND AND THE OTHER ENGLISH COLONIES.

The Old Testament spirit in New England—Roger Williams—The first Jew in Massachusetts—Judah Monis, instructor in Hebrew at Harvard—Newport—Jews from Holland bring there the first degrees of Masonry—The cemetery immortalized by Longfellow—Jacob Rodrigues Rivera introduces the manufacture of sperm oil—Aaron Lopez, the greatest merchant in America—Immigration from Portugal—Rabbi Isaac Touro—Visiting rabbis—First Jews in Connecticut—Philadelphia—Congregation Mickweh Israel—Easton's wealthy Jews—Maryland—Dr. Jacob Lumbrozo—General Oglethorpe and the first Jews of Georgia—Joseph Ottolenghi—The Carolinas—Charleston.

Although "the Puritans of England and America appropriated the language of our judges and prophets" and the spirit of the Old Testament was the most potent force in the foundation and the conduct of the early Commonwealths of New England, still it was not a typical or recognized leader of those who deemed themselves members of a new Hebrew theocratic democracy, but rather an outcast from their ranks, who first granted full religious liberty to the Jews and bade them welcome. This man was Roger Williams (1600?-1684), the former clergyman of the Church of England, who later (1631) became a Puritan pastor in Salem, Mass., and was expelled for denying the right of the magistrates to punish Sabbath-breaking, and was four years later "banished from the jurisdiction of the Puritans of America, and driven into the wilderness to endure the severity of our northern winter and the bitter pangs of hunger."[1]

[1] Oscar S. Straus, "The Origin of the Republican Form of Government in the United States," p. 48.

There was at least one Jew in Massachusetts before the arrival of the first Jews in New Amsterdam, and he is mentioned only as being assisted—or forced—to quit the colony. The reference to him is dated May 3, 1649, when it is stated that the court allows Solomon Franco, the Jew, six shillings per week out of the treasury for ten weeks for subsistence till he can get his passage into Holland (see Kohut, *The Jews of New England* in "Publications," XI, p. 78). Several other Jews are mentioned as having lived there in the latter part of the seventeenth and in the first three-quarters of the eighteenth centuries. But owing to the intolerance and religious zeal of the Puritans, they either moved to other parts or embraced Christianity. When a Jew named Joseph Frazon (or Frazier) died in Boston, in 1704, his body was sent to Newport for burial.

The most distinguished among the early converts was Judah Monis (born in Algiers about 1680; died in Northborough, Mass. in 1764). He was baptized in the College Hall at Cambridge, Mass., on March 22, 1722, and was afterward active in the cause of his new faith, although he observed throughout his life the Jewish Sabbath. He was an instructor in Hebrew at Harvard University, from 1722 till 1759, when on the death of his wife he resigned and removed to Northborough. Besides some insignificant missionary pamphlets, he was the author of the first Hebrew grammar printed in America (Boston, 1735).

It was in the smallest of the original colonies, which is now likewise the smallest State in the Union, Rhode Island, founded by the pioneer of religious liberty in the New World, that the Jews established their oldest congregation on the North American continent. Providence was founded in 1636, Portsmouth and Newport about two years later, and the last named place, which soon became one of the most important cities in the colonies, excelling even New York as a commercial center and port of entry until after the Revolution, began to attract Jews soon after their arrival in these parts of the country. The earliest authentic mention of Jews in Newport is in 1658, when fifteen Jewish families are said to have arrived from Holland, bringing with them the first degrees of Masonry which they proceeded to confer on Abraham Moses in the house of Mordecai Campanall.[1] But there is reason to believe that Jews from New Amsterdam and Curaçao settled there a year or two before. A congregation seems to have been organized in 1658 under the name "Jeshuat Israel." The cemetery, immortalized by Longfellow and Emma Lazarus, was acquired by Campanall and Moses Packeckoe, in 1677, but it is possible that there existed an earlier Jewish cemetery.

Still even in Rhode Island it was only tolerance; the recognition of equal rights was yet to come with the Declaration of Independence. In reply to a petition of the Jews, the General Assembly of Rhode Island, in 1684, affirmed the right of the Jews to settle in the colony, declaring that "they may expect as good protection here as any stranger being not of our nation residing among us in His Majesty's colony ought to have, being obedient to His Majesty's laws."

More Jewish settlers arrived from the West Indies in 1694; but the great impulse to the commercial activity which raised Newport to the zenith of its prosperity was given by a number of Portuguese Jews who settled there about the middle of the eighteenth century. Most prominent among those were Jacob Rodrigues Rivera (died at an advanced age in 1789), who arrived in 1745, and Aaron Lopez, who came in 1750. The former introduced into America the manufacture of sperm oil, having brought the art with him from Portugal, and it soon became one of the leading industries; Newport, whose inhabitants were engaged in whale fishing, had seventeen manufactories of oil and candles and enjoyed a practical monopoly of this trade down to the Revolution.

Aaron Lopez (died May 28, 1782), who was Rivera's son-in-law, became the great merchant prince of New England. (Ezra Stiles says of him, that for honor and extent of commerce he

[1] See Oppenheim, "The Jews and Masonry," in "Publications" XIX, pp. 9 ff., for an interesting treatment of the discussion about the authenticity of this statement.

was probably surpassed by no merchant in America.) The advantages of this important seaport were quickly comprehended by this sagacious merchant, and to him in a larger degree than to any one else was due the rapid commercial development that followed. He was the means of inducing more than forty Jewish families to settle there, the heads of many of which were men of wealth, mercantile sagacity, high intelligence and enterprise. In fourteen years after Lopez settled there, Newport had 150 vessels engaged in trade with the West Indies alone, besides an extensive trade which was carried on as far as Africa and the Falkland Islands. The Jews were even then, nearly three hundred years after the expulsion, transferring to the liberal English colonies the wealth and the still more valuable business ability and commercial connections which they could not freely or safely employ as Marranos in Portugal. The emigration of secret Jews from that country increased after the great earthquake at Lisbon (1755), and a considerable portion went to Rhode Island. One of the vessels from that unhappy city, bound for Virginia, was driven into Narragansett Bay, and its Jewish passengers remained at Newport.

Isaac Touro (died Dec. 8, 1783) came from Jamaica to Newport, in 1760, to become the minister of its prosperous congregation, and occupied the position until the outbreak of the Revolution, when he returned to end his days in Jamaica. Until the time of his arrival worship was held in private houses, but in 1762 the congregation, which numbered between sixty and seventy members, decided to erect a Synagogue. The building, which is still standing, was completed and dedicated in 1763. There is evidence that the Jewish population of Newport, even before the Revolution, contained considerable German and Polish elements. According to one historian, the city numbered before the outbreak of hostilities 1,175 Jews—which was probably a majority of the Jews in all the colonies—while more than 300 worshipers attended the Synagogue.

Many Jewish rabbis from all parts of the world were attracted to Newport in those times. The above-named Ezra Stiles

(1727-95), the famous president of Yale University, who was a preacher in Newport at that time, mentions several of them in his diary. He met one from Palestine in 1759, two from Poland, 1771 and 1772, respectively, a Rabbi Bosquila from Smyrna, a Rabbi Cohen from Jerusalem and Rabbi Raphael Hayyim Isaac Carregal (b. Hebron, Palestine, 1733; d. Barbadoes, 1777), who preached at Newport in Spanish in 1773, and became an intimate friend of the Christian theological scholar.

The arrival of a Jewish family from the West Indies to New Haven, Conn., in 1772, is noted by Stiles, who was a native of that place, in his diary as follows: "They are the first real Jews at that place with exception of the two brothers Pinto, who renounced Judaism and all religion." This is substantially accurate in regard to New Haven, although one David, the Jew, is mentioned in the Hartford town records as early as 1659 (or 1650), and the residence of several Jews is implied in the entry which was made in the same records under date of September 2, 1661: "The same day ye Jews which at present live at John Marsh, his house, have liberty to sojourn in ye town for seven months." They are mentioned at a subsequent period, too, which proves that they were permitted to remain longer than the allotted seven months. But all trace of them is lost afterwards, and almost two centuries had passed until the first Synagogue was erected in Hartford.

* * * * *

The Jews of New Amsterdam who had difficulties with Peter Stuyvesant in 1655 about their right to trade on the South River, which was subsequently re-named the Delaware (see above, chapter 9) were probably the first to set foot in what later became the colony and still later the State of Pennsylvania. This was twenty years before William Penn (1644-1718) became part proprietor of West Jersey, and more than a quarter of a century before he came over to America (1682) and founded the city of Philadelphia in the colony of Pennsylvania, which he received as a grant from the King of England in the preceding year.

The first Jewish resident of Philadelphia was Jonas Aaron, who was living there in 1703. A number of other Jews settled there in the first half of the eighteenth century and some of them, including David Franks (1720-93), Joseph Marks and Sampson Levy, became prominent in the life of the city. Isaac Miranda came there earlier (1710) and held several State offices, but he was a convert to Christianity, and his preferment cannot be considered a Jewish success. A German traveler mentions the Jews among the religious sects of Philadelphia in 1734. In 1738 Nathan Levy (1704-53) applied for a plot of ground to be used as a place of burial, and obtained it Sept. 25, 1740. This was the first Jewish cemetery in the city, and was henceforth known as the "Jews' burying ground," situated in Spruce street, near Ninth street. It later became the property of the Congregation Mickweh Israel, which had its beginnings about 1745 and is believed to have worshipped in a small house in Sterling alley. The question of building a Synagogue was raised in 1761, as a result of the influx of Jews from Spain and the West Indies, but nothing was then accomplished in that direction. In 1773, when Barnard Gratz (born in Germany, 1738; died in Baltimore, 1801) was parnas and Solomon Marache, treasurer, a subscription was started "in order to support our holy worship and establish it on a more solid foundation," but no Synagogue was built until about ten years later. Barnard Gratz and his brother, Michael (b. 1740), with whom he came to Amreica about 1755, were among the eight Jewish merchants of Philadelphia who signed the Non-Importation Resolution in 1765. The others were Benjamin Levy, David Franks, Sampson Levy, Hyman Levy, Jr.; Mathias Bush and Moses Mordecai.

Jews were to be found in Lancaster, Pa., as early as 1730, before the town and county were organized, and the name of Joseph Simon was preserved as the best known of the first arrivals. Myer Hart (d. about 1795) and his wife, Rachel, and their son, Michael (b. 1738), were one of the eleven original families that are classed as the founders of Easton, Pa., about 1750. Myer Hart heads the list of those furnishing material for the erection of a schoolhouse in Easton in 1755. He is first described as a shopkeeper and later as an innkeeper, and he was naturalized April 3, 1764. In 1780 his estate was valued at £2,095, and that of his son, Michael, at £2,261, these two being the heaviest taxed individuals in the county. At that period there were two other Jewish merchants residing at Easton, Barnard Levi and Joseph Nathan.

There is a tradition that Schafferstown, Pa., had a Synagogue and a Jewish cemetery in 1732, but the facts have not been verified, and there is a suspicion that the supposed Jews were German pietists who assumed Biblical names.

To the south of Pennsylvania the older colony of Maryland, which was established in 1634, "adopted religious freedom as the basis of the State;" but this boon was reserved for Christians only, although there is no record that the statutory death penalty for those who denied the trinity was ever carried out in practice. The physician, Jacob Lumbrozo (d. May, 1666), who hailed from Lisbon, Portugal, and came to Maryland about January, 1656, and later became an extensive land owner, was committed for blasphemy in 1658, but this did not prevent him from enjoying a lucrative practice and engaging in various mercantile pursuits in subsequent years. He was even granted letters of denization on Sept. 10, 1663, which vested him with all the privileges of a native or naturalized subject. But his case seems to have been exceptional, probably owing to his medical skill and his wealth. But in general, colonial Maryland was no place for Jews, and even after it became a part of the United States it was one of the last to remove the civil disabilities of its Jewish citizens.

Another Marrano physician from Lisbon, Dr. Samuel (Ribiero) Nuñez, who escaped from the clutches of the Inquisition and arrived, in 1733, in the newly founded colony of Georgia, found a more congenial place of refuge. Georgia was in respect to the Jews the reverse of New Netherlands; the trustees of the colony in England were opposed to permitting Jews to settle there, but General James Edward Oglethorpe (1696-

1785), the Governor, was very friendly disposed towards them. Nuñez was one of forty Jewish immigrants who unexpectedly arrived at Savannah in the second vessel which reached the colony from England (July 11, 1733). The Governor, one of the noblest figures of colonial times, bade them welcome, and considered them a good acquisition to the new colony. The first settlers were of Spanish and Portuguese extraction,[1] but Jews who apparently came from Germany took up their residence there less than a year afterwards. Both bands of settlers received equally liberal treatment, and they soon organized a congregation (1734). The first male white child born in the colony was a Jew, Isaac Minis. Abraham de Lyon, of Portugal, introduced the culture of grapes into Georgia in 1737, while others of the early settlers engaged in the cultivation and manufacture of silk, the knowledge of which they likewise brought with them from Portugal. A dispute with the trustees of the colony respecting the introduction of slaves caused an extensive emigration to South Carolina in 1741, and resulted in the dissolution of the congregation. But in 1751 a number of Jews returned to Georgia, and in the same year the trustees sent over Joseph Ottolenghi (d. after June, 1774) to superintend the somewhat extensive silk industry of the colony. Ottolenghi soon attained prominence in the political life of the colony and was elected a member of the General Assembly, where he served from 1761 to 1765. Several other Jews renderd distinguished services to Georgia, but they belong to the period of the Revolution, which will be treated separately in the following part. A new congregation was started in 1774.

"Jews, heathens and dissenters" were granted full liberty of conscience in the liberal charter which the celebrated English philosopher, John Locke (1632-1704) drew up for the governance of the Carolinas (1669), and the spirit of tolerance was always retained there. Still few Jews were attracted there at the beginning, and about thirty years later we know of only one

[1] For a list of their names see "Publications" XVII, pp. 168-69.

Jew, Solomon Valentine, as living in Charleston. A few others followed him, and in 1703 a protest was raised against "Jew strangers" voting for members of the Assembly. About the middle of the eighteenth century the number of Jews in Charleston suddenly increased through the above-mentioned exodus from Georgia, and the first Synagogue of the Congregation Bet Elohim was established in 1750. Its first minister was Isaac da Costa, and among its earliest members were Joseph and Michael Tobias, Moses Cohen, Abraham da Costa, Moses Pimenta, David de Olivera, Mordecai Sheftal, Michael Lazarus and Abraham Nuñez Cardozo. The first Synagogue was a small building on Union street; its present edifice is situated at Hassell street. A Hebrew Benevolent Society, which still survives, was also organized at an early date. A German-Jewish congregation was also in existence in the last quarter of the eighteenth century. Several prominent Jews of London purchased large tracts of land in South Carolina, near Fort Ninety-six, which became known as the "Jews' Land." Moses Lindo who arrived from London in 1756, became engaged in indigo manufacture, which he made one of the principal industries in the colony. Another London Jew, Francis Salvador (d. 1776), was the most prominent Jew in South Carolina at the time of the outbreak of the Revolutionary War.

PART III.

THE REVOLUTION AND THE PERIOD OF EXPANSION.

CHAPTER XI.

THE RELIGIOUS ASPECT OF THE WAR OF INDEPENDENCE.

Spirit of the Old Testament in the Revolutionary War—Sermons in favor of the original Jewish form of Government—The New Nation as "God's American Israel"—The Quebec Act—The intolerance of sects as the cause of separation of Church and State—A Memorial sent by German Jews to the Continental Congress—Fear expressed in North Carolina that the Pope might be elected President of the United States—None of the liberties won were lost by post-revolutionary reaction, as happened elsewhere.

The spirit of the old Testament which was prevalent among the early settlers of New England was perhaps still more manifest there at the time of the outbreak of the Revolutionary War of Independence. The ever-increasing antagonism which was aroused by the attempt of the Parliament of England to regulate and to tax the colonies, found expression in Biblical terms to an extent which can hardly be appreciated in the present time. The people in America had to fight over again the same battles for constitutional liberties which the English had fought before them, and George III., so far as his claims over the colonies were concerned, relied as much upon the kingly prerogative, the doctrine of "Divine Right," as ever did James I. All of these pretensions, all the questions of right and liberty had to be re-argued. To refute this false theory of kingly power it was not only expedient but necessary to revert to the earliest times, to the most sacred record, the Old Testament, for illustration and for argument, chiefly because the doctrine of Divine Right of a King by the Grace of God and its corollaries, "unlimited submission and non-resistance," were deduced, or rather distorted, from the New Testament, having been brought into the field of politics with the object of enslaving the masses through their religious creed. "It is, at least, an historical fact—says the historian Lecky—that in the great majority of instances the early Protestant defenders of civil liberty derived their political principles chiefly from the Old Testament, and the defenders of despotism from the New. The rebellions that were so frequent in Jewish history formed the favorite topic of the one, the unreserved submission inculcated by St. Paul, the other."[1]

While there were many free thinkers or Deists among the intellectual leaders of the Revolution, the masses of the colonists were intensely religious, and an argument from Scripture carried more weight with them than any other. Education was limited at that period in the colonies; there were not many newspapers, they were rarely issued more than once a week, and the number of subscribers was but few. The pulpit had their place, and the pastors in their sermons dealt with politics not less than with religion. Sermons were for the people the principal sources of general instruction. These pastors, in the way of history, knew above all that of the Jewish people, and they were the first to bring before their audiences the ideals of the old Hebrew commonwealth. Rev. Jonathan Mayhew (1720-66), whose discourse, in 1750, against unlimited submission was characterized as "the morning gun of the Revolution," declared in a later oration on the "Repeal of the Stamp Act" which he delivered in Boston on May 23, 1766: "God gave Israel a king in His anger because they had not sense and virtue enough to like a free common-

[1] Lecky, *Rationalism in Europe*, vol. II, 168, quoted in Straus, *Origin of Republican Form of Government in the United States,* pp. 19 *ff.*, which see for an extensive treatment of this subject.

wealth, and to have Himself for their King—where the spirit of the Lord is there is liberty—and if any miserable people on the continent or isles of Europe be driven in their extremity to seek a safe retreat from slavery in some far distant clime—O let them find one in America." Rev. Samuel Langdon (1723-97), President of Harvard College, delivered an election sermon before the "Honorable Congress of Massachusetts Bay" on the 31st of May, 1775, taking as his text the passage in Isaiah I, 26, "And I will restore thy judges as at first," in which he said: "The Jewish government, according to the original constitution, which was divinely established, if considered only in a civil view, was a perfect republic. And let them who cry up the divine right of Kings consider, that the form of government which had a proper claim to a divine establishment was so far from including the idea of a King, that it was a high crime for Israel to ask to be in this respect like other nations, and when they were thus gratified, it was rather as a just punishment for their folly. . . The civil polity of Israel is doubtless an excellent general model, allowing for some peculiarities; at least some principal laws and orders of it may be copied in more modern establishments." Almost everybody at that time knew by heart the admonitions of Samuel to the children of Israel, describing the manner in which a King would rule over them.

Sermons drawing a parallel between George III. and Pharaoh, inferring that the same providence of God which had rescued the Israelites from Egyptian bondage would free the colonies, were common in that period; and they probably had more effect with the masses than the great orations of the statesmen or the philosophical essays of the publicists which came down to us in the literature of the Revolution. The success of the War of Independence was also accepted in that sense. The election sermon preached by the Rev. Dr. Ezra Stiles, President of Yale College, on May 8, 1783, at Hartford, before Governor Trumbull and the General Assembly of the State of Connecticut, may be cited as an instance. Dr. Stiles took for his text Deut. XXVI, 19: "And to make you high above all nations which he has made, in praise, and in name, and in honor, etc." This sermon takes up one hundred and twenty closely printed pages, and assumes the proportions of a treatise on government from the Hebrew Theocracy down to the then present, showing by illustration and history that the culmination of popular government had been reached in America, transplanted by divine hands in fulfilment of Biblical prophecy from the days of Moses to the land of Washington; and discussing from an historical point of view "the reasons rendering it probable that the United States will, by the ordering of heaven, eventually become this people." He referred to the new nation as "God's American Israel" and to Washington as the American Joshua who was raised up by God to lead the armies of the chosen people to liberty and independence.[1]

The committee which was appointed on the same day the Declaration of Independence was adopted, consisting of Dr. Franklin, Mr. Adams and Mr. Jefferson, to prepare a device for a seal for the United States, at first proposed that of Pharaoh sitting in an open chariot, a crown on his head and a sword in his hand, passing through the dividing waters of the Red Sea

[1] Another great American clergyman, Dr. Henry M. Field (1822-1907), who wrote about a century later, also found in the Jewish polity much that was later adopted in the Constitution of the United States. In his work *On the Desert* (New York, 1883), he says: "Perhaps it does not often occur to readers of the Old Testament that there is much likeness between the Hebrew Commonwealth and the American Republic . . . . . At the bottom there is one radical principle that divides a republic from a monarchy or an aristocracy; it is the natural equality of men—that "all men are born free and equal"—which is fully recognized in the laws of Moses as in the Declaration of Independence. Indeed, the principle is carried further in the Hebrew Commonwealth than in ours; for not only was there equality before the laws, but the laws aimed to produce equality of condition in one point, and that a vital one—the tenure of land, of which even the poorest could not be deprived, so that in this respect the Hebrew Commonwealth approached more nearly to a pure democracy." See a more extensive quotation in Simon Wolf's *The American Jew as Patriot, Soldier and Citizen*, pp. 494-98.

in pursuit of the Israelites: with rays from a pillar of fire beaming on Moses, who is represented as standing on the shore extending his hand over the sea, causing it to overwhelm Pharaoh.[1]

Great religious animosity was also aroused by the "Quebec Act," which was passed by the British Parliament in 1774, for the purpose of preventing Canada from joining the other colonies. It guaranteed to the Catholic Church the possession of its vast amount of property, and full freedom of worship. The object which it was intended to effect by the passage of this act was purely one of State policy, and as far as Canada herself was concerned it was a wise and diplomatic step. But with the exception perhaps of the Boston Port Bill, it was the most effectual in alienating the colonies. It was construed as an effort on the part of Parliament to create an Established Church, and not that alone, but the establishment of *that* Church which was most hateful to and dreaded by the great majority of the people in the colonies.

It was not due to lack of religious sentiment that the ultimate bond between the colonies was a strictly secular one, and that Church and State were forever separated in the Constitution of the United States. It was rather due to the great and insurmountable differences in the religious beliefs among the various parties to the confederation; it may be said that it was strong sectarianism which forced upon them a non-sectarian government. The religious complexion of no two of the American colonies was precisely alike. The various sects at the time of the Revolution were grouped as follows: The Puritans in Massachusetts, the Baptists in Rhode Island, the Congregationalists in Connecticut, the Dutch and Swedish Protestants in New Jersey, the Church of England in New York, the Quakers in Pennsylvania, the Baptists, Methodists and Presbyterians in North Carolina, the Catholics in Maryland, the Cavaliers in Virginia, the Huguenots and Episcopalians in South Carolina, and the Methodists in Georgia. Owing to these diversities, to the consciousness of

[1] A drawing of this design is printed as the frontispiece of Mr. Straus's above-named work.

danger from ecclesiastical ambition, the intolerance of sects as exemplified among themselves as well as in foreign lands, it was wisely foreseen that the only basis upon which it was possible to form a Federal union was to exclude from the National Government all power over religion.

The seperation of Church and State was therefore a practical necessity, based on causes which were deeply rooted in the life of the people. It was almost a forced step on the way of development, not an enthusiastic outburst in favor of an abstract principle. This is why the ground which was then gained was never lost again, why there was no reaction and no reversion to the former order of a religious establishment as happened in France after the great revolution which began in 1789. The moderate, self-restrained liberalism of the colonists held its own after the struggle was over and kept on progressing slowly. The violent radicalism of the older country went so far that many steps had to be retraced, and the fight of separating Church and State had to be fought out all over again in our own time, more than a century after all religion was abolished during the reign of terror.

A letter sent by an unnamed German Jew on behalf of himself and his brethren to the President of the Continental Congress, in which the wretched condition of the Jews in Germany at that time is depicted, and their desire to become subjects of the thirteen provinces is expressed, appeared in the *Deutsches Museum* of June, 1783, and four years later a separate edition of it was published under the title, *Schreiben eines deutschen Juden an den Nord Amerikanischen Präsidenten.*[1] As there is no record of its reception or discussion in America, it probably attracted very little attention. The same is also true of the letter which Jonas Phillips (b. in Rhenish Prussia, 1736; d. in New York,

[1] See Dr. M. Kayserling, *A Memorial Sent by German Jews to the President of the Continental Congress,* in "Publications" VI, pp. 5-8, where it is also stated that the letter was wrongly attributed to Moses Mendelssohn (1729-86).

Jan. 28, 1803), of Philadelphia, sent to the Federal Convention in relation to the removal of the test oath in Pennsylvania which discriminated against Jews and those who did not subscribe to Christian doctrines (Sept. 7, 1787). When the fundamental law of the land was adopted there were no exciting debates about the question of religious liberty. The clause abolishing religious tests in the Federal Constitution passed almost unanimously; the State of North Carolina alone voted against it, and as there were hardly any Jews there at that time, the fear of the Roman Catholics was the only cause for the illiberal stand taken by its representatives. The extent of that fear can be understood from the fact that when the State Convention of North Carolina to adopt the Federal Constitution convened in Hillsborough, in July, 1788, pamphlets were circulated "pointing out in all seriousness the danger of the Pope being elected President should the Constitution be adopted." (See Hühner, *Religious Liberty in North Carolina,* "Publications," XVI, p. 42). The time for religious liberty as well as for independence in national affairs had come and was accepted as a matter of course, and it is the exceptional glory of the American Revolution that all the liberties won were retained and the young nation was enabled to continue on the way of progress unhindered by post-revolutionary reaction, and to devote its energies to the solution of the problems which the Revolution left unsolved, and to new problems which arose after that period.

CHAPTER XII.

THE PARTICIPATION OF JEWS IN THE WAR OF THE REVOLUTION.

Captain Isaac Meyers of the French and Indian War of 1754—David S. Franks and Isaac Franks—David Franks, the loyalist—Solomon and Lewis Bush—Major Benjamin Nones—Other Jewish Soldiers, of whom one was exempted from duty on Friday nights—The Pinto brothers—Commissary General Mordecai Sheftal of Georgia—Haym Solomon, the Polish Jew, and his financial assistance to the Revolution.

There were only about two thousand Jews in the colonies at the time when the war broke out, mostly well-to-do merchants of Spanish and Portuguese descent, of whom a considerable number had formerly lived in England or had trade connections with the mother country and with its various dependencies. Class interest and personal predilection for old associations were therefore in favor of their being in sympathy with the ruling power over the sea; still the number of Jewish loyalists was small. The largest number cast their lot with the colonists, and performed useful service in various ways—as merchants abstaining under non-importation agreements from buying English goods, as tradesmen furnishing supplies, as officials assisting the movements of the army, and as officers and soldiers in the line. In most of the colonies the Jews were then still barred from elective office by clauses in the charters and restrictive laws; but this did not prevent them from participating in the work of liberating the country, while on the other hand there was no desire manifested to exclude them from doing their patriotic duty, from which they were excluded in the middle of the preceding century by the less liberal burghers of New Netherlands.

The names of more than forty Jews who served in the continental armies of the Revolution have been preserved, and most of the data about them is to be found in Mr. Simon Wolf's valuable work.[1] As they almost all belonged to the wealthier class, it is but natural that the number of officers is disproportionately large in this small band. Four of them reached the rank of Lieutenant-Colonel, three became Majors, and there were at least half a dozen Captains. Nor were these the first Jews to bear arms or to hold military rank in the colonies. As early as 1754, during the French and Indian War, Isaac Meyers, a Jewish citizen of New York, called a town meeting at the "Rising Sun" Inn and organized a company of bateau men of which he became the captain. Two other Jews are named as taking part in the same war. Both of them served in the expedition across the Allegheny Mountains in the year above named.

Two members of the Franks family served creditably in the Continental army, while a third (they were probably cousins) became known through his sympathy for England. David Salisbury Franks, who is described as a "young English merchant," settled in Montreal, Canada, in 1774, and was active both in business and in the affairs of the Jewish community. On May 3, 1775, he was arrested for speaking disrespectfully of the king, but was discharged six days later. In 1776 General Wooster appointed him paymaster to the American garrison at Montreal, and when the army retreated from Canada he enlisted as a volunteer and later joined a Massachusetts regiment. In 1778 he was ordered to serve under Count d'Estaing, then commanding the sea forces of the United States; upon the failure of the expedition he went to Philadelphia, becoming a member of General Benedict Arnold's military family. In 1779 he went as a volunteer to Charlestown, serving as aide-de-camp to General Lincoln, and was later recalled to attend the trial of General Arnold for improper conduct while in command of Philadelphia,

[1] *The American Jew as Patriot, Soldier and Citizen*, by Simon Wolf, edited by Louis Edward Levy, Philadelphia, 1895.

in which trial Franks was himself implicated. He was aide-de-camp to Arnold at the time of the latter's treason, in September, 1780; on October 2 he was arrested, but when the case was tried the next day he was honorably acquitted. Not satisfied with this, Franks wrote to General Washington asking for a court of inquiry; on November 2, 1780, the court met at West Point and completely exonerated him. In 1781 he was sent by Robert Morris to Europe as bearer of dispatches to Jay in Madrid and to Franklin in Paris. On his return Congress reinstated him into the army with the rank of Major. On January 15, 1784, Congress resolved "that a triplicate of the definitive treaty [of peace] be sent out to the ministers plenipotentiary by Lieut.-Col. David S. Franks" and he again left for Europe. The next year he was appointed Vice-Consul at Marseilles; in 1786 he served in a confidential capacity in the negotiations connected with the treaty of peace and commerce made with Morocco, and on his return to New York in 1787 brought the treaty with him. On January 28, 1789, he was granted four hundred acres of land in recognition of his services during the Revolutionary War.

His relative, Isaac Franks (b. in New York, 1759; d. in Philadelphia, 1822), was only seventeen years old when he enlisted in Colonel Lesher's regiment, New York Volunteers, and served with it in the battle of Long Island. On September 15 of the same year he was taken prisoner at the capture of New York, but effected his escape after three months' detention. In 1777 he was appointed to the quartermaster's department, and in January, 1778, he was made foragemaster, being stationed at West Point until February 22, 1781, when he was appointed by Congress ensign in the Seventh Massachusetts Regiment. He continued in that capacity until July, 1782, when he resigned on account of ill-health. He settled in Philadelphia, where he later held various civil offices, and was in 1794 appointed by Governor Mifflin Lieutenant-Colonel of the Second Regiment of Philadelphia County Brigade of the Militia of the Commonwealth. It was at his house at Germantown (now No. 5442

Main Street) that President Washington resided during the prevalence of yellow fever in 1793, when the seat of government was removed to that suburb of Philadelphia. His portrait, painted by his friend, Gilbert Stewart, is now in the Gibson collection of the Pennsylvania Academy of Fine Arts in Philadelphia.

The third and loyalist member of the family, David Franks (b. in New York, 1720; d. in Philadelphia, 1793), son of Jacob Franks, settled in Philadelphia early in life, and was elected a member of the provincial Assembly in 1748. He supplied the army with provisions during the French and Indian War, and in 1755 he assisted to raise a fund for the defense of the colony. On November 7, 1765, he signed the Non-Importation Resolution; his name is also appended to an agreement to take the King's paper money in lieu of gold and silver. During the Revolution he was an intermediary in the exchange of prisoners, as well as "an agent to the contractors for victualing the troops of the King of Great Britain." He was twice imprisoned by the Colonial Government as an enemy to the American cause, and after his second release, in 1780, he left for England. He returned in 1783 and lived the last ten years of his life in Philadelphia.

Solomon Bush, a native of Philadelphia, the son of Matthias Bush, was an officer in the Pennsylvania militia for ten years. In 1777 he was appointed by the Supreme Council of Pennsylvania Deputy Adjutant-General of the State militia. In September of that year he was dangerously wounded during a skirmish and had to be taken to Philadelphia. When the British captured the city in December, 1777, he was taken prisoner, but released on parole. In 1779 he was promoted to the rank of Lieutenant-Colonel, and was pensioned in 1785.

A Colonel Isaacs of the North Carolina militia is mentioned as "wounded and taken prisoner at Camden, August 16, 1780; exchanged July, 1781." (Wolf, *l. c.*, p. 49.)

Lewis Bush became First Lieutenant of the Sixth Pennsylvania Battalion on January 9, 1776, and Captain on June 24 of

Col. Isaac Franks.

the same year. He was transferred to Colonel Thomas Hartley's additional Continental Regiment in January, 1777, and was commissioned Major March 12, 1777. He participated in a number of battles, and at the battle of Brandywine, on September 11, 1777, he received wounds from which he died four days later.

Benjamin Nones (d. 1826), a native of Bordeaux, France, emigrated to Philadelphia in 1777, and at once took up arms on behalf of the colonies. He served as a volunteer in Captain Verdier's regiment under Count Pulaski during the siege of Savannah, and on September 15, 1779, received a certificate for gallant conduct on the field of battle. He attained the rank of Major, and it is stated that he was with General De Kalb at the battle of Camden, S. C., on August 16, 1780.

Jacob de Leon and Jacob de la Motta were captains under de Kalb; Captain Noah Abraham was called out with the battalion of Cumberland County militia of Pennsylvania, July 28, 1777. Aaron Benjamin (d. 1829), who started as an ensign in the Eighth Connecticut Regiment January 1, 1777, rose three years later to the rank of Regimental Adjutant. Manuel Mordecai Noah (1747-1825) served under General Marion; Isaac Israel rose to the rank of Captain in the Eighth Virginia Regiment in 1777, and Nathaniel Levy, of Baltimore, is mentioned as having served under Lafayette. There is a record of a certificate issued by the New York Committee of Safety, in January, 1776, which read as follows: "Hart Jacobs, of the Jewish religion, having signified to this committee that it is inconsistent with his religious profession to perform military duty on Friday nights, being part of the Jewish Sabbath, it is ordered that he be exempted from military duty on that night of the week. . . ." (See "Publications," XI, p. 163.)

Three, and probably four, brothers of the old Pinto family who resided in Connecticut, took an active part in the Revolution. Abraham Pinto was a member of Company X, Seventh Regiment, of that State, in 1775; William Pinto (of whom it it not certain that he was a brother) appears as a volunteer in

1779 and 1781. Jacob Pinto, who was in New Haven as early as 1759, appears to have been a member of a political committee in that city in 1775, and his name is found among those of other influential citizens of the place in a petition to the Council of Safety for the removal of certain Tories in 1776. Solomon Pinto served as an officer of the Connecticut line throughout the war, and was wounded in the British attack on New Haven July 5 and 6, 1779. He was one of the original members, in his State, of the Society of the Cincinnati, which at the beginning included only meritorious officers of the Revolutionary army.

Mordecai Sheftal (b. at Savannah, Ga., 1735; d. there 1797), who was one of the first white children born in Savannah, being the son of Benjamin Sheftal, who came there in 1733, was the chairman of the Revolutionary Parochial Committee of his native city. In 1777 he was appointed Commissary-General to the troops of Georgia, and in October of the following year he became Deputy Commissary of Issues in South Carolina and Georgia. His imprisonment after Savannah was taken by the British attracted much attention and the description of it forms an interesting part of the local history of that period. In 1782 Sheftal appeared in Philadelphia, which was then the haven for pariot refugees, as one of the founders of the Mickweh Israel congregation. In the following year, in common with other officers, he received a grant of land in what was called "The Georgia Continental Establishment" as a reward for services during the war. He subsequently figures as one of the incorporators of the Union Society (1786), which is still one of Savannah's representative organizations; and his name is also closely associated with the early history of Freemasonry in the United States.

Sheftal and the above-named Manuel Mordecai Noah, besides their active service in the army, also contributed large sums to the cause of the Revolution. Other Jews advanced considerable sums, some of them almost beyond their means. The list of those who rendered valuable and timely assistance includes Benjamin Levy, Hyman Levy, Samuel Lyons, Isaac Moses and Benjamin Jacobs.

There was one, however, who gave more than all of them together, who gave away practically all he possessed, and neither he nor his rightful heirs ever recovered the large debts which the new nation owed to him. This man was Haym Salomon (b. in Lissa, Poland, now a part of Prussia, in 1740; d. in Philadelphia, Jan. 6, 1785). He probably traveled extensively before coming to America, because he could speak German, French and Italian, besides Polish and Russian, an accomplishment which could hardly have been acquired by a Jew in Poland in that period. He settled in New York, and there married Rachel, a daughter of Moses B. Franks (a brother of Jacob Franks). He was arrested by the British as an American spy soon after they occupied New York in September, 1776, and was kept in confinement for a considerable period. When his linguistic proficiency became known he was turned over to the Hessian General, Heister, who gave him an appointment in the commissariat department. He used the greater liberty which was now accorded him to be of service to the French and American prisoners, and to assist a number of them to effect their escape. On August 11, 1778, he escaped from New York and settled in Philadelphia. He soon became a prominent exchange broker, and did considerable business with Robert Morris (1734-1806), the financier of the American Revolution,[1] who was Superintendent of Finance for the colonies in 1781-84. He also became broker to the French consul and the treasurer of the French army which came to assist Washington, and fiscal agent to the French minister to the United States, Chevalier de la Luzerne. In these capacities large sums passed through his hands and he became the principal individual de-

[1] Aaron Levy (b. in Amsterdam, 1742; d. in Philadelphia, 1815), who was also of great assistance to the colonies in their struggle for independence, was a partner of Robert Morris in various enterprises in Pennsylvania. The town of Aaronsburg, Center County, Pa., was founded by Levy and is named after him. (See "Jew. Encyclopedia," s. v., Aaronsburg and Levy, Aaron.)

positor of the Bank of North America, which was founded by Morris. The latter, who kept a diary, mentions in it nearly seventy-five separate transactions in which Salomon's name figures in the negotiations of bills of exchange, by which means the credit of the government was maintained in this period; Salomon practically being the sole agent employed by Morris for this purpose. Most of the money advanced by Louis XVI. to the cause of the Revolution and the proceeds of the loans negotiated in Holland passed through his hands.

He advanced aid to numerous prominent men of this period. James Madison, in a letter (Aug. 27, 1782) urging the forwarding of remittances from his State which he represented in Philadelphia, wrote: "I have for some time been a pensioner on the favor of Haym Salomon, a Jew broker." On September 30 of the same year he writes: "The kindness of our little friend in Front Street, near the coffee house, is a fund which will preserve me from extremities, but I never resort to it without great mortification, as he obstinately rejects all recompense. The price of money is so usurious that he thinks it ought to be extorted from none but those who aim at profitable speculation. To a necessitous delegate he gratuitously spares a supply out of his private stock." James Wilson (1742-98), another famous delegate to the Continental Congress, who sometimes acted as Salomon's attorney, relates that without his client's aid, "administered with equal generosity and delicacy" he would have been forced to retire from the public service.

Haym Salomon died suddenly, at the age of forty-five, leaving a widow and two infant children, named Ezekiel and Haym M. The inventory of his estate showed that he had lent to the government more than $350,000, but although these certificates of indebtedness were almost all that was left of his wealth, they were never paid, and all efforts of his heirs in later times to recover from Congress payment on these claims, or even to obtain a token of recognition for his great services, have thus far proved unsuccessful.

Salomon also took an active part in Jewish communal affairs in Philadelphia and was one of the original members of the Congregation Mickweh Israel. In 1784 he was treasurer of what was probably the first Jewish charitable organization in that city.

His son, Hyam M. Salomon, lived in New York and was a dealer in powder and shot, occupying a store in Front Street in the time of the great fire of 1835. William Salomon (b. in Mobile, Ala., Oct. 9, 1852) of New York is a great-grandson of Hyam Salomon.

CHAPTER XIII.

THE DECLINE OF NEWPORT; WASHINGTON AND THE JEWS.

England's special enmity to Newport caused the dispersion of its Jewish congregation—The General Assembly of Rhode Island meets in the historic Newport Synagogue—Moses Seixas' address to Washington on behalf of the Jews of Newport and the latter's reply—Washington's letters to the Hebrew Congregations of Savannah, Ga., and to the congregations of Philadelphia, New York, Richmond and Charleston.

The breaking out of the Revolution put an end to the commercial prosperity of Newport. Its situation upon the ocean, which made it before so favorable for commerce, had now an opposite effect, and left it more exposed to attacks from the enemy than any other place of equal importance, in North America. Its inhabitants had especially provoked the hostility of the mother country, as it was one of the first places to manifest a spirit of resistance to the British Government by burning an armed vessel of war that came to exact an odious tax. It could expect no mercy and received none, when 8,000 British and Hessian troops occupied it in 1776. Four hundred and eighty houses were destroyed, its commerce was ruined and its commercial interests never recovered from this blow, which fell with crushing effect upon the Jewish residents.

The congregation was dispersed, the Synagogue was closed, and Rabbi Isaac Touro went with his family to Jamaica, where he remained until his death in 1782. Aaron Lopez, who was a heavy sufferer, accompanied by a majority of the foremost Jews of Newport, removed to Leicester, Mass., and their stay in that town had a favorable effect on its development. Others went to Philadelphia and other places. When Newport was evacuated, in 1779, after the enemy destroyed its wharves and fortifications and carried off its library and records, some of the exiles began to return. When the General Assembly of the State of Rhode Island convened for the first time after the evacuation, it met in the historic Synagogue (Sept., 1780). Aaron Lopez was one of a number of the Leicester colony who set out for their former home, but he was drowned on the way, and his body was later recovered and buried in the old cemetery.

But those who returned did not remain long. New York had become the great commercial center after the Revolution, and the important Newport merchants left one by one for that city; others went to Philadelphia, Charleston or Savannah. The congregation was, however, still in existence when President Washington visited Newport in August, 1790, and he was on that occasion formally addressed by Moses Seixas on behalf of the Jews of Newport as follows:

Sir:—Permit the children of the stock of Abraham to approach you with the most cordial affection and esteem for your person and merit, and to join with our fellow-citizens in welcoming you to Newport.

With pleasure we reflect on those days of difficulty and danger when the God of Israel, who delivered David from the peril of the sword, shielded your head in the day of battle, and we rejoice to think that the same spirit which rested in the bosom of the greatly beloved Daniel, enabling him to preside over the provinces of the Babylonian Empire, rests and ever will rest upon you, enabling you to discharge the arduous duties of Chief Magistrate of these States.

Deprived, as we have hitherto been, of invaluable rights of free citizens, we now—with a deep sense of gratitude to the Almighty Disposer of all events—behold a government erected by the majesty of the people, a government which gives no sanction to bigotry and no assistance to persecution, but generously affording to all liberty of conscience and immunities of citizenship, deeming every one, of whatever nation, tongue or language, equal parts of the great governmental machine. This so ample and extensive Federal Union, whose base is philanthropy, mutual confidence and public virtue, we cannot but acknowledge to be the work of the great God, who rules the armies of the heavens and among the inhabitants of the earth, doing whatever deemeth to Him good.

For all the blessings of civil and religious liberty which we enjoy under an equal and benign administration, we desire to send up thanks to the Ancient of days, the great Preserver of men, beseeching Him that the angel who conducted our forefathers through the wilderness into the promised land may graciously conduct you through all the difficulties and dangers of this mortal life; and when, like Joshua, full of days and of honors, you are gathered to your fathers, may you be admitted into the heavenly paradise to partake of the water of life and the tree of immortality.

To this letter, which bears unmistakable traces of having been originally composed in Rabbinical Hebrew, the Father of His Country replied as follows:

TO THE HEBREW CONGREGATION OF NEWPORT, RHODE ISLAND.

Gentlemen:—While I have received with much satisfaction your address, replete with expressions of esteem, I rejoice in the opportunity of assuring you that I shall always retain a grateful remembrance of the cordial welcome I experienced in my visit to Newport from all classes of citizens.

The reflection on the days of difficulty and danger, which are passed, is rendered the more sweet from the consciousness that they are succeeded by days of uncommon prosperity and security. If we have the wisdom to make the best use of the advantage with which we are now favored, we cannot fail under the just administration of a good government to become a great and happy people.

The citizens of the United States of America have the right to applaud themselves for having given to mankind examples of an enlarged and liberal policy worthy of imitation. All possess alike liberty of conscience and immunities of citizenship. It is now no more that toleration is spoken of as if it were by the indulgence of one class of people that another enjoyed the exercise of their inherent natural rights, for happily the Government of the United States, which gives to bigotry no sanction, to persecution no assistance, requires only that they who live under its protection should demean themselves as good citizens in giving it on all occasions their effectual support.

It would be inconsistent with the frankness of my character not to avow that I am pleased with your favorable opinion of my administation and fervent wishes of my felicity. May the children of the stock of Abraham, who dwell in this land, continue to merit and enjoy the good will of the other inhabitants, while everyone shall sit in safety under his own vine and fig-tree and there shall be none to make him afraid. May the Father of all mercies scatter light and not darkness in our paths and make us all in our several vocations useful here and, in His own due time and way, everlastingly happy.[1]

G. WASHINGTON.

In the year following this correspondence the Synagogue was closed for lack of attendance, and it was not reopened for nearly a century. The above-named Moses Seixas, who for many years was cashier of the Bank of Rhode Island, was one of the last Jews in Newport of that period. Moses Lopez, the nephew of Aaron, is reputed to have been the last one who remained there, and ultimately he, too, left for New York, where he died in 1830. Sentiment caused the descendants of many of the original families to direct that their remains should be buried in the old cemetery, where tombstones show interments during the entire period down to 1855. Abraham Touro (d. in Boston, 1822), the son of Rabbi Isaac Touro, bequeathed a fund for perpetually keeping the Synagogue in repair, and also made provisions for the care of the burial ground. His brother Judah Touro of New Orleans replaced the old cemetery wall with a massive one of stone, with an imposing granite gateway (1843); and, at his own request, he himself was buried there. The street on which the Synagogue is situated is known as Touro Street. The city also possesses a park known as Touro Park. Though the Touro fund provided for the support of the minister also, the Synagogue remained closed until 1883, when the Rev. A. P Mendes, on appointment by the Congregation Shearith Israel of New York (which became the legal proprietor of both Synagogue and cemetery of Newport), became minister and conducted services until his death in 1891.

* * * * *

There are extant two other letters written by George Washington to Jewish communities which felicitated him upon his ad-

[1] A fac-simile of Washington's reply is found in the "Jewish Encyclopedia," vol. IX, between pp. 294-95.

vancement to the presidency. One is in reply to an address signed by Levi Sheftal as president, in behalf of the Hebrew Congregations of Savannah, and is as follows:

TO THE HEBREW CONGREGATIONS OF THE CITY OF SAVANNAH, GEORGIA.

Gentlemen:—I thank you with great sincerity for your congratulation on my appointment to the office which I have the honor to hold by the unanimous choice of my fellow-citizens, and especially the expressions you are pleased to use in testifying the confidence that is reposed in me by your congregations.

As the delay which has naturally intervened between my election and your address has afforded me an opportunity for appreciating the merits of the Federal Government and for communicating your sentiments of its administration, I have rather to express my satisfaction rather than regret at a circumstance which demonstrates (upon experiment) your attachment to the former as well as approbation of the latter.

I rejoice that a spirit of liberality and philanthropy is much more prevalent than it formerly was among the enlightened nations of the earth, and that your brethren will benefit thereby in proportion as it shall become still more extensive; happily the people of the United States have in many instances exhibited examples worthy of imitation, the salutary influence of which will doubtless extend much further if gratefully enjoying those blessings of peace which (under the favor of heaven) have been attained by fortitude in war, they shall conduct themselves with reverence to the Deity and charity towards their fellow-creatures.

May the same wonder-working Deity, who long since delivered the Hebrews from their Egyptian oppressors, planted them in a promised land, *whose providential agency has lately been conspicuous in establishing these United States as an independent nation,* still continue to water them with the dews of heaven and make the inhabitants of every denomination participate in the temporal and spiritual blessings of that people whose God is Jehovah.

G. WASHINGTON.

The third address was from the Hebrew Congregations in the cities of Philadelphia, New York, Richmond and Charleston, dated December 13, 1790, and signed on their behalf by Manuel Josephson, to which the President returned the following:

Gentlemen:—The liberality of sentiment towards each other, which marks every political and religious denomination of men in this country, stands unparalleled in the history of nations.

The affection of such a people is a treasure beyond the reach of calculation, and the repeated proofs which my fellow-citizens have given of their attachment to me and approbation of my doings form the purest sources of my temporal felicity.

The affectionate expressions of your address again excite my gratitude and receive my warmest acknowledgment.

The power and goodness of the Almighty, so strongly manifested in the events of our late glorious revolution, and His kind interposition in our behalf, have been no less visible in the establishment of our present equal government. In war He directed the sword, and in peace He has ruled in our councils. My agency in both has been guided by the best intentions and a sense of duty I owe to my country.

And as my intentions have hitherto been amply rewarded by the approbation of my fellow-citizens, I shall endeavor to deserve a continuance of it by my future conduct.

May the same temporal and eternal blessing which you implore for me rest upon your congregations.

G. WASHINGTON.

CHAPTER XIV.

OTHER COMMUNITIES IN THE FIRST PERIODS OF INDEPENDENCE.

Rabbi Gershom Mendez Seixas—Growth of the Jewish community of Philadelphia on account of the War—Protest against the religious test clause in the Constitution of Pennsylvania—Benjamin Franklin contributes five pounds to Mickweh Israel—Secession of the German-Polish element—New Societies—Jewish lawyers; Judge Moses Levy—Congressman H. M. Phillips—The Bush family of Delaware—New Jersey and New Hampshire—North Carolina: the Mordecai family and other early settlers.

While the Jewish community of New York was not entirely dispersed, like that of Newport, by the outbreak of the Revolution, a great majority resolved to leave the city before it was occupied by the British (Sept. 15, 1776). The patriotic minister of the Congregation Shearit Israel, Rabbi Gershom Mendez Seixas (b. in New York, 1745; d. there July 2, 1816), who was the spiritual head of the community since 1766, early espoused the cause of the colonies, and it was mostly due to his influence that the congregation closed the door of its Synagogue on the approach of the British. Most of those who left went to Philadelphia; Rabbi Seixas himself first went to Stratford, Conn., where he remained about four years, and where several of his former congregants joined him. In 1780 he, too, went to Philadelphia, but returned to New York after the war (March, 1784), when the Synagogue was reopened and he resumed his former position. He later (1787) became a trustee of Columbia College, and was one of its incorporators whose name appeared on the charter.

There was, however, notwithstanding the statement of Dr. Benjamin Rush that "the Jews in all the States are Whigs," a sprinkling of Tories in New York Jewry, who remained at home, and some of them occasionally held services in the Synagogue during the British occupation, under the presidency of Lyon Jonas, and subsequently of Alexander Zuntz, a Hessian officer, who settled in New York. On the reorganization of the congregation at the close of the Revolution, Hyman Levy succeeded Zuntz as president, and the congregation presented an address of congratulation to Governor Clinton on the outcome of the war. Rabbi Seixas was one of the fourteen ministers who participated in the inauguration of Washington as President, in New York, on April 30, 1789. A list of the residents of New York in 1799 whose residences were assessed at £2,000 or over includes the names of Benjamin Seixas, Solomon Sampson, Alexander Zuntz and Ephraim Hart.

The community was still small—not quite half as large as that of Newport in the preceding period; there were only about 500 Jews in New York at the commencement of the War of 1812. But it was slowly growing and several of the first communal institutions date from that time. A Hebrah Gemilut Hasodim, for the burying of the dead, was organized in 1785; the Polonies Talmud Torah was founded in 1802, with a fund which Myer Polonies bequeathed to the congregation for that purpose in the preceding year. The Hebrah Hesed we-Emet was organized in the same year.

The Jewish community which gained most in the time of the war was that of Philadelphia. The little building in Sterling Alley, where the Congregation Mickweh Israel prayed at that time, soon became too small, and a three-story brick house, in Cherry Alley, between Third and Fourth Streets, was hired. But even the new place was soon too small, and a plain building was constructed on a lot in Cherry Street, west of Third Street, which was bought for the purpose. It was dedicated on September 13, 1782, by Rabbi Seixas. A list of the members of the congregation at that time contains 102 names[1] and the percentage of Ashkenazic (German and Polish) names is much larger than in similar lists of earlier dates.

A year after the Synagogue was built the Jews of Philadelphia for the first time appeared as an organized body in any public proceeding. On the 23d of December, 1783, the minister, Gershom Mendez Seixas; the parnass, Simon Nathan; and Asher Myers, Barnard Gratz and Haym Salomon, as members of the *Mahamad* or Board of Trustees, in behalf of themselves and brethren, addressed the Council of Censors in relation to the declaration required to be made by each member of the Assembly, which affirmed that "the Scriptures of the Old and the New Testaments were given by Divine inspiration," and also in relation to that part of the Constitution which declared that "no other test should be required of any other civil magistrate in that State." They represented that the provisions deprived them of the right of ever becoming representatives. They did not covet office, they said, but they thought the provision improper, and an injustice to the members of a persuasion that had always been attached to the American cause. This memorial appeared to have had no immediate effect; but it doubtless had its influence in procuring the ultimate modification of the test clause in the Constitution of Pennsylvania.

Rabbi Seixas was succeeded in Philadelphia by the Rev. Jacob Raphael Cohen (d. Sept., 1811), who was formerly a reader or hazzan in Montreal, Canada, and New York. The congregation was weakened by the departure of a considerable number of members after the war, and probably also by the death of Haym Salomon, who was one of its most generous contributors, and found itself in financial difficulties about the year 1788. After an application to the General Assembly of Pennsylvania for permission to set up a lottery to pay the amount due on the Synagogue building was not granted, the congregation issued a gen-

[1] See Hyman Polock Rosenbach, *The Jews in Philadelphia prior to 1800*, pp. 22-23, *ff.*, Philadelphia, 1883.

eral appeal to citizens of all sects. Among the non-Jews who sent in contributions in response to this appeal was the great Benjamin Franklin (1706-90) and the astronomer, David Rittenhouse (1732-96), the former contributing five pounds and the latter two.

In April, 1790, the Legislature passed an act to allow the Hebrew Congregation to raise eight hundred pounds sterling by a lottery. The managers were: Manuel Josephson, Solomon Lyon, Solomon Hays, Solomon Etting, William Wistar and John Duffield. The last two were not Jews, but were placed among the trustees probably to give the project some influence with members of other denominations.

The inevitable secession of the Ashkenazic element took place in 1802, when the "Hebrew-German Society Rodef Shalom," one of the earliest German-Jewish congregations in America was formed. It was reorganized and chartered in 1812. Among its earliest rabbis were Wolf Benjamin, Jacob Lipman, Bernhard Illowy, Henry Vidaver, Moses Sulzbacher and Moses Rau.

A Society for the Visitation of the Sick and for Mutual Assistance was organized in October, 1813, with Jacob Cohen as its first president. In 1819 several ladies organized the still existing Female Hebrew Benevolent Society, of which Miss Rebecca Gratz (1781-1869), who was reputed to be the prototype of Rebecca in Walter Scott's "Ivanhoe," was the first secretary. Several other benevolent and educational societies date their origin from the first half of the Nineteenth Century, and have helped to give the Jewish community of Philadelphia that substantiality and compactness of organization which is missing in other large cities of the United States.

At the same time progress was being made in other directions, too. The aptitude of the Jew for the legal profession could not be displayed and utilized as early as his well known medical skill, which he exercised even in the dark ages. But as soon as the opportunity of emancipation was offered, good jurists appeared and soon occupied a prominent place at the bar and also on the bench. The earliest Jewish practitioner in Pennsylvania, of whom there is a record, was Moses Levy (d. May 9, 1826), whose admission to the bar dates as far back as 1778, and who a year later was admitted to practice in the Supreme Court of that State. He held various offices and finally became Presiding Judge of the District Court of the City and County of Philadelphia (1822), after having served twenty years as Recorder. At least three other Jews were admitted to the practice of law in Philadelphia in the eighteenth century; Samson Levy (d. 1831) in 1787, Daniel Levy of Northumberland county (d. 1844) in 1791, and Zalegman Phillips (1779-1839) in 1799. About a dozen more were admitted during the first half of the nineteenth century, among them being the latter's son, Henry Mayer Phillips, who was admitted in 1832, and was, twenty-four years later, elected to represent the fourth district of Pennsylvania in the 35th Congress. (See Henry S. Morais, *The Jews of Philadelphia,* index.)

* * * * *

The number of Jews in the remainder of the thirteen original colonies was at that time very small and they were mostly scattered. While there are, for instance, records of Jews who lived or traded in Delaware as early as 1655, there was no Jewish community in that State until about two centuries later. But there was at least one Jewish family in Wilmington, Del., immediately after the Revolution, several members of which participated in that struggle. David Bush joined the Washington Lodge of Freemasons of Wilmington on December 16, 1784.[1] He was its Senior Warden in 1789, its Treasurer in 1791 and again Senior Warden in 1795. He was the father of Major Lewis Bush, who has been mentioned in a former chapter (page 90), and of three other sons, two of whom also held offices

[1] See Oppenheim, The Jews and Masonry, in "Publications," vol. XIX, 1-94, for the sources of most of the references to Masonry in this work.

in the same lodge in the last decade of the eighteenth century. Joseph Capelle (Carpelles ?) was Master of the lodge in 1792.

The colony of New Jersey, whose Indians, according to a description by William Penn, closely resembled Jews, had very few real Israelites in Colonial times, despite its proximity to New York on one side and to Pennsylvania on the other. In the test established in West Jersey for office-holders in 1693, the candidate had to declare on oath or affirmation that he "professes faith in God the father, and Jesus Christ his eternal son. . ." In the East Jersey Bill of Rights was inserted the provision "that no person or persons that profess faith in God, by Jesus Christ his only son, shall at any time be any way molested. . . . Provided this shall not be extended to any of the Romish religion." But, as it is justly observed by Mr. Friedenberg (see "Publications," XVII, p. 36), these provisions were not at all aimed against the Jews, of whom there were hardly any in the colony at that time, but against heathens, atheists, infidels and Catholics, especially against the latter. No Jews were naturalized in New Jersey before the Revolution. David Hays is known to have resided on a plantation in Griggs Town, Somerset County, in 1744, when he offered it for sale; and Myers Levy, a Dutch Jew, is reported to have absconded from Spottsville, in East New Jersey, in 1760, leaving many debts behind. Another Jew, Nathan Levy, a shop keeper of Philipsburg, Sussex County, West Jersey, is mentioned many years later. There was only, as far as it is known, one Jew in the New Jersey troops of the Continental Army: Asher Levy or Lewis, a grandson of the well-known Asser Levy of New Amsterdam. He was commissioned ensign in the first regiment, September 12, 1778. "The New Jersey Journal" was established by David Franks at Camden in 1778 and existed about four years.

The first families with Jewish names which are mentioned in the records of New Hampshire, were the Moses and the Abrams family "descendants of Jewish Christians." The Abrams family, according to tradition, is descended from two brothers who came from Palestine to New England at an unknown date, their names being William Abrams, who was a ship's carpenter and fell into the sea and was drowned, and John, the other brother, who settled at Amesbury, Mass. ("Publications," XI, p. 79). In the list of grants to settlers on the road, between Wolfsborough and Leavits Town (Ossipee), issued in 1770, on condition that each settler had to give a bond for £30 that a house would be erected by him within a year, grant No. 11 was made to Joseph Levy. In 1777 mention is made of William Levi, of Somersworth, as a private in the 2d New Hampshire Continental Regiment. Abraham Isaac settled in Portsmouth about the close of the Revolution and was active in Masonic affairs. A local historian writes of him that "he and his wife were natives of Prussia and Jews of the strictest sect. They were the first descendants of the venerable Patriarchs that ever pitched their tents in Portsmouth, and during their lives were the only Jews among us. He acquired a good property and built a house on State street. Their shop was always closed on Saturday." Mr. Isaac died February 15, 1803, and on the stone which marks his grave in the North Burying Ground is an epitaph written by the poet J. M. Sewall, author of the popular revolutionary song "Vain Britons Boast No Longer."

It has already been mentioned in a former chapter (page 86) that there were hardly any Jews in North Carolina at the time when its representatives voted at the Constitutional Convention against the abolition of religious tests. The provision of its State Constitution of 1776, which read "That no person who shall deny the being of God or the truth of the Protestant religion . . . shall be capable of holding any office or place of trust or profit in the Civil Department within the State" was doubtless aimed primarily at Roman Catholics, though it necessarily included Jews, Quakers, Mohamedans, etc. Jews did not become directly interested in the struggle for religious liberty in that State until the first decade in the Nineteenth Century, and the description of it will be found in the following chapter.

The annals of Freemasonry, which usually disclose the earliest Jewish settlers in various localities in the eighteenth century, do not contain any Jewish names in the lodges of that fraternity until its very close. Jacob Mordecai (b. in Philadelphia, 1762; d. in Richmond, 1838), the son of Moses Mordecai (b. in Bonn, Germany, 1707; d. in Philadelphia, 1781), was Master of Johnston Caswell Lodge No. 10, of Warrenton, N. C., in 1797, 1798 and 1799. He was the founder and proprietor of a female seminary in that city which enjoyed a good reputation. One of his sons, Major Alfred Mordecai (1804-87), was probably the first Jewish graduate of the United States Military Academy of West Point.[1] Zachariah Hart (also spelled Harte) was a member of David Glasgow Lodge, in Glasgow County, in 1798 and 1799. Abraham Isaacs was Senior Warden of St. Tammany Lodge No. 30, of Wilmington, in 1798. Aaron Lazarus (1777-1841), who is mentioned as one of the first Hebrews to reach Wilmington and later became one of the first directors of the Wilmington & Weldon Railroad Company, was a member of the same lodge in 1803. There were about half a dozen other Jewish Masons in the lodges of Wilmington, Newbern and of Beaufort County about that time.

[1] A description of this highly interesting Jewish family, by Gratz Mordecai, is found in "Publications," VI, pp. 39-48.

CHAPTER XV.

THE QUESTION OF RELIGIOUS LIBERTY IN VIRGINIA AND IN NORTH CAROLINA.

Little change in the basic systems of State institutions—Patrick Henry, Madison and Jefferson on religious liberty in Virginia—The similarity between the Virginia statute and the conclusions of Moses Mendelssohn pointed out by Count Mirabeau—The first congregation of Richmond—Article 32 of the Constitution of North Carolina against Catholics, Jews, etc.—How Jacob Henry, a Jewish member of the Legislature, defended and retained his seat in 1809—Judge Gaston's interpretation—The first congregation of Wilmington, N. C.—Final emancipation in 1868.

The provision in Article VI of the Constitution of the United States (§3) that "no religious test shall ever be required as a qualification to any office or public trust under the United States" settled the matter only as far as the National Government was concerned. Each of the independent and sovereign States could solve this problem in its own way, though most of them have already adopted full religious freedom. But it must be remembered that the basic institutions of the States were not directly changed by the Revolution, and in some of them they were not changed at all. In some instances Royal Charters remained, with some alterations, as State Constitutions; English common law remained in force even to this day, unless otherwise provided for by special enactment. The colonies were too free originally to require or desire a sudden radical change when they threw off the British yoke. They kept on progressing by the slow process of evolution, but not at an equal pace, each emphasizing the questions in which its inhabitants were mostly interested.

Uniform or simultaneous action was not to be expected under such conditions.

Virginia, the State of Washington and of Jefferson, the "mother of presidents" and the home of the framers of the National Constitution, began to consider the question of religious liberty seriously soon after peace was declared. It was not a new question even then, for as early as 1776, when a new Constitution for the Commonwealth was drafted, there occurred a significant discussion about the difference between toleration and rights. The Declaration of Rights, reported by a committee of which Colonel Mason was chairman, contained a provision relative to religious liberty whose authorship is attributed to Patrick Henry (1736-99). It provided that all men should enjoy the fullest toleration in the exercise of religion. Madison strongly opposed the use of the word toleration, which recognized liberty of worship not as a right but as a favor granted to dissenting denominations. At his instance the provision was amended to read: "All men are equally entitled to the free exercise of religion, according to the dictates of conscience."

But even this was still far from actual separation of Church and State in Virginia. Even the annual assessments, which had been theretofore levied in favor of the Episcopal Church, were not abolished outright, they were simply suspended from year to year, until, at Jefferson's instance, the grant was defeated in 1779. In that year he introduced a measure entitled "A bill for establishing religious freedom," which, after two readings, was sent throughout the State to secure the sense of the people relative to it before taking final action at the next legislature. It was permitted to languish unacted upon for several years, and during that time an agitation was kept up against the spirit which it embodied. Various measures were suggested, about 1784, looking to establish Christianity in Virginia instead of any single Christian sect, as before the Revolution, and for securing governmental support to all Christian sects. The theory of the advocates of such measures was, that while there should be no actual persecution of non-Christian sects, the State ought to establish Christianity as the religion of the great majority of the people, and that the Revolution had evolved merely the principle that no single Christian sect should be preferred over any other. On November 11, 1784, a resolution drafted by Patrick Henry was reported to the Lower House of the Legislature, providing that "the people" of the Commonwealth, according to their respective abilities, ought to pay a moderate tax or contribution for the support of the Christian religion, or of some Christian church denomination or communion. . . ." In spite of Madison's opposition, it was adopted by a vote of 47 to 32, and a special committee, of which Mr. Henry was chairman, was appointed to draft such a bill.[1]

It was clearly understood that this measure was intended to curtail the rights of Jewish and other non-Christian residents. Beverly Randolph, writing about this subject to James Monroe, says: "The only great point that has been discussed since the sitting of the Assembly has been a motion for a general assessment, upon more contracted ground than I could ever have expected. The generals on the opposite sides were Henry and Madison. The former advocated, with his usual art, the establishment of the Christian religion in exclusion of all other Denominations. By this I mean that Turks, Jews and Infidels were to contribute to the support of a religion whose truth they did not acknowledge. Madison displayed great learning and ingenuity, with all the powers of a close reasoner; but was unsuccessful in the event, having a majority against him. I am, however, inclined to think that the measure will not be adopted. . . . The supporters of this holy system will certainly split whenever they come to enter upon the minute arrangements of the business."

"A bill establishing a provision for teachers of the Christian religion" was brought in December 23, 1784, and after it was

[1] See Max J. Kohler, *Phases in the History of Religious Liberty in America* . in "Publications," XI, pp. 53-73, where the subject is extensively treated and the sources are given.

amended, but without materially changing its substance, it passed its second reading. But on the next day (December 24) Madison was able to secure the passage of a resolution postponing the third reading till the following November, and copies of the bill were ordered to be printed and distributed in every county of the Commonwealth. The people were requested to signify their opinion respecting the adoption of such a measure to the next session of the legislature. An active and thorough discussion of the bill followed throughout the State. Madison prepared a "Memorial and Remonstrance" against the bill, which was extensively circulated and signed.

Madison made no mistake in suggesting this appeal to the people. When the Assembly met in October, 1785, the table of the House of Delegates almost sunk under the weight of the accumulated copies of the memorial against the bill which came from different counties, each with its long and dense columns of subscribers. The fate of the assessment was sealed. The manifestation of the public judgment was too unequivocal and overwhelming to leave the faintest hope to the friends of the measure, and it was abandoned without a struggle. The declaratory act for the establishment of religious liberty, which had been drawn by Jefferson as one of the committee of revisors and presented to the legislature in 1779, was then taken up and passed into a law. Madison's "Memorial and Remonstrance" had cleared away every obstruction.

In a letter to Madison, dated December 16, 1786, Jefferson, who was then our Minister to France, wrote: "The Virginia Act for religious freedom has been received with infinite approbation in Europe, and propogated with enthusiasm. I do not mean by the governments, but by the individuals who compose them. It has been translated into French and Italian, has been sent to most of the courts of Europe, and has been the best evidence of the falsehoods of those reports which stated us to be in anarchy. It is inserted in the new Encyclopædia, and is appearing in most of the publications respecting America. In fact, it is comfortable to see the standard of reason at length erected, after so many ages during which the human mind has been held in vassalage by kings, priests and nobles; and it is honorable for us to have produced the first legislature who had the courage to declare that the reason of men may be trusted with the formation of his own opinions."

In the following year Count Mirabeau (1749-91) the most distinguished of the advocates of Jewish emancipation in France, calls attention in his essay *On Moses Mendelssohn and the Political Reform of the Jews* (1787) to the striking similarity of the enactment of Virginia to the conclusions at which the Jewish philosopher of Berlin arrived by abstract reasoning; assuming that Mendelssohn never saw the preamble of the American law, which was drafted by Jefferson four years before the publication of "Jerusalem" in 1783. It is clear, however, that about seven years later, when the great French Revolution, which was influenced by the American Revolution much more than is commonly supposed, was in full swing, even the debates of the Constitutional Convention of Virginia of 1776 had become known to the friends of religious liberty in France. In the course of a petition in favor of their own emancipation, addressed by the French Jews to the National Assembly on January 29th, 1790, they said: "America, to which politics will owe so many useful lessons, has rejected the word toleration from its code, as a term tending to compromise individual liberty and to sacrifice certain classes of men to other classes. To tolerate is, in fact, to suffer that which you could, if you wish, prevent and prohibit."

There were not many Jews in Virginia in the time when this momentous question was discussed and solved. Individual Jews are mentioned in the Seventeenth Century, but the first record of a congregation occurs in connection with the address to Washington, mentioned above (page 102), which was sent by the Hebrew congregations of Philadelphia, Richmond, New York and Charleston. The minute-book of the Congregation Bet Shalom of Richmond, Va., dates back to the year 1791, and it is assumed that the first or Sephardic congregation was organized in that year. The first place of worship was in a room of a three-story brick building on the west side of 19th street, between Franklin and Grace streets, where one of the members resided. It later moved to a small brick building, erected on the west side of 19th street in the rear of the Union Hotel, which then stood on the corner of Main street. After some years a lot was purchased from Dr. Adams on the east side of Mayo street, above Franklin street, on which a commodious synagogue was erected, in which the congregation worshipped for upwards of three-quarters of a century. The burial ground on Franklin street, near 21st street, which is now enclosed with a substantial granite wall, was conveyed by Isaiah Isaac to Jacob I. Cohen, Israel I. Cohen, David Isaac, Moses Mordecai, Jacob I. Cohen, Jr., Simon Gratz, Aaron Levy, Moses Jacob and Levy Myers, as trustees, on October 21st, 1791. It was used until about 1816, when Benjamin Wolfe, then a member of the Common Council of the City of Richmond, made application on behalf of the congregation for a new piece of ground, which was granted by an ordinance passed on the 20th day of May, giving for that purpose an acre of land belonging to the City of Richmond lying upon Shockoe Hill.[1]

* * * * *

North Carolina, like Virginia, had an Established Church until a short time before the outbreak of the Revolution, all citizens being required to pay toward its support, and dissenting clergymen being denied the privilege of performing even the marriage ceremony. But when the Dissenters won their fight against the Establishment, they took an uncompromising stand against the complete emancipation of Roman Catholics, Jews and others not belonging to a Protestant denomination. The opposition to Jews was mainly theoretical or academic, as there were practically no Jews in North Carolina at that time. In happy con-

[1] See Jacob Ezekiel, *The Jews of Richmond*, in "Publications," IV, pp. 21-27.

trast to some Old World countries of the present time, opposition to Jews in the United States developed only in parts of the country where they were least known. In all the original States which had considerable Jewish communities, like New York, Pennsylvania and Rhode Island, full religious liberty was firmly established before the adoption of the Federal Constitution.

Like Virginia, too, North Carolina adopted a Constitution in 1776. It provided for liberty of worship and even excluded clergymen from being members of the Senate, House of Commons or Council of State. But when it came to the question of holding office, an exception was incorporated in Article 32 which read as follows:

"That no person who shall deny the being of God or the truth of the Protestant religion or the Divine Authority, either of the Old or New Testament, or who shall hold religious principles incompatible with the freedom and safety of the State, shall be capable of holding any office or place of trust or profit in the Civil Department within the State."

This article was doubtless aimed primarily at Roman Catholics; but the prohibition being a sweeping one, it necessarily included Jews, Quakers, Mohamedans, Deists, etc. While there was some opposition to the adoption of this section, it seems to have expressed the predominating opinion of the State on that point, for, as it was noted above (page 86), the delegates of North Carolina voted at the Federal Constitutional Convention of 1787 against the clause abolishing religious tests. The entire question was again discussed at the State Convention which was called in 1788 to ratify the Constitution of the United States, and the narrower view prevailed. The Convention resolved neither to ratify nor reject the Constitution, but that a Declaration of rights be laid before Congress and twenty-six amendments proposed. North Carolina was therefore unrepresented in the extra session of the first Congress which adopted the first amendment, "That Congress shall make no laws respecting the establishment of religion or prohibiting the free exercise thereof." This amendment was partly a concession to that State, implying a guaranty that even should a Papist or a Mohamedan be elected President, he should not be able to force his religion on those unwilling to accept it. After its adoption, North Carolina adopted the Constitution, in November, 1789.

Despite all this prejudice, section 32 of the State Constitution soon came to be regarded a dead letter. As a matter of fact, a Catholic was elected Governor in 1781. It was not until 1809 that the whole subject again came prominently to the front in the case of Jacob Henry, a Jew, who was elected a member of the Legislature for Carteret County. He had served throughout the year 1808 and had apparently been re-elected for 1809, and then a fellow member asked to have his seat declared vacant on account of his faith.

Henry delivered a notable address in the Assembly in defense of his rights to his seat. It made a strong impression at that time, and was later republished as an example of fine composition in a work known as the *American Orator.*[1] He was permitted to retain his seat, but the principle at issue was rather avoided than settled. It was decided that the article prohibiting non-Protestants from holding office in any civil department of the State did not exclude such persons from serving in the Legislature, because the legislative office was above all civil offices. The view was more pointedly defined by saying that Catholics and Jews could make the laws, but could neither execute nor interpret them. Actually, however, both executive and judicial offices were held by non-Protestants, before and after that incident.

When a distinguished Roman Catholic, William Gaston (1778-

[1] See Leon Hühner, *Religious Liberty in North Carolina,* in "Publications," XVI, pp. 37-71, for the facts and the sources, and also for Henry's speech, which is too long to be reproduced here. The speech is also found in *Selections for Homes and Schools,* by Marion L. Misch, pp. 305-10, issued by the Jewish Publication Society of America in 1911.

1844), was chosen Justice of the Supreme Court of North Carolina (1834) a doubt arose, even in his own mind, whether he could accept the office. But he resorted to an even more ingenious interpretation of the Constitution, which was subsequently followed in other cases as well. He argued that the word "deny" implied an overt act, and that "the Constitution does not prescribe the faith which entitles to or excludes from civil office, but demands from all those who hold office, that decent respect of the prevalent religion of the country which forbids them to impugn it, to declare it false, to arraign it as an imposition upon the credulity of the people."

While the acceptance of this decision made it possible for every one to hold office, the efforts to abolish the religious test altogether did not cease. The question was again thoroughly debated at the Convention which came together in 1835 to amend the State Constitution. There were practically no Jews in the State even then, but some of the distinguished members of the Convention championed the cause of absolute religious liberty and worked for the abolition of the entire article which prescribed the test. Their efforts, however, were not successful, and the change which was adopted emancipated only the Catholics, by substituting the word "Christian" for "Protestant."

The small Jewish Congregation of Wilmington, N. C., which was organized in 1852 for burial purposes, began about four years later to circulate a petition for the removal of the existing disability. A bill to that effect was introduced in the Legislature in the same year (1858), but the committee to which it was referred reported that while it considered the objectionable clause "a relic of bigotry and intolerance unfit to be associated in our fundamental law with the enlightened principle of representative government . . . it is highly inexpedient to alter or amend the Constitution by legislative enactment in any particular whatsoever."

When the Constitution of North Carolina was again changed by the Convention of 1861, which voted for secession and joined the Confederacy, the article in question was changed in phraseology only. The word "Christian" was omitted, but the clause still debarred from holding office a "person who shall deny the being of God or the Divine Authority of both the Old and the New Testament." The convention of the period of reconstruction, which met in 1865, afforded no relief, but the Constitution which it framed was rejected by the people at the polls in the following year, though on other grounds. It was not until the Constitutional Convention of 1868 that Jewish emancipation was accomplished in North Carolina. The time was ripe for the abolition of all religious tests, and there appears to have been no debate on that point. Only "persons who shall deny the being of Almighty God" were, and still are, debarred from holding office in that State, as no change has been made in this regard since 1868.

CHAPTER XVI.

THE WAR OF 1812 AND THE REMOVAL OF JEWISH DISABILITIES IN MARYLAND.

The Jewish community almost at a standstill between the Revolution and the War of 1812—Stoppage of immigration and losses through emigration and assimilation—No Jews in the newly admitted States—The small number of Jews who fought in the second war with England included Judah Touro, the philanthropist—The Jewish disabilities in Maryland—A Jew appointed by Jefferson as United States Marshal for that State—The "Jew Bill" as an issue in Maryland politics—Removal of the disabilities in 1826.

The hopes of the Jews of western Europe were raised by the French Revolution, which gave the Jews of France full citizenship. The Napoleonic wars brought liberty and Jewish emancipation in the countries and principalities which were conquered by the great Corsican, and even where this was not achieved it became a probability for the near future. The disturbed state of Europe made foreign travel, and especially emigration over sea, hazardous, and there were hardly any new arrivals of Jews from the Old World during the quarter century following the establishment of the United States Government. There were, on the other hand, numerous departures of Jews for England and its American colonies, especially Jamaica, during and after the Revolution, and the losses through baptism and mixed marriages, which account for the disappearance of a large number of colonial Jewish families, retarded the natural growth of the communities. As a result it is doubtful whether there were as many Jews in the United States at the time of the outbreak of the second war with England, in 1812, as there were in the Revolutionary period. Neither had their wealth or importance increased in those times; it seems that there was even some deterioration in both, caused no doubt by the lack of new blood which is indispensable to small communities.

There were hardly any Jews in the three new States which were admitted to the Union in the eight years of Washington's administration. In Vermont, which came in in 1791, there was no Jewish Congregation until the last quarter of the nineteenth century. Kentucky (1792) and Tennessee (1796) had very few Jews until a later period, and the stray Jewish sounding names which are met with in various records in the first half century of their existence as States are not safe material for the foundation of a history of the Jews in these Commonwealths. Ohio, which was admitted in 1803, had very few Jews at that time, and the immense territory of Louisiana, which was purchased from Napoleon in the same year, had practically none, as Jews never thrived in the French possessions in the New World, except in colonies like Martinique,[1] where there was a Jewish community prior to it being occupied by the French (1635).

The number of Jews who took part in the War of 1812 was therefore smaller than that of the participants in the War of Independence, and the disproportionately large percentage of officers shows that they still belonged mostly to the wealthier classes. In the list which is enumerated in the valuable work of Mr. Simon Wolf, which was mentioned above, there are mentioned thirteen officers, of whom one, Nathan Moses of Pennsylvania, achieved the rank of Colonel, and two, Mayer Moses of South Carolina and Mordecai Myers of Pennsylvania, were captains. (General Joseph Bloomfield of New Jersey, who is included in the list, was not a Jew, see "Publications," XI, p. 190.) The balance comprises three lieutenants, one adjutant, one ensign, two sergeants, three corporals and twenty-seven

[1] See *Jewish Encyclopedia*, VIII, pp. 353-54, s. v., Martinique; and also Oppenheim in "Publications," XVIII, pp. 17-18.

privates. Among the latter were Jacob Hays and Benjamin Hays of New York, father and son; and Judah Touro, the philanthropist, who was dangerously wounded at the battle of New Orleans in January, 1815.

The War of 1812 gave the impetus to a renewal of the agitation for the removal of the disabilities of the Jews of Maryland, the only State which had a considerable Jewish community in such a disadvantageous position. The church establishment in Maryland terminated with the fall of the proprietary rule and the emergence into statehood. With it fell, too, the force of the legislation which for a century and a half had declared the profession of Jewish faith a capital offence, as was already mentioned in a previous chapter (page 77).[1] But part of the old spirit remained under the new conditions, and the new State Constitution of 1776, which granted free exercise of religion, provided for "a declaration of belief in the Christian religion" as a necessary qualification for holding public office. But this did not prevent a gradual influx of Jews during and after the Revolutionary War, which is to be attributed to the commercial and industrial advantages of Baltimore. The first formal effort to effect the removal of the disability was made in December, 1797, when Solomon Etting (b. in York, Pa., 1764; d. in Baltimore, 1847), Bernard Gratz (b. in York, Pa., 1764; d. in Baltimore, 1801) and others presented a petition to the General Assembly at Annapolis in which they averred "that they are a sect of people called Jews, and thereby deprived of many of the valuable rights of citizenship, and pray to be placed upon the same footing with other good citizens." The committee to whom this petition was referred reported the same day that they "have taken the same into consideration and conceive the prayer of the petition is reasonable, but as it involves a constitutional question of considerable importance they submit to the House the pro-

[1] See J. H. Hollander, *Civil Stotus of the Jews in Moryland,* in "Publications," II, pp. 33-44; the article *Maryland* in the "Jewish Encyclopedia" and Blum's *History of the Jews of Baltimore.*

priety of taking the same into consideration at this advanced stage of the session." This disposition of the petition put a quietus upon further agitation for the next five years. In the meantime (1801) Reuben Etting (b. in York, Pa., 1762; d. in Philadelphia, 1848), a brother of the above-mentioned Solomon, was appointed by President Jefferson United States Marshal for Maryland, which presented the anomalous condition of a man who could not be chosen constable under the State laws, holding a highly responsible Federal office. A second petition with the same object in view as the first was presented to the General Assembly in November, 1802, and this time it came to a vote, but it was refused, thirty-eight voting against it and only seventeen in its favor. The attempt was renewed in 1803 and in 1804, when it was again defeated by a vote of thirty-nine to twenty-four. This fourth defeat disheartened the few determined spirits upon whom the brunt of the struggle had thus far fallen, and the formal agitation ceased for a time.

The arrival in Baltimore from Richmond, Va., in the year 1808, of the Cohen family, consisting of the widow and six sons of Jacob J. Cohen, a soldier of the Revolution (a native of Rhenish Prussia, who came to America in 1773 and died in 1808), and other arrivals in that period, helped to increase the material importance and the communal influence of the Jews of Baltimore. After Solomon Etting and several members of the Cohen family served with distinction in the defense of Baltimore and in subsequent military engagements, the injustice of the Jewish disabilities became more manifest. The sympathy of a group of men active in public life was enlisted, and these conducted the legislative struggle for full emancipation of the Jews in the General Assembly from 1816 to 1826. The most prominent figure in this group, which included Thomas Brackenridge, E. S. Thomas, General Winder, Colonel W. G. D. Worthington and John V. L. MacMahon, was Thomas Kennedy of Washington county.

The "Jew Bill' became a clearly defined issue in Maryland

politics, and here we see again the American peculiarity mentioned above (page 118), that those who knew the Jew best were his most ardent defenders. Several representatives from country districts, where Jews were known by name only, failed of reelection because they had voted for the repeal of Jewish disabilities; while, on the other hand, a disposition favorable to Jewish emancipation became at an early date a sine qua non of election from Baltimore. The successful effort of Jacob Henry to retain his seat in the Legislature of North Carolina, which has been described in the previous chapter, was effectively used by the friends of the Jews in Maryland. Speaking on the Jew Bill in 1818, Mr. Brackenridge alluded to the incident as follows: "In the State of North Carolina there is a memorable instance on record of an attempt to expel Mr. Henry, a Jew, from the legislative body of which he had been elected a member. The speech delivered on that occasion I hold in my hand. It is published in a collection called "The American Orator," a book given to your children at school and containing those republican truths you wish to see earliest implanted in their minds. Mr. Henry prevailed, and it is a part of our education as Americans to love and cherish the sentiments uttered by him on that occasion." Six years later Col. Worthington, in the course of a speech on the same subject, also recalled Henry's triumph in glowing terms. Some of the addresses delivered on that subject were considered of sufficient importance to be republished separately after the question was settled; one collection of them entitled "Speeches on the Jew Bill in the House of Delegates in Maryland" was published in Philadelphia in 1829.

Finally, in 1822, a bill to the desired effect passed both houses of the General Assembly; but the Constitution of Maryland required that any act amendatory thereto must be passed at one session and published and confirmed at the succeeding session of the Legislature. Accordingly, recourse was necessary to the session of 1823-24, in which a confirmatory bill was introduced accompanied by a petition from the Jews of Maryland. The bill was confirmed by the Senate, but defeated in the House of Delegates after a stirring debate, and all formal legislation hitherto enacted was rendered nugatory. But the time was ripe for this act of justice, and on the last day of the following session of the Legislature (Feb. 26, 1825) an act "for the relief of the Jews of Maryland," which had already received the sanction of the Senate, was passed by the House of Delegates by a vote of twenty-six to twenty-five. The bill provided that "every citizen of this State professing the Jewish religion" who shall be appointed to any office of profit or trust shall, in addition to the required oaths, make and subscribe a declaration of his belief in a future state of rewards and punishments, instead of the declaration now required by the government of the State. In the following year a brief confirmatory act was passed and the battle for Jewish emancipation was won. Theoretically there still remained a discrimination, which was not eliminated until many years afterwards; but practically there was no formal disability. Solomon Etting and Jacob I. Cohen, both of whom had been throughout the moving spirits of the legislative struggle, were promptly elected in Baltimore (Oct., 1826) as members of the City Council, and the former ultimately became president of that body. A number of Jews later occupied and still occupy important political positions in Maryland commensurate with their individual ability and with the prominence of Jews in the business and professional life of the State.

CHAPTER XVII.

MORDECAI MANUEL NOAH AND HIS TERRITORIALIST-ZIONISTIC PLANS.

Noah's family; his youth and his early successes as journalist and as dramatist—His appointment as Consul in Tunis and his recall—His insistence that the United States is not a Christian nation—Editor and playwright, High Sheriff and Surveyor of the Port of New York—His invitation to the Jews of the world to settle in the City of Refuge which he was to found on Grand Island—Impressive ceremonies in Buffalo which were the beginning and the end of "Ararat"—His "Discourse on the Restoration of the Jews"—Short career on the bench—Jewish activities.

While the last vestiges of discrimination against the Jews were being removed in Maryland, a grandiose plan for solving the Jewish problem through colonization in America was conceived by one of the most prominent Jews of New York. This man was Mordecai Manuel Noah (b. in Philadelphia, July 19, 1785; d. in New York March 22, 1851). He was of Portuguese descent, a son of Manuel Mordecai Noah of South Carolina, who served in the Revolutionary army, and a cousin of Henry M. Phillips (b. in Philadelphia, 1811; d. there 1884), who was a member from the fourth district of Pennsylvania in the Thirty-fifth Congress (elected as a Democrat in 1856), and besides occupying various positions of honor and trust, also served as Grand Master of Free Masons of his native State. Noah was left an orphan at the age of four, and was brought up by his maternal grandfather, Jonas Phillips (b. in Germany, 1736; d. in Philadelphia, 1803). Noah was apprenticed to a carver and gilder, but his studious habits and abilities attracted the attention of some prominent men, and it is said that the financier, Robert Morris, procured the cancellation of his indentures and obtained for him an appointment as clerk in the office of the Auditor of the United States Treasury.

Upon the removal of the national capital to Washington, young Noah resigned his clerkship and accepted employment as a reporter at the sessions of the Pennsylvania Legislature at Harrisburg, where he acquired his first experience in journalism. Several years later he removed to Charleston, S. C., where he became in 1809 the editor of "The City Gazette" and became an ardent advocate of war with England. This was against the prevailing spirit of the wealthy seaport town, and it involved him in many quarrels and in several duels, in one of which he killed his opponent. It was also in this city that his first play, "Paul and Alexis," or "The Orphans of the Rhine," was performed for the first time. It was afterwards taken to England, where it was somewhat altered, and with its name changed to "The Wandering Boys" was brought out in 1820 at the Park Theatre in New York with great success.

After declining an appointment as Consul to Riga, Russia, in 1812, Noah was appointed by President Madison a year later as American Consul to Tunis, with a special mission to Algiers. He sailed from Charleston in a vessel bound for France, which was captured by the British fleet off the French coast. He was brought to England as a prisoner of war, but being regarded as a person of importance he was allowed to remain at liberty upon his parole, and to utilize the time in travelling through the country. After some months he was released and proceeded by the way of Spain to his post of duty. He was soon engaged in the work for which he was specially commissioned—to ransom the American prisoners then held in slavery by the Algerians. He was to endeavor to release the captured sailors in such wise as to lead the Algerians to believe that the relatives and friends of the captives, and not the American government, was interested in their ransom. Noah effected this in a creditable manner under the circumstances; but he was compelled to expend a sum exceeding the amount allowed him by his government. Noah's political opponents at home made use of this apparent irregularity to effect his recall. Mr. Monroe, then Secretary of State, wrote to him that it was not known at the time of his appointment that his religion would be any obstacle to the exercise of his consular functions, but that recent information, on which entire reliance could be placed, proved that it would have a very unfavorable effect; that the President therefore had deemed it expedient to revoke his commission, and that upon the receipt of this letter he should consider himself as no longer in the service of the United States.[1] Noah finally extricated himself from all his difficulties, and later was thoroughly vindicated, his actions approved and his advances remitted.

One of his official acts as Consul deserves special mention. The war between the United States and England was still raging, when one day an American privateer came into the harbor of Tunis with three English East Indiamen loaded with valuable cargoes as prizes. The prizes and cargoes were turned over to the American Consul to sell at auction. The British Minister protested against such sale on the ground of a clause in the treaty with England which provided that no Christian power should sell a British prize or its cargo in an Algerian port. Noah admitted the *bona fides* of the stipulation, but contended that under proper interpretation of international law the United States could not be held to be a Christian nation within the meaning of the treaty and hence was excepted from the inhibition. To prove his contention he exhibited the Constitution of the United States with its provisions against sectarianism and religious tests, and finally cited the Joel Barlow Treaty with Turkey of 1808, ratified by the United States Senate, which declared that the United States made no objections to Mussulmen because of their religion and that they are entitled to and should receive

[1] Daly, p. 112, et seq.; see also Wolf, *Mordecai Manuel Noah,* Philadelphia, 1897, and *Jewish Encyclopedia,* s. v., Noah.

all the privileges of citizens of the most favored nations. This argument was sustained by the Bey and the prizes were accordingly sold in Tunis. Noah's contention thus became established as a principle of international law which has never since been challenged. It was perhaps this stand taken by Noah in declaring the American nation to be non-Christian which convinced the government at home that his faith was "an obstacle to the exercise of his consular functions."

On his return to America Noah settled in New York (1816), where he resided for the rest of his life in the enjoyment of many honors and great popularity. He was successively the editor of the "National Advocate," "New York Enquirer," "Evening Star," "Commercial Advertiser," "Union" and "Times and Messenger." In 1819 he published in New York his "Travels in England, France, Spain and the Barbary States" in which he described his experiences abroad, the services he had rendered to his government in Tunis and the manner in which he was requited. His occupation as a journalist, which brought him into frequent connection with the theatre, led him to return to dramatic authorship, and he was reputed to be one of the most popular American playwrights of his day. Most of his plays were based on American history, but some of them dealt with other themes, like his successful melodrama "Yousef Carmatti, or The Siege of Tripoli."

He also took an active part in politics, and was appointed High Sheriff of New York in 1822; but when the office was made elective a short time afterwards he was defeated after an exciting campaign. He was a supporter of General Jackson, and was later appointed by him Surveyor of the Port of New York.

But during all these varied activities he never forgot, as he was indeed seldom permitted to forget, that he was a Jew. He had strong convictions on the subject of Jewish nationality and devoted considerable attention to the Jewish question in general. Finally, in 1825, he turned to his long cherished scheme of the restoration of the Jews to their past glory as a nation. For this purpose he acquired, with the aid of some of his friends, an island thirteen miles in length and about five miles broad, called Grand Island, in the Niagara River, opposite Tonawanda, not far from Buffalo, N. Y., and issued a proclamation to the Jews of the world, inviting them to come and settle in the place, which he named "Ararat, a City of Refuge for the Jews."

The plan had its practical side and attracted considerable attention. Noah was at that time perhaps the most distinguished Jewish resident in America, and could by no means be considered a visionary. The tract was chosen with particular reference to its promising commercial prospects, being close to the Great Lakes and opposite to the newly constructed Erie Canal; and Noah deemed it "pre-eminently calculated to become in time the greatest trading and commercial depot in the new and better world." After heralding this project for some time in his own newspapers and in the press, religious and secular, generally, Noah selected September 2, 1825, as the date for laying the foundation stone of the new city. Impressive ceremonies, ushered in by the firing of cannon, were held, and participated in by state and federal officials, Christian clergymen, and even American Indians, whom Noah identified as the "lost tribes" of Israel, and who were also to find refuge in this new "Ararat."

It was found on that day that there were not boats enough in Buffalo to carry to Grand Island all who wished to go there, and the celebration, in consequence, took place in Buffalo. A procession, headed by a band of music, was formed, composed of military companies and several Masonic bodies in full regalia, after which came Noah, as Governor and Judge of Israel, wearing a judicial robe of crimson silk trimmed with ermine, followed by fraternal officers and dignitaries. After marching through the principal streets of Buffalo, the procession entered the Episcopal Church, where exercises, including a long oration by Noah, were held; the close of the ceremonies being announced by a salvo of twenty-four guns.

The celebration in Buffalo was the beginning and the end of

the scheme. There was no response to the proclamation, the city was never built, and the monument of brick and wood which was erected upon the island on the site of the contemplated town fell to pieces, and in the course of time wholly disappeared. The only relic of the enterprise is the foundation stone of the proposed city, which is preserved in the rooms of the Buffalo Historical Society, with the inscription of 1825 still legible.

Noah's plan was to establish "Ararat" as a merely temporary city of refuge for the Jews, until in the fulness of time a Palestinian restoration could be effected. The failure of this project of a "temporary asylum" did not weaken his belief in the ultimate redemption of the Jews and their return to the Holy Land. Nearly twenty years after the unsuccessful attempt to concentrate the Jews on Grand Island, Noah delivered the greatest oration of his life, "A Discourse on the Restoration of the Jews," which was soon afterwards published in book form (New York, 1844), in which he urged the return to Palestine as the only solution of the Jewish question, which had become acute in Europe in the troublesome times preceding the upheavals of 1848.

Noah resigned the office of Surveyor of the Port of New York in 1833, after having held it about four years. After eight years of intense journalistic and political activity, he was, in 1841, appointed by Governor Seward an Associate Judge of the New York Court of Sessions. He had no sooner commenced to discharge his judicial duties than James Gordon Bennett, in the "New York Herald," began to assail and ridicule him. Noah himself made no complaint, but others took up the defence of the court's dignity and Bennett was indicted for libel. Noah himself was not anxious to have the case prosecuted, asserting that the attack on him was the result of an old editorial quarrel, in which he had been to a considerable degree the aggressor. Bennett came off with a small pecuniary fine. Noah shortly afterwards resigned from the bench, to avoid sitting upon the trial for forgery of a certain member of Congress whom he had known from boyhood.

He took an active part in Jewish communal affairs of New York City, and was in 1842 elected president of the Hebrew Benevolent Society. He was also president of the Jewish Charity Organization of New York, and remained at its head when it was merged into a B'nai Berith lodge. Among his works of Jewish interest deserves also to be mentioned a translation of the "Book of Jashar," which he published in 1840.

He married Rebeccah Jackson of New York, and their offspring numbered five sons and a daughter. He died in the 66th year of his age, and was the last Jew that was buried within the limits of old New York City.

PART IV.

THE SECOND OR GERMAN PERIOD OF IMMIGRATION.

CHAPTER XVIII.

THE FIRST COMMUNITIES IN THE MISSISSIPPI VALLEY.

Impetus given to immigration to America by the reaction after the fall of Napoleon—The second period of Jewish immigration—First legislation about immigration (1819)—The first Jew in Cincinnati—Its first congregation, Bene Israel—Appeals to outside communities for funds to build a synagogue—The first Talmud Torah—Rabbis Gutheim, Wise and Lilienthal—Cleveland—St. Louis—Louisville—Mobile—Montgomery and its alleged Jewish founder, Abraham Mordecai—Savannah and Augusta—New Orleans—Judah Touro.

The reaction in Western Europe after the fall of Napoleon in 1815 gave an impetus to emigration to America. This was especially true of Germany and more particularly of the German Jews. Those who had already tasted the sweets of freedom could not so easily endure the returning hardships of the galling exceptional laws and discriminations, as did their fathers and grandfathers who knew not the experience of better conditions. While the struggle for political and religious liberty was carried on with increased intensity in the various German states and principalities, many ventured to come out to the New World in quest of more favorable conditions and better opportunities. This new immigration, which continued for about half a century, until the Jews in all the German states were emancipated, much exceeded the immigration of the preceding two centuries, while it now appears almost insignificant in comparison with the large influx from the Slavic countries in the last thirty years. These Jewish immigrants of the second period, which is usually called the German period (though a considerable number came from Austria-Hungary, Russian-Poland and even Russia proper), were in one essential point more like the Slavic Jews who came after them than like the Sephardim of former times; they came poor, and grew up with the country. The Spanish and Portuguese Jews as a class were wealthy; some of them brought more capital with them than was found in the localities in which they settled. Their wealth and their business connections made them welcome or secured them sufferance at a time and at places—in the Old World as well as in the New—where a poor Jew, coming to earn his living as a peddler or craftsman, would probably never have been admitted. But better times had come; an immensely large country, which had now increased its territory by the Louisiana Purchase, and doubly secured its independence by the successful issue of the second war with its former masters, now needed men even more than money, and the immigrant who came to cast his lot with the new nation was welcome. A substantial part of the Jewish immigrants of this new era remained in the older communities, which were thereby largely increased. But many penetrated far into the South and the West; new settlements were founded in scores of places, and almost in each case a congregation was formed as soon as there were a sufficient number of Jews to warrant such an undertaking. As there was no longer any struggle between the Jews, as such, and the surrounding non-Jewish world, the history of the Jews of a locality is mainly the history of its communal institutions and of its individual members, who reflect credit on it by their distinction in various fields of activity. We shall now follow the formation of these new communities in various parts of the country, with an effort to understand the spirit which moved the early settlers in their Jewish activities, which helped them to rise to an eminent position in their new home and to be useful to their fellow citizens, as well as to their co-religionists who arrived at a later period.

* * * * *

There are no statistical figures for the number of immigrants who arrived in the second decade of the nineteenth century; but what may be considered as an official declaration (in the voluminous report of the Immigration Commission, issued in 1910) states that after the year 1816 "an unprecedented emigration from Europe to the United States occurred. It is estimated that no less than 20,000 persons arrived in 1817." The sudden demand for passage caused overcrowding, disease and death in the steerage of the sailing vessels, which resulted in the first "legislative interference" by a law which "became effective March 2, 1819, containing provisions intending to regulate the number of passengers on each vessel and proper victualing of each vessel." A provision of this law also marked the beginning of statistics relative to immigration into the United States. And as there was now a certain percentage of Jews among the arrivals of each year, it may be presumed that the Jews of that time were as much interested in these earliest provisions relating to immigration, as we are to-day in that perennial question.

Some of the pioneers of this new Jewish immigration came from England, but as in the earlier period of the Spanish Jews, the Germans and the Polish soon followed, or came simultaneously. A typical instance was that of Cincinnati, where the first Jewish congregation in the Ohio Valley was formed. The first Jew to settle there was Joseph Jonas (b. in Exeter, England, 1792; d. in Cincinnati, May 5, 1869), who came to America in 1816 and lived for a short time in New York and in Philadelphia. He left the latter city on the second day of January, 1817, and arrived in Cincinnati on the eighth of March. He was a watchmaker by trade, and had little difficulty in establishing himself. He was a curiosity at first, as many in that part of the country had never seen a Jew before. Numbers of people came from the country round about to see him, and he related in his old age of an old Quakeress who said to him: "Art thou a Jew? Thou art one of God's chosen people. Wilt thou let me examine thee?" She turned him round and round and at last exclaimed: "Well, thou art no different to other people."[1]

Jonas remained the only Jew in Cincinnati for about two years, when he was joined by Lewis Cohen of London, Barnet Levi of Liverpool and Joseph Levy of Exeter. These four, with David Israel Johnson of Brookville, Ind. (a frontier trading-station), conducted in the autumn of 1819 the first Jewish service in the western portion of the United States. Solomon Buckingham, Moses Nathan and Solomon Menken came there from Germany in 1820. The last named established the first wholesale dry goods house in Cincinnati. The six Moses brothers, one of whom, Phineas (d. 1895), lived to the age of ninety-seven, arrived in the following two years, and about this time Joseph Jonas was joined by his three brothers, Abraham, Samuel and George; their parents and a fourth brother, Edward, coming some time afterwards. Services were held only on Rosh ha-Shanah and Yom Kippur until 1824, when the number of Jewish inhabitants reached about twenty. (See "Publications," IX, p. 155, for fourteen Jewish names from the Cincinnati Directory of 1825.) In the first month of that year the Congregation "Bene Israel" was formally organized, and at a meeting held some time thereafter it was resolved to build a suitable house of worship.

There was not, however, sufficient wealth in the new community to enable the congregation to undertake the work unaided, and an appeal was sent to the older congregations in the United States and also to England, for help in the proposed un-

[1] See Philipson, *The Jewish Pioneers in the Ohio Valley,* in Publications, VIII, pp. 43 et, seq.; also Markens, pp. 100-104, and *Jewish Encyclopedia,* s. v. Cincinnati.

dertaking. A copy of this appeal has been preserved (in "Publications," X, pp. 98-99) and reads as follows:

TO THE ELDERS OF THE JEWISH CONGREGATION AT CHARLESTON.

GENTLEMEN: — Being deputed by our Congregation in this place, as their committee to address you in behalf of our holy Religion, separated as we are and scattered through the wilds of America as children of the same family and faith, we consider it as our duty to apply to you for assistance in the erection of a House to worship the God of our forefathers, agreeably to the Jewish faith; we have always performed all in our power to promote Judaism and for the last four or five years we have congregated where a few years before nothing was heard but the howling of wild beasts and the more hideous cry of savage man. We are well assured that many Jews are lost in this country from not being in the neighborhood of a congregation, they often marry with Christians, and their posterity lose the true worship of God forever; we have at this time a room fitted up for a synagogue, two manuscripts of the law and a burying ground, in which we have already interred four persons, who, but for us, would have lain among the Christians; one of our members also acts as Shochet. It will therefore be seen that nothing has been left undone, which could be performed by eighteen assessed and six unassessed members. Two of the deceased persons were poor strangers, one of whom was brought to be interred from Louisville, a distance of near 200 miles.

To you, Gentlemen, we are mostly strangers and have no further claim on you, than that of children of the same faith and family, requesting your pious and laudable assistance to promote the decrees of our holy Religion. Several of our members are, however, well known both in Philadelphia and New York—namely Mr. Samuel Joseph, formerly of Philadelphia; Messrs. Moses Jonas and Mr. Joseph Jonas, the two Mr. Jonas's have both married daughters of the late Rev. Gerson Mendes Seixas of New York. Therefore with confidence, we solicit your aid to this truly pious undertaking, we are unable to defray the whole expense, and have made application to you as well as the other principal congregations in America and England, and have no doubt of ultimate success.

It is also worthy of remark that there is not a congregation within

500 miles of this city, and we presume it is well known how easy of access we are to New Orleans, and we are well informed that had we a synagogue here, hundreds from that city who now know and see nothing of their religion, would frequently attend here during holidays.

We are, Gentlemen, your obedient servants,

S. Joseph Chan,
Joseph Jonas,
D. I. Johnson,
Phineas Moses.

I certify the above is agreeable to a Resolution of the Hebrew Congregation of Cincinnati.

July 3, 1825.

Joseph Jonas, Parnas.

Both the congregation in Charleston and that in Philadelphia sent contributions, and so did some individuals in New Orleans and in Barbadoes, W. I. It was some time, however, until the necessary amount was collected. The congregation was chartered by the General Assembly of Ohio in 1830, and the synagogue was dedicated in the year 1836. The first official reader was Joseph Samuels; he was succeeded by Henry Harris, who was followed in 1838 by Hart Judah. In the same year was organized the first benevolent association. The first religious school was founded in 1842, but it existed only a short time. A Talmud Torah was established in 1845, which gave way in the following year to the Hebrew Institute, of which James K. Gutheim (b. in Prussia, 1817; d. in New Orleans, 1886) was the founder. This also flourished but a short time, for with the departure of Rabbi Gutheim for New Orleans in 1848 the institute was closed.

A considerable number of German Jews arrived in the city during the fourth decade of the nineteenth century. They were not in sympathy with the existing congregation, in which the influence of the English Jews was predominant, and determined to form another congregation. The Bene Yeshurun congregation was accordingly organized by these Germans in September, 1841, and it was incorporated under the laws of the state in 1842. Its first reader was Simon Bamberger, and when Gutheim, who followed him, left it, he was succeeded by H. A. Henry and A. Rosenfeld. The assumption of the office of rabbi in the Bene Yeshurun congregation by Isaac M. Wise in April, 1854, and in the Bene Israel congregation by Max Lilienthal (b. in Munich, 1815; d. in Cincinnati, 1882) in June, 1855, gave the Jewish community of Cincinnati a commanding position and made it a Jewish center and the home of a number of movements which were national in scope. But their activity in general Jewish matters does not properly belong to the history of Jews in Cincinnati, and will be treated in a succeeding chapter. Three other congregations were formed before the close of the period of German-Polish immigration: the Adath Israel, organized in 1847; the Ahabat Achim, organized in 1848; and the Shearit Israel, in 1855.

The first Jew who is known to have settled in Cleveland, O., was a Bavarian, Simson Thorman, who came there in 1837. He was soon joined by Aaron Leventrite and by others of his countrymen, and the thriving city, which had then about 6,000 inhabitants, soon had twenty Jews, who organized the Israelitish Society in 1839. In 1842 there was a split, and the seceding part formed the Anshe Chesed Society; but four years later these two again united and formed the Anshe Chesed congregation, the oldest existing congregation in Cleveland. The first services were held in a hall on South Water street and Vineyard lane, with Thorman as president and Isaac Hoffman as minister or reader. A burial ground was purchased in 1840. New dissensions arose in 1848 in the rapidly increasing community and resulted in the withdrawal of a number of members, who in 1850 formed the Congregation Tifereth Israel, which from the beginning represented the reform element. Isidor Kalish (b. in Krotoschin, Prussia, 1816; d. in Newark, N. J., 1886) was its first rabbi until 1855, and he was followed by Wolf Fassbinder, Jacob Cohen, G. M. Cohen, Jacob Mayer, Aaron Hahn and the present incumbent, Moses J. Gries (b. in Newark, 1868), who assumed his position in 1892. The rabbis of the older congregation were: Fuld, 1850; E. Hertzman, 1860-61; G. M. Cohen, 1861-66; Nathan, 1866-67; Gustave M. Cohen, 1867-75; Moritz Tintner (b. in Austerlitz, Austria, 1828; d. in New York, May 11, 1910), 1875-76; and M. Machol (b. in Kolmar-in-Posen, 1845) since 1876.

The first Jewish congregation in St. Louis, Mo., was organized about the same time as that of Cleveland, though individual Jews were living there more than thirty years before. The Bloch, or Block, family of Schwihau, Bohemia, settled there about 1816, the pioneer being Wolf Bloch. Eliezer Block was an attorney-at-law there in 1821. Most of the early arrivals intermarried with Christians, and were lost to Judaism. It was not until the Jewish New Year in 1836 that the first religious services were held, when ten men rented a little room over a grocery store at the corner of Second and Spruce streets. The Achduth Israel or United Hebrew Congregation was organized in 1839, Abraham Weigel (d. 1888) being the first president and Samuel Davidson the first reader. Services were held for many years in a private house in Frenchtown. The first building used as a synagogue was located in Fifth street, between Green and Washington avenues. According to Markens (p. 108), Bernard Illowy (b. in Kolin, Bohemia, 1814; d. near Cincinnati, O., 1871), one of the leading conservative rabbis of America in his time, a pupil of the great Rabbi Moses Sofer (1763-1839), of Presburg, Hungary, was elected to the rabbinate of the St. Louis congregation in 1854. Its temple on Sixth street, between Locust and St. Charles streets, was dedicated in 1859. Rev. Henry J. Messing (b. 1848) held the position of rabbi for about thirty years. The B'nai El congregation, which was organized in 1852, moved into its own house of worship in 1855. Rabbi Moritz Spitz (b. in Csaba, Hungary, 1848), editor of the "Jewish Voice," has been at the head of this congregation since 1878. The third of the earlier congregations, Shaare Emet, was organized in 1866, with H. S. Sonnenschein (b. in Hungary, 1839; d. in Des Moines, Ia., 1908) as its first rabbi.

The first Jewish organization of Louisville, Ky., is mentioned in the year 1832, and two brothers named Heymann, or Hyman, from Berlin, were known to have settled there as early as 1814. Several Polish Jews from Charlestown, S. C., and some German Jews from Baltimore arrived there about 1836, and were soon joined by new arrivals direct from Germany. They bought a graveyard, built a mikweh and engaged a *shochet*. A few wealthy Jews came from Richmond, Va., but they did not associate with the others and were soon absorbed by the non-Jewish population. The first regular minister was J. Dinkelspiel (1841), and the congregation, which was named Adath Israel, was incorporated in 1842. B. H. Gotthelf was elected cantor and *shochet* in 1848 and later became Hebrew teacher of a school which was opened in 1854. In 1850 a synagogue was built on Fourth street, between Green and Walnut streets, which was consumed by fire in 1866. A regular preacher, L. Kleeberg, was then engaged and remained till 1878. Another congregation was chartered by the legislature in 1851, but it was not properly organized until 1856, when it changed its name from "The Polish House of Israel" to Bet Israel.

Farther to the south congregations were organized about that time in Mobile, Ala., and in two other towns of that state. The most prominent among the early settlers of Mobile was Israel I. Jones, who arrived there from Charleston, S. C., and organized the Congregation Shaare Shamayyim, the oldest in the state, in 1844. B. L. Tim, from Hamburg, in whose residence the first services were held; I. Goldsmith, S. Lyons, D. Markstein, Solomon Jones and A. Goldstucker, all from Germany, were among the first members. The first synagogue was dedicated in December, 1846, with Mr. Jones as President and Rev. de Silva as minister. The latter died in New Orleans in 1848 and was succeeded by Baruch M. Emanuel, who served for five years. Montgomery, which is said to have been founded by Abraham Mordecai, an intelligent Jew, who dwelt fifty years in the Creek Nation, and confidently believed that the Indians were originally of his people (see "Publications," XIII, pp. 71-81, 83-88), had its first Jewish society for relieving the sick, organized in 1846. Its first twelve members were from Germany and Poland. In 1849 this Chevra, which held religious services on Rosh ha-Shanah and Yom Kippur, was enlarged into a regular congregation called Kahal Montgomery or Temple Beth Or. Isaiah Weil was the first president and the number of members was about thirty. No rabbi was employed until about fifteen years later. There is also a record of a congregation which was organized in Claiborne, Ala., in 1855, and had an officiating rabbi. Most of the Jews, however, left the town and the congregation passed out of existence.

While the older Jewish community of Savannah, Ga., which dated from the eighteenth century, was strengthened by the new immigration, a new community, in Augusta, grew up in the first half of the nineteenth century. A Mr. Florence and his wife came there from Holland in 1825. Isaac Hendricks arrived with his family from Charleston, S. C., in 1826, and it is believed that Isaac and Jacob Moise, also Charlestonians, reached Augusta about the same time. Jews from Germany began to arrive in 1844. Isaac Levy, who came there about 1840, was for many years City Sheriff, and Samuel Levy was for two years Judge of the Superior Court and for ten years Judge of the Court of Ordinary (Markens, p. 113). There is reason to believe that the sixth Governor of Georgia, David Emanuel (d. 1808), who assumed the office March 3, 1801, and after whom the largest county in the state, Emanuel, was named, was a Jew, or at least of Jewish Descent.[1] The number of Jews in Augusta went on increasing until about 1846, when the congregation B'nai Israel, which is still in existence, was organized.

The prominent figure of the philanthropist Judah Touro (b. in Newport, R. I., 1775; d. in New Orleans, 1854) looms large in the early Jewish history of New Orleans. Touro was edu-

[1] See Leon Hühner, *The first Jew to hold the Office of Governor of one of the United States* in "Publications," XVII, pp. 187-95.

Judah Touro.

cated by his uncle, Moses Michael Hays (1739-1805), who had become an eminent merchant of Boston, and was later employed in his counting house. Touro came to New Orleans about a year before Louisiana was purchased by the United States from France in 1803. He opened a store and built up a thriving trade in New England products, and soon became one of the wealthiest and most prominent merchants of the growing city. He gave liberally to many charities and public spirited enterprises in New Orleans and elsewhere, at a time when large gifts for such purposes were not as common as they are now. When he donated $10,000 towards the erection of the Bunker Hill Monument in 1840, those interested in raising the necessary funds had almost given up their project in despair. Though the cornerstone was laid in 1826, on the fiftieth anniversary of the battle which it was to commemorate, Amos Lawrence's generous offers of aid met with no material response, even when aided by the eloquent appeals of Edward Everett (1794-1865) and Daniel Webster (1782-1852), until Touro privately offered to duplicate Lawrence's donation, provided the remaining necessary $30,000 would be raised. On the dedication of the monument in 1843, when Daniel Webster was the orator of the day, the generosity of the chief donors was praised in the lines read by the presiding officer, which became very popular at that time.[1] At his death he left, among many other bequests, a large sum in trust to Sir Moses Montefiore (1784-1885) for the poor Jews of Jerusalem. His name is connected with the oldest and largest Jewish institutions in New Orleans, while Boston, Newport and other communities have benefited by his generosity.

[1] The lines read as follows:

Amos and Judah—venerated names!
Patriarch and prophet, press their equal claims,
Like generous coursers running neck and neck,
Each aids the work by giving it a check.
Christian and Jew, they carry out a plan—
For though of different faith, each is in heart a man.

Alexander Isaacs and Asher Philips were also among the arrivals at New Orleans early in the last century. Morris Jacobs and Aaron Daniels were the Senior Wardens, and Abraham Plotz, Asher Philips and Abraham Green, the Junior Wardens of a benevolent society named Shaare Chesed. In that capacity they bought the first Jewish cemetery in New Orleans, which was located just beyond the suburb of Lafayette, in the Parish of Jefferson, fronting on Jackson street, where the first interment, that of Hyam Harris, took place on June 28, 1828. The first congregation adopted the name of the benevolent society, and worshipped in a room on the top floor of a building in St. Louis street. The oldest existing synagogue, the Shaare Chesed Nefuzot Judah, commonly known as the Touro synagogue, was organized in its present form in 1854. The other congregations belong to a later period, which will be described in a subsequent part.

Another prominent Jew, the greatest in American public life—Judah P. Benjamin—also lived in New Orleans in this period. But he took no interest in Jewish affairs, and his career belongs to the chapters in which the participation of Jews in the dispute about slavery and in the Civil War will be described.

CHAPTER XIX.

NEW SETTLEMENTS IN THE MIDDLE WEST AND ON THE PACIFIC COAST.

Increase in general immigration—Estimated increase in the number of Jews—The natural dispersion of small traders over the country—Chicago—First congregations and other communal institutions—Indiana—Iowa: Polish Jews settle in Keokuk and German Jews in Davenport—Minnesota—Wisconsin—Congregation "Bet El" of Detroit, Mich.—The first "minyan" of gold seekers in San Francisco—"Mining congregations"—Solomon Heydenfeldt—Portland, Ore.

The tide of immigration, which began to rise still higher than before in the second quarter of the nineteenth century, now consisted to a considerable part of Germans, and a goodly portion of them were Jews from Germany and the surrounding countries. The official figures for the number of immigrants who came to the United States in 1826 are 10,837; for 1832, 60,482; in 1842 it rose to 104,565. The rise was very unequal, with marked recessions sometimes to less than half in the intervening years; but when measured by decades the increase was constant, and after 1845 there were only two years—1861 and 1862—in which the number of immigrants fell below 100,000. While there are no figures obtainable as to the number of Jews which came in those years, it is certain that they soon outnumbered many times the few comparatively small communities which existed before that period. The estimates made by representative Jews at various times, giving the number of Jews in the country in 1818 as 3,000, in 1826 as 6,000, in 1840 as 15,000 and in 1848 as 50,000, are merely guesses, but they give a fair idea of the estimated ratio of increase in those thirty years. The experience of to-day is that whenever actual figures are obtained they prove to be in excess of the estimate made by communal leaders, and it is probable that the same results would be disclosed in the former times, too. On the other hand, care must be exercised to guard against exaggerated estimates, made for various reasons, but mainly for political effect.

As a large part of the Jewish immigrants then took to peddling or other forms of trade on a small scale, it was natural for them to disperse over all the states and territories, though, as we shall see farther on, many settled in the larger cities, in which the number of Jews soon rapidly multiplied. The problem of congestion never arose, or could arise, among business people, no matter how small their business might be at the beginning. It arose at a later period of immigration, which brought to our shores large numbers of laborers, both skilled and unskilled, with whom living near their centers of occupation was an economic necessity as well as a convenience. This is why no artificial aid or encouragement was at that time necessary to the scattering of Jewish immigrants over all habitable places, and why many of them became pioneers and early settlers in new communities. The same thing happens now, too, with that small part of the immigrants which still take to trading as their first vocation.

Thus we find in Chicago, the future metropolis of the great Middle West, a Jew by the name of J. Gottlieb, arrived within a year after its incorporation as a town, in 1837. Isaac Ziegler (1808-93), a peddler, came there in 1840; in the same year came also the brothers Benedict (d. 1854) and Nathan Shubert and P. Newburg, tailors. The last named became a tobacco dealer and later removed to Cincinnati. Benedict Shubert became a leading merchant tailor and built the first brick house in Chicago, on Lake street, where he carried on his business for a number of years. About twenty Jews from Germany, including Jacob Rosenberg (d. 1900) and the brothers Julius, Abraham (b. in Bavaria, 1819; d. in Chicago, 1871) and Moses Kohn, came to

Chicago between 1840 and 1844, and about as many in the following three years. A "Jewish Burial Ground Society," of which Isaac Wormser was president, was organized in 1845, and bought from the city one acre of ground on the north side (now within the confines of Lincoln Park) for a cemetery. It was abandoned in 1857, when it was already within the city limits.

The first religious services were held in a private room above a store on Wells street (now Fifth Avenue) on Yom Kippur of the same year, Philip Newburg and Mayer Klein officiating as readers. Only an exact *minyan* or ten men attended those services, which had to be discontinued whenever one left the room. The second services, with about the same number of attendants, were held on Yom Kippur, 1846, also in a private room, above the dry goods store of Rosenfeld & Rosenberg, 155 Lake street, Philip Newburg and Abraham Kohn officiating. A scroll of the Torah which the brothers Kohn had brought with them from Germany was used on both occasions.

The "Kehilat Anshe Maarab" was organized with about twenty members in 1847. L. M. Leopold (b. in Wurtemberg, 1821; d. in New York, 1889) was the first president, and Rev. Ignatz Kunreuther (1811-84) was elected rabbi, shochet and reader. He held the position six years, when he retired to private life, and later engaged in the real estate and loan business. The first synagogue, which was built on Clark street, between Adams and Quincy streets (where the new post office now stands), was dedicated Friday, June 13, 1851. Rev. Liebman Adler (b. in Saxe-Weimar, 1812; a. 1854; d. in Chicago, 1892), father of the prominent architect, Dankmar Adler (1844-1900), was the second rabbi of the congregation, and held the position for more than twenty years. The Hebrew Benevolent Society was organized in 1851 and is still in existence. The second congregation, under the name "B'nai Sholom," consisting mostly of natives of Prussian-Poland, was established in 1852. The "Jüdische Reformverein," which subsequently led to the organization of the Sinai Congregation, was organized in 1858, with

Leopold Mayer as president and Dr. Bernhard Felsenthal (b. in Germany, 1822; d. in Chicago, Jan. 12, 1908) as secretary. The Hebrew Relief Association, which later built the Michael Reese Hospital, the first Jewish hospital in Chicago, was instituted in 1859. Henry Greenbaum (b. in Germany, 1833) was its first president. Isaac Greensfelder became treasurer, and Edward S. Salomon, who afterwards served with distinction in the Civil War, was brevetted to the rank of Brigadier-General, and later served for four years as Governor of Washington Territory (1871-74), was its first secretary. Salomon was elected Clerk of Cook County in 1861.[1]

The oldest Jewish congregation in Illinois outside of Chicago is that of Peoria, surnamed Anshe Emet, which was organized in 1860.

In the neighboring State of Indiana, which was admitted to the Union in 1816, Jews began to settle about the same time as in Illinois, and there are four communities which date back to the period before the Civil War. The oldest Jewish congregation in the state is the Achdut we-Sholom of Fort Wayne, which was instituted in 1848. The Congregation Ahawat Achim of Lafayette is but one year younger, while the congregation of Evansville dates from about the same time. The first Jewish settlers in Indianapolis, the capital, which now had the largest community, were Moses Woolf, and Alexander and Daniel Franco, who came there from England in 1849. A family of Hungarian Jews named Knefler arrived soon afterwards. Adolph Rosenthal and Dr. J. M. Rosenthal came in 1854, and Herman Bamberger, who later became a leading merchant, arrived in 1855. The first congregation was organized in 1856, but more than a decade passed until it was housed in its own building.

Jewish immigrants also soon penetrated west of Illinois, into

[1] See H. Eliassof, *The Jews of Chicago,* in "Publications," XI, which also appeared separately.

that part of the Louisiana Purchase which was organized as the Iowa Territory in 1838. Its pioneer Jew was Alexander Levi (b. in France, 1809) who arrived to this country in 1833 and kept a store in Dubuque in 1836. He was the first foreigner to be naturalized in Iowa, and was a justice of the peace in 1846. A Mr. Samuel Jacobs was surveyor of Jefferson County in 1840, and Nathan Louis and Solomon Fine are mentioned as peddlers in Fort Madison in 1841. They settled in Keokuk and later in McGregor, both of which places had a number of Jews in those early days. It is stated (see Glazer, *The Jews of Iowa,* Des Moines, 1905) that about one hundred Jewish peddlers arrived in Iowa in the decade following its admission as a state (1846). Burlington and Keokuk were the centers for peddlers, who were mostly from Poland and Russia, while most of the German Jews preferred Davenport, which was largely settled by Germans. According to the above-mentioned authority, the first *minyan* was held in Keokuk in 1855, on Passover, and in that year the Jews of that place organized a society which later became the Congregation B'nai Israel. In Davenport a congregation having the same name was organized in 1861, which is still in existence. Among those who participated in public affairs was William Krouse (b. about 1823), who arrived in Iowa in 1843, and furthered the movement to remove the capital from Iowa City to Fort Des Moines, where he resided. He was the founder and one of the directors of the first public school in that city. His brother Robert was one of the earliest settlers of Davenport.

Farther to the north, there were only individual Jewish traders in Minnesota before the Civil War, and the three brothers Samuels, from England, who had an Indian trading post at Taylor Falls, on the Minnesota side of the St. Croix River, seem to have been the first Jewish settlers in that state. Morris Samuels, a captain in the Union army, was one of them. Isaac Marks, who resided in Mankato about that time, had a trading post near that place. About 1857 some Jews came to St. Paul and engaged in general business, which likewise consisted mostly in trading with the Indians. But there was no communal organization there or in any other part of the state until about fifteen years afterwards.

There is a record of one Jew who resided in Green Bay, Wisconsin, as early as 1792. His name was Jacob Franks (see "Publications," IX, p. 151, ff.). But we know little of other Jews there prior to the time of its admission to the Union in 1848. Shortly afterward the Congregation Bene Yeshurun was organized in Milwaukee by Löbl Rindskopf, Leopold Newbauer, Emanuel Silverman and others. Alexander Lasker and Marcus Heiman were its first cantors, in the order named. Isidor Kalish, M. Folk, Elias Epstein and Emanuel Gerechter later succeeded one another as rabbis.

Still farther to the north, Michigan, which became a state eleven years before Wisconsin, received its first Jewish settlers about the same time. About a dozen families of Bavarian Jews settled in Detroit in 1848. According to an account written by Dr. Leo M. Franklin (b. in Cambridge City, Ind., 1870; rabbi of Temple Bet El, Detroit, since 1899), it was due to Isaac Cozens, and more especially to his wife, Sophie, with whom he arrived in Detroit from New York about 1850, that the Bet El Society was established in that year. In April, 1851, steps were taken to incorporate the congregation by "the undersigned Israelites of the City of Detroit for the purpose of forming a society to provide themselves a place of public worship, teachers of their religion and a burial ground, and give such society the name of Congregation 'Bet El'." The signatures attached to the petition for incorporation are those of Jacob Silberman, Solomon Bendit (d. in St. Clair, Mich., 1902), Joseph Friedman, Max Cohen, Adam Hirsch, Alex. Hein, Jacob Long, Aaron Joel Friedlander, Louis Bresler and C. F. Bresler; an exact *minyan,* or the minimum number, required for the formation of a synagogue. Like most congregations of that period, Bet El was Orthodox in its ritual, but it was not long before the Reform spirit began to create divisions in the community. In 1861 a large number of the members withdrew because of the introduction of an organ and a mixed choir into the synagogue, and they formed the Congregation Shaare Zedek, of which Rev. A. M. Hershman is now the rabbi. The first rabbi of Congregation Bet El was Rev. Samuel Marcus, and he was followed by a number of well known rabbis, including Liebman Adler, Isidor Kalish, Kaufman Kohler, Henry Zirndorf and Louis Grossman.

A large number of Jews crossed the continent or came by boats from various parts of the world, along with the heavy tide of travel towards the Pacific Coast, when the discoveries of gold in California in 1849 began to attract great multitudes. There was a *minyan* in San Francisco on Yom Kippur of that year in a tent owned by Louis Franklin. Among those who participated were H. Joseph and Joel Noah, a brother of Mordecai M. Noah. The organization of the Jewish community was completed between July and October of the following year, when two congregations came into existence about the same time. The Shearit Israel congregation, which comprised the Polish and English elements, was organized in August, 1850, under the leadership of Israel Solomons. The Germans and Americans united in the Congregation Emanuel, the name of whose president, Emanuel M. Berg, is signed on a contract dated September 1, 1850, for the renting of a room on Bush street, below Montgomery, as a place of worship. About a dozen "mining congregations" sprang up in as many different places in California in the following ten years; Sonora had a Hebrew Benevolent Society as early as 1851; Stockton, a Congregation Re'im Ahubim in 1853. In Los Angeles the founding of a benevolent society was brought about by Carvalho, a Sephardic Jew, who was a member of General Fremont's expedition. Religious services were held there in 1852. In Nevada City a Hebrew Society was organized in 1855, which numbered twenty members about two years later. In Jackson a congregation was organized for the autumn holidays in 1856, and it erected the first synagogue in the mining districts. The building still stands, but it is used for other purposes, as the Jews have left the place long ago. Fiddletown, Grass Valley, Shasta, Folsom, Marysville and Jesu Maria all had temporary congregations which did not long survive the "gold fever." (See "Jewish Encyclopedia," s. v., California.) Sacramento is the only place in the state outside of San Francisco which has Jewish organizations—a congregation and two societies, which originated in this period.

A majority of the Jews from the mining communities who did not return to the East finally drifted into San Francisco, which from the beginning had the largest and most important Jewish community of the Pacific Coast. The foremost among the Jews who attained eminence in the new state, which was admitted into the Union in 1850, was Solomon Heydenfeldt (b. in Charleston, S. C., in 1816; d. in San Francisco, 1890). He removed to Alabama at the age of twenty-one, where he was admitted to the bar and practiced law for a number of years in Tallapoosa County. He was obliged to leave the state on account of his views on the slavery question, and came to San Francisco in 1850. He was elected Associate Justice of the Supreme Court of California two years later and held the office with distinction from 1852 to 1857. His brother Elkan and Isaac Cardozo were members of the Legislature of California in 1852, while another Jew, Henry A. Lyons, was also a member of the Supreme Court of the state about that time. A. C. Labatt, one of the pioneers, was an alderman of San Francisco in 1851, when Samuel Marx was United States appraiser of the port and Joseph Shannon was county treasurer. Many Jews who began their careers in San Francisco later became eminent merchants and financiers, like the four brothers Seligman, the three brothers Lazard, the Glaziers and the Wormsers, all of whom settled later in New York. Michael Reese, one of the extensive realty brokers; Moritz Friedlander, who later became one of the largest grain dealers in the country; and Adolph Sutro, the engineer, were also among those whose modest beginnings belong to that period. To the same class belong also Louis Sloss and

Lewis Gerstle, who later founded the Alaska Commercial Company.

What may be considered as an overflow of the Jewish immigration to California reached Oregon about a decade before it attained statehood in 1859. Most of the first Jewish settlers, who originally came from various parts of Southern Germany, arrived in Oregon from New York and other eastern states by way of Panama and California, and settled principally in Portland. Its first congregation, Bet Israel, was organized in 1858, the founders being Leopold Mayer, M. Mansfield, B. Simon, Abraham Frank, Jacob Mayer, H. F Bloch, Samuel Levy and others. Rev. H. Bories was the first Hazan and Rev. Dr. Julius Eckman the first rabbi and preacher. He was succeeded by Rev. Dr. Isaac Schwab, who later went to St. Joseph, Mo. A burial society, or cemetery association, was organized some time before and the first benevolent society about a year later. The Jewish community of Portland has practically remained the only one in the state to this day, and though not large numerically, it has been from the beginning one of the most influential and important of the Jewish communities of the country. A proportionately larger number of Portland Jews have been elevated to high positions in the service of the city, state and nation than those of any other community. But they mostly belong to a later period which will be treated in a subsequent part of this work.

CHAPTER XX

THE JEWS IN THE EARLY HISTORY OF TEXAS. THE MEXICAN WAR.

The first settler in 1821—Adolphus Sterne, who fought against Mexico and later served in the Texan Congress—David S. Kaufman—Surgeon-General Levy in the army of Sam Houston—A Jew as the first meat "packer" in America—Major Leon Dyer and his brother Isadore—Mayor Seeligsohn of Galveston (1853)—One Jew laid out Waco; Castro County is named after another—Belated communal and religious activities—The War with Mexico, in which only a small number of Jews served—David Camden de Leon and his brother Edwin, U. S. Consul-General in Egypt.

The history of the Jews of Texas begins at the time when the largest state of the American Union was still a part of Mexico. The first Jewish settler of whom any record is preserved was Samuel Isaacs, who came there from the United States in 1821 with Austin's first colony of three hundred. He received a Spanish grant of land as a colonist, and is later mentioned once more as the recipient of a bounty warrant for 320 acres of land, located in Polk county, for services in the army of Texas in 1836-37. When Abraham Cohen Labatt (b. in Charleston, S. C., in 1802; d. in Texas after 1894), who has been mentioned in the preceding chapter, visited Velasco, Texas, in 1831, he found there two Jews—Jacob Henry from England and Jacob Lyons from Charleston—who had been there for some years engaged in business. When the former of the two died without issue he left his fortune for the building of a hospital at that seaport

Adolphus Sterne (b. in Cologne, Germany, 1801; d. in New Orleans, 1852) was one of the first settlers in Nacogdoches, in the eastern portion of Texas, where he came from New Orleans in 1824. He knew several European languages and soon mastered various Indian dialects, which made him very useful to the insurgents against Mexican rule, whose cause he espoused. He was sentenced to death for his share in the Fredonian war against Mexico. He was saved by a general amnesty which had been declared by that time, and took an oath of allegiance to the Mexican government, which he kept faithfully until Texas became an independent republic in 1836. After having been Alcalde and official interpreter under the old order, he served in both the upper and the lower houses of the Texas Congress. Dr. Joseph Hertz came with his brother Hyman to Nacogdoches about 1832; Simon Schloss (b. in Frankfort-on-the-Main, 1812) came there in 1836. David S. Kaufman (b. in Cumberland County, Pa., in 1813; d. in Washington, D. C., 1851), a graduate of Princeton College, came there from Louisiana in 1837. In 1838 he was elected a Representative in the Texas Congress; was twice re-elected and was twice chosen Speaker of the House. In 1843 he was elected to the Senate, where, in 1844, as a member of the Committee on Foreign Relations, he presented a report in favor of annexation to the United States. When this plan was carried out he was elected one of the first members of the House of Representatives from Texas, serving from 1846 until his death five years afterwards. Albert Emanuel (b. 1808) came there from Germany in 1834, and was one of the first volunteers in the Texas army, serving in the battle of San Jacinto. He later settled in New Orleans, where he died in 1851. Samuel Mass (who married a sister of Offenbach, the composer) and Simon Weiss were two other natives of Germany who settled in Nacogdoches about that time. Four Jews are known to have fought at Goliad under Fannin (March 26, 1836), one of whom, Edward J. Johnson (b. in Cincinnati, O., 1816) was slain, together with his chief, after the surrender to the Mexicans.

Moses Albert Levy served as surgeon-general in Sam Houston's army throughout the Texas-Mexican war. Dr. Isaac Lyons, of Charleston, served as surgeon-general under General Tom Green in the war of 1836. Among other Jews who rendered notable service to the Republic of Texas were the brothers Leon and Isadore Dyer, natives of Germany, who, at an early age, came with their parents to Baltimore, where the older Dyer founded a meat-packing establishment, which is said to have been the first in America. Leon Dyer (b. 1807; d. in Louisville, Ky., 1883), who settled in New Orleans, was quartermaster-general of the state militia of Louisiana in 1836, when Texas called for aid in her struggle for independence. With several hundred other citizens of New Orleans, he responded, and, coming to Galveston, he received a commission as major in the Texas forces, signed by the first President, Burnett. The Louisiana contingent was assigned to the force of General Green, and saw much active service. Major Dyer also served on the guard which took General Santa Anna, the captive President of Mexico, from Galveston to Washington in the following year. His brother, Isadore Dyer (b. 1813; d. in Waukesha, Wis., 1888), settled in Galveston as a merchant in 1840, and was one of its public spirited citizens. He was one of the earliest grand masters of the Order of Odd Fellows in Texas. The first Jewish religious services in Galveston were held at his house in 1856.

Henry Seeligsohn (b. in Philadelphia, 1828; d. 1886) came to Texas in 1839, and was elected first lieutenant of the Galveston Cadets, an organization composed of young boys, which rendered efficient service. His father was Michael Seeligsohn (d. 1868), who was elected Mayor of Galveston in 1853. Levi Myers (sometimes also called Levi Charles or Charles Levi) Harby (b. in Georgetown, S. C., 1793; d. in Galveston, 1870), who was a midshipman in the United States Navy in 1812 and was taken prisoner by the British, also participated in the Texan war of independence. A. Wolf was killed in the battle of Alamo in 1836, and his name is inscribed on the Alamo monument at

Austin. Jacob de Cordova (b. in Spanish Town, Jamaica, 1808; d. in Texas, 1868) removed to Galveston from New Orleans in 1837 and was the founder of several newspapers, represented Harris county in the Texas Legislature in 1847, and laid out the city of Waco in 1849. Henry Castro (b. in France, 1786; d. in Monterey, Mexico, 1861), a descendant of a wealthy Marrano family, entered, in 1842, into a contract with President Sam Houston of Texas to settle a colony west of the Medina. Houston also appointed him consul-general in France for the Republic of Texas. Between 1843 and 1846 Castro sent to Texas about 5,000 emigrants from the Rhenish provinces, who settled in the towns of Castroville, Quihi, Vandenburgh and O'Harris. Castro county, in northwest Texas, was named in honor of this early promoter of immigration to Texas, who sank large sums in the venture.

There was little communal and religious activity in the stirring times of the early development of Texas, and the first communal organizations appeared a considerable time after Jews settled in some localities. The first Jewish cemetery in Texas was established in Houston in 1844, where the first synagogue in the state was built exactly ten years later. The Jews of Galveston acquired their first burial ground in 1852; religious services were held since Yom Kippur 1856, but no congregation was organized until twelve years later. In San Antonio almost twenty years passed between the acquisition of a cemetery (1854) and the organization of the first congregation. All the other Jewish communities in the rapidly growing state date their foundation from a later period.[1]

* * * * *

The war with Mexico, which began in 1846, was the least popular of all the wars in which the United States has engaged,

[1] See the papers contributed by Rev. Henry Cohen, of Galveston, Tex., to the "Publications," Vols. II, IV, V, on the Jews of Texas (the last being on Henry Castro) and his article "Texas" in the Jewish Encyclopedia, Vol. XII.

and this probably accounts for the small number of Jews who volunteered to participate in what was practically an attack on a weak neighbor. The number of Jews in the country was now more than ten times as large as in the time of the wars with England; but there are only about a dozen more names in the list of the Jewish soldiers of the Mexican war (in the above-mentioned work of Mr. Simon Wolf) than in the list of the year 1812. New York now had the largest Jewish community, and was represented by no less than fifteen in that small band of less than sixty, in which there was only one from Pennsylvania (Gabriel Dropsie, Co. E, 1st Regiment), one from New Jersey (Sergeant Alexander B. Weinberg) and five from Maryland. The others were mostly from the South, a large proportion of them having participated in the earlier struggle between Texas and Mexico.

The most prominent Jewish soldier of the Mexican war was David Camden de Leon (b. in South Carolina, 1813; d. in Santa Fé, N. M., 1872). He graduated as a physician from the University of Pennsylvania in 1836 and two years later entered the United States army as an assistant surgeon. He served with distinction in the Seminole war of 1835-42, which was the most bloody and stubborn of all wars against Indian tribes. For several years afterwards he was stationed on the Western frontier. He served throughout the Mexican war and was present at most of the battles. At Chapultepec he earned the sobriquet of "the Fighting Doctor," and on two occasions led a charge of cavalry after the commanding officer had been killed or wounded. He twice received the thanks of Congress for his distinguished services and for his gallantry in action. He was afterwards again assigned to frontier duty, and in 1856 became surgeon, with the rank of major. Like most Southern officers in the regular army, de Leon resigned his commission at the outbreak of the Civil war and joined the Confederacy, for whose government he organized the medical department, becoming its first surgeon-general. Edwin de Leon (b. in Columbus, S. C., 1818;

d. 1891), the journalist and author, who was appointed by President Pierce consul-general to Egypt, and was later a confidential agent of the Confederate States in Europe, was a brother of David C. de Leon.

Leon Dyer and Henry Seeligsohn, whose participation in the struggles of Texas was described at the beginning of this chapter, also served as officers in the war with Mexico. The names of Captain Michael Styfft, who served on the staff of General Zachary Taylor, and of Lieutenant-Colonel Israel Moses, who was promoted from the rank of assistant-surgeon, have also been preserved. Among those who were killed in action was Sergeant Abraham Adler of the New York Volunteers.

CHAPTER XXI.

THE RELIGIOUS REFORM MOVEMENT.

Political liberalism and religious radicalism of the German Jewish immigrant—The struggle with Orthodoxy hardly more than an animated controversy—No attempt made here by the Temple to swallow the Synagogue, as was the case in Germany—The first Reformers of Charleston, S. C.—Isaac Leeser, the conservative leader, the first to make a serious effort to adjust Judaism to American surroundings—Dr. Max Lilienthal—Isaac M. Wise, the energetic organizer of Reform Judaism—Dr. David Einhorn—Dr. Samuel Adler—Bernhard Felsenthal—Samuel Hirsch.

The Jewish immigrants, who were penetrating into various parts of the country in that period, formed only a portion of the new arrivals. The bulk of them, as in later times, remained in the East, principally in New York City, where not less than ten new congregations were established in the second quarter of the nineteenth century. While the proportion of those unaffiliated with a synagogue was probably smaller then than it is now, the tendency to establish very small synagogues was also less, so that the existence of a dozen congregations in New York about the year 1850 may denote a larger Jewish population at that time than an equal or even a larger number would imply at the present time. It would also not be safe to insist that there were not at that time in existence several congregations whose names were not preserved on account of their insignificance or for other reasons.

The German element, which predominated in this second period of Jewish immigration, was mostly under the influence of the liberalism, which was then prevalent in Germany. But the political liberal of central Europe at that time found in the United States all, and in some respects more than, he was striving for in the Old Country, including that national unity which was then only a pious dream in Germany. Aside from the question of slavery, which was not yet acute in the North at the beginning of that period, the German liberal found here all his ideals realized: perfect equality for all white men without distinction of creed or nationality; absolute freedom of speech and of the press; more individual liberty and better opportunities for work, for trade and for enterprise than could be thought of in the localities from which he came. It was natural for most of them to sympathize with the abolitionist movement, and later they were among the first to join the newly formed Republican party. But even the political radical or revolutionary of the other side of the ocean had little to object to in the democracy which he found here fully developed, and he soon became a patriotic, and to some extent a conservative, American citizen.

It was different in regard to the religious liberalism or radicalism which was then occupying the minds of the Jews of Germany. The conditions in that country made religious reform one of the burning questions of the day among them; some saw in its adoption a sure means of obtaining the much coveted political emancipation, while others thought it the only protection against the frightfully increasing number of conversions which were then occurring. Orthodox Judaism was certainly losing ground in Germany at that time, and it was difficult to foresee where it would stop or how much of it would remain. Wherever there was a struggle between the old order of things in religious matters and the new, the latter was certain to prevail. Within a few decades the real old style Orthodoxy almost totally disappeared from most parts of Germany. retaining a foothold only in the province of Posen and in isolated localities like Mayence and Frankfort-on-the-Main. Elsewhere even those who did not join the extreme reformers adopted a conservatism which was far from the old

Orthodoxy. The bulwark of Orthodoxy—the poor Jewish masses—was itself disappearing: the old style rabbis who survived were in despair, and when they died modern German preachers were chosen to fill their places. It seemed as if the temple was swallowing the synagogue, and the religious radical was victorious decades before the political radical obtained even a part of what he desired.

The conditions in this country were entirely different. Emancipation had been achieved, and there was practically no Jewish question as far as the outside world was concerned. There were no wholesale desertions from the camp of Judaism, but that slow drifting away of a part of the wealthier class, which is not an unusual phenomenon wherever and whenever there is no legal restriction or stubborn prejudice to prevent gradual assimilation. There was also a steady replenishment, or rather an augmentation, of the poorer Orthodox classes, among whom the Polish and Russian element was steadily increasing, a prejudice which is almost national keeping them apart from the Germans, who were rapidly advancing in wealth, social and political position, as well as in religious radicalism. The old American element which remained true to traditional Judaism, the considerable part of the Germans who would not accept reform, and the masses of later arrivals, gave to Orthodox Judaism in America a strength which it never possessed in Germany after the close of the eighteenth century. The steady increase in immigration from the Slavic countries easily filled up the places of those whose improved material and social condition caused them to drop out of the ranks of the Orthodox; just as those who rose to wealth and joined the reformers filled up the places left vacant by those who advanced beyond Reform Judaism into that complete assimilation into which it must lead those of its devotees who emphasize its progressive side and neglect the eternal and historical sides.

These conditions reduced the struggle between Orthodoxy and Reform to something hardly above an animated controversy in the denominational periodicals, and its historical value consists chiefly as an indicator of material progress. There was no class-struggle between the wealthy Jews and their poorer brethren who came after them in increasingly larger numbers, and there was no real conflict between the former's and the latter's religious views for the same reason. Accession to the ranks of wealth usually meant affiliation with a Reform congregation, where the poor man could not afford to join and would not be welcome if he came. While several of the young enthusiasts who came over permeated with the fighting spirit of the German reformers might have thought at the beginning of continuing the struggle in the Old-World fashion until the "enemy" was annihilated, it did not take them long to discover the futility of such efforts. The task of Reform Judaism in America was plainly not to conquer the Orthodox synagogue or to win recruits from the ranks of those who wished to remain faithful to traditional Judaism, but to enroll under its banner the affluent American or Americanized Jews who were on the point of drifting away altogether. The view of the extremely conservative, who considered these reformers as already lost to Judaism, has been shared by a large majority of the Jews of the United States for the last sixty or seventy years. But aside from condemning public declarations which were offensive to the Orthodox spirit and which were occasionally made by reformed bodies or by their conspicuous representatives, the Orthodox masses have, as usual, displayed more fortitude than aggressiveness in religious matters. This accounts for the presence of numerous leaders, agitators and organizers in the Reform camp, where newly assumed positions had to be defended to one's own satisfaction even if there was no formidable attack; while Orthodoxy easily held its own by force of increasing numbers, even if its tenacity was relaxed by the stress of circumstances.

The autonomy of congregation, which is a characteristic feature of new Jewish settlements, and which remained permanently in a country where there are no general laws about religion and no special relations with the government to force on the Jews official representatives, was also favorable to the spread of Reform. Still, the first attempt which was made in Charleston, S. C., in 1824, to imitate the Reform movement of Germany was a failure. The "Reformed Society of Israelites," which was established there in that year by twelve former members of the Congregation Bet Elohim, who left the latter religious body because a memorial for the reformation of the ritual was rejected by the vestry without discussion, had but a brief existence. But Charleston was losing its comparative importance and was attracting less Jewish immigration than the northern seaport communities. So there was a continual drifting away into indifference, and when a new synagogue was built to replace the one which was destroyed by the great conflagration of 1838, the petition of thirty-eight members that an organ be placed in the new structure, was granted. There was again a split in the congregation, which did not become united until it was greatly reduced by the ravages of the Civil War.

It was the rabbi of the Charleston congregation (Gustav Poznanski), a man imbued with the spirit of the Reform Temple of Hamburg, who decided, as an authority on Jewish matters, that an organ in the synagogue was permissible according to religious law. This is typical of numerous later cases in which an autonomous congregation, subject to no other religious authority and not connected with any other religious body, accepted the authority of its own rabbi to modify its ritual and its religious practices in accordance with his personal views or inclinations. Several other "Reform Vereine" in the East and the Middle West had a more lasting success, because they obtained able and energetic leaders from among the young German scholars who came over at that time, and who were, so to speak, in duty bound to continue the spread of Reform in their new home. But curiously enough, and perhaps emblematic of the ultimate course of American Judaism, the first real and successful attempt to adjust Judaism to its surroundings in the United States was not made by an adherent of the Reform movement, but by its strongest and

Rabbi Isaac Leeser.

ablest opponent which this country has developed. Long before the new leaders of that movement arrived and began to spread their ideas and ideals in the German language, there arose a vigorous and diligent pioneer who introduced the English sermon in the American synagogue, who established the first influential Jewish periodical, a man whose strong intellect and organizing abilities left their impress on the Jewish community of the entire country—Rabbi Isaac Leeser.

He was born in Neuenkirchen, Prussia, in 1806, and received his secular education in the gymnasium of Münster. But he was also instructed in Hebrew and was well versed in several tractates of the Talmud, when he left for the United States at the age of eighteen. He came to this country in May, 1824, and settled in Richmond, Va., being employed in the business of his uncle, Zalma Rehiné, for the following five years. He went to a school for a short time, but studied much in his leisure hours, increasing not only his secular knowledge but also his acquaintance with Jewish lore. He early evinced interest in religious affairs, and was soon assisting Rev. Isaac B. Seixas (1782-1839), of the Portuguese Congregation of Richmond, in teaching religious classes. In 1828 an article in the "London Quarterly" reflecting on the Jews was answered by Leeser in the columns of the "Richmond Whig" and attracted considerable attention on account of its excellence. This ultimately led to his being elected Minister of Congregation Mickweh Israel in Philadelphia in 1829.

He came to Philadelphia in that year and resided there for the remainder of his life. He preached his first English sermon in 1830 and in the same year appeared his translation of Johlson's "Instruction in the Mosaic Religion." In the following ten years appeared several volumes of his articles and discourses, a Hebrew Spelling Book, and a Catechism. In 1843 he established "The Occident and American Jewish Advocate," which he edited for twenty-five years, until his death, when it was continued for one year longer by Mr. (now Judge) Mayer Sulzberger, who had latterly assisted Rabbi Leeser in its direction. In 1845 appeared his translation of the Bible, which "became an authorized version for the Jews of America." Besides writing, editing and translating, he visited various parts of the United States, where he lectured on divers topics relating to Judaism, always advocating and spreading that enlightened conservatism for which he consistently stood all his life.

The Hebrew Education Society, the Board of Hebrew Ministers, and the Jewish Hospital of Philadelphia owe their foundation to his active efforts; and he also advocated a union of all the Jewish charities of that city, which was consummated some years after his decease. The Board of Delegates of American Israelites, the first American Jewish Publication Society and the Maimonides College (of which he was the first president) were also created mostly through his influence.

After serving twenty-one years at the Mickweh Israel synagogue, Rabbi Leeser retired in 1850 and held no clerical position until 1857, when the Bet El Emet Congregation was organized by a number of his friends. He became its rabbi, continuing until his death, on February 1, 1868. The opinion that he was "the most distinguished of Hebrew spiritual guides in this country"[1] is hardly exaggerated.

The first among the prominent leaders of the Reform movement to arrive in this country was Dr. Max Lilienthal (b. in Munich, Bavaria, 1815; d. in Cincinnati, O., 1882). He played an important part in the attempt of the Russian Government to spread secular knowledge among the Jews of that country by drastic means; but when he seemed to be at the height of his career he suddenly left Russia under circumstances which have never been thoroughly explained, and came to the United States in 1845. Settling in New York he first became the rabbi of the Congregation Anshe Chesed on Norfolk street, and later of Sha'ar ha-Shomayyim, on Attorney street. These were Ortho-

[1] Henry S. Morais, *The Jews of Philadelphia,* p. 45.

Dr. Isaac M. Wise.

dox congregations, and there was considerable friction between the religious members and the rabbi, who was inclined towards Reform. He gave up the rabinate in 1850 and established an educational institute, at the same time becoming one of the most active spirits in the "Verein der Lichtfreunde," a society formed in 1849 for the discussion and spreading of the teachings of Reform. In 1855 he was elected rabbi of the Congregation Bene Israel, of Cincinnati, O., and held the position until his death. He wrote many articles and several works of prose and poetry, both in German and in English, and was an active communal worker, a teacher, and even participated in the municipal affairs of Cincinnati, serving as a member of the Board of Education, as a director of the Relief Union and of the university board. But he was eclipsed and practically reduced to the position of assistant to the man who surpassed him as a leader and organizer, and who became the recognized head of the reformed Jews of the West.

This man was Isaac Mayer Wise (b. in Bohemia, 1819; d. in Cincinnati, 1900), who came to this country in the summer of 1846 and after a brief stay in New York became the rabbi of Congregation Bet El of Albany (organized 1838), the first, and then the only, congregation of that city. He had received an old-fashioned rabbinical education at home, but he soon developed here into a radical reformer and introduced in his synagogue many novel features and practices, often in the face of strong opposition. A split in the community followed, in 1850, and his followers organized a new congregation, the Anshe Emet, of which he remained rabbi for four years. In 1854 he was chosen rabbi of Congregation Bene Yeshurun in Cincinnati, and held the position for the remaining forty-six years of his life. He established there "The Israelite" (now "The American Israelite") soon after his arrival in Cincinnati, and through this organ he advocated, with much energy, his ideas of Reform and the plans of organization which he succeeded in carrying out, after many failures and setbacks, about twenty years later, when the time for unification and organization had arrived. He also established, in 1855, a German weekly, the "Deborah," by means of which he reached a part of the Jewish public which did not read English. He wrote much for his periodicals, and was also the author of numerous books on theological and historical subjects, and also several novels, and even two plays (in German). But his chief strength was his ability as an organizer. The Union of American Hebrew Congregations, the Hebrew Union College (opened 1875) and the Central Conference of American Rabbis (organized 1889) owe their existence to him.

David Einhorn (b. in Bavaria, 1809; d. in New York, 1879), who came to America in his mature years, had played a somewhat prominent part in the Reform movement in Germany, where he held several important rabbinical positions. His scholarly attainments were of a high order; but he was even more radical than Wise and Lilienthal, whom he strongly opposed soon after his arrival to this country in 1855. He became in that year the rabbi of Har Sinai Congregation in Baltimore, Md. (organized in 1843), and soon afterward he began to issue there a monthly magazine in German under the name of "Sinai," in which he advocated his views of Reform. In 1861 Einhorn was compelled to leave Baltimore on account of his anti-slavery views, which he courageously expressed despite the local sympathy with the South. He went to Philadelphia, where he became rabbi of Kenesset Israel, removing to New York in 1866, where he became the rabbi of Congregation Adath Yeshurun, a position which he held until a short time before his death. In later years he became reconciled to his former opponents in the Reform camp, and was the leading spirit in the rabbinical conference which was held in Philadelphia in 1869.

Dr. Samuel Adler (b. in Worms, Germany, 1809; d. in New York, 1891) was a preacher and assistant rabbi in his native city until 1842, when he became rabbi of Alzey, Rhine Hesse, and remained there about fifteen years. He also participated in the rabbinical conferences in Germany, in which the Reform movement was to some extent systematized; and he was considered one of its representatives there when he was called, in 1857, to become rabbi of Congregation Emanuel of New York. This was the first avowedly Reform congregation in the city, and has since become the wealthiest Jewish congregation in the country. It was organized in 1845. Its first place of worship was a private house on the corner of Clinton and Grand streets, and its first rabbi-preacher, L. Merzbacher (d. 1856) began his duties at a salary of $200 per annum. Dr. Adler was brought as his successor, and held the position until he was retired as rabbi emeritus in 1874, being succeeded by Dr. Gustav Gottheil (b. in Pinne, Prussian-Poland, 1827; d. in New York, 1903). Adler was in his time practically the only Reform rabbi in New York, and neither his disposition, which was that of a scholarly retired man, nor the local circumstances, which were influenced by the fact that the Poles and Russians had a large majority even in the supposedly German period, were favorable to the spread of Reform. He was the possessor of a large library of rabbinica, which was after his death presented by his family to the Hebrew Union College. Dr. Felix Adler (b. in Alzey, 1851), the founder of the Society for Ethical Culture, is his second son.

The last of the American pioneer Reform rabbis whose activities date back to the time before the outbreak of the Civil War was Bernhard Felsenthal (b. in Germany, 1822; d. in Chicago, 1908). While originally intended for a secular career, he was a thorough Talmudical scholar, and for a decade before he came to this country (in 1854) he was a teacher in a Jewish congregational school. After three years spent in Madison, Ind., as rabbi and teacher, he removed to Chicago, where he became an employee of a Jewish banking firm. In 1858 the Jüdische Reformverein of Chicago was formed, with Felsenthal as its secretary and guiding spirit. In the following year he published a pamphlet in favor of Reform which attracted much attention; and two years later, after the Reformverein developed into Sinai Congregation, he became its first rabbi. In 1864 he took charge of

Zion Congregation, the second Reform congregation of Chicago, and held the position until he was retired as rabbi emeritus, in 1887. While he was theoretically an extreme radical in religious matters, his extensive knowledge of rabbinical literature and his love for Jewish learning, added to his generous disposition and real affection for Jewish scholars of the old type, helped to make his relations with the Orthodox Jews more pleasant than in the case of other representative rabbis of his class. He was probably the only Reform rabbi in this country who was really beloved among the masses of the immigrants from the Slavic countries, and he thus exemplified a possibility of a better understanding between the different wings of American Judaism, which was then, and partly still is, by many considered difficult of accomplishment.

Samuel Hirsch (b. in Rhenish Prussia, 1815; d. in Chicago, 1889) belonged to this group, although he did not arrive in America until 1866, after having served as chief rabbi of Luxembourg for nearly a quarter of a century. He succeeded David Einhorn in Philadelphia, where he remained for twenty-two years. After retiring from the ministry he removed to Chicago, where he spent his last days with his son, Dr. Emil G. Hirsch (b. in Luxembourg, 1852), the eminent preacher and professor of rabbinical literature at the University of Chicago. Samuel Hirsch belonged to the extreme wing of radical reformers, and was one of the first to advocate the holding of special services in the Temple on Sunday. His chief work was written in Germany, "Die Religionsphilosophie der Juden" (Leipsic, 1842), of which only one part appeared. It is an effort to explain Judaism from the Hegelian point of view, but as it was written long before he arrived in this country, it has no interest for American Jewish history except, perhaps, as an instance of the influence of the German method of abstract theorizing on the uncompromising radical pioneers of the American Reform movement.

CHAPTER XXII.

CONSERVATIVE JUDAISM AND ITS STAND AGAINST REFORM.

"The poor Jews of Elm street and the rich Jews of Crosby street"—Rabbis Samuel M. Isaacs, Morris J. Raphall and Jacques J. Lyons—Sabato Morais—Kalish and Hübsch, the moderate reformers—Benjamin Szold—Dr. Marcus Jastrow's career in three countries—Alexander Kohut—Russian Orthodoxy asserts itself in New York, and the Bet ha-Midrash ha-Godol is founded in 1852—Rabbi Abraham Joseph Ash and his various activities—Charity work which remains subordinate to religious work in the synagogue.

In New York, too, it was not a radical appealing to a wealthy congregation, but a conservative in a neighborhood where the poorer Jews dwelt, who first introduced the English sermon in the synagogue. Reference is made by a correspondent from New York (see "Orient," 1840, p. 371) to "the poor Jews of Elm street and the rich Jews of Crosby street" in that period; and it was, characteristically enough, in the synagogue of the Bene Yeshurun, then situated at Elm street, that the innovation was made. Samuel Mayer Isaacs (b. in Leeuwarden, Holland, 1804; d. in New York, 1878), the son of a Dutch banker who removed to England, was called to the rabbinate of that congregation in 1839. When members who seceded from that synagogue formed the Congregation Sha'are Tefilah, in 1847, Rabbi Isaacs went with them and remained with his new charge until his death. He was an able exponent of conservative Judaism and was the founder of the "Jewish Messenger" (1857), which was continued after his demise by his son, Professor Abraham Samuel Isaacs

(b. in New York, 1852), until 1902, when it was merged with another Jewish periodical. Like Leeser, Rabbi Isaacs was a good organizer, and influenced the foundation of various Jewish institutions.

His successor as rabbi of the Elm street congregation was Rabbi Morris Jacob Raphall (b. in Stockholm, Sweden, 1798; d. in New York, 1868), who was, like Isaacs, also the son of a banker. Raphall was a linguist and a good rabbinical scholar, and while in England he delivered lectures on Hebrew poetry, and also began there the publication of the "Hebrew Review and Magazine of Rabbinical Literature," which was discontinued in 1836. For some time he acted as secretary to Solomon Herschell (1762-1842); he also made translations from Maimonides, Albo and Wessely; he participated in the translation of part of the Mishna, and began a translation of the Penteteuch, of which one volume appeared. After being for eight years minister of the Birmingham Synagogue, he sailed for New York in 1849, and remained with the Bene Yeshurun until shortly before his death. Raphall was the only prominent Northern rabbi who defended the institntion of slavery in the pulpit, as well as in one of his works, entitled "Bible View of Slavery."

Rev. Jacques Judah Lyons (b. in Surinam, 1814; d. in New York, 1877), who was a rabbi in his native city for several years, came to the United States in 1837, went to Richmond, Va., where he was minister of the Congregation Bene Shalom for two years, came to New York in 1839, and became rabbi of the Spanish and Portuguese Congregation, which had removed from Mill street to Crosby street in 1834. He held the position thirty-eight years," successfully combating every movement to change the form of worship in his congregation."

Leeser's successor in the pulpit of Mickweh Israel in Philadelphia was also a prominent conservative, Sabato Morais (b. in Leghorn, Italy, 1823; d. in Philadelphia, 1897). After having spent five years in London as the master of a Jewish Orphans' School, he arrived in Philadelphia in 1851, and "until his death

Photo by Gutekunst, Phila.

Rabbi Sabato Morais.

his influence was a continually growing power for conservative Judaism. . . Though his ministry covered the period of greatest activity in the adaptation of Judaism in America to changed conditions, he, as the advocate of Orthodox Judaism withstood every appeal in behalf of ritualistic innovations and departures from traditional practice," proving thereby how much the personality of the rabbi counts in this country in deciding the religious attitude of his congregation. When Maimonides College was established in Philadelphia, in 1867, Morais was made professor of the Bible and Biblical literature; and he held the chair during the six years that the college existed. He was the founder and the first president of the faculty of the Jewish Theological Seminary, which was established in New York in 1886, which position, as well as that of Professor of Bible, he held until his death. Henry Samuel Morais (b. in Philadelphia, 1860), the writer on Jewish historical subjects and the first editor of the Philadelphia "Jewish Exponent" (established 1887), is a son of Sabato Morais.

Isidor Kalisch (b. in Krotoschin, Prussian-Poland, 1816; d. in Newark, N. J., 1886) was another scholarly rabbi of that period, who came to the United States in 1849, after having studied at several European universities. While he was more inclined toward Reform, he is chiefly known for his literary works and translations, which cover a wide range of Jewish subjects in Hebrew, German and English. He officiated as rabbi in various communities, beginning with Cleveland, O., and ending in Newark, N. J., to which city he removed from Nashville, Tenn., after he retired from the ministry in 1875. Supreme Court Justice Samuel Kalisch (b. in Cleveland, O., 1851) of Newark is his son.

Rev. Adolph Hübsch (b. in Hungary, 1830; d. in New York, 1884) was also a moderate Reformer with a good Rabbinical education. He came to New York in 1866 and became rabbi and preacher of the Congregation Ahabat Chesed, which grew considerably under him. He was one of those who yielded to the temptation of the time to tamper with the Siddur, and his edition of it, which was adopted by several other congregations for a certain time, was an addition to the curiosities of American Jewish liturgical literature.

Henry S. Jacobs (b. in Kingston, Jamaica, 1827; d. in New York, 1893), who came to Richmond, Va., as rabbi of Congregation Bet Shalom in 1854 and later held similar positions in Charleston, S. C., New Orleans and New York (Shearit Israel, 1873-74; Bene Yeshurun, 1874-93), also belongs to the group of conservative rabbis of that period, who did much to uphold traditional Judaism as a living faith without treating it as a movement or considering themselves as agitators. His conciliatory attitude enabled him to act as president of the Board of Jewish Ministers of New York from its organization until his death.

Benjamin Szold (b. in Hungary, 1829; d. at Berkely Springs, W. Va., 1902), who came to Baltimore in 1859 as rabbi of Oheb Shalom congregation and remained with it as rabbi until 1892 and as rabbi-emeritus until his death, was an opponent of radicalism who influenced his congregation to adopt a more consevative course relating to prayers. The changes in the contents of the Siddur, or traditional Prayer Book, are a characteristic of the extremely individualistic period in the Reform movement, when almost every leader of prominence tried his hand at it, and when the aim seemed to be to make the services in each temple or Reform-synagogue as unlike that of the other as possible. Most of those special "siddurim" have neither literary nor historical value, and deserve to be mentioned only as the curiosities or vagaries of an epoch of transition in American Judaism. Szold used the prevailing method for the purpose of inducing his congregation to retrace its steps; and his "Abodat Israel," which closely followed traditional lines, soon displaced the more radical "Minhag America," not only in his own synagogue but in a number of others. It was re-published several times, once with an English translation. His commentary on Job (Baltimore, 1886), written in Hebrew, is one of the best works of that nature produced in the United States. Miss Henrietta Szold, the translator and writer on Jewish subjects, is his daughter.

Of the same age, and to some extent imbued with the same views as Szold, was Mordecai or Marcus Jastrow (b. in Ragosen, Prussian-Poland, 1829; d. in Germantown, Pa., 1903), who had a remarkable career as rabbi in two countries before he came to America. Jastrow had a thorough rabbinical education, and also a degree of Ph.D. from the University of Halle. In 1858 he became the preacher of the modern or "German" congregation at Warsaw, Russian-Poland, and threw himself into the study of the Polish language and of the condition of the Jews of Poland. His work "Die Lage der Juden in Polen", which appeard anonymously (Hamburg, 1859), proves him to have possessed much valuable information and clear views on the condition of the Jews of Poland; while a collection of Polish sermons which was published in Posen (1863) attest to his mastery of the language. He took the part of the Poles against their Russian oppressors, and participated in the demonstrations against the killing of five Poles in a suburb of Warsaw in February, 1861, which led to the beginning of the second Polish insurrection. Jastrow was imprisoned, together with the great Rabbi Berush Meisels, and after being held more than three months, was expelled from Russia. His widely circulated patriotic Polish sermons, his efforts to bring the Jews and Christians together in protest against the Muscovite tyranny, and his imprisonment, made him one of the most popular men in the old Polish capital at that time. He occupied the position of rabbi at Mannheim, Germany, for a short time in 1862, but his sympathy with Poland was too strong to permit him to remain there when, on the supposed pacification of that unhappy country, the order for his expulsion was revoked in November of that year. He soon returned to Warsaw, but a few months later the actual insurrection broke out, and, his passport being cancelled while he was visiting Germany, he could not return to Russia.

He then (1864) accepted a position as rabbi at Worms, Hesse, where he remained until 1866, when he was chosen rabbi of the Congregation Rodeph Shalom in Philadelphia.

In the first years of his American rabbinate, Jastrow ably seconded the efforts of Leeser to preserve conservative Judaism in the East against the advance of radical Reform, and continued to oppose that tendency after Leeser's death. Jastrow was one of the professors of Maimonides College, and later collaborated with Szold in the revision of the "Siddur Abodat Israel" and in its translation into English. Besides his activity in local Jewish affairs and in other Jewish matters of a more general nature, he contributed to many European and American Jewish periodicals and was for several years the chief editor of a new translation of the Bible into English, which was undertaken under the auspices of the Jewish Publication Society of America. He also found time to compile his great work, "A Dictionary of the Targumim, the Talmud Babli and Yerushalmi, and the Midrashic Literature" (London and New York, 1886-1903), and in his last years was editor of the department of the Talmud in the "Jewish Encyclopedia." Two of his sons are renowned American scholars. The older, Prof. Morris Jastrow (b. in Warsaw, 1861), has occupied the chair of Semitic languages at the University of Pennsylvania since 1892, and is one of the foremost Orientalists in the country. The younger, Joseph Jastrow (b. in Warsaw, 1863), has been prof. of Psychology at the University of Wisconsin since 1888, and a recognized authority on his special subject. He was in charge of the psychological section of the World's Columbian Exposition in Chicago in 1893, and served as president of the American Psychological Association for the year 1900.

The last of the important rabbis to come here from a Western European country was Alexander Kohut (b. in Hungary, 1842; d. in New York, 1894), the lexicographer and Orientalist, whose "Aruch Completum" (Vienna, 1878-92), to which he devoted twenty-five years of his life, is still the standard work on the

Photo by Gutekunst, Phila.

Dr. Marcus Jastrow.

subject. The first four volumes were printed during his residence in Hungary, where he was rabbi first at Stuhlweissenburg, then at Fünfkirchen, and lastly at Grosswardein (1880-84). The last four appeared during his sojourn in America, whither he came in 1885, when he was chosen rabbi of Congregation Ahabat Chesed in New York. He was at once recognized as an eminent conservative leader, and was associated with Morais in founding the Jewish Theological Seminary, in which he became professor of Talmudic methodology. In March, 1894, while delivering a eulogy on Kossuth, he was stricken in the pulpit, and died after lingering several weeks. A volume containing memorial addresses and tributes to his memory was published by his congregation in 1894. Another volume, containing essays by forty-four noted scholars in Europe and America, entitled "Semitic Studies in Memory of Rev. Dr. Alexander Kohut," was published in Berlin in 1897 by his son, George Alexander Kohut (born in Stuhlweissenburg, 1874), the bibliographer and writer on Jewish subjects.

Extreme Russian Orthodoxy asserted itself in New York about the middle of the nineteenth century. There were numerous Jews from Russia in the country long before that, and the immigration from Russian-Poland increased heavily after 1845, when Jews in the Kingdom of Poland were first conscripted in the army, in violation of a promise made by the Government that this was to be postponed until they were granted equal rights with non-Jewish subjects. The first Russian congregation in America was founded June 4, 1852, with twelve members, which soon increased to about twenty-three, several of whom, however, were natives of Germany who were dissatisfied with the Reform tendencies of the congregations to which most of their countrymen belonged.[1] The first place of worship was in a garret of the

[1] The list of these members as given by J. D. Eisenstein in his *History of the first Russian-American Jewish Congregation* in Publications IX, pp. 63-74, is as follows: Benjamin Lichtenstein, Judah Middleman, Abraham Benjamin (of Hamburg), Abraham Joseph Ash, Joshua

house, No. 83 Bayard street, for which a monthly rental of eight dollars was paid. B. Lichtenstein was the first Parnass or president, I. Cohen the secretary, H. S. Isaacs the reader and Abraham Joseph Ash (Eisenstadt? b. in Semyatich, Russia, 1813; d. in New York, 1888), who came to America in that year and was a Talmudical scholar, acted as rabbi without compensation.

The place on Bayard street was soon too small for the rapidly increasing congregation, and it removed in November of the same year to larger quarters on the first floor of a house on the corner of Canal and Elm streets, for which a monthly rental of twenty-five dollars was paid, although there was a carpenter-shop on the floor above. In another six months the continual increase necessitated another removal, this time to the top floor of a former court house at the corner of Pearl and Centre streets. There was a German congregation, "Bet Abraham," on the first floor of the same building; but it soon moved out and, changing its name to "Sha'are Zedek," located in Henry street and was known as the Henry Street Synagogue, until it moved uptown several years ago.

During the three years which the first Russian congregation, which called itself simply the Bet ha-Midrash, remained on Pearl street, Mr. Ash became the regularly appointed rabbi at a salary of two dollars a week, and Joshua Falk ha-Kohen, author of "Abne Joshua" (a commentary on Pirke Abot, New York, 1860), delivered occasional sermons without compensation. About this time a quarrel between Rabbi Ash and Judah Middleman, who was also a Talmudical scholar, about the recognition of a shochet, in which the rabbi would not submit to the decision of European rabbinical authorities, led to the first split in the

Rothstein, Israel Cohen, Abba Baum, David Lasky, Leib Cohen, Baruch Solomon Rothschild, Elijah Greenstein, Feibel Philips (the scribe), Abraham Reiner, Tobias Schwartz, Abraham Levy (of Raczki), Hyman Harris, Leibel Raczker, Samuel Hillel Isaacs, Jerahmel Chuck (of Berlin), Isidor Raphall and Jacob Levy. The first twelve were the original members.

congregation. Middleman and his followers withdrew and formed a separate *minyan* on Bayard street, which later became the congregation Bene Israel (Kalwarier, organized 1862), which now has its synagogue on Pike street.

A Portuguese Jew by the name of John Hart, who visited the Pearl street synagogue to say kaddish on his Jahrzeit, or anniversary of his parents' death, influenced his friend, Samson Simpson, the founder of Mount Sinai Hospital (b. in Danbury, Conn., 1780; d. in New York, 1857), to donate three thousand dollars, which formed the largest part of the fund with which the Welsh Chapel, No. 78 Allen street, was purchased and turned into a synagogue. It was dedicated June 8, 1856. New quarrels between the rabbi's adherents and the officers of the congregation led to a lawsuit, and later to another split; this time Rabbi Ash and twenty-three of his followers left the synagogue, and they formed a new congregation which they named "Bet ha-Midrash ha-Godol," which was dedicated August 13, 1859, the first location being the top floor of the house on Forsyth street, on the southwest corner of Grand street. Henry Chuck was the first president of the new congregation; Mayer Salwen, secretary; Israel Cohen, reader, and Nathan Mayer, beadle and collector.

About the time of the beginning of the Civil War, Rabbi Ash left the rabbinate and engaged in business, in which he was successful for a time. During these years he became one of the largest contributing members and acted for a time as the highest officer of the congregation. But reverses came and he again became a rabbi, which, with a short interruption in 1876, when he became a dealer in "Kosher" wine, he remained until his death. The congregation removed from Forsyth street to the corner of Clinton and Grand streets in 1865, and from there moved into its own new building at 69 Ludlow street, which was dedicated September 27, 1872. This building was sold in 1885 when the congregation purchased the Methodist church at Nos. 52-60 Norfolk street, which has been known as the Bet ha-Midrash ha-Godol for the last quarter of a century.

This synagogue, which was increasing in wealth and membership, made progress in true Orthodox fashion. A system of baking strictly kosher matzoth for Passover was introduced in 1870. An extra shochet, Asher Lemil Harris, was engaged for the special meat market which supplied the members. A "Hebra Mishnayot" for the daily study of the Mishna was organized in the same year and a "Hebrah Shas," for the study of the Talmud every evening after the services, was organized in 1874 by Rabbi Ash and Judah David Eisenstein (b. in Mesericz, government of Siedlce, Russian-Poland, 1855; a. 1872), who is now the editor and publisher and practically the author of the Hebrew Encyclopedia "Ozar Israel."

The congregation also did a considerable amount of direct and unorganized charity work, the money often being contributed by members or visitors who were called to the reading of the Torah on Saturdays or other formal occasions. Poor transients and immigrants were assisted, some were taken into the houses of the more wealthy members for Sabbaths and festivals. Many of them were assisted to become peddlers, and were even instructed in the rudiments of the occupation. The poor of the Holy Land were also remembered by special donations once a year. But charity work never overshadowed the religious work. The affairs of the synagogue remained paramount, which is one of the principal reasons why congregations of this kind retain their truly Orthodox character. The increase of wealth brought the employment of the first professional cantor, Judah Oberman (1877), who was succeeded by Simha Samuelson in 1880. Other large congregations were now growing up on the East Side, where the Jewish population was increasing very fast; but the further development of its religious and communal life belongs to a later period.

CHAPTER XXIII.

INTERVENTION IN DAMASCUS. THE STRUGGLE AGAINST SWISS DISCRIMINATION.

The Damascus Affair; the first occasion on which the Jews of the United States requested the government to intercede in behalf of persecuted Jews in another country—John Forsyth's instructions to American representatives in Turkey, in which those requests were anticipated —A discrimination in a treaty with Switzerland to which President Fillmore objected, and which Clay and Webster disapproved—The case of a Jewish-American citizen in Neufchatel—Newspaper agitation, meetings and memorials against the Swiss treaty—President Buchanan's emphatic declaration, and Minister Fay's "Israelite Note" about the Jews of Alsace—Question is settled by the emancipation of the Swiss Jews.

The Jewish community of the United States as a whole had no difficulties with the outside world and no serious internal problems in the period of expansion which is treated in this part. The results of the treaty between our Government and that of Russia, which was concluded in 1832, in which the rights of American Jews to enter Russia on the same conditions as other American citizens were not safeguarded as explicitly as ought to have been done in dealing with a power so unfriendly to the Jews, had not become apparent until nearly a half century afterwards, and must be ascribed more to oversight and ignorance of Russia's treatment of Jews than to wilful neglect. Several unfavorable local decisions against Jews as such, mostly in cases of violation of Sunday laws, or of exemption claimed by Jews from attending court on Saturday,[1] were of an immediately more pain-

[1] See A. M. Friedenberg, *Calendar of American-Jewish Cases,* Publications, XII, pp. 87 *et seq.*

ful nature; but this question also did not become acute until a much later period, when there grew up communities containing large poor Orthodox masses, for whom the observance of two day's rest was a great economic hardship. An occasional objection to a public functionary's forgetfulness about there being other citizens than Christians, which was sometimes noticed in Thanksgiving Day Proclamations (see Dr. Lilienthal's correspondence about a case of that nature with Governor Salmon P. Chase of Ohio, in "Publications," XIII, pp. 30-36) would soon itself be forgotten by Jew and gentile alike. The Jews were occasioning and experiencing very little difficulties, contributing to the work of developing the country, and thus unconsciously assisting in preparing themselves and the general population for the larger influx of immigrants which were to come later.

The Jews of America were therefore prepared to participate with the Jews of Western Europe in arousing public sympathy and causing diplomatic intervention in the case of the thirteen unfortunate Jews of Damascus who were imprisoned and tortured under the Blood Accusation of 1840. While the distance and the absence of the present means of quick communication delayed the action taken by the Jews of America until after the necessary assistance was rendered by European governments at the instance of the most influential Jews of England and France, the steps taken by the Jews here and the noble response of the Government under President Martin Van Buren (1782-1862) is of real historical value, and has been so regarded by Jost.[1] It was for the first time that the Jews of the United States interested themselves and enlisted the interest of the government in the cause of suffering Jews in another part of the world, and thus participated in that consolidation of the Jewish public spirit which resulted from this memorable occurrence, and which jus-

[1] Jost, *Neuere Geschichte der Israeliten*, ii. pp. 360-68. See also Jacob Ezekiel, *Persecution of the Jews in 1840,* "Publications," VIII, pp. 141-45, and Joseph Jacobs, *The Damascus Affair of 1840 and the Jews of America,* ibid x, pp. 119-28.

tifies the statement made by Mr. Jacobs that "in a measure, modern Jewish history may be said to date from the Damascus affair of 1840." There were now emancipated Jews in some countries who not only dared to come out in open protest against anti-Jewish outrages in other countries, but could also interest civilized governments to take official notice of such outrages—something unknown in former times. The American government, on its part, did not even wait for the request of the Jews to intercede in behalf of the victims of barbarous cruelty; but of its own accord it sent instructions to its representatives in Turkey and in Egypt to do all in their power for the unfortunate Jews.

The first meeting of Jews "for the purpose of uniting in an expression of sympathy for their brethren at Damascus, and of taking such steps as may be necessary to procure for them equal and impartial justice" was held in New York on August 19, 1840; and a letter containing the Resolution which was adopted there was sent to President Van Buren under the date of August 24, to which the following reply was received:

Washington, August 26, 1840.

Messrs. J. B. Kursheedt, Chairman, and Theodore J. Seixas, Secretary.

Gentlemen:—The President has referred to this Department your letter of the 24th inst., communicating a resolution unanimously adopted at a meeting of the Israelites in the City of New York, held for the purpose of uniting in an expression of sentiment on the subject of the persecution of their brethren in Damascus. By his direction I have the honor to inform you, that the heart-rending scenes which took place at Damascus, had previously been brought to the notice of the President by a communication from our Consul at that place, in consequence thereof, a letter of instruction was immediately written to our Consul at Alexandria, a copy of which is herewith transmitted for your satisfaction.

About the same time our Charge d'Affairs at Constantinople was instructed to interpose his good offices in behalf of the oppressed and persecuted race of the Jews in the Ottoman Dominions, among whose kindred are found some of the most worthy and patriotic of our own citizens, and the whole subject which appeals so strongly to the universal sentiment of justice and humanity was earnestly recommended to his zeal and discretion. I have the honor to be, gentlemen,

Very respectfully,

Your obedient servant,

JOHN FORSYTH.

The letter by Mr. John Forsyth (1780-1841) to the Consul, which is mentioned in the above communication, was as follows:

Washington, August, 14, 1840.

JOHN GLIDDON, ESQ., United States Consul at Alexandria, Egypt.

Sir:—In common with all civilized nations, the people of the United States have learned with horror the atrocious crimes imputed to the Jews of Damascus, and the cruelties of which they have been the victims. The President fully participates in the public feeling, and he cannot refrain from expressing equal surprise and pain, that in this advanced age, such unnatural practices could be ascribed to any portion of the religious world, and such barbarous measures be resorted to, in order to compel the confession of imputed guilt; the offences with which these unfortunate people are charged, resemble too much those which, in less enlightened times, were made the pretexts of fanatical persecution or mercenary extortion, to permit a doubt that they are equally unfounded.

The President has witnessed, with the most lively satisfaction, the effort of several of the Christian Governments of Europe, to suppress or mitigate these horrors, and he has learned with no common gratification their partial success. He is moreover anxious that the active sympathy and generous interposition of the Government of the United States should not be withheld from so benevolent an object, and he has accordingly directed me to instruct you to employ, should the occasion arise, all those good offices and efforts which are compatible with discretion and your official character, to the end that justice and humanity may be extended to these persecuted people, whose cry of distress has reached our shores. I am, sir,

Your obedient servant,

JOHN FORSYTH.

The following letter was addressed to David Porter (1780-1843; the father of Admiral David D. Porter), who was then United States Minister to Turkey:

DEPARTMENT OF STATE.

Washington, August 17, 1840.

DAVID PORTER, ESQ.

Sir:—In common with the people of the United States, the President has learned with profound feelings of surprise and pain the atrocious cruelties which have been practiced upon the Jews of Damascus and Rhodes, in consequence of charges extravagant and strikingly similar to those, which, in less enlightened ages, were made pretexts for the persecution and spoliation of these unfortunate people. As the scene of these barbarities are in the Mahomedan dominions, and, as such inhuman practices are not of an infrequent occurrence in the East, the President has directed me to instruct you to do everything in your power with the government of his Imperial Highness, the Sultan, to whom you are accredited, consistent with discretion and your diplomatic character, to prevent or mitigate these horrors,—the bare recital of which has caused a shudder throughout the civilized world; and in an especial manner, to direct your philanthropic efforts against the employment of torture in order to compel the confession of imputed guilt. The President is of the opinion that from no one can such generous endeavors proceed with so much propriety and effect, as from the representative of a friendly power, whose institutions, political and civil, place upon the same footing, the worshippers of God, of every faith and form, acknowledging no distinction between the Mahomedan, the Jew, and the Christian. Should you, in carrying out these instructions, find it necessary or proper to address yourself to any of the Turkish authorities, you will refer to *this distinctive characteristic* of our government, as investing with a peculiar propriety and right, the interposition of your good offices in behalf of an oppressed and persecuted race, among whose kindred are found some of the most worthy and patriotic of our citizens. In communicating to you the wishes of the President, I do not think it advisable to give you more explicit and minute instructions, but earnestly commend to your zeal and discretion, a subject which appeals so strongly to the universal sentiments of justice and humanity.

I am, sir, your obedient servant,

JOHN FORSYTH.

The Jews of Philadelphia held, on August 27, a meeting for the same purpose in the vestry of the Mickweh Israel Synagogue, at which were present, besides the prominent Jews of the city, several representative Christian clergymen—Dr. Ducachet, Rector of St. Stephens, Dr. Ramsay, a Presbyterian minister, and the Rev. Mr. Kennedy—all of whom spoke. Isaac Leeser was the principal orator, and he argued that as both Christianity and Islam are derived from Judaism, if the last advocated ritual murder, the daughter-religions would equally be guilty of the same practice. He contrasted the position of the Eastern Jews with that of their brethren in this happy land, and declared that while the Jews everywhere felt themselves true citizens of the lands in which they dwelt, they still retained full sympathy with their co-religionists throughout the world, especially when charges were brought against them which affected the honor and good fame of their religion. A series of resolutions were adopted and sent to Washington, whence Mr. Forsyth replied in similar terms to those he had used in his letter to the Jews of New York, and likewise enclosed a copy of his letter to Consul Gliddon at Alexandria. Another meeting was held in Richmond, Va., where a resolution was adopted thanking the President "for the prompt and handsome manner in which he has acted in reference to the persecution practiced upon our brethren in Damascus."

The Jews of the United States were also in open sympathy with the liberal movements in Central Europe, especially in Germany, which culminated in the revolutions of the year 1848. While there was no active co-operation or direct assistance in those times of slow communication, those who wrote from America described the conditions prevailing here as well-nigh ideal from the liberal point of view. A poem by Sigmund Herzl, entitled "Auf! Nach Amerika!" which appeared in the "Central Organ," published in Vienna in 1848 by Isidor Bush (b. in Prague, Bohemia, 1822; a. in New York, 1849; d. in St. Louis, Mo., 1898), in which America is described as a place where true brotherly love reigns supreme, where ignorance and base prejudice are entirely unknown, may be taken as an example of the expression of that sentiment. When the great Jewish champion of the liberal movement in Germany, Gabriel Riesser (b. in Hamburg, Germany, 1806; d. there 1863), visited America in 1856, he was greeted by many former German revolutionary soldiers—both Jewish and Christian—and in New York they gave a public dinner in his honor. German Jews in Philadelphia formed a Riesser Club, which existed for a number of years. (See Albert M. Friedenberg in "Publications," XVII, pp. 204-5.)

* * * * *

The first diplomatic difficulties which the Government of the United States experienced on account of discrimination against its Jewish citizens occurred about this time, and—strangely enough—it was not with Russia, but with the Swiss Confederation. A general convention between the two republics was drawn and signed at Berne, November 25, 1850, by Mr. A. Dudley Mann, American Minister to Switzerland, on the part of the United States, and by Messrs. Druey and Frey-Hérosée on the part of the Swiss Confederation. This treaty and a copy of the instructions under which Mr. Mann acted, together with his dispatch of November 30, 1850, explanatory of the Articles of Convention, were transmitted to the United States Senate on February 13, 1851, by President Millard Fillmore (1800-74). Neither the treaty nor the papers accompanying it were ever made public, the ban of secrecy imposed by the Senate having never been removed. But President Fillmore himself, in the message transmitting the treaty, objected to it in the form in which it was presented. He said: "There is a decisive objection arising from the last clause in the First Article. That clause is in these words: *On account of the tenor of the Federal Constitution of Switzerland, Christians alone are entitled to the enjoyment of the privileges guaranteed by the present Article in the Swiss Cantons. But said cantons are not prohibited from ex-*

tending the same privileges to citizens of the United States of other religious persuasions.

"It is quite certain [continues the President] that neither by law, nor by treaty, nor by any other official proceeding is it competent for the Government of the United States to establish any distinction between its citizens founded on differences in religious beliefs. Any benefit or privilege conferred by law or treaty on one must be common to all, and we are not at liberty, on a question of such vital interest and plain constitutional duty, to consider whether the particular case is one in which substantial inconvenience or injustice might ensue. It is enough that an inequality would be sanctioned, hostile to the institutions of the United States and inconsistent with the Constitution and the laws. Nor can the Government of the United States rely on the individual Cantons of Switzerland for extending the same privileges to other citizens of the United States as this article extends to Christians. It is indispensable not only that every privilege granted to any of the citizens of the United States should be granted to all, but also that the grant of such privileges should stand upon the same stipulation and assurance by the whole Swiss Confederation, as those of other articles of the convention.[1]

The two most prominent men in American public life at that time, Senator Henry Clay (1777-1852) and Secretary of State Daniel Webster (1782-1852), strongly disapproved the discrimination which the proposed treaty provided. The former wrote: "I disapprove entirely the restrictions limiting certain provisions of the treaty, under the operation of which a respectable portion of our fellow-citizens would be excluded from their benefits. This is not the country nor the age in which unjust prejudices should receive any countenance." Webster wrote about the same time to a Jew who addressed him on the subject (presumably J. M. Cordozo): "The objections against certain specialties of the Swiss Convention concerning the Israelites which you urge in your letter to me have not escaped the attention of the Department, and I hasten to inform you that they will be laid

[1] See Sol. M. Stroock *Switzerland and the American Jews,* "Publications" XI, pp. 7-52, and Cyrus Adler, *Jews in American Diplomatic Correspondence,* ibid XV, pp. 25-39, for ample treatment of the subject, including numerous documents and copious references.

before the Senate with the convention. (The letter is dated February 11, 1851.)

In the meantime, although it was asserted on behalf of Switzerland that the discriminations which it insisted upon were only "a precautionary measure . . . a safeguard against the immense itinerant (Jewish) population of Alsace," the two Cantons of Basle vigorously executed a decree of banishment against the Jews which was promulgated November 17, 1851. The law was suspended for a few months because of a note sent by Emperor Napoleon III. to the Council of the Federation, in which he said "That France will expel all Swiss citizens established in France in case the two Cantons should insist on carrying out this law against the Jews." But while the negotiations were pending, the two Cantons carried out the law of expulsion, and no further steps were taken by France. About this time there was set on foot in this country a movement to procure religious toleration abroad for American citizens generally. It appears to have been aimed at the persecution of American Protestants in Catholic countries, and the movement to secure redress in this direction culminated in a resolution introduced in the House of Representatives, December 13, 1852, by John A. Wilcox, of Mississippi, which declared "that the representatives of this Government at foreign courts be instructed to urge such amendments of all existing treaties between the United States and the other powers of the world as will secure the same liberty of religious worship to all American citizens residing under foreign flags which is guaranteed to all citizens of every nation of the whole world who reside under the flag of our Union."

Objection was made to this resolution as an encroachment upon the powers of the Executive, and action was delayed for a long time. A resolution of a similar nature, which was reported to the Senate from the Committee on Foreign Relations, February 17, 1853, met the same fate. But all these discussions had the effect of the Senate refusing to ratify the treaty with Switzerland in the form in which it was sent to it. Mr. Mann thereupon proceeded to negotiate another treaty which, while striking from it the clause objected to by the President and the other notable men mentioned above, yet in another form inserted a clause, the effect of which was the same as that of the clause which had been stricken out. Article I of this new treaty read as follows:

The citizens of the United States of America and the citizens of Switzerland shall be admitted and treated upon a footing of reciprocal equality in the two countries, where such admission and treatment shall not conflict with the constitutional or legal provisions, as well Federal as State and Cantonal of the contracting parties.

Despite the previous and many subsequent protests from numerous Jews, and also despite the attention of the government, which was attracted to the case of A. H. Gootman, an American-Jewish citizen, who was ordered expelled from the Canton of Neufchatel in 1853, the treaty containing the above article was ratified by the Senate November 6, 1855. Ratifications were exchanged two days afterward, and the treaty was proclaimed November 9, 1855, by President Franklin Pierce (1804-69), when William Learned Marcy (1786-1857) was Secretary of State.

In 1856 the above mentioned Mr. Gootman, who had remained in Neufchatel by special permission, again requested, through the American minister to Switzerland, Mr. Theo. S. Fay, the intervention of the United States Government against his expulsion. In his letter to the State Department Mr. Fay states it as a matter of fact that the treaty between the two republics "does not grant to Israelites the right of domicile in Switzerland," and in a second letter he says "that it may be superfluous to repeat that the obnoxious clause in the treaty was unavoidable without a revision of the federal constitution of Switzerland." He also repeats "that the admission of American Jews would necessitate that of Jews of other nations, and particular inconvenience is apprehended from the usurious Israelitish population of the French province of Alsace." This second

Gootman case became generally known, and public sentiment was aroused against the treaty. The result of the agitation was apparent even in the general press of the country, and many protest meetings were held, memorials drawn and forwarded to Washington and committees appointed to consider the matter. A delegation of prominent Jews went to the Capital in October, 1857, and presented a memorial to President James Buchanan (1791-1868), who gave an explicit promise to remedy the wrong of which the Jews complained.

The declaration of the President on the subject was so emphatic that most of the leaders and promoters of the agitation were completely satisfied that the question was already settled in their favor. Dr. Einhorn wrote in his "Sinai": "We feel satisfied that the Israelites of the United States may feel implicit confidence in the Executive, and that their rights as citizens of the United States will be zealously maintained." Dr. Wise, in the "Israelite," wrote: "No doubt was left in the minds of the delegates, but that this matter is settled as far as we are concerned." Rabbi Leeser, however, was not so well satisfied, and he did not agree that all agitation ought now to cease, but thought it "advisable for all the congregations that have not yet acted to draw up memorials and send them to the President, to show at least that the interest in the question was not confined to the four States represented at Washington on the 31st of October."

Another long diplomatic correspondence followed, with reciprocal requests for information about the condition of the Jews in both countries, with urgent requests from Washington that something be done, and with explanations from Mr. Fay that the Cantonal laws or constitutions would have to be changed before favorable action could be expected. In November of the same year Mr. Fay wrote: "I would wish carefully to avoid offering encouragement to the Hebrews." But he was now working diligently to carry out the desire of the President, and was even collecting material to disprove the charges made by the Swiss against the Alsatian Jews. In November, 1858, he wrote to Secretary of State Lewis Cass (1782-1866): "That the mouths of all foreign governments and preceding treaty makers have been until now closed by a plea about the Alsatian Jews. I think that after the renseignements which I am now collecting no Swiss authority will ever dare to advance that objection against us as an argument, and I am more and more of the opinion that it may become expedient to denounce our treaty until the expunction of the offensive clause." The results of Mr. Fay's investigations were incorporated in his "Israelite Note," which was transmitted to the Secretary of State on June 3, 1859, and to the Federal Council of Switzerland on the same day. It had a salutary effect on Switzerland, where the Federal Council assisted in its circulation. A German edition of it was printed in St. Gall in 1860. The cause of the Jews in Switzerland gained much from this intervention of the representative of a foreign government in their behalf; and the consequences were felt in other countries where the struggle for Jewish emancipation was then going on. According to a letter written by Mr. Fay in October, 1859, the Bavarian Minister told him that should he succeed in Switzerland, the Israelites of Bavaria would also be emancipated.

The case of the Jews was making considerable progress, and other enlightened governments also made representations to Switzerland in favor of the Jews; still nothing definite was accomplished under Buchanan's administration, either. In March, 1861, Rabbi Leeser expressed, in the "Occident," his regret, that nothing was done, and wrote that he expected that nothing would be done until "Switzerland herself will render the laws harmless by repealing through her Cantonal Councils all inequality laws existing against us." This prediction proved correct; for while the succeeding Secretary of State, William H. Seward (1801-72) took up the matter with Mr. George G. Fogg, who was then minister to Switzerland, several years passed before another favorable report reached the State Department on the subject. The appointment by the Government of the United States of a Jewish citizen, Mr. Bernays, as its Consul to Zürich created a stir in both countries, and clearly indicated the favorable disposition of the administration of President Abraham Lincoln (1809-65) towards the Jews.

In 1864 Mr. Fogg wrote to Mr. Seward that the President of the Confederation, Mr. Dubs, had informed him that the Federal Council were then disposed to so amend the treaty that no discrimination founded on religious belief should thereafter be made or endured by citizens of the United States within the limits of the Swiss Confederation. The remaining Cantons were removing the Jewish disabilities one after another; but in some of them, as in Basle, the hotbed of opposition and prejudice against the Jews, full civil rights were not granted until 1872, although the right of residence was freely accorded ten years earlier. The new Swiss Constitution, which was adopted in 1874, at last established full religious liberty, and also made the question of treatments of aliens a Federal, as distinguished from a Cantonal, matter. It was not until then that the question was solved, so to speak, automatically; but it is conceded that the efforts of the Government of the United States contributed to the result, although it could not attain its object by direct diplomatic negotiations.

PART V.

THE CIVIL WAR AND THE FORMATIVE PERIOD.

CHAPTER XXIV.

THE DISCUSSION ABOUT SLAVERY. LINCOLN AND THE JEWS.

Pro-slavery tendencies of the aristocratic Spaniards and Portuguese—David Yulee (Levy)—Michael Heilprin and his reply to Rabbi Raphall's *Bible View on Slavery*—Immigrants of the second period as opponents of slavery—Two Jewish delegates in the Convention which nominated Abraham Lincoln, and one member of the Electoral College in 1860—Two other Jews officially participate in Lincoln's renomination and re-election in 1864—Abraham Jonas—Encouragement from the Scripture in original Hebrew.

As almost all the early Jewish settlers in America belonged to the wealthy classes, and most of them were in everything, except as to their faith, aristocratic Spaniards or Portuguese, it was natural for them to accept the institution of slavery as they found it, and to derive as much benefit from it as other affluent men. There were numerous Jewish slave holders in various parts of the New World, including the West Indies, New York and New England, long before and down to the American Revolution. There are several early references even to American-Jewish slave dealers. The growth of democracy and changed economic conditions had gradually put an end to slavery in the north soon after the beginning of the nineteenth century; but in the South slavery remained common, among Jews as well as among others. Public opinion in the South not only sanctioned slavery, but considered it the basis of its prosperity and predominance; and the prominent Jew of that part of the country was simply acting and feeling like his non-Jewish neighbors and fellow-citizens when he owned slaves or defended the institution at every possible opportunity. And those Jews who attained high political or social position in the South were by force of circumstances pro-slavery men. There was no lack of individual instances of Jews who evinced special tenderness for the black man, and even went so far as to liberate the negroes of whom they were the owners. It is thus related of the philanthropist Judah Touro "that the negroes who waited upon him in the house of the Shepards—with whom he lived for forty years —were all emancipated by his aid and supplied with the means of establishing themselves; and the only slave he personally possessed he trained to business, then emancipated, furnishing him with money and valuable advice." The American and Foreign Anti-Slavery Society, in its report in 1853, noted that some Jews in the Southern States "have refused to have any right of property in man, or even to have any slaves about them" and that the cruel persecutions they themselves were subjected to tended to make them friends of universal freedom.[1] But these were exceptional, not typical cases, and not more common among Jews than among gentiles.

It was therefore natural to find in a man like David Yulee (originally David Levy, b. in St. Thomas, W. I., 1811; d. in New York City, 1886), who after studying at Richmond, Va., became a planter in Florida, a stanch supporter and defender of slavery. He was a Delegate to Congress from the Territory of Florida from 1841 to 1845, bearing the name of Levy. When Florida was admitted as a state in 1845, Levy, who had then assumed the name of Yulee, was elected a United States Senator

[1] See Max J. Kohler in article *Antislavery Movement in America* in "Jew. Encyclopedia."

from that state, being the first Jew who was elected to the upper house of the American Congress. He served a full term and later he was elected for another term, beginning in 1855 which he did not finish, because he retired in January, 1861, to join the Confederacy, later serving as a member of the Confederate Congress. We find even a resident of the far West, Judge Samuel Heydenfeldt, of California—mentioned in a former part—who, as a native of the South, was a strong partisan of the Confederacy, going so far as to withdraw from a lucrative practice in the courts, because he felt that he could not subscribe to the "iron clad" oath of loyalty required by law as a condition precedent to argument in every case (see *Friedenberg,* in "Publications," X, p. 138).

In the religious controversies which went on at the time when the question of slavery began to absorb the attention of the American people, the Jews also took part on both sides. It has already been mentioned that Dr. Einhorn was forced to quit Baltimore on account of the strong stand against slavery which he took in his sermons and in his German monthly "Sinai." Rabbi Sabato Morais found in Philadelphia, and so did Rabbis Bernhard Felsenthal and Liebman Adler in Chicago, more congenial surroundings for their work against slavery. Rabbi Morris J. Raphall, of New York, came out in 1860 with a strong sermon, which later appeared in a pamphlet, entitled *"Bible View on Slavery,"* in which he attempted to prove that since the Bible, which is the highest law, sanctioned slavery, it was futile to invoke an alleged "higher law" against it. There was, of course, no lack of replies and refutations to this argument, but none was so strong or attracted so much attention as one that came from the pen of a scholar who represented the very latest class of Jewish immigrants to the United States.

This man was Michael Heilprin (b. in Piotrkow, Russian-Poland, 1823; d. in Summit, N. J., 1888), the son of Pinhas Mendel Heilprin (b. in Lublin, Russian-Poland, 1801; d. in Washington, D. C., 1863). His father, who was a scholarly

Michael Heilprin.

merchant of the old Polish-Jewish type and the author of several works in Hebrew, was his only teacher, and brought him up in that spirit of enlightened Orthodoxy which was not antagonistic to the acquisition of secular learning. Michael's almost phenomenal memory and diligence helped him to master many languages and to become proficient in numerous sciences, which enabled him later to become one of the associate editors and an important contributor to *Appleton's New American Cyclopaedia.* The Heilprins removed to Northern Hungary about 1843. where Michael established himself as a bookseller in Miskolcz. He soon mastered the Hungarian language, and his articles and poems in the cause of liberty attracted much attention during the stormy days of 1848 and 1849. He became the friend and confidant of Louis Kossuth (1802-94) and other leaders, and when the short-lived independent Hungarian government was established, he became secretary of the literary bureau which was attached to its ministry of the interior. After the suppression of the Revolution he spent some time in Cracow and in France, but returned to Hungary in 1850, and settled as a teacher in Satoralja-Ujhely, where his second son, the well-known American naturalist, Angelo Heilprin, was born in 1853 (d. in New York, 1907); the elder son, Louis, the encyclopedist (b. in Miskolcz, 1851), died in New York in 1912.

Michael Heilprin came to the United States in 1856 and settled in Philadelphia, where for two years he taught in the schools of the Hebrew Education Society. He "saw but one struggle here and in Hungary," and his sympathies were actively engaged in the anti-slavery movement. In 1858 he settled in Brooklyn, where he resided until 1863, when he removed to Washington, returning to New York in 1865. On January 16, 1861, he contributed a fiery denunciation and an exhaustive scholarly refutation of Raphall's views to the *New York Tribune* which commanded wide attention; and owing to this vehement but convincing repudiation of alleged Jewish pro-slavery views,

Heilprin succeeded in arousing the public in a more marked degree than any other Jewish anti-slavery champion.

The bulk of the Jewish immigrants who came from Germany in the forty years preceding the Civil War were almost unanimous against slavery, because they were under the influence of the liberal movements of the Old World. These immigrants were intensely interested in the anti-slavery movement and were among the first and the most enthusiastic members of the newly formed Republican party. The two Jews who were chosen delegates to the National Convention of that party in 1860, which nominated Abraham Lincoln for the Presidency, and the Jewish member of the Electoral College which ratified the choice of the people in that year, were all natives of Germany. The oldest among them was Sigismund Kaufman (b. in Darmstadt, 1824; d. in Berlin, 1889), who participated in the German Revolution of 1848-49, and coming to America, became a representative of the German Republican element in the United States. He took an active part in the leadership of German social and fraternal organizations in New York, was a director of the Hebrew Orphan Asylum, and held the position of Commissioner of Immigration. He addressed anti-slavery meetings in English, German and French, and was considered one of the influential politicians of New York in his time. He was chosen a Presidential Elector for the State of New York in 1860.

Moritz Pinner (b. in Germany about 1828), one of the members of the Republican State Convention which was held in St. Louis on February 12, 1860, was elected a delegate to the National Republican Convention to be held in Chicago the following May. He was opposed to the Presidential candidate who was put forward by that convention, and when it adopted the unit rule, thereby forcing him to vote against his own favorite candidate (Seward), he offered his resignation; but the convention adjourned without taking action on it. He was at the Chicago Convention as a delegate, but abstained from voting, on account of his declination to be bound by the decree of the

Photo by Klauber, Louisville.

Lewis N. Dembitz.

State Convention, which is one of the reasons why his name does not appear on the official roll of the Missouri delegates. Pinner, who later removed to Elizabeth, N. J., was actively engaged for a number of years before the outbreak of the war in circulating anti-slavery literature in Missouri, and was for some time the editor of a German periodical devoted to the same cause.[1]

The third and youngest of the three Jews who directly participated in the official part of the work of nominating and electing Abraham Lincoln to the Presidency in 1860, was Lewis Naphtali Dembitz (b. in Zirke, Province of Posen, Prussian-Poland in 1833; d. in Louisville, Ky., 1907), who had been a practicing attorney at Louisville since 1853. He was previously occupied as a journalist and had at a later time written several works on legal and general, as well as on Jewish, subjects. Dembitz took an active interest in Jewish affairs and held various communal positions in local and national bodies. He was considered one of the leaders of Conservative Judaism in America, and is best known as the author of *Jewish Services in the Synagogue and Home* (1898). At the Convention of 1860 he was a delegate from the city of Louisville, where he resided for more than a half century, and where he held the position of Assistant City Attorney from 1884 to 1888.

The one Jewish delegate to the Convention which re-nominated Mr. Lincoln in 1864 was likewise a native of Germany, while the one Jewish member of the Electoral College which re-elected him was of German parentage. The former was Maier Hirsch (1829-76), a merchant of Salem, Oregon, who was one of the six delegates from that state to the Republican National Convention of 1864. He settled in Oregon in 1852, when he came to the United States from Würtemberg. He settled in New York in 1874, where he died two years later. Maier Hirsch was a brother of Solomon Hirsch, who was United

[1] See Markens, *Lincoln and the Jews* in "Publications," XVII, pp. 10-65, for a more detailed treatment of the subject of this chapter.

States Minister to Turkey from 1889 to 1892, and of Edward Hirsch, at one time State Treasurer and later a State Senator of Oregon.

The Presidential elector of 1864 was A. J. Dittenhoefer (b. in South Carolina, 1836), who came with his parents to New York when he was four years old, and has resided there continually since. He served as Justice of the Marine (now City) Court, and held several positions of trust and honor in the Republican Party, of which he was one of the earliest members in New York.

Among the personal friends of Lincoln was Abraham Jonas (b. in Exeter, England, 1801; d. in Quincy, Ill., 1864), whose four sons, strangely enough, fought in the Confederate Army. Jonas, who first lived in Kentucky, was a member of the Legislature of that State in 1828-30 and in 1833; and in the last named year he was also chosen Grand Master of Masons of the State of Kentucky. He removed to Illinois in 1838, and there also became Grand Master of the newly organized Masonic Grand Lodge, which was founded in 1839. He was elected a member of the Illinois Legislature in 1842, retiring from his mercantile pursuits on being admitted to the bar in 1843. He served as Postmaster of Quincy from 1849 to 1852. Jonas, with Lincoln, was chosen by the Illinois State Republican Convention, held at Bloomington on May 29, 1856, a Presidential elector on the Fremont ticket. A confidential letter which Lincoln, after his first nomination in 1860 wrote to Jonas, denying that he was affiliated with the American or "Know Nothing" party, is preserved in the authoritative Lincoln biography by Nicolay and Hay. During his last illness, when he knew that the doctors had no hope for his recovery, Jonas's only wish was to see his son, Charles H., a member of the Twelfth Arkansas Regiment, who was at that time a prisoner of war on Johnson's Island, Lake Erie. This wish was communicated by telegraph to Lincoln, who issued an order, dated June 2d, 1864, to "Allow Charles H. Jonas, now a prisoner of war at Johnson's Island, a parole of three weeks to visit his dying father, Abraham Jonas, at Quincy, Ill." Benjamin F. Jonas (b. in Williamstown, Ky., 1834; d. in New Orleans, 1911), who served in the artillery of Hood's Corps in the Army of Tennessee, and who, after serving several terms in the Legislature of Louisiana, was elected a United States Senator from that state, serving from 1879 until 1885, was one of the above mentioned four sons of Abraham Jonas who served in the Confederate Army.

The admiration which Jews felt for Lincoln was probably best expressed by the silk flag which City Clerk Abraham Kohn of Chicago sent to the President-elect before his departure for Washington in February, 1861. It was painted in colors, its folds bearing Hebrew characters lettered in black with the third to ninth verses of the first chapter in Joshua, the last verse being: "Have I not commanded thee? Be strong and of good courage; be not afraid neither be thou dismayed; for the Lord thy God is with thee whithersoever thou goest."

CHAPTER XXV.

PARTICIPATION OF JEWS IN THE CIVIL WAR. JUDAH P. BENJAMIN.

Probable number of Jews in the United States at the time of the outbreak of the Civil War—Seddon's estimate of "from ten to twelve thousand Jews in the Southern Army"—Judah P. Benjamin, the greatest Jew in American public life—His early life and his marriage—Whig politician, planter and slave owner—Elected to the United States Senate and re-elected as a Democrat—Quits Washington when Louisiana seceded and enters the cabinet of the Confederacy—Attorney-General, Secretary of War and Secretary of State—His foreign policy—His capacity for work—When all is lost he goes to England and becomes one of its great lawyers—His last days are spent in France.

The highest estimate of the number of Jews in the United States about the time of the outbreak of the Civil War was about four hundred thousand (Jonas P. Levy in 1858; see "Publications," XI, p. 39), while the lowest, given by Mr. Simon Wolf in his work, which is the standard authority on the participation of the Jews in the war,[1] thinks it "altogether doubtful whether there were more than 150,000, if that many, when hostilities commenced." But it is certain that even if the higher estimate is nearer the truth, the Jews took their full share in the struggle and "that the enlistment of Jewish soldiers, North and South, reached proportions considerably in excess of their ratio to the general population." Mr. Wolf has collected data to the effect that over seven thousand Jews took part in the conflict on both sides, but he has by no means been able to come near com-

[1] *The American Jew as Patriot, Soldier and Citizen*, p. 6.

From Pierce Butler's "Judah P. Benjamin."

Judah P. Benjamin.

pleteness. Neither the Government of the United States nor that of the Confederacy took notice of the religion of its soldiers; a large number of the young German-Jewish volunteers were far from being strict adherents of religion, while many among the native Jews had American names and could not be easily recognized as Jews. Mr. Seddon, the Secretary of War of the Confederacy, when requested, in the fall of 1864, to grant a furlough to Jewish soldiers who would like to keep Rosh ha-Shanah and Yom Kippur, is quoted as replying that he believed that there were from ten to twelve thousand Jews in the Southern Army, and that it would perhaps disintegrate certain commands if the request was granted. While this number is probably an exaggeration, it cannot be very far from the truth, and considering the comparatively small number of Jews in the South at that time, this is a really remarkable showing.

The number of Jews who distinguished themselves by their bravery and who attained high rank and other forms of recognition, was also correspondingly large, especially if we consider their inexperience in war. But before treating of the men who gained eminence on the field of battle, and of the others whose creditable record in the war helped them to attain positions of prominence in other walks of life afterwards, we shall speak of the one man who occupied a really commanding position in this gigantic struggle, the greatest Jew in American public life—Judah P. Benjamin.

He was the son of Philip (b. about 1782) and Rebecca de Mendes Benjamin, who emigrated from London, England, to St. Thomas, W. I., in 1808, shortly after their marriage, where the son was born August 6, 1811. The Benjamins removed to the United States, where they originally intended to go, about 1818, and settled in Charleston, S. C. Judah Philip entered Yale University in 1825, and left in 1827, without taking a degree. A year later he came to New Orleans, where he taught English, learned French and studied law as a notary's clerk. He was admitted to the bar in 1832 and a year later married his former pupil, Natalie St. Martin, who remained all her life a devout Roman Catholic. The marriage was not a happy one, and when their only child which survived infancy was about five years old, Mrs. Benjamin moved permanently to France to educate her, and Mr. Benjamin saw them only on his visits to Paris, which he made almost annually.

Benjamin was associated with Thomas Slidell, who later became Chief Justice of Louisiana, in the preparation of the *Digest of the Reported Decisions of the Superior Courts in the Territory of Orleans and State of Louisiana,* which was published in 1834. He soon afterward became interested in politics, and was elected to the lower house of the General Assembly of Louisiana on the Whig ticket in 1842. When he was forced by weakened eyesight to relinquish his law practice for a time, he took up sugar planting, in which he likewise succeeded very well. The plantation, however, was ruined by a flood, and Benjamin removed to New Orleans, together with the members of his family, whom he brought over from South Carolina. They were his mother (d. 1847), his oldest sister, the widow of Abraham Levy (whom she married in 1826), and his younger sister, who later became the mother of Julius Kruttschnitt (b. in New Orleans, 1854), the railroad manager. As a planter Benjamin became a slave owner, and some of his slaves, who were still living at the beginning of the present century, "would tell visitors all sorts of tales of the master of long ago—none but kindly memories and romantic legends of the glory of the old place."[1]

He soon became one of the recognized leaders of the Whig party in his state, and "no small share of the flashes of success that came to it in the last decade of its existence in Louisiana is attributable to his energy and political sagacity." He was, according to the journalistic custom of that time, savagely as-

[1] Pierce Butler, *Judah P. Benjamin,* Philadelphia, 1907, p. 62. This complete biographical work is the only one of its kind written of an American Jew, and practically supersedes all that was written about Benjamin before.

sailed by the newspapers which opposed him, and he was even charged, in 1844, with belonging to the "Know Nothing" party, despite the fact that he was himself foreign born. But he agreed with that party in his opposition to the granting of suffrage to immigrants into the state, even to natives of Northern States, in whom he saw a source of danger to the South.

His seat in the Constitutional Convention of 1844 being contested, he resigned and was re-elected by a much larger majority. When he again took his seat at the convention which re-assembled in New Orleans, Benjamin was the recognized leader of the delegates of that city in its disputes with the representatives of the country districts. One of his speeches at that convention proved that he clearly foresaw the war in 1845, though he was then considered an alarmist. He was elected a State Senator in 1852, and soon became a leading candidate for the United States Senate. He received the nomination by an unexpectedly large majority and was elected in the same year, as a Whig. When that party was split by the antagonism between the North and the South, he came out openly in 1855 with the declaration that it did not exist any more as a national party. He urged the necessity of uniting in one great Southern party, on a platform "on which we can all stand together to meet with firmness the coming shock." When the formation of such a party proved impracticable, he turned to the Democratic party and became more friendly to the administration. His first really powerful speech in the Senate was delivered May 2d, 1856, on the Kansas bill, in which he distinctly and calmly enunciated the right of secession.

In 1859 Benjamin was re-elected to the United States Senate by a majority of one vote (that of the last "Know Nothing" in the Louisiana Legislature). He was now one of the prominent Senators, and chairman of the Judiciary Committee. He was in favor of secession only as a last resort; but he thought that this last resort was reached after Lincoln's election in 1860. He delivered two powerful orations in the Senate in the following winter, and a memorable farewell speech, February 4, 1861, on the right of Louisiana to secede. His last speech in the capital was delivered before the Washington Artillery on Washington's birthday, and soon after, in New Orleans, he took leave from his family, whom he was never to see again.

Louisiana had already seceded from the Union on January 26, 1861, and one month later, February 25, Benjamin was named by the President of the new Confederacy, Jefferson Davis (1808-89) as his Attorney-General. Benjamin assumed his new office at the new capital, Montgomery, Ala.; but there was hardly any work for him to do as an Attorney-General to a government that practically had no courts. But he was often called upon by President Davis to perform other services which required tact and delicacy, and he soon gained the latter's confidence to a marked degree. On September 17, 1861, Benjamin was named Secretary of War ad interim, to succeed Secretary Walker, acting also as Attorney-General until November 15 of that year. He proved unpopular in his new office, and was blamed by a Congressional committee for not sending ammunition to General Wise, who lost an important battle about that time. But as a matter of fact there was nothing to send, and the President and his Secretary of War preferred to accept official blame to disclosing the dearth and scarcity of powder to a committee of the Confederate Congress, fearing that it might become known to the Yankees. Benjamin shouldered the odium, as usual; but he rose in the estimation of Davis and the other leaders who were conversant with the true state of affairs. Thus it happened that while almost everybody in the South expected Benjamin to be dismissed in disgrace, the surprising news was published on March 27, 1862, that he was promoted to the office of Secretary of State.

His new Department was the one for which he was pre-eminently fit; and while he could not, in the nature of things, accomplish all that was expected of him, he earned the undying fame which was best expressed in the description of him as the "Brains of the Confederacy." The great problem was to obtain assistance from a maritime power, the only one who could help the blockaded Confederacy, which was prevented by the blockade from selling its chief staple article—cotton. Spain, though a slave power herself at that time, was unfriendly to the former persistent filibusters, and her distrust could not be overcome. France was too friendly with England and would not interfere without the latter's consent or co-operation, so that even if the South could send out a new Benjamin Franklin to Paris he could accomplish little. Benjamin, like almost all Southern statesmen, believed that England will be unable to get along without cotton, and ignoring or misunderstanding the moral forces which the cause of the North awakened in Europe, he displayed more independence at the beginning than was justifiable. Later, when he was in England, Benjamin declared: "I did not believe that your government would allow such misery to your operatives, such loss to your manufacturers, or that the people themselves would have borne it." Benjamin believed that recognition (by England and France) even without intervention would end the war, and he might have been right if recognition came early.

Mason, the Southern representative in England, made little headway, and even had his cause been stronger, he was no match for Adams, the minister of the North. Slidell, Benjamin's friend, was apparently more successful in France. Benjamin authorized him to offer France a cotton subsidy valued at over sixty million francs for breaking the blockade or even for simple recognition of the Confederacy. Emperor Louis Napoleon (1808-73) seemed to have been favorably inclined, and Mercier, the French minister at Washington, who visited Richmond with Lincoln's permission, was so influenced by Benjamin that he became almost enthusiastic. But communications were unsteady and unsafe, and some dispatches came seven months after they were sent from Paris. As an instance: Benjamin received from Slidell on February 27, 1863, a message written December 27, 1862, stating that the envoy to France was "without any dispatch from you later than April 15th." The fall of New Orleans, May 1, 1862, blasted the hopes of early intervention.

Benjamin worked very hard as Secretary of State, although there were no ambassadors to be received and no social functions to be attended in Richmond. It has been stated on good authority that President Davis consulted with his Secretary of State more freely than with any other member of his cabinet, and finding him always willing and able, got in the habit of referring to the State Department anything that did not beyond any hope belong to some other department. Benjamin's assistant secretary, L. O. Washington, writes of him: "He was ever calm, self-poised, and master of all his resources. His grasp of a subject seemed instantaneous. His mind appeared to move without friction. His thought was clear." Mrs. Jefferson Davis wrote: "Mr. Benjamin was always ready for work; sometimes with half an hour recess, he remained with the Executive from ten in the morning until night. . . . Both the President and the Secretary of State worked like galley slaves, early and late. Mr. Davis came home fasting, a mere mass of throbbing nerves, and perfectly exhausted; but Mr. Benjamin was always fresh and buoyant."

When New Orleans fell, his little family, after privations and misadventures, moved to La Grange, Ga., where he could again supply them with money. When the fortune of the Confederacy began to wane, his unpopularity increased, and attacks upon the score of his religion and race, which were never neglected by his opponents during his entire career, were now redoubled. He was especially blamed for the desperate plan, which was carried out through the desire and influence of General Robert E. Lee (1807-70) of enlisting negroes in the Confederate army. On February 9, 1865, Benjamin made, at a mass meeting in Richmond, the last public speech of his life. His power over his audience was still great, but all was lost. Richmond fell in less than two months. After an anxious week at Danville, he accompanied President Davis to Greensboro, where the fugitive government halted for a few days. Taking leave from Mr. Davis, to whom he could no longer be of any assistance, he escaped to the West Indies, where he visited his native place for the last time, and after many dangers and adventures he arrived in England, July 22, 1865.

* * * * *

Although England did not recognize the Confederacy, many sympathized with it, and Benjamin, whose fame preceded him, was received in London with great friendliness, despite the order which he gave as Secretary of State, expelling from the Confederate States all British Consuls, because they persisted in acting under orders from their superiors in Washington. He was befriended by many of the important men of the time in London, including both Benjamin Disraeli (Earl of Beaconsfield, 1804-81) and William E. Gladstone (1809-98). Having been born in an English colony, the son of an Englishman, he simply returned to his original allegiance, seemingly trying to forget his experience of more than forty years as an American. He never made a political address or a public declaration after leaving America.

His subsequent career as an English barrister, as one of the greatest of barristers in his time, was wonderful, especially when we remember that it was begun when he was over fifty-five years of age; with a past history which was so crowded with activity and exciting experience to wear out any man. He wrote there his *Treatise on the Law of Sale of Personal Property, with References to the American Decisions, to the French Code and Civil Law* which became a legal classic on both sides of the Atlantic. His income from his law practice was for some years as high as £15,000 annually, which was much rarer then than it is now. In 1872 he received a "patent of precedence," which gave him rank above all other Queen's Counsels. About 1877 he began to build a new house on Avenue d'Jena (No. 41), in Paris, in which city his wife and only child continued to reside, even after he settled in England. A bad accident caused by an attempt to jump off a tram-car, in 1880, left him a sick man for the rest of his life. Diabetes developed, and in February, 1883, he was forced to announce his retirement from the English Bar. After a notable banquet given in his honor by the Bench and Bar—the first of its kind in England—he retired to his mansion in Paris, where he died May 6, 1884, about seventy-three years old. He was buried according to the rites of the Catholic Church, although it is not believed that he was converted to Christianity. His wife survived him seven years. His only daughter, Ninette, who married Captain Henri de Bousignac, of the French army, died without issue in 1898.

CHAPTER XXVI.

DISTINGUISHED SERVICES OF JEWS ON BOTH SIDES OF THE STRUGGLE.

More "brothers in arms" and a larger proportion of officers in the Confederate Army than in that of the North, because most Southern Jews were natives of the country—Some distinguished officers—A gallant private who later became a rabbi—Paucity of Southern records—Generals Knefler, Solomon, Blumenberg, Joachimsen and other officers of high rank in the Union Army—New York ranks first, Ohio second and Illinois third in the number of Jews who went to the front—Two Pennsylvania regiments which started with Jewish colonels—Commodore Uriah P. Levy, the ranking officer of the United States navy at the time of the outbreak of the war, is prevented by age from taking part in it.

The disproportionately large number of Jews who served in the Confederate army was already alluded to in the former chapter. Another proof of it is the preponderance among the Jews in that army of instances of "brothers in arms" (as Mr. Wolf calls them), i. e., of groups of several brothers who went to the front with their neighbors to fight the battles of the state and the section of the country in which they lived. Six brothers Cohen—Aaron, Jacob H., Julius, Edward, Gustavus A. and Henry M.—came from North Carolina. South Carolina contributed the five brothers Moses—Percy, Joshua L., Horace, J. Harby and A. Jackson. The four brothers Jonas have been mentioned in a former chapter, but they also had a fifth brother who, like their father, embraced the Union cause. Raphael Moses and his three sons were four Southern soldiers from

Georgia, while Alabama sent also three Moses brothers: Mordecai, Henry C. and Alfred. Three brothers Cohen came from Arkansas, Virginia and Louisiana each sent three brothers surnamed Levy, while of the three brothers Goldsmith two came from Georgia and one from South Carolina. The reason for the presence of so many brothers in arms in the Confederate army is given by the above named authority as due to the fact that the Jews of the Southern States were, in a much larger proportion than those of the North, natives of the soil or residents of long standing. While the Jews of the North were much more numerous, they were, for the most part, immigrants of a comparatively recent date, and therefore less intensely imbued with the spirit of the conflict.

There were about twenty-three Jewish staff officers in the Confederate army, which is likewise a larger number than those who held similar positions in the Union army, and probably for the same reason given above. The most distinguished of them were: Surgeon-General David de Leon, who participated in the Mexican war (see page 162); Assistant Adjutant-General J. Randolph Mordecai, and Colonel Raphael J. Moses, who served on the staff of General Longstreet and was chief commissary for the State of Georgia. Adolph Meyer (b. in New Orleans, 1842; d. there 1908), who later served nine terms as a member of the House of Representatives in Washington from the First District of Louisiana (52d to 60th Congresses, inclusive), entered the Confederate army in 1862, and served until the close of the war on the staff of Brigadier-General John S. Williams of Kentucky. There were also about a dozen Jewish officers in the Confederate navy, one of whom, Captain Levy Myers Harby (b. in Georgetown, S. C., 1793; d. in Galveston, Tex., 1870), who had previously served in the war of 1812, in the Mexican war and in the Bolivian war, and, after resigning from the service of the United States and joining the Confederacy, distinguished himself in the defence of Galveston, and was in command of its harbor at the close of the Civil War.

Photo by Harris & Ewing, Wash., D. C.

Hon. Simon Wolf.

Lionel Levy, a nephew of Judah P. Benjamin, served as Judge-Advocate of the Military Court of the Confederate Army. Among those who served as privates in the ranks who deserve to be mentioned was Samuel Ullman of the 16th Infantry Regiment of Mississippi, who served gallantly through the war, being twice wounded, and later (1891-94) was rabbi of Emanuel Congregation of Birmingham, Ala. There have also been preserved the names of twenty-five Jews among the Confederate prisoners who died in Elmira, N. Y., during the time which they were detained there. A list of seventeen soldiers interred at the Jewish burying ground of Richmond, Va., contains the names of one captain, three lieutenants, and one corporal, which is an exceptionally large ratio of officers for the Civil War on either side. Even in the South the Jews could at that time be numbered by tens of thousands, with a much larger proportion of poor men, or immigrants, than in former times, and the relative number of officers was perforce much smaller than at the time of the Revolution or of the War of 1812. Still the Jews of the South were then, as it was stated above, much more assimilated or Americanized than those of the North, and the records of the Confederate army were less carefully kept or preserved. Thus it happens that, while judging from inference and some general statements, it may appear that the number of Jews in the armies of the Confederacy was almost as large as, if not larger than, their number in the Union Army, the actual records compiled by Mr. Wolf tell an entirely different story. His lists contain about six thousand names of Jews who supported the Union cause, while among those who defended secession and slavery there were only about a fifth of that number whose names and identity he ascertained.

It is also to the Union army that we have to go to find Jewish officers who commanded regiments on the battlefields. Brevet Major General Frederick Knefler, a native of Hungary, who rose to the colonelcy of the 79th Indiana Regiment and subsequently became a Brigadier-General, and was made Brevet Major-General for meritorious conduct at Chickamauga, is classed as a Jew. Edward S. Solomon (known also as Salomon; b. in Sleswick-Holstein, 1826; d. 1909) emigrated to the United States after receiving a high school education in his native town, and settled in Chicago, where he was elected alderman in 1860. At the outbreak of the war he joined the 24th Illinois Infantry as second-lieutenant, participating in the battles of Frederickton and Mainfordsville, Kentucky, and was promoted to the rank of major in 1862. He then resigned and assisted in the organization of the Eighty-second Illinois Infantry, in which regiment he became lieutenant-colonel, and afterwards became its colonel. He took part, under General Howe, in the battles of Chancellorville, Gettysburg, Chattanooga, Lookout Mountain and Missionary Ridge. In 1865 he was brevetted brigadier-general. When peace was restored he returned to Chicago and became clerk of Cook County, Ill. In 1870 he was appointed by President Ulysses S. Grant (1822-85) governor of Washington Territory, and held the position about four years. After resigning, in 1874, he settled in San Francisco, where he was twice elected to the Legislature of California, and also held the office of District Attorney of San Francisco.

Leopold Blumenberg (b. in Prussia, 1827; d. in Baltimore, 1876) served with distinction in the Prussian-Danish war of 1848-49 and was promoted to the rank of first lieutenant. He came to the United States in 1854 and settled in Baltimore, where he engaged in a profitable business, which he abandoned at the outbreak of the war. He helped to organize the Fifth Maryland Regiment, in which he became a major. His work for the Union cause excited the animosity of local secessionists, who attempted to hang him, and he was forced to have his house barricaded and guarded for several nights. Blumenberg was acting colonel of his regiment near Hampton Roads. He was later attached to Mansfield's corps at the Peninsular campaign, and commanded his regiment as colonel at Antietam, where he was severely wounded. When he had partly recovered he was appointed by President Lincoln provost-marshal of the third Maryland district, which position he held for two years. President Andrew Johnson (1808-75) gave him a position in the revenue department and commissioned him brigadier-general, United States Volunteers, by brevet. General Blumenberg was a member of the Har-Sinai Congregation and of the Hebrew Orphan Asylum of Baltimore.

Philip J. Joachimsen (b. in Breslau, Germany, 1817; a. 1831; d. in New York, 1890) was appointed Assistant Corporation Attorney of the City of New York soon after his admission to the bar, in 1840, and fifteen years later he became Assistant United States District Attorney, being afterward appointed Substitute United States Attorney under a special provision of an act of Congress. (*Markens 223.*) During his term of office he secured the first capital conviction for slave trading, and also the conviction of some Nicaraguan filibusterers. He organized and commanded the 59th New York Volunteer Regiment and was injured at New Orleans. He was made brigadier-general by brevet. In 1870 he was elected a Judge of the Marine Court of the City of New York and served a full term of six years. Judge Joachimsen was active in Jewish communal affairs, and was the first president of the Hebrew Orphan Asylum (1859). Twenty years later he organized the Hebrew Sheltering Guardian Society.

General William Mayer rendered valuable service during the Draft Riots in New York City, for which he received an autograph letter of thanks from President Lincoln. Subsequently General Mayer devoted himself to journalism and was the editor of several German newspapers.

Marcus M. Spiegel, the son of a rabbi of Oppenheim-on-the-Rhine, enlisted in the 67th Ohio Infantry Regiment and was promoted step by step until he became lieutenant-colonel, and for bravery manifested on the battle field, was appointed Colonel of the 120th Ohio Infantry. He was wounded at Vicksburg, and after joining his regiment again, fell at Snaggy Point, on the Red River, Louisiana. But for his untimely death, Colonel Spiegel would have been promoted to the rank of Brigadier-General, to which he was recommended by his superior officers.

Max Einstein (b. in Würtemburg, 1822; a. 1844) had considerable military experience prior to the outbreak of the war. He was a silk merchant, and became First Lieutenant of the Washington Guards in 1852. In the following year he joined the Philadelphia (Flying) Artillery Company and was chosen its Captain. He became Aide-de-Camp (with the rank of Lieutenant-Colonel) to Governor James Pollock of Pennsylvania in 1856. In 1860 he was elected Brigadier-General of the Second Brigade of Pennsylvania Militia. In the succeeding year he organized the 27th Pennsylvania Infantry Regiment, which was mustered into service May 31, 1861, for a three years' term. This regiment, under Colonel Einstein's command, succeeded in covering the retreat of the Union Army in the first battle of Bull Run and won credit by its conduct. Einstein was subsequently appointed by President Lincoln United States Consul at Nüremberg, Germany, and later served as United States Revenue Agent at Philadelphia.

It is worth noting as an example that this one regiment had nearly thirty Jewish officers, most of them in minor positions, and about sixty privates in the ranks. This was, of course, an exceptional case, but Jews were represented in most of the regiments, especially those of Philadelphia, almost if not quite as much as in the regiments of those states which sent a larger contingent of Jewish soldiers to the front than Pennsylvania. The first of those states was New York, with nearly two thousand, which had already at that time achieved the distinction of having the largest Jewish community in the New World. Ohio, which came second, with 1,134, and Illinois, with 1,076, clearly indicated the growing importance of the Middle West for the new immigration. Indiana contributed over five hundred—almost as many as Pennsylvania—while Michigan had more than two hundred of its Jewish inhabitants in the Union Army. New England had the smallest representation, for the number of Jews there was very small at that time.

There was still another Pennsylvania regiment, the 65th (Fifth Cavalry), known as the "Cameron Dragoons" (on account of its being recruited under the authority of an order issued by Secretary of War Simon Cameron (1799-1889) July 6, 1861), which first went to the front under the command of a Jewish colonel. His name was Max Friedman (b. in Mühlhausen, Germany, 1825), and he came to the United States in 1848, settling in Philadelphia. He served as Major of a Regiment in the State Militia prior to the Civil War. Colonel Friedman remained with his regiment in the field until a severe wound received at the battle of Vienna, Virginia, forced him to resign in the following month. He later (1869) settled in New York as the cashier of the Union Square National Bank, of which he was one of the organizers.

Abraham Hart (b. in Hesse-Darmstadt, 1832), who arrived in this country at the age of eighteen, was a captain in the 73d Pennsylvania Infantry Regiment, and when Colonel Kolter, under whom he served, was elevated to the command of a brigade in General Blenker's Division of the Army of the Potomac, Captain Hart was detailed as Adjutant-General of the brigade. Moses Isaac of New York attained the same rank, that of adjutant-general in the Third Army Corps of the Army of the Potomac, and participated in the battles of the Peninsular campaign, subsequently serving under General Banks. Another New York Jew, of whom little else is known besides a brief notice by Mr. Wolf (p. 285), was Lieutenant-Colonal Leopold C. Newman, of the 31st Infantry Regiment of that state, whose foot was shattered by a cannon ball in the battle of Chancellorville (May 2, 1863), and he was taken to Washington, where he died. President Lincoln visited him at his bedside, and brought along his commission promoting him to the rank of Brigadier-General.

While the number of Jewish soldiers was proportionally large, and many of them became distinguished for bravery and were promoted to responsible positions, it was in the other branch of the service, the Navy, in which a member of the Jewish community attained the highest rank up to that time. Commodore Uriah Phillips Levy (b. in Philadelphia, 1792; d. in New York, 1862) held the highest rank in the United States Navy prior to the outbreak of the Civil War, though his age prevented him from participating in that struggle. Levy sailed as a cabin boy before he was eleven years old, and at the age of fourteen he was apprenticed as a sailor, and also attended a naval school for one year, becoming a second mate four years later. He soon rose to be first mate, and was master of a schooner at twenty. While he was on a cruise on the "George Washington," of which he was part owner as well as master, a mutiny took place, his vessel was seized and he was left penniless; but he managed to return to the United States, and after obtaining the necessary means, he secured the mutineers, brought them to the United States and had them convicted.

Levy received his commission from the United States Navy as sailing master in October, 1812, when the war with England had already begun. Until June 13 he served on the ship "Alert," doing shore duty; then he went on the brig "Argus," bound for France. The "Argus" captured several prizes, and Levy was placed in command of one, but the prize was recaptured by the English, and Levy and the crew were kept as prisoners for sixteen months in England. In 1816 he was assigned as sailing master to the "Franklin," and in March, 1817, he was appointed lieutenant in the Navy, which appointment was confirmed by the Senate.

Levy had many difficulties in the Navy, partly due to his promotion from the line, which is never popular among officers who receive their training at the Naval Academy, and partly, as he himself and many others thought, on account of his faith and descent. He fought a duel, in which he killed his opponent,

Commodore Uriah P. Levy.

was court-martialed six times, and finally dropped from the list as captain, to which rank he had been promoted. He defended his conduct before a court of inquiry in 1855, which restored him to the navy as captain. Subsequently he rose to the rank of commodore.

Levy was the descendant of an old Philadelphia family, always acknowledged his Jewish allegiance, and was one of the charter members of the Washington Hebrew Congregation. He purchased Monticello, the home of Thomas Jefferson, whom he greatly admired, and it is still owned by the family, the present owner being Congressman Jefferson M. Levy, a nephew of the commodore. A statue of Jefferson, presented to the government by Uriah P. Levy, is still standing in the Statuary Hall of the Capitol in Washington. Levy is buried in the portion of Cypress Hills Cemetery in New York which belongs to Congregation Shearit Israel (of which another nephew, Louis Napoleon Levy, a brother of the Congressman, is president), and on his imposing tombstone is recorded that "he was the father of the law for the abolition of the barbarous practice of corporal punishment in the United States Navy."

CHAPTER XXVII.

THE FORMATIVE PERIOD AFTER THE CIVIL WAR.

Ebb and flow of immigration between 1850 and 1880—Decrease and practical stoppage of Jewish immigration from Germany—The breathing spell between two periods of immigration, and the preparation for the vast influx which was to follow—The period of great charitable institutions—Organization and consolidation—The Hebrew Union College and the Union of American Hebrew Congregations—The Independent Order B'nai Brith—Other large fraternal organizations and their usefulness—Important local institutions in New York, Philadelphia, Chicago, etc.

The number of immigrants arriving in the United States increased in the middle of the last century, and reached its highest point of that period in 1854, when the new arrivals numbered 427,833. It then began to diminish, and fell to about 150,000 in 1860, and to less than 90,000 in each of the two first years of the Civil War, 1861 and 1862. In the following year it began to rise again, and in the two last years of the war, when the final outcome was already easily foreseen in the Old World, it was considerably above the three years preceding the beginning of the conflict. In 1865 there came 247,453; in 1867 (when the present system of figuring by the fiscal year, ending June 30, was adopted) they numbered 298,967, and only a little less in 1868. In 1869 it rose to 352,569; in 1870 to 387,203. After a slight relapse in 1871 to 321,350, it rose in 1872 to 404,806 and in 1873 to 459,803, when the current receded again on account of the slackening of all business activity which followed the panic of that year. It sank to as low as

138,469 in 1878, rose again to 177,826 in 1879, and to 457,257 in 1880, when the country had fully recovered from the effects of the panic, as well as from the ravages of the great struggle.

But while Germans formed a large part of those who arrived in the two or three decades after the war, the number of Jews who left that country was now very small, and sank to almost nothing about 1880. What was described by a Jewish traveler[1] as the second German-Jewish migration to America, which began about 1836, and to which "Bavaria contributed the largest quota of (Jewish) immigrants, because of her peculiarly harsh (anti-Jewish) marriage laws and commercial restrictions," practically ended in the decade of the Civil War, when the Jews were emancipated in most of the German states. The progress made by these immigrants in less than one generation can be best illustrated by quoting two passages from the same article by Mr. Kohler: "The early German settlers commonly arrived here without means, frequently without any education other than of the most rudimentary character." Subsequently (p. 102) he quotes a German-American politician, who wrote in 1869: "The German Jews in America gain in influence daily, being rich, intelligent and educated, or at least seeking education. They read better books than the rest of the Germans. . ."

This progress was largely accelerated by the great business activity which followed the war. A large number of the German-Jewish immigrants amassed wealth, and the stoppage of the arrival of new poor immigrants, or rather of poor relatives, reduced the number of the needy and helpless among them to an insignificant fraction. It may be said that it was during these fifteen years (1865-80), between the preceding large German-Jewish immigration and the following incomparably larger Russian-Jewish influx, that the Jews of the United States succeeded in bringing their communal house to order, and in preparing for their

[1] See Kohler, *German-Jewish Migration to America* in "Publications" IX, 96 ff.

historic mission of receiving the great masses which were soon to be driven thither from the Slavic countries by the iron hand of persecution. Most of the large charitable institutions, which are the pride of American Judaism, and have served to relieve want and pain in various forms, actually date from that period. The date of organization or original foundation is in most cases much earlier. But at the beginning these institutions were more like the small charities which are now founded by poor immigrants. There were very few great Jewish institutions in the United States prior to the Civil War, although most of the magnificent organizations in the older communities justly claim a continued existence from ante-bellum days. The largest number and the most important of them grew to their imposing size and vast usefulness in "the seventies," i. e., in that breathing spell which the Jews of America had between two periods of immigration.

The tendency to organize, to consolidate and take up the work of American Judaism in earnest, which characterized that period, manifested itself in the conferences of the Reform Rabbis, although as occasions for squabbles about destructive innovations and for extremely radical declarations, they deserve to be classed as ephemeral sensationalism rather than events of historical importance. It was at the third of these conventions, held in Cincinnati in June, 1871, that it was decided to establish the Hebrew Union College and to organize the Union of American Hebrew Congregations. The last named organization, which was founded in July, 1873, with thirty-four congregations, numbering about 1,800 members,[1] now comprises about two hundred congregations, with a total membership of nearly twenty thousand, and includes practically the entire American and Americanized German elements which are affiliated with Jewish religious institutions. The College, which was established two years later, has

[1] Rev. Joseph Krauskopf, *Half a Century of Judaism in the United States*, in "The American Jews' Annual" for 5648, p. 87.

Julius Bien.
Principal organizer of the Ind. Order B'nai B'rith.

educated nearly one hundred and fifty American Rabbis, some of whom have attained eminence as preachers and communal workers.

The Independent Order B'nai B'rith (Sons of the Covenant), which seems destined to be the great Jewish international organization of the future, though founded in 1843, did not assume its commanding position until about a quarter of a century afterward. It had less than 3,000 members in 1857. Three years after the close of the Civil War its membership rose to 20,000, which was probably a larger proportion of the Jewish population of the country at that time than it ever had before or after. It now has about 34,000 members, distributed in the seven districts into which it has divided the United States, and in Germany, Austria and Roumania, where there are flourishing lodges. A lodge has also recently been established in England. The guiding spirit of the order was Julius Bien (b. in Hesse-Nassau, Germany, 1826; d. in New York, 1909), who was its president in the years 1854-57 and 1868-1900. His successor was Leo N. Levi (b. in Victoria, Tex., 1856; d. in New York, 1904), who was in turn succeeded by the present incumbent, Adolf Kraus (b. in Bohemia, 1850; a. 1865), an eminent attorney, who has resided in Chicago since 1871, where he has served as President of the Board of Education, Corporation Counsel of the city and President of the Civil Service Commission.

While no other Jewish fraternal organization succeeded in accomplishing as much as the B'nai B'rith in communal or charitable work and in representing general Jewish interests for a number of years, other organizations of the same kind, which kept more strictly to the activities for the benefits of their own members, also originated in that period. They are the Order Brith Abraham (organized 1859) and its offshoots, the Kesher shel Barzel (founded 1860), the Independent Order Brith Abraham (1887), the Free Sons of Israel (1849), and the Free Sons of Benjamin (1879). The two Brith Abraham Orders, the second of which was formed by a secession from the first, have grown very fast of late years, the former having about 70,000 members of both sexes and the latter about twice that number. Like most of the other Jewish orders which originated later, the bulk of their membership consists of immigrants of the last period from the Slavic countries. Aside from the pecuniary benefits which members and their families derive from these organizations at lower rates than they could have obtained elsewhere, the educational value of these bodies is also great, for many obtain there the first glimpse of the systematic working of an organization which is amenable to its own rules.

As much, if not more, progress was made in that time with the founding of institutions which are considered as local in their character, but which in large communities like New York, Philadelphia or Chicago ultimately helped more people at a larger cost than many of the national organizations. The United Hebrew Charities of New York was organized in 1874, two years after the incorporation of the Home for Aged and Infirm Hebrews. The Mount Sinai Hospital was originally the Jews' Hospital (organized 1857), but it was then a small institution, and its large structure (which was abandoned for a still larger one in 1901) which first bore the name of Mount Sinai was erected in 1870. The Hebrew Benevolent Orphan Asylum, which was organized in its original form in the first quarter of the last century, had only thirty children, in a rented house, in 1860. Its first building, on the corner of Third avenue and Seventy-seventh street, was erected in 1862, and its magnificent structure on Amsterdam avenue more than twenty years afterwards. The Hebrew Sheltering Guardian Orphan Asylum Society was organized in 1879. The Hebrew Free School Association, which gave the impetus to the organization in later years of important educational institutions, like the Hebrew Technical Institute, the Technical School for Girls, and ultimately also to the Educational Alliance (originally The Hebrew Institute, organized 1891), originated in that period and existed until about 1899. The Young Men's Hebrew Association was organized in 1874.

Philadelphia likewise enjoyed much communal activity in that formative period of American-Jewish history. The first Jewish theological seminary in America, Maimonides College, was opened there in 1867 and existed for six years. The Hebrew Education Society, which was organized in 1848 and opened its school with twenty-two pupils in 1851, opened a second school in the vestry room of the Bene Israel Synagogue on Fifth street in 1878, and a third school on the northwest corner of Marshall street and Girard avenue in 1879. The first Jewish Hospital Association of that city was incorporated in 1865. The Jewish Maternity Association was founded in 1873. The Jewish Foster Home, which erected its first small building in 1855, was organized in its present form in 1874, since which time it has become one of the most important communal institutions there. The Young Men's Hebrew Association was organized in 1875, a year later than the one in New York.

The first Jewish Hospital in Chicago was erected on Lasalle avenue in 1868. It was destroyed by the great fire of 1871, and eight years later the funds which made possible the erection of the Michael Reese Hospital were donated for that purpose. The United Hebrew Charities of Chicago, originally the United Hebrew Relief Association, was organized in 1859, and changed its name later. The United Hebrew Charities of St. Louis was organized in 1875.

CHAPTER XXVIII.

NEW SYNAGOGUES AND TEMPLES. IMMIGRATION FROM RUSSIA PRIOR TO 1880.

Continued increase in the wealth and importance of the German-Jewish congregations—New and spacious synagogues and temples erected in various parts of the country in the "sixties" and the "seventies" —Problems of Russian-Jewish immigration prior to 1880—Economic condition of the Jewish masses in Russia worse in the "golden era" than under Nicholas I.—Emigration from Russia after the famine of 1867-68 and after the pogrom of Odessa in 1871—Presumption of the existence of a Hebrew reading public in New York in 1868—The first Hebrew and Yiddish periodicals.

The charitable institutions which were founded or enlarged in this period were not the only indication of the improved and settled condition of the Jews who came here in the preceding half century. These institutions were later to be even more enlarged, and numerous others were to be established to meet the demands made upon them in the following quarter century. It is to the synagogues or temples which date from these times that we have to turn in order to gain a true conception of the general condition of the Jews. In this respect there is a striking similarity between the condition of the Sephardim at the beginning of the nineteenth century and the German Jews at the end of its third quarter. In both cases the numerical growth almost stopped with the cessation of immigration from the home country. The small number of arrivals and the natural increase were barely enough to replace the losses through death and through estrangements which were caused by outright defections or by the slower process of mixed marriages. And just as the

Spanish and Portuguese element in American Judaism, which had barely held its own after the suspension of the Inquisition, permitted the surviving Marranos to remain where they were, and improved conditions in Western Europe obviated the necessity of the Sephardim of Holland, France or England looking for new homes, so did the much larger and more active German element practically stop growing numerically after the emancipation of the Jews in the German States. The number of Jews who arrived here from Germany after 1880 is insignificant, and the same may be said of the relative number of German-Jewish synagogues which were established after that time.

As a matter of fact the formation of German congregations stopped several years earlier. The better cohesiveness and discipline among the Americanized Jews made splits a very rare occurrence. Only in large cities the removal of many members of a congregation too far from the location of its synagogue caused the formation of new congregations, consisting mostly of members of older bodies, with some accessions of immigrants from the Slavic countries. In the smaller cities there is even now only one German-American congregation, usually dating from before the Civil War or from the decade following it. In the larger cities there may be several of them of about the same age, except in some communities, like Charleston, S. C., where the Spanish and the Germans are fused in the one Reform congregation, or in New York, where each section of the community is sufficiently large to have several congregations of its own.

It is therefore not to the increase in the number of German-Jewish congregations, but to their increase in wealth and importance, as demonstrated by the increase in the size and splendor of the synagogues and temples, that we have to look for proof of the great progress which was made in that period. The most representative congregations of New York have been described in the preceding parts of this work. In Philadelphia a new, spacious synagogue of its oldest congregation, Mickweh

Israel, was dedicated in 1860, and the new beautiful temple of the Congregation Rodef Shalom, "one of the earliest German-Jewish congregations in America," was built in 1870. Kehillat Anshe Maarab of Chicago had its first large synagogue ready (converted from a church) in 1868. The second oldest congregation, Bene Shalom, erected its first temple, on the corner of Harrison street and Fourth avenue, in 1864, "at that time the handsomest Jewish house of worship in Chicago." The third eldest, Sinai Congregation, purchased the site of its temple in 1872 (after the fire of 1871 had destroyed its former house of worship), and the structure was finished four years later. In distant California, Temple Emanuel, of San Francisco, was dedicated in 1866. In the District of Columbia (Washington) the first synagogue was dedicated in 1863 and the second in 1873. The old congregation of Savannah, Ga., erected a new and much larger synagogue in 1876.

Temple Achdut we-Shalom of Evansville, Ind., which was erected in 1856, was replaced by a more costly one in 1874. In Indianapolis, the capital and largest city of that state, a new temple was dedicated in 1868, about three years after the cornerstone was laid. The first temple of the Congregation Adath Israel of Louisville, Ky., was finished in 1868; about three years later congregations were organized in Owensboro and Paducah, in the same state. Temple Sinai of New Orleans, La., of which Dr. Maximilian Heller (b. in Prague, Bohemia, 1860), has been rabbi since 1887, dates from 1870. In Monroe, in the same state, a congregation was organized in that year, and in Shreveport, La., several years before. The synagogue of the Baltimore Hebrew Congregation, which was erected in 1845, was enlarged in 1860, while the "Chizzuk Amoonah," which seceded from it in 1871, erected its synagogue on Lloyd street five years later.

The older synagogues of both Boston, Mass., and Detroit, Mich., date from the same period. Mount Zion Congregation of St. Paul, Minn., was founded in 1871. Meridian, Natchez, Port Gibson and Vicksburg, in the State of Mississippi, have synagogues which originated within the decade of the war. The same is true of Kansas City, St. Joseph and St. Louis, in Missouri, and of Temple Israel of Omaha, Neb. The first houses of worship of Hoboken and Jersey City, N. J., were established about 1870, while in the largest city of that state, Newark, the synagogue (built 1858) of the Congregation B'nai Jeshurun (organized 1848) was replaced by an imposing temple which was dedicated in 1868.

In the State of New York, outside of its chief city, the same can be seen. The first considerable synagogue of Albany, that of Congregation Beth El, was erected in 1865. The first congregation of Buffalo, organized in 1847, built its own synagogue in 1874. In both of these cities, like in many others, larger and more costly temples were erected later; but there was much less wealth in the country in general after the Civil War, and a building costing fifty thousand dollars which was erected in the "sixties" or the "seventies" represented perhaps a further advance from preceding times than one three times as costly indicated in the "nineties." In some instances, like that of Rochester, where the first Jewish community was organized in 1848, the purchase of a spacious church building early in its career (1856) postponed the necessity of a large edifice until later. It was not until Rabbi Max Landsberg (b. in Berlin, 1845; a. 1871) had been with the Congregation "Berith Kodesh" of Rochester for nearly a quarter century that the present fine temple was erected (1894). In other communities divisions or splits made it impracticable to build large houses of worship until a later time; so we find that in Syracuse, where the first religious organization was formed in 1841, and the first synagogue was opened in 1846, a building erected in 1850 sufficed for the needs of the congregation more than half a century afterwards. This was because a new congregation was formed in 1854; another secession took place in 1864 and one more congregation was founded in 1870. Brooklyn, on account of its proximity to New York City, could not develop a really independent communal life until it had a very large Jewish population, and in some respects has not done so even yet. The Keap Street Synagogue, which dates from the period which we deal with in this chapter, was the largest of its kind in the city for many years.

* * * * *

The marked diminution or practical cessation of Jewish immigration from Germany by no means meant a stoppage of Jewish immigration. There was a steady flow of immigration from Russia, which, beginning with the exodus from Russian-Poland of 1845 (see above, page 189), has actually never ceased until this day, although it did not assume the immense proportions of the last thirty years. The "Aufruf" on behalf of the Russian-Jewish refugees, which Rabbi S. M. Schiller (Schiller-Szinessy, b. in Alt-Ofen, Hungary, 1820; d. in Cambridge, England, 1890) published in the *Orient* for 1846 (pp. 67-68), is a sufficient indication of the comparative antiquity of a problem which many suppose never arose until after the anti-Jewish riots in 1881. What is even less known in Western countries is that the economic condition of the Jews in Russia was much worse in the so-called "golden period" under Czar Alexander II. (1818-81) than under his more despotic predecessor. There was a popular saying among the Russian-Jews at that time—when it could not have occurred to anybody that these years of starvation would later be considered a golden age—that Czar Nicholas I. (1796-1855) wanted the persons of the Jews but left them their goods, while his son was less concerned about the persons, but despoiled them of their goods. This allusion to the passage in the Pentateuch (Gen. 14, 21), in which the king of Sodom says to Abraham "Give me the persons and take the goods to thyself," meant that Nicholas, who first began to enroll Jews in the Russian army and attempted to convert as many Jews to Christianity as possible, afforded the Jews in general better opportunities to earn a living than the more liberal Alexander. The fact that no proper provision was made for the Jews in the re-adjustment which followed the emancipation of the serfs, and that even the slight concessions, like the permission to skilled artizans to live outside of the "Pale of Settlement," were never carried out honestly, is at the bottom of much of the Jews' trouble there.

In less than five years after the emancipation of the Russian serfs there came a crisis, occasioned by the hard times which followed the crop failure of 1867, which caused "a state of distress in East Prussia and a famine on the other side of the border."[1] The Jews of Germany did much to alleviate the distress of the large number of Russian Jews who lived at that time in East Prussia, and also to send relief to the needy co-religionists of Western Russia. But then, as now, the suffering was too widespread and the general condition too hopeless to be relieved by almsgiving, and the result was an exodus of considerable magnitude. This new exodus was treated in a series of articles in the *Allgemeine Zeitung des Judenthums* of 1869 entitled "Auswanderung der Juden aus den Westrussischen Provinzen" (Emigration of Jews from the provinces of Western Russia). M. Anatole Leroy-Beaulieu (in his *Les Immigrants juifs et le Judaisme aux Etats-Unis,* Paris, 1905, p. 5) tells of 500 Jewish emigrants from Russian-Polland which the Alliance Israelite Universelle sent to the United States in 1869 from the famine stricken districts. The great anti-Jewish riot in Odessa on Passover, 1871, which shattered the hope of the Jews for emancipation in the then near future, and marked the beginning of the reaction which culminated in the reign of the following Czar, was also followed by cosiderable emigration of Jews. Many remained in Prussia, which was yet open for Russian subjects; but a large number proceeded to the United States, or went there after remaining for some time in England.

The Jewish population of the United States, and especially of the City of New York, was therefore constantly increasing,

[1] See Dr. Isaac Rülf (1834-1902), *Die Russische Juden,* Memel, 1892, p. 4 ff.

though neither the number of Jews nor the relative proportion as to country of origin is possible to ascertain for that time. Judge Daly (p. 56) quotes Joseph A. Scovil, author of "Old Merchants of New York" as saying (in 1868), "There are now 80,000 Israelites in this city, and it is the high standard of excellence of the old Israelite merchant of 1800 that has made the race occupy the proud position it now holds in this city and in the nation." Daly himself thought the number to be somewhat smaller. He says (p. 58), "The Jews have now (1872) in New York twenty-nine synagogues, and as a proportional part of the population they are now estimated at about 70,000."

Whether the lower estimate or the higher is nearer the truth, it is clear that there were already in New York a large number of Jews, and that a considerable portion of them were from Russia. A rare little volume in rabbinical Hebrew, entitled *Emek Rephaim,* against the heresy of the Reform Jews, which was published by the author, Elijah Holzman, a shochet from Courland, in New York, in 1868, is a good indication that there were already here at that time a sufficient number of readers of that language to warrant the publication of a work of that nature. As only the intellectual aristocracy among the Jews of the Slavic countries reads Hebrew and a large majority of the Russian-Jewish immigrants of that period belonged to the poorest and most ignorant classes, the belief in the existence of a Hebrew reading public, even if it proved to be a mistaken one, implies the presence of a large number of Russians.

The first attempts to establish periodicals for this public soon followed. Hirsch Bernstein (b. in Wladislavov or Neustadt-Schirwint, government of Suwalki, 1846; d. in Tannersville, New York, 1907) arrived in New York in 1870, and in the same year established the first Judaeo-German or Yiddish paper, and also the first periodical publication in the Neo-Hebraic language in the United States. The Yiddish publication, called "The Post," had a brief existence; but the second, *ha-Zofeh be' Erez ha-Hadashah,* of which Mordecai ben David Jalomstein

Kasriel H. Sarasohn.

(b. in Suwalki, 1835; a. 1871; d. in New York, 1897) was editor for most of the time, appeared weekly for more than five years. His brother-in-law, Kasriel H. Sarahson (b. in Paiser, Russian-Poland, 1835; d. in New York, 1905), who arrived in the United States in 1866, and settled in New York, founded there, in 1874, the weekly "Jewish Gazette," which, with its daily edition, the *Jewish Daily News* (established 1886), later became the most prosperous Jewish periodical publications in any country. Jalomstein was the principal contributor to these publications for about twenty years. Another Yiddish weekly, the *Israelitische Presse,* was founded in Chicago in 1879, by Nachman Baer Ettelson and S. L. Marcus. It had a Hebrew supplement, and existed for several years. The Jewish press in general will be treated in a later chapter; but it deserves to be mentioned here that some of the best representative Jewish papers of the country, like the *American Hebrew* of New York and the *Jewish Exponent* of Philadelphia (both founded in 1879) and the *Jewish Advance* of Chicago (founded 1878; existed about four years) contributed to place the Jews of the country in the proper condition for the reception of the large number of persecuted Jews which were soon to arrive.

PART VI.

THE THIRD OR RUSSIAN PERIOD OF IMMIGRATION.

CHAPTER XXIX.

THE INFLUX AFTER THE ANTI-JEWISH RIOTS IN RUSSIA IN 1881.

The country itself is well prepared for the reception of a larger number of Jewish immigrants—Absence of organized or political Anti-semitism—Increase in general immigration in 1880 and 1881—Arrival of the "Am Olam"—Imposing protest meetings against the riots in Russia—Welcome and assistance—Emma Lazarus—Heilprin and the attempts to found agricultural colonies—Herman Rosenthal—Failures in many States—Some success in Connecticut and more in New Jersey—Woodbine—Distribution—Industrial workers and the new radicalism.

The favorable economical and political conditions of the country itself were, however, the best preparation for the reception of a larger number of Jewish immigrants from Russia, who came as the result of the greatest Jewish migration since the exodus from Egypt. The strong congregations, the well-organized charities and the considerable number of wealthy Jews who were able and willing to assist the refugees, as well as the numerous able, energetic and tireless workers who did their best to alleviate the sufferings of the new arrivals and to help them to find their way in the new surroundings—all these were necessary and to some degree indispensable to solve as much of the problem as circumstances would permit. But all would have been useless if there was not room for new immigrants to settle here, and work for them to do. It would also have been well nigh impossible to take full advantage of the opportunities which this country offers to willing workers, were it not for the absence of that organized or official anti-Semitism which is found in one form or another in almost all civilized countries outside of the English-speaking world. Individual instances of social antipathy and personal dislike, or even hatred, of Jews, were not rare in the United States, at that period or at any other. But the Jew baiter was never encouraged, or even approved, by the all-powerful public opinion of the country at large; sympathy for the suffering Jew was easily aroused, and those who pleaded the cause of the victim of persecution were not hampered by open opposition or by covert political influences.

There was a sudden increase in immigration in the two years preceding the Russian influx. The country was recovering from the panic of 1873 and from the effect of the contraction of the currency which was incident to the resumption of specie payment by the government at the beginning of 1879. The number of immigrants who came here in 1876 was 169,986; in 1877 it fell to 141,857; in 1878 to 138,469. There was a slight rise in 1879 to 177,826; but in 1880 it jumped to 457,257 and in 1881 (in the fiscal year ending June 30, when there was as yet no increased immigration from Russia on account of the riots) to 669,431. The people who came were needed, as is the case with the million or more who had come here in the three years preceding the panic of 1907 and again in the last two or three years, which is proven by the fact that they are easily absorbed. Not only the general conditions, but even the times, were favorable for an increased Jewish immigration. There was neither economic nor national or racial cause for abstaining from giving those who fled from the *pogroms* the best public and open-hearted welcome that Jewish refugees ever received when coming in masses from one country to another.

The first of the anti-Jewish riots of that period took place in

Yelisavetgrad, on April 27, 1881. Another outbreak in Kiev followed on May 8, and there were "over 160 towns and villages in which cases of riot, rapine, murder and spoliation have been known to occur during the last nine months of 1881" (Joseph Jacobs, "Persecution of the Jews in Russia, 1881," p. 13). These riots, and the relief which was afforded to its victims, and especially to those who left Russia by way of Germany and Austria, have created a small literature of their own; but the subject in general belongs rather to the history of the Jews in Russia than to the present work, which can only be concerned with the emigrants after their arrival here. The first to arrive as a direct result of the riots, and among whom the new tendencies which were called forth by the calamities were prevalent to an appreciable degree, were included in a group of about 250 members of the "Am Olam" ("Eternal People") Society which came to New York July 29, 1881.

Unlike the time of the Damascus affair in 1840 (see above, p. 193), the Jews of America not only took the leading part in arousing public opinion against the outrages, but they could do much more than enlist the sympathies of their non-Jewish fellow-citizens: they collected money to aid the sufferers and bade them welcome to these shores. A call for "A meeting of the citizens of New York without distinction of creed, to be held on Wednesday evening, February 1st, 1882, . . for the purpose of expressing their sympathy with the persecuted Hebrews in the Russian Empire," was signed by about seventy-five of the most prominent non-Jewish citizens of New York, headed by ex-President U. S. Grant. The memorable meeting was held in Chickering Hall, and was presided over by Mayor William R. Grace; it was addressed by distinguished men in various walks of life, including three Christian clergymen, and had a marked effect on public opinion. It was on the same day that a similar meeting, at which the Lord Mayor presided, was held in London, at the Mansion House. Two weeks later (February 15) a meeting of the same nature with the same excellent moral result was held in Phila-

Emma Lazarus

delphia, where four clergymen, two of them Protestant Bishops and one representing the Roman Catholic Archbishop, were among the speakers. The Hebrew Immigrant Aid Society collected over $300,000 for the new arrivals, and nearly two-thirds of that sum was contributed by residents of this country, the balance coming from Germany, England and France. Some groups of immigrants were given a public welcome; temporary quarters were built for their accommodation on Ward's Island and at Greenpoint, L. I., where several thousand were housed and maintained until they found employment.

There was one other voice raised at that time in behalf of the Jew and of Judaism, only to be prematurely silenced forever a few years afterwards. The most gifted poet which American Jewry has produced, Emma Lazarus (b. in New York 1849; d. there 1887) was aroused, and her noble spirit reached its full height, by the stirring events of the martyrdom of the Russian Jew. Like so many other intelligent Jews in various countries, Emma Lazarus, the daughter of an old Sephardic family of social position, the friend of Emerson and other noted literary men, was up to that time mainly interested in general and classic subjects, and devoted to them her poetical and literary talents. "She needed a great theme to bring her genius to full flower, and she found that theme in the Russian persecution of 1881 . . . Her poetry took on a warmer, more human glow; it thrilled with the suffering, the passion, the exaltation of a nation of the Maccabees."[1] Her family, though nominally Orthodox, had hitherto not participated in the activities of the synagogue or of the Jewish community. But contact with the unfortunates from Russia led her to study the Bible, the Hebrew language, Judaism and Jewish history. She suggested, and in part saw executed, plans for the welfare of the immigrants. The fruit of her latter literary activity include *"Songs of the Semite"* (1882); *"An Epistle to the Hebrews"*; poems like *"The Banner of the Jew," "The*

[1] Adele Szold in *Emma Lazarus, a biographical sketch,* in "The Hebrew Standard" for December 1, 1905.

New Ezekiel," and *"By the Waters of Babylon: Little Poems in Prose"* (1887), her last published work. A collection of her works, in two volumes, appeared after her death (1889), and in 1903 a bronze tablet commemorative of her was placed inside the pedestal of the Statue of Liberty in New York harbor. (See *Jewish Encyclopedia,* s.v. Lazarus, Emma, by Miss Henriette Szold.)

The number of those who received direct assistance was only a small fraction of the arrivals from Russia at that time. According to the opinion of the author of the article *United States* in the "Jewish Encyclopedia," "The various committees and societies assisted about five per cent. of the total Jewish immigrants." One of the most active and self-sacrificing of the workers for the refugees, Michael Heilprin, who was himself brought up under the influence of the *Haskalah* movement, was, like all Maskilim of the old school, a strong believer in the theory that the Jewish problem was to be solved by inducing or helping the Jews to become agriculturists. Many of the immigrants who belonged to the class described as *Intellectuals* or *Intelligents,* whose dreams of political liberty and assimilation in Russia were shattered by the pogroms, also entertained fantastic notions about the virtue of agriculture. They fell in with all colonization plans, for which they had more enthusiasm than natural aptitude, and this gave rise to a series of experiments in the colonizing of Russian immigrants, none of which were immediately successful, though it contributed to the inception of a small class of Jewish farmers which is slowly growing in the United States, and in which many see considerable promise for the future.

The first Jewish agricultural colony of that period was founded on Sicily Island, Catahoula Parish, Louisiana. The settlers, including thirty-five families from Kiev and twenty-five from Yelisavetgrad, had been partly organized in Russia. Its leading spirit was Herman Rosenthal (b. in Friedrichstadt, Courland, 1843; a. 1881), who is now chief of the Slavonic department of the New York Public Library. Before the colony was fairly

Photo by Schill, Newark, N. J.

Herman Rosenthal.

started it was literally swept away by an overflow of the Mississippi in the spring of 1882, and the colonists scattered; a few of them, however, settling as independent farmers in Kansas and Missiouri. In July, 1882, Rosenthal headed another group of twenty families which formed the colony Cremieux, in Davison county, in the present State of South Dakota. It led a precarious existence for about three years and was finally abandoned. Another attempt, which was made by the Alliance Israelite Universelle, with the formation of a colony surnamed "Betlehem Yehudah," in the same region, was no more successful. Colonies founded in the same year in Colorado and Oregon met with no better fate. The colonies founded in North Dakota (one), in Kansas (five), in Michigan (one), and in Virginia (two) remain but memories. Those founded later in Connecticut were more successful, and some of them are still in existence and even growing. The most successful were those established in New Jersey, where four of the nine which were founded there since 1882 are still in existence and, considering the drawbacks of such enterprises, are in a flourishing condition. They are: Alliance, Salem county, founded by the Alliance Israelite in 1882; Carmel, Cumberland county, founded by the aid of Michael Heilprin in the same year; Rosenhayn, in the same county, which owes its origin to six families which were settled there by the Hebrew Emigrant Aid Society of New York in 1883; and Woodbine, Cape May county, which was founded by the trustees of the Baron de Hirsch Fund in 1891, and is the largest as well as the most thriving of all Jewish colonies in America. Woodbine now has over two thousand inhabitants, and is an incorporated borough with a government of its own, which was instituted in 1903, with Professor Hirsch Loeb Sabsovich (b. in Berdyansk, Russia, 1860; a. 1888), the former superintendent of The Baron de Hirsch Agricultural and Industrial School of that place, as the first Mayor. He was succeeded by M. L. Bayard, who is likewise a native of Russia.

While the assistance rendered to the needy immigrants, and

the large sums expended in the formation of colonies and in supporting them, attracted the most attention, a larger number were effectively helped by being distributed over various parts of the country where they could engage in trade or find work for which they were much better fitted than for farming. The largest number received little, if any, assistance, except such as was rendered by their relatives or countrymen whom they found here. The least successful and those who became helpless or dependent from various causes were assisted by the old charitable institutions, which were enlarged or strengthened by the new demands made upon them, and by new ones which sprang up everywhere as the occasion required. But the bulk of the new comers succeeded remarkably well, and many of them were soon in a position to assist those who came after them, and to contribute to charities from which they received assistance but a short time before, or to found new charitable institutions which were conducted in a manner more suitable to the character of the immigrants.

The number of applicants to Jewish charitable institutions was increasing, and so was the number of people who crowded the districts in the larger cities where Jews live together. But in both cases there was going on a continual change, due to the steady inflow of new immigrants, on the one hand, and on the other to the steady rising in the social and economic scale, and the continued departure to other and better neighborhoods or to other cities. The same people did not apply for charity or dwell in tenement houses long. They soon made room for those who came after them, and what seemed to the superficial observer a solid, unmovable mass of poverty and helplessness which presented a very difficult problem, was in reality in a state of constant flux. This transient, fleeting mass slowly spread over the country, until we find communities of Jewish immigrants practically in every city in the Union, and hardly a place without some individuals of that class. Most of those Jewish immigrants living in smaller places, as well as almost all of them who live in more comfortable quarters in the large cities or their suburbs, passed through the tenement house districts or the so-called "Ghetti"; which proves that the distribution considered by some as a desirable process which must be artificially accelerated, is actually being accomplished by the free movement of individuals and is hardly noticed.

The number of those who remained, though temporarily, in the congested centers of population, especially in New York, was very large, and was constantly becoming larger, because more immigrants came in each year than the number of those who left those centers. This mass was hardly affected by the small withdrawals from it for the purpose of colonization. It was too large and was replenished too fast to be able to disperse as small traders over the country or to go in business even on a small scale in the cities, as did the smaller number of Jewish immigrants who came in the former periods. And so, after all deductions are made, including those who went to become farmers and those who went to become peddlers, of those whose intelligence and the learning which they brought with them enabled them, sometimes with a little aid, to pursue their studies; and those whose business acumen or the small capital which they brought, enabled them to engage in trade and to prosper in a short time—after all these deductions, there remained a very large class, steadily increasing by the excess of arrivals over departures, which could do the only thing which poor people can do in a country where capital is abundant and industries flourish—go to work. The Jewish immigrants soon began to fill the factories and the shops, especially those of the clothing trade, which was then to a certain extent already in Jewish hands. The trades to which they flocked began to extend fast; immigrant workers themselves soon ventured to open small shops, where they employed those who came after them. While wages were comparatively small and "sweating" was common, the earnings were so much above what the poor man can make in Russia, and the standard of living so much higher than the one to which the laborer is accustomed over there, that even those who worked under what an

American would consider the worst circumstances, soon saved enough money to begin sending for their families, their relatives, and even their friends. The great mass was solving its own problem by hard work and by thrift; it built up and multiplied the industries in which it was occupied, and thus made it easy to absorb the newcomers year by year and to become a part of the great industrial army which is doing the work of the country.

Thus there arose a third and new class of Jewish immigrants, unlike the first or Sephardic small groups who came here usually with large means and took their position among the higher classes as soon as they arrived; also unlike the second and larger groups of German, Polish and Hungarian Jews who came in the second period, most of whom began as peddlers and artizans, but ultimately became merchants or professional men. Among the immigrants of the third period, which began in 1881, there were many men of means and skilled men who at once joined the better situated classes. There were also among them a large number who took up peddling or petty trade with various degrees of success. But the agriculturists and the industrial workers, or proletariat, are distinctive features of the new period. The colonist was mostly assisted and usually failed; then he joined the trading or the working classes in the cities. The industrial classes took care of themselves and fared much better. Even their new problems presented difficulties which were more apparent than real. The seeming persistence in errors which are characteristic of those who are here only a short time is easily explained when it is considered that in cities like Philadelphia or Chicago there are always thousands, and in New York there are always tens of thousands, of Jewish immigrants from Slavic countries who came to this country within the last year. So there is always at hand a mass which is not aware of what a similar mass—which to the outsider seems the same—did a year before; and what seem to be repetitions year after year of the same actions which lead to the same results or to the same lack of results, are actually experiments made but once by each successive wave of immigration and soon abandoned, only to be taken up later as a novel experience by those who come later.

As the worker succeeded the trader, so the political extremist comes to the fore in this period, as the radical in religious matters did in the former. Many of the "intellectuals" sympathized with the revolutionary movement in Russia, and were infected by the Socialistic virus which is the bane of that movement and has made its success well nigh impossible. While the German or Austrian revolutionary of the "forties" or "fifties" wanted nothing for his fatherland which the people of the United States did not already enjoy, the Russian theorist was dreaming of a social revolution and of fantastic victories for the peasantry and the proletariat which should put Russia far in advance of the civilization of the "rotten West." There was plenty of opportunity under the freedom of speech and of the press prevailing in this country "to continue the struggle against capital" among the sweat-shop workers. For a while the Socialist agitator became the most active leader among the immigrant masses; the "maskilim," or half-Germanized, Hebrew scholars were forced into the background, and the large Orthodox majority confined itself to the ever-increasing number of synagogues and kept quiet, as usual. But as the years went by and the immigrants of the beginning of the period became more Americanized and more conservative, it became clear that radicalism was a passing phase in the development of the Russian-Jewish immigrant, that the largest number outgrow it in several years at the utmost, and that the extreme movements depend almost entirely on the new arrivals who are attracted by its novelty, and on those who cater to them. Excepting what may be described as a pronounced tendency to Socialism in the Yiddish sensational press—differing in degree more than in kind from the general press of that type—the Socialist movement has not held its own proportionally among the Russian immigrants, and the fears of some of their friends that the neighhorhoods where the noisy agitation was carried on would develop into politically Socialistic strongholds, were dispelled almost before the first decade of this period was over.

CHAPTER XXX.

COMMUNAL AND RELIGIOUS ACTIVITIES AMONG THE NEW COMERS.

Congregational and social activities among the new comers—Ephemeral organizations—The striving after professional education—Synagogues as the most stable of the new establishments—"Landsleut" congregations—The first efforts to consolidate the Orthodox community of New York—The Federation of Synagogues—Chief Rabbi Jacob Joseph—Other "chief rabbis" in Chicago and Boston—Prominent Orthodox rabbis in many cities—Dr. Philip Klein—The short period in which the cantor was the most important functionary in the Orthodox synagogue—Synagogues change hands, but are rarely abandoned.

A large majority of the Russian immigrants, like the overwhelming majority of the Jews in Russia, were Orthodox Jews, and the younger men who were temporarily attracted by the radical movements which were, in Russian fashion, mostly antireligious, began drifting back into the synagogues as soon as they grew older and became more settled and more Americanized. The older and the middle-aged needed congregational life from the moment of their arrival, and this gave rise to the establishment of a surprisingly large number of new synagogues in all places where the new arrivals settled. The situation in New York is again typical; the twenty-nine congregations in 1872 increased more than tenfold in about sixteen years, which far exceeds the growth of charitable institutions, of labor-organizations and of fraternal or self-education societies, all of which were springing up at that time in large numbers. The legal restrictions which make the organization of any form of societies a difficult matter in Russia, were to some extent responsible for the formation of numerous organizations here for the most variegated number of purposes. The ease with which a charter or papers of incorporation could be obtained, tempted many to form themselves into organizations to enjoy that privilege; while the equally novel experience of being permitted to form organizations without obtaining charters, to hold meetings and elect officers without fear of interference by the authorities, was another strong inducement to overdo things in the matter of organizations. But that same lack of experience was also the cause of unfamiliarity with voluntary corporate existence and of inability to hold the organization together after it was formed. A large percentage of the societies formed existed only a short time; the same was true of all forms of organizations, especially of labor unions. Only those which were subject to the discipline of a central body—notably lodges which form part of the larger and better conducted orders—showed a better proportion of survivals.

The conditions prevailing in Russia were also largely the cause of the disproportionately large number of young people who attempted, by their own efforts or assisted by their often hard pressed parents, to study for the professions. Under the educational restrictions in Russia only the highly gifted or the children of the wealthy could hope to enter the higher institutions of learning; here the same opportunities were open to all alike, with free education up to the universities. It was natural for the poor to strive to make use of those opportunities, and to spare no efforts to enter the ranks of the college graduates, who are looked upon by the Russian populace as superior beings.

But in the course of years, as the proportion of those who are more Americanized became larger, and the newer arrivals, though they kept on coming in increasing numbers, were in a constantly diminishing minority as compared with the entire mass of immigrants, there was a decrease in the number of hastily conceived and immature organizations, and a larger proportion of those which were formed had sufficient strength to survive. Of late years there has been even a slackening of the rush for higher or professional education among the children of the poorer classes; which is also partly due to the more exacting requirements for entrance into the better class of colleges and universities.

All these economic, fraternal and educational activities—the last, of course, only as far as it concerns adults who could not benefit by the public school system—and the agitation about political and economic questions, and, to some extent, even the occupation of the immigrants, were novel experiences and largely temporary. The only activity which might be considered as normal, and to which there was a constant reversion even among those who abandoned it abruptly—one may almost say, violently—was that relating to the synagogue. As compared with other institutions, a surprisingly small number of congregations formed by the immigrants succumbed; and the steady increase in the number and solidity of these religious establishments, as well as of the Talmud Torahs, or religious schools, and later of the Yeshibot or strictly Orthodox Talmudical academies, are the best proof of Israel's taking root in the United States. Most of the work of a public or semi-public character in the new Jewish settlements or communities, including even the work of numerous charitable institutions ministering to wants which are due to the exigencies of immigration, cannot in the nature of things be otherwise than temporary, even if they last for decades. It is only the building of synagogues which represents that continuity of Jewish existence throughout the centuries, which unites us with the Jews of other countries and other times, and demonstrates the ability and the willingness of the Jewish masses to support the old faith under all circumstances.

These thousands of small synagogues all over the country, of which there are now about eight hundred in New York, bear also strong marks of Slavic, especially Russian, influence. The only place where it was safe for Jews to gather and have intercourse in that country was the synagogue, which for that reason served not only as a house of worship, but also as a meeting room, and, to some degree, as a club house. Here it served all these purposes for the old-fashioned Jew, to whom the new social organizations which grew up here remained strange or became repugnant after a short contact. In addition to this, the—exceedingly unchurchlike—small synagogue is usually composed of members who come from the same town in the Old Country, or from the same district. The "landsleute" meet there, receive the newest arrivals and the latest news from home; it is not unfrequently made the headquarters for extraordinary charitable activity when the home town is visited by a conflagration or a "Pogrom."

The tendency is to break away from those little synagogues and to join larger ones in the more comfortable neighborhoods, as well as to enlarge them by admitting members who hail from other towns and even from other countries. But the changes are mainly accomplished by slow transition, the gaps which are left by departures are easily filled up by new arrivals; so that the transformation is much nearer to a slow process of evolution than to the "decay of Judaism in this country" of which many are complaining. The earliest manifestation of this new development was the first effort which was made, less than a decade after the beginning of the new immigration, to consolidate the Orthodox Jewish community of New York under the leadership of a great rabbinical authority, and to raise the expense of the new institution by the same method by which the Jewish communities of Russia are financed—by an income from the Kosher-meat business.

In Russian-Poland, as in Germany or Austria, members of the Jewish community pay a direct tax for the support of the rabbinate and the communal institutions, and while the Jewish taxpayers elect the officers who assess them, the tax or "etat" is collectible by force, i. e., with the aid of the police authorities, if it is not paid voluntarily. Only those members of the community who pay comparatively larger sums are entitled to vote for communal officers, so that the poorer classes are taxed without being represented in the governing body of the community, and the very poor are not taxed at all. In Russia proper, including Lithuania and the balance of the "pale of settlement," where the masses of the Jews dwell, the "Korobka" or tax on Kosher meat (more correctly a tax on the slaughtering of animals for Kosher food) takes the place of the "etat" of Poland and the "Kultussteuer" of some western countries. This indirect tax, which rests more heavily on the poor, is less felt and therefore considered less burdensome, though it is and always has been hated by the Jewish masses in Russia. The absolute separation of Church and State in this country made any form of enforced taxation out of the question. And when the want of a recognized religious authority for the large mass of Orthodox Jews of New York began to be seriously felt, and the question of providing for his salary and for other communal needs of a general nature, for which the individual synagogues did not feel themselves bound to provide, became a subject for discussion among the public spirited Jews in the community, the plan of a control over the business of Kosher meat, over which the new rabbi should have complete religious supervision, suggested itself as the only practicable solution of the problem.

A Federation of Congregations, comprising about fifteen of the more important Orthodox synagogues, was consequently formed in 1888, and one of the greatest rabbinical authorities of Russia, Rabbi Jacob Joseph (b. in Krozh, government of Kovno, Russia, 1840; a. 1888; d. in New York, July 28, 1902), who was at that time the preacher of the old Jewish community of Wilna, was brought over as Chief Rabbi of the Federation. He was received with great honor by the Orthodox masses, and was recognized by them as the greatest rabbi that ever came to this country. But the federation of synagogues soon fell to pieces; the scheme of controlling the supervision of the Kosher meat supply failed almost from the beginning. There was too much prejudice against a form of "Korobka" even among the Orthodox masses, despite the fact that they continued to pay, as they still do, a higher price for Kosher meat, and a systematization of the busi-

Chief Rabbi Jacob Joseph.

ness could produce a large revenue for communal purposes without a further increase in the price. Many independent Orthodox rabbis did not submit to the authority of the great rabbi; his influence was weakened, and several years afterward he fell the victim of a severe illness, which incapacitated him for hard work or for leadership. But the failure of the system was due to the impossibility of conducting Jewish affairs in America after patterns designed in and for Russia. The chief rabbi personally was revered by the multitudes of religious Jews, and when he died after a lingering illness, his funeral (July 30, 1902), though it was marred by a disturbance in which a number of persons were injured, was one of the most imposing ever seen in New York.

Several other attempts to choose chief rabbis, with the hope of uniting or solidifying under them the Orthodox congregations of a large city, were not more successful. The most notable of them was the selection, by a union of congregations which was formed for that purpose in Chicago, of another great Talmudical scholar, Rabbi Jacob David Wilowski (Ridbaz, b. in Kobrin, government of Kovno, 1845), as its chief rabbi in 1903. Rabbi Wilowski, who was Rabbi Joseph's predecessor in Wilna, first came to the United States in 1900 in the interest of his great work on the Talmud Yerushalmi. It was during his second visit to this country that the effort to detain him as the spiritual head of a united Orthodox community in the second largest city of the New World was made. But a strong opposition, which centered around Rabbi Zebi Simon Album, made his position untenable, and he resigned after holding it for ten months. After travelling for more than a year over the United States, he left (1905) for the Holy Land and settled in Safed, where he still resides. It was again seen in his case, and confirmed because it occurred fifteen years after the importation of the first and greatest chief rabbi in the greatest Jewish community, that both the rabbis and the religious laymen are too independent here to submit to a chief rabbi, regardless of his importance as a Talmudical authority. The last to assume the title was Rabbi Gabriel Zeeh Margolioth (b. in

Wilna, 1848; a. 1906), who is considered the greatest rabbinical scholar among the Orthodox rabbis of the United States. Rabbi Margolioth held the office of Chief Rabbi in Boston about four years, until his removal (1911) to New York to become rabbi of the "Adat Israel."

In most of the other large cities there are prominent Orthodox rabbis who are held in high esteem and recognized as spiritual leaders of the religious masses, although their actual jurisdiction extends only over the one or several congregations of which they are the appointed rabbis. The best known of that class in New York was the "Moscower Rab" Chayyim Jacob Vidrevitz (b. in Dobromysl, government of Mohilev, 1836; a. 1891; d. in New York, 1911). Among the living, Rabbi Moses Zebullon Margolioth (b. in Krozh, 1851; a. 1889), formerly of Boston; Rabbi Abraham Eliezer Alperstein (b. in Kobrin about 1854; a. 1881), formerly of Chicago; and Rabbi Shalom Elhanan Jaffe (b. in Wobolnik; government of Wilna, 1858; a. 1889), formerly of St. Louis, are among the better known of the numerous Orthodox rabbis of New York.

Outside of New York Rabbi Abraham Jacob Gerson Lesser (b. in Mir, government of Minsk, 1835; a. about 1880), formerly of Chicago, and for about the last ten years in Cincinnati, is considered the dean of the Orthodox rabbis in this country. He is the author of several rabbinical works, one of which was translated into English by Mr. H. Eliassof. Of about the same age is the nestor of the Chicago rabbinate, Rabbi Eliezer Anixter, who occupied the rabbinical position there for about forty years. In Philadelphia Rabbi Bernhard Louis Levinthal (b. in Kovno, 1864; a. 1891) occupies a leading position and is perhaps the most Americanized of the strictly Orthodox rabbis in the country. Rabbi Moses Simon Sivitz (b. in Zittawan, government of Kovno, 1853; a. 1886), formerly of Baltimore (1886-89), and Rabbi Aaron Mordecai Ashinsky (b. in Reygrod, Russian-Poland, 1866), formerly of Detroit, Mich., and Montreal, Canada, are the foremost representatives of the Orthodox element in Pittsburg, Pa. Rabbi Asher Lipman Zarehy (b. in Kovno, 1862; a. 1892), formerly of Brooklyn, N. Y. (1892), and of Des Moines, Ia. (1893-1903), is at the head of the United Orthodox Hebrew Congregations of Louisville, Ky.

The number of prominent Orthodox rabbis among the immigrants who came from other countries than Russia is comparatively very small. The Hungarians, who belong to an earlier period, slowly draw nearer to the German and American element in religious matters. The Austrians or Galicians, who began to arrive in larger numbers somewhat later than the Russians, took a longer time to settle down to local conditions, and being at liberty to return to their old home whenever they liked, the large number who went back, only to return again in a few years, retarded the gradual development of their communal life. They are, on the other hand, much more successful, relatively, in their social organizations, such as lodges and "landsleut" societies, on account of the larger liberty of organization which they enjoyed at home. Their leading rabbi in New York was Rabbi Naftali Reiter (born in Hungary, 1844; a. 1887; d. in New York, 1911), who officiated as rabbi of the Congregation Magen Abraham Dukler (Attorney street), the leading Galician synagogue of New York from 1893 until his death. The leading Hungarian rabbi of New York is Dr. Hillel ha-Kohen or Philip Klein (b. in Baraeska, Hungary, 1849; a. 1891), who occupies a unique position in the Jewry of New York and of the country, being recognized as a Talmudical authority, and at the same time possessing the secular learning obtained by studying at the University of Berlin. Dr. Klein was rabbi of Libau, Russia, for ten years before he came to this country to officiate as rabbi of the Hungarian Congregation Oheb Zedek of New York, which position he still holds.

* * * * *

At the beginning of the period of development among the Jewish immigrants from Slavic countries it was, however, not the rabbi, but the hazzan or cantor who was considered the most important functionary of the Orthodox congregation, especially of the larger ones. The number of wealthy members was insignificant, and while the smaller congregations holding services in rented rooms could subsist on the modest contributions and donations from regular attendants and from those who came occasionally for the high holidays or on account of marriages, the naming of newborn children, "jahrzeiten," etc., the large synagogue with a building of its own, which was usually heavily mortgaged, often had a hard struggle for existence. The rabbi, unless he was a popular preacher, was considered as a somewhat superfluous burden; he received only a small salary, or none at all, having to rely for a living on the emoluments of the rabbinical office. But a popular cantor attracted new members and also large audiences on the special occasions when a charge for admission was made. His salary was therefore considered a profitable investment, and some of the best known cantors of Russia were induced to come to America, especially to New York.

The most renowned among the synagogue singers who were brought over in that period were Israel Michalovsky (b. in Suwalki, Russian-Poland, 1831; a. 1886; d. in New York, 1911), Israel Cooper (b. in Alusenitz, government of Kamenetz-Podolsk, 1840; a. 1885; d. in New York, 1909), and Pinhas Minkovsky (b. in Byelaya Tzerkov, 1859), who, after spending a short time in New York, returned, in 1892, to Odessa, whence he came. But the circumstances under which the influence of the cantor was predominant were abnormal and could not last long. The improvement in the general material conditions, the increase in the number and proportion of wealthy members, and the growing sense of duty and responsibility in religious matters, helped to bring the rabbi nearer to the front, where he belongs. There are even now many excellent and well paid hazzanim in the large cities, and the Orthodox rabbis are yet far from the security of tenure and of income which is enjoyed by the rabbis in the Old World. But some sort of an equilibrium has been restored, and the rabbinate has gained, morally as well as materially.

In the last few years many of the larger synagogues in the older Jewish neighborhoods of the great cities have been again in a precarious financial condition, which is due to the removal of its older and wealtheir members to the more fashionable quarters or to the suburbs. But no one would think now, as it was thought a quarter century before, of attempting to strengthen the position of a snyagogue by the importation of a famous hazzan. In many cases the well-to-do older members feel it to be their religious duty to keep up the large synagogues which they built in districts which are now inhabited mostly by the poorer and later arrivals, though they themselves now live too far to reach it, and have built new synagogues in their new neighborhoods and have even engaged English-speaking rabbis to deliver sermons. In other instances the immigrants of latter years are ready and willing to take over the synagogues, sometimes by the simple method of joining as members and obtaining control by becoming the majority. It also happens that the synagogue itself is removed to a location to which most of the members have moved, and the old building is sold to a smaller or to a newly formed congregation. But, as it was stated above, the number of congregations which disbanded, and of synagogue buildings which are abandoned for other purposes, is small. The continuance of immigration and the steady increase among the earlier comers of the number who affiliate themselves with the religious community obviates the necessity of giving up old religious organizations at the time when new ones are being established all over the country.

CHAPTER XXXI.

NEW COMMUNAL AND INTELLECTUAL ACTIVITIES.

The Jewish Alliance of 1891 as the first attempt to form a general organization in which the immigrants of the latest period should be officially recognized—Some of the prominent participators—The new Exodus of 1891—The Baron de Hirsch Fund—Various activities—Decrease in the numbers and proportion of the helpless and the needy—The American Jewish Historical Society—The Jewish Publication Society of America—The Jewish Chautauqua—Participation in the World's Columbian Exposition in 1893—The Council of Jewish Women.

In less than a decade after the first influx from Russia, an attempt was made to establish some form of co-operation between the immigrants of the new period and the American or Americanized Jews who belonged to the former periods. The latter were complaining that the burden of charities was becoming too heavy, while from the former, especially from the more intelligent immigrants who were interested in Jewish matters, there arose even at that early date a demand for recognition and a share of responsibility in communal work. The theory that the two elements, described respectively as the German and the Russian, must be brought nearer together, and that the latter element must be prepared to take over the hegemony of the Jewish community from the former, just as the German took it over from the Sephardim, was already then, as it is to some extent still now, a favorite with those who consider themselves representatives of the immigrants. And it was the effort to apply part of this theory to practice, and perhaps, according to some, to put it to the test, that a call was issued for a convention of the Jewish Alliance of America, which met in Philadelphia on February 15, 1891.

Nineteen cities were represented, some of them as far as San Francisco, Cal. (by Bernhard Marks), and Portland, Ore. (David Solis-Cohen). Boston was represented by David Blaustein (b. in Lida, Russia, 1866; a. 1886), who later became eminent as an educator and communal worker. The Hon. Simon Wolf (b. in Rhenish Bavaria, 1836; a. 1848), a recognized representative in Washington of the Jews of the country, came from the capital. There were twenty delegates from Baltimore, including Samuel Dorf and B. H. Hartogensis. Chicago sent six men, including Dr. A. P. Kadison and Leon Zolotkoff (b. in Wilna, 1865(?); a. 1887). Among the seven delegates from New York were the Russian immigrants Nicholas Aleinikoff and P. Caplan, and the native American, Ferdinand Levy (b. in Milwaukee, Wis., 1843), who served in the Union army with his father and two brothers during the Civil War, and held various offices in New York City and in Jewish fraternal organizations. The largest contingent was, of course, from Philadelphia, its fifty-four delegates including many well-known men from both elements, like the inventor, Louis E. Levy (b. in Bohemia, 1846), Dr. Solomon Solis-Cohen, a native of Philadelphia; Bernhard Harris, who was chosen secretary, and Dr. Charles D. Spivak (b. in Krementshug, Russia, 1861; a. 1882), who was president of the temporary organization.

A constitution was adopted and a permanent organization formed, of which a well known local Jewish philanthropist, Simon Muhr (b. in Bavaria, 1845; d. in Philadelphia, 1895), was elected president; Simon Wolf, treasurer, and Bernhard Harris, secretary. The board of trustees which was elected included, as representatives of New York, the communal leader, Daniel P. Hays (b. in Pleasantville, N. Y., 1854), and the educator, Henry M. Leipziger (b. in Manchester, England, 1854). There was some enthusiasm in numerous communities for the plan which was "to unite Israelites in a common bond for the purpose of more effectually coping with the grave problems presented by enforced emigration . . ." and thirty-one branches were formed throughout the country.[1] But the entire plan came to nothing. In February, 1892, the Jewish Alliance was consolidated with "The American Committee for Ameliorating the Condition of the Russian Refugees," which was organized in New York apparently for the purpose of heading off the activity of the Alliance. Both organizations were soon forgotten, and the historical value of the Alliance consists chiefly in its having been the first formal manifestation of a desire which was partly satisfied in an entirely different manner fifteen years later by the formation of the American Jewish Committee.

There was another recurrence of persecutions in Russia in the same year, which did not take the sensational form of massacre and pillage, but had as much or even more effect in forcing Jews to leave the country. Relentless expulsions from Moscow and from villages in which the Jews have dwelt peacefully and on good terms with their neighbors forced tens of thousands to leave the country, and as many of them now had relatives or friends in the United States, it was natural for them to turn their faces towards the New World. Conditions were again favorable, for several reasons. The tide of general immigration, which fell from 788,992 in 1882 to 334,203 in 1886, rose after some vaccillations in the following three years to 455,302 in 1890, to 560,319 in 1891 and to 623,084 in 1892. In the year ending June 30, 1893, which includes a few months of the hard times which began in the spring of that year, the number of immigrants was still as high as 502,917, and it is only in the following twelvemonth, when only 314,467 arrived, and in 1895, when immigration fell to 279,948, which was the lowest number since 1879, that the deterrent effects of the panic of 1893 were visible.

Not only had the Jews in general made progress in the decade after 1881, and were better able to cope with the new situation because they discovered their own strength in the work

[1] See Morais, *The Jews of Philadelphia*, p. 142, and also *Constitution of the Jewish Alliance of America*, etc., Philadelphia, 1891.

of helping their less fortunate brethren, and had also learned by experience that the new element adjusted itself to the new surroundings with remarkable rapidity, but there was also a new agency to assist in the work of helping some of the newcomers to find their way to work and independence. The great Jewish philanthropist, Baron Maurice de Hirsch (b. in Munich, Bavaria, 1831; d. in Hungary, 1896), some time before the new increase of immigration from Russia, created and endowed the Baron de Hirsch Fund for the ameliorating of the condition of certain Jewish immigrants in the United States. The fund, which he originally endowed with the sum of $2,400,000 (and which had grown later to nearly a million more), was incorporated under the laws of the State of New York, February 12, 1891, the trustees being: M. S. Isaacs, president; Jacob H. Schiff (b. in Frankfort o. t. Main, 1847; a 1865), vice-president; Jesse Seligman (b. in Bavaria, 1827; d. in California, 1894), treasurer; Dr. Julius Goldman (who later became president), honorary secretary. The other trustees were Henry Rice (b. in Bavaria, 1835; a. 1850), who for many years was president of the United Hebrew Charities of New York; James H. Hoffman and Oscar S. Straus (b. in Germany, 1850; a. 1854), of New York, and Mayer Sulzberger (b. in Hildesheim, Baden, 1843; a. 1848) and William B. Hackenburg (b. in Philadelphia, 1837), of Philadelphia. Adolphus S. Solomons (b. in New York, 1826; d. in Washington, 1910) was the first general agent. The present trustees are: Eugene S. Benjamin, president; Jacob H. Schiff, vice-president; Murry Guggenheim, treasurer; Max J. Kohler, honorary secretary; Nathan Bijur, Abram I. Elkus, Henry Rice, Louis Siegbert, S. G. Rosenbaum, all of New York City; Mayer Sulzberger, W B. Hackenburg and S. S. Fleischer, of Philadelphia. H. L. Sabsovich succeeded A. S. Solomons as general agent.

The trustees of this fund, which has an annual income of about $125,000, at first used the amount at their disposal in relieving the immediate necessities of the refugees, and in order to make the immigrants self-supporting, a number of them were given instruction in the work which is required in the manufacture of elothing, white goods, etc. The United Hebrew Charities of New York was made the agent through which the material necessities were relieved, and certain sums are still granted by the fund to institutions which make a specialty of assisting immigrants. On the other hand, the fund itself is receiving assistance from the Jewish Colonization Association (I. C. A., to which Baron de Hirsch left a large share of his fortune) in the activities which it carries on through the Jewish Agricultural and Industrial Aid Society for the encouragement of farming, and the Industrial Removal Office, for the distribution of workingmen from the crowded centers of population to places further inland (both of these institutions were organized in 1900). When the great pressure due to the rapid immigration had somehwat relaxed, the trustees carefully matured their plans of education and of colonization, doing a large amount of good with the various forms of instruction, including technical as well as elementary knowledge; while the colonization plans, which resulted in the establishment of the colonies which have been mentioned in a former chapter, meet with so many difficulties that progress is made at a less rapid pace.

The Jews of America were thus even better prepared to receive a large number of Jewish immigrants at the beginning of the last decade of the nineteenth century than they were ten years before. There was also at this time a smaller number and a much smaller proportion of helpless people among the Russian refugees, for those who lived in the interior of Russia, outside of the "pale of settlement", and would have remained there had it not been for the expulsions, were as a rule active and fairly successful men, and therefore better able to take care of themselves than those whom poverty or lack of employment forced to emigrate. Many more found relatives and friends here than in 1881-82, and among those who were here there were also many more who could be of assistance to new arrivals than in former times. As a matter of fact, Jewish immigration from the Slavic countries had then assumed its natural form, which it has retained ever since, except in the years following the massacres in the present century. Most men come to kinsmen or personal friends, who are willing and able to assist them in finding their way. A large majority consists of wives and children, of parents and other near relatives, who come because they were sent for and because the breadwinner or the most energetic member of the family has previously established himself here and demands their precense, or feels certain that they will soon be able to provide for themselves. The helpless Jewish immigrant who has nowhere to go and nothing to do when he arrives, is now very rare, and has been rare for the last two decades.

The number of the new immigrants needing assistance immediately after their arrival had been reduced to such a small fraction that those having the interest of the Jewish masses at heart began to express their opinion that it would perhaps be better if organized charity would leave them alone altogether. At first this opinion was uttered mostly in the Yiddish press or at meetings of immigrants. But in time there came not only a still further improvement in the general condition of the Jews, and also a further diminution in the number of helpless immigrants, but the voice of the immigrant-citizen became more potent in communal affairs. The folly of appeals, in which the wants of that class were exaggerated, became apparent; a large number of the employees of charitable institutions, and even some of the directors, were now Russian or Galician or Roumanian Jews, with a closer acquaintance with the needs, and also with the lack of needs, of the new arrivals. Much of the friction due to the resentment against help, which was rendered sometimes with more ostentation than the circumstances required, was obviated under the altered conditions, and the ground was prepared for a new co-operation of all elements of the community.

The foundation about this time of the American-Jewish Historical Society, whose objects are the collection and preservation of material bearing upon the history of the Jews in America, may be taken as an indication that the times were now again considered normal in the Jewish community. It was organized in June, 1892, with Oscar S. Straus as president, and Dr. Cyrus Adler (b. in Van Buren, Ark., 1863) as secretary. The latter is now (since 1899) its president, and Albert M. Friedenberg and Dr. Herbert Friedenwald, secretaries. It has thus far issued twenty annual volumes of its "Publications," which form an invaluable collection of material on the subject, much of which has been used in the preparation of this work. The president and both secretaries, as well as its curator, Leon Hühner, and some of its officers and members of its Executive Council, like Professor Richard J. H. Gottheil (b. in Manchester, England, 1862; who came here with his father, Rabbi Gustave Gottheil (1827-1903) of Temple Emanuel, New York, in 1873), of Columbia University; Professor Jacob H. Hollander (b. in Baltimore, 1871), of Johns Hopkins University, and Max J. Kohler (b. in Detroit, Mich., 1871), are among the most important contributors of papers and monograms on various historical subjects to the publications of the society.

Another society of a kindred nature, but appealing to a wider circle, The Jewish Publication Society of America (organized in Philadelphia, 1888; incorporated there 1896), began to attain prominence about that time. It has published for distribution among its members and also for sale to the general public about sixty books on a large variety of subjects, some of them, like the English edition of Graetz's History of the Jews, Schechter's "Studies in Judaism" and the earliest works of fiction by Israel Zangwill, are highly valuable. Morris Newburger (b. in Hohenzollern-Sigmaringen, 1834; a. 1854) was its first president and held the office for fourteen years, until he was succeeded by the present incumbent, Edwin Wolf, in 1902. The leading spirit of the society is the chairman of its Publication Committee, Mayer Sulzberger, the eminent communal leader and Jewish bibliophile, who has been a Judge of the Court of Common Pleas in Philadelphia since 1895. The secretary of that committee, Henrietta

Miss Sadie American.

Szold, has done much useful work in translating or preparing for publication a considerable part of the works which the society has published.

This society is the third of its kind in the United States. The first, which was called the "American Jewish Publication Society," was founded by Isaac Leeser in 1845, and in the same year an auxiliary society was established at Richmond, Va. It published fourteen works between that year and 1849; but went out of existence after its plates and books were destroyed by fire, in 1851. The second, The Jewish Publication Society, was established in New York in 1873, by Leopold Bamberger, Benjamin I. Hart, Myer Stern, Edward Morrison and several others of New York, William B. Hackenburg (b. in Philadelphia, 1837) of Philadelphia and Simon Wolf of Washington. Rabbis Gustave Gottheil, Moses Mielziner (b. in Schubin, Posen, 1828; d. in Cincinnati, 1903, where he had been Professor of Talmud in the Hebrew Union College since 1879, and Wise's successor as president) and Frederick de Sola Mendes (b. in Jamaica, W. I., 1850; since 1874 rabbi of Congregation Shaarey Tefilla); Marcus Jastrow of Philadelphia, and Maritz Ellinger (b. in Germany, 1830; a. 1854; d. 1907), editor of the "Menorah" and of the "Jewish Times," constituted its publication committee. It existed only for two years.

The Jewish Chautauqua Society, "for the dissemination of knowledge of the Jewish religion by fostering the study of its history and literature, giving popular courses of instruction, issuing publications, establishing reading circles, holding general assemblies, and by such other means as may from time to time be found necessary and proper," is also a product of this new period of spiritual and literary activity in the American-Jewish world. It was founded in 1893 by Dr. Henry Berkowitz (b. in Pittsburg, Pa., 1857; since 1892 rabbi of the Congregation Rodeph Shalom, Philadelphia), who is still its chancellor. It now has about three thousand members.

The World's Columbian Exposition, which was held in Chicago in the year 1893, offered the Jews on opportunity to participate in the great event in diversified ways. What they did and what they exhibited as artists, scientists, manufacturers and merchants does not belong to the subject of this work, which is mostly concerned with Jewish matters. But the Jews participated, as such, in the World's Parliament of Religions which was held in Chicago at that time. Among the separate denominational congresses which constituted that Parliament was also a Congress of Jewish Women, the first of its kind ever held. This congress resulted in the organization of the National Council of Jewish Women, "to further united efforts in behalf of Judaism by supplying means of study; by an organic union to bring about closer relations among Jewish women; to furnish a medium of interchange of thought and a means of communication and of prosecuting work of common interest; to further united efforts in the work of social betterment through religion, philanthropy and education." Hannah G. Solomon and Sadie American, respectively chairman and secretary of the congress, were elected president and secretary of the council. In 1896 the word "National" was eliminated from the name, on account of the entrance of sections from Canada. The council now consists of more than sixty sections and is doing noble work in pursuance of its program. Miss American still retains the office of secretary, while Mrs. Solomon was succeeded as president by Mrs. Marion L. Misch, of Providence, R. I.

CHAPTER XXXII.

THE LABOR MOVEMENT AND NEW LITERARY ACTIVITIES.

Difficulty of securing data for the history of the Labor Movement among Jewish immigrants—John R. Commons' characterization of a Jewish labor union—A constantly changing army of followers under the same leaders—The movement under the control of the radical press—The leaders as journalists and literary men—They popularize the press and teach the rudiments of politics—The voter —The "Heften"—Neo-Hebrew periodicals—The Yiddish stylists—The plight of the Hebraists.

Any attempt to give even the merest outline of the history of the labor movement among the immigrant Jews in the United States would lead into a maze of unreliable figures, exaggerations, and conflicting statements, not only between opponents, but also among those most friendly to their cause. The Russian Jew, in America, like the Russian himself at home, has not yet learned to divorcè trade unionism from politics; his labor organizations are either organized and managed by Socialistic agitators and politicians, and in the end split from within on account of the continuous wars among the adherents of various schools of Socialistic principles and tactics; or, if it is not Socialistic, and would not permit the machinery of its organization to be used for the benefit of the party—or, rather, of one of the Socialistic parties—it is opposed, and sometimes ruined, by open attacks or by neglect. And so it comes that as long as a labor union is typically Jewish, i. e., as long as it differs from the American trade union in its being much more political and being more interested in a general struggle against capital or against the present order of society, it leads a precarious existence. The small number of labor unions whose members are exclusively Jewish immigrants, which are strictly trade unions and permit their members to have their own political views or preferences, are usually affiliated with American central labor bodies, and belong to the history of the labor movement of the country rather than to one which deals with the Jews as a separate entity.

But the radicalism of the laborer as such, and the radicalism of the union which he enters and upholds, is like the radicalism of the immigrant in general and like his dwelling in tenement houses: a passing phase which seems permanent because new arrivals take up the place of those who are continually dropping out from the ranks on account of their improved material and educational condition. Isaac A. Hourwich (b. in Wilna, 1860; a. 1892), the economist and statistician, in his attempt to review the labor movement among the Jews in this country, could do no better than to quote the following characterization from the pen of a recognized specialist on the subject:

> The Jew's conception of a labor organization is that of a tradesman rather than that of a workman. In the clothing manufacture, whenever any real abuse arises among the Jewish workmen, they all come together and form a giant union, and at once engage in a strike. They bring in 95 per cent. of the trade. They are energetic and determined. They demand the entire and complete elimination of the abuse. The demand is almost always unanimous, and is made with enthusiasm and bitterness. They stay out a long time, even under the greatest of suffering. During a strike large numbers of them are to be found with almost nothing to live upon and their families suffering, still insisting, on the streets and in their halls, that the great cause must be won. But when once the strike is settled, either in favor of or against the cause, they are contented, and that usually ends the union, since they do not see any practical use for a union when there is no cause to fight for. Consequently the membership of a Jewish union is wholly uncertain. The secretary's books will show 60,000 members in one month and not

5,000 within three months later. If, perchance, a local branch has a steady thousand members, and if they are indeed paying members, it is likely that they are not the same members as in the year before.[1]

This is, with the modifications pertaining to time and place, the history of practically every trades-union organization among the Jewish immigrants from the Slavic countries. From the first union of Jewish tailors, which was organized in New York in 1877, through the time of the first comprehensive strike of workers in the clothing trade in that city in 1890, the still larger one in 1894; down to the great waist makers' strike in 1909 and the great strikes in New York, Chicago and Cleveland in 1910 and 1911, the leadership has remained almost the same for about a quarter century. Abraham Cahan (b. in Podberezhye, near Wilna, 1860; a. 1882), who was the first to deliver Socialist speeches in Yiddish in the United States, is still practically at the head of that movement among his countrymen. Morris Hillquit (b. in Riga, Russia, 1870; a. 1887) began his activity as a Socialist leader among the immigrants before he was of age, and is now a recognized leader of the Socialists of the country, being also the author of a History of Socialism in the United States. Joseph Barondess (b. in Kamenetz-Podolsk, 1867; a. 1885), the leader of the second great cloak makers' strike, who is now a communal worker and a leader among the Zionists, is still looked upon as a representative of the Jewish working classes in New York. The same conditions prevail in other large cities; only there the movement began somewhat later, and the local leaders seldom attained lasting prominence even locally; for the movement is more than anything else a newspaper movement, and those who control the Yiddish Socialist press in New York are masters of the situation in every center of population where there is a Socialist movement among the Jewish immigrants.

[1] John R. Commons, in his report on "Immigration and Its Economic Effects," quoted in the article "Trade Unionism" in *The Jewish Encyclopedia*, vol. XII.

As the radical press is the means by which the unstable and mostly temporary labor organizations are held in control, it has played a much more important part in the entire Jewish labor movement than the general labor press has played in the much stronger and more lasting American labor movement. This is again on account of its political radicalism, which appeals to a wide circle of readers, who may be neither trade union laborers nor even Socialists. In its latest phase of development the Jewish radical press becomes a sensational afternoon paper, only with a stronger tinge of "red" than the journal of the same type printed in the vernacular. This preponderance of the literary side of the movement had the results which were to be expected: it produced better writers than labor leaders, more talented literary artists than organizers or disciplinarians. And while most of the radical periodicals also succumbed sooner or later, they had a more lasting effect on the development of the immigrant than the extremist labor organizations. This is also a reflex of Russian conditions, where the labor movement is entirely in the hands of the "intelligencia" or learned classes, though for an entirely different reason, the laborers themselves being mostly illiterate. Here every Jewish labor leader is a journalist or an author, often both; and they belong more properly to the chapters treating of Jewish literature in America.

The agitator among the immigrants has also rendered other highly useful service, besides the impetus which he gave to the development and popularization of the Yiddish press. The average laborer immigrant from Russia knew very little of newspapers, although practically every one of them could read his mother tongue—Judeo-German or Yiddish. But the Russian government did not permit at that time the publication of popular newspapers, and we find, for instance, in the year 1886, three daily papers in Russia in the old Hebrew language, which is understood by the more educated classes, and not one in Yiddish. But little as the immigrant knew about newspapers, he knew less, or actually nothing at all, about politics. The explanation of the aims of the one party for which the agitator wanted to win him had to be preceded by introductory explanations of the nature and functions of parties generally, of their utility as a means of inaugurating reforms, and their power to carry them out when a successful campaign places the government in their hands. The Socialist agitator was thus the first teacher of civics, and he was a very active worker for the cause of naturalization. He was anxious that the immigrant workingman should become a citizen and build up with his vote the Socialist party which the native laborer was so slow to recognize.

But the large majority of the Jewish laborers had enough of Socialism by the time they were entitled to citizenship; the number of voters of that party increased very slowly, and, like the above-mentioned case of the unions, they were not the same from year to year. While the Jewish population was increasing rapidly in some parts of New York and other large cities, and the number of non-Jewish, or rather non-immigrant, voters in some districts became very small or practically disappeared, the number of Socialist votes was fluctuating, and never became a majority or even a plurality in a district. While the leaders were preaching that all opportunities were now gone and all avenues of advancement were closed for the poor man, every individual among their followers was struggling to raise himself above his surroundings. Americanization meant the abandonment of extreme views on all subjects, and the naturalized immigrant, even when he remained a manual worker, was soon voting for one of the two great American parties. He still retained a leaning towards radical reform, for the Russian mind is much inclined to theorizing; but he would now seldom go further than support an American reformer or join one of the movements instituted by the better elements for the purpose of purifying city governments. But as the reform element usually signalizes its accession to power by a severe enforcement of Sunday-closing laws and other interferences with personal liberty which smack of persecution, the immigrant Jew usually joins the other disappointed classes to turn the reformers out of office at the next election.

There was a slow and steady turning away from the dry and monotonous radical literature of that period, which was a counterpart of the turning away from extreme politics. In one respect the change in literary tastes or requirements amounted to a revulsion—one might almost say, to a revolution. The first attempt to publish in Yiddish a sensational novel in weekly or semi-weekly installments, popularly known as "Heften," which was made in New York about 1890, met with extraordinary success. The number of such ventures soon multiplied, and the sales were large in other cities as well as in the place of publication. The Yiddish periodical press became endangered, but it saved—and revenged—itself by beginning to publish one, two and sometimes as much as three serial stories in daily installments, a practice which in a short time ruined the business of the "Heften."

It was also about this time that the "Maskilim" or half-Germanized Hebrew scholars, who were forced to the background by the domination of the radicals at the beginning of the "Russian period," began to forge to the front again. The number of Jews who could read Hebrew was fast increasing, the proportion of intelligent and well-educated men being much larger among those who were forced to emigrate than among the earlier immigrants. Well known Hebrew scholars who arrived in that period began the publication of Hebrew periodicals, and while none of the publications survived, some of them existed for a number of years and exerted a certain influence; besides contributing to develop the talents of new writers and to lay the foundation for a Neo-Hebrew literature in America, which is progressing slowly but surely.

One of the first of the Hebrew editors of the new period was Ephraim Deinard (b. in Courland, 1846; a. 1888), the author and traveler. He established the weekly "Ha-Leomi" (Nationalist) in New York in 1889, and it existed for about two years. Another traveler and author, Wolf (or William) Schur (b. in Utian,

Russia, 1844; d. in Chicago, 1910), established his weekly "Ha-Pisgah" (The Summit), which appeared in New York and Baltimore in the years 1890-94 and in Chicago in 1897-1900. The "ha-Ibri" (The Hebrew), also a weekly, was founded by K. H. Sarasohn and edited by Gerson Rosenzweig (b. in Karatchin, in the government of Grodno, Russia, 1861: a. 1888) during the time of its existence, from 1892 to 1898. Of the Hebrew monthlies of that period only the "Ner he-Maarabi" (Western Light), which appeared in 1895-97, edited first by Abraham H. Rosenberg (b. in Pinsk, 1838; a. 1891) and afterwards by Samuel B. Schwarzberg, deserves to be mentioned.

In one respect the Hebrew and the Yiddish writers were struggling with the same difficulty—that of making themselves understood to the largest possible number of readers. The method prevailing in Russia of writing as hard or using as high a language as possible so that the highly intelligent reader—the title to which every reader of a newspaper there at that time laid claim—should take pride in being able to understand the contents, would not attract readers here as it does where scarcity of printed matter makes the public accept with eagerness whatever is offered. But the Hebrew writer came here with a style that may be termed aristocratic, and the Yiddish writer, who had to begin everything anew, had hardly any style. It was all easy as far as the work of the agitator was concerned; denunciations and accusations are always easily understood, and this alone is one of the reasons of their popularity. But when it came to the parts where the writer wanted to describe or to explain, especially in the scientific or semi-scientific articles which a public that had no systematic schooling so eagerly devoured, the language of most of the writers was inadequate and not easily understood.

Thus it comes that, although most of the Yiddish periodicals of that time were advocating, some of them with great vehemence, certain principles, or leading certain movements, the earliest reputations were made by stylists who were not identified with particular movements. The highest popularity among the reading masses was attained by Abner Tannenbaum (b. in Shirwint, Russia, 1848; a. 1887), whose perspicuous writing, whether as the author of the "Heften," which he inaugurated, or on his favorite subject, popular science, simply could not be misunderstood. George Selikovich (b. in Retovo, government of Kovno, Russia, in 1863; a. 1887), a linguist and a good Hebrew stylist, is another writer whom everybody could easily understand, and who acquired popularity with the public to whom Yiddish periodical literature was brought down here, for the first time in its history. Nahum Meir Schaikewitz (Shomer, b. in Nesvizh, government of Minsk, Russia, 1849; a. 1888; d. in New York, 1905), the novelist and playwright, also appealed to the masses with his easy flowing style, and was a favorite here with the same classes which used to read his works and see his plays in the old country.

The recognition accorded to these writers, none of whom were agitators or even party men, proves that even in the time when it seemed that the "ghetti" or neighborhoods of the Jewish immigrants were seething with movements and agitations, the great masses were not much interested in them; though the curious crowded the largest meeting rooms, and many who were not yet sure of their newly found freedom were inclined to test it by participating in a march or some other form of demonstration which was forbidden in their old home. Some writers, on the other hand, who followed the Russian usage of subordinating their art to the cause which they were advocating, were extolled by their partisans as great geniuses, but had a much smaller public than the above-mentioned literati.

The writers of Hebrew, who by reason of their training and inclination held more aloof even from their own public, have not yet solved the great question of style; which partly accounts for the remarkable fact that their periodical literature has actually vanished in the two decades in which the possible number of their readers has increased almost tenfold. Some of the best known Hebrew literati from the Old World came here since the establishment of the Neo-Hebrew periodicals which were mentioned above: men like the poet Menahem Mendel Dolitzki (b. in Byelostok, 1856; a. 1892); the exegete Abraham Baer Dobsevage (b. in Pinsk, 1843; a. 1891; d. in New York, 1900); the philosopher Joseph Loeb Sosnitz (b. in Birz, 1837; a. 1891; d. in New York, 1910); the grammarian Moses Reicherson (b. in Wilna, 1827; a. 1890; d. in New York, 1903), and the knight-errant of Hebrew literature, Naphtali Hirz Imber (b. in Zloczow, Galicia, 1856; a. 1892(?); d. in New York, 1909). But neither they nor others less known, who could perhaps be more productive under more favorable circumstances, could accomplish much even in those branches of literary journalism where Yiddish has not penetrated. They were not entirely idle, and some of the results of their literary labor will be mentioned in the proper place in a following part of this work. But they have not influenced the Jewish spirit and have contributed little to the general intellectual development of the community. The traditional war for progress which they waged in their old homes, where they were often the only learned or enlightened men in the community, had no place in a world where general education is so easily accessible; and they could not feel at home in the ranks of the conservatives, where they belong in this country. Most of them floundered until the rise of the Zionist movement, which they joined halfheartedly. Many took to teaching of Hebrew, and are still waiting for the expected revival of interest in Hebrew literature which the new nationalism is supposed to produce.

CHAPTER XXXIII.

RELATIONS WITH RUSSIA. THE PASSPORT QUESTION.

The normal rate of Jewish immigration is but slightly affected by the panic of 1893—Oppressiveness of the Sunday Laws are felt by the new immigrants—The Extradition Treaty with Russia—Beginning of the struggle about the Passport Question—The first Resolution against Russia's discrimination, introduced in Congress by Mr. Cox in 1879—Diplomacy and diplomatic correspondence—More resolutions—Rayner, Fitzgerald, Perkins—Henry M. Goldfogle—John Hay's letter to the House—More letters, speeches and discussions—The Sulzer Resolution and the last step to abrogate the Treaty of 1832.

The large increase in Jewish immigration from Russia after the renewed persecutions of 1891, like the general increase in the beginning of the last decade of the nineteenth century, lasted only till the effects of the hard times, which began in the spring of 1893, began to be felt. But the increase in Jewish immigration was more than ordinarily large, or what might be considered for those times as abnormal, only in one year—1892. If this year, in which there arrived 76,417 Jews from Russia,[1] should be eliminated, it is seen that Jewish immigration fell off much less in proportion than general immigration. The general figures are: 560,319 for 1891; 502,917 for 1893; 314,467 for 1894; and 279,948 for 1895. The number of Jewish immigrants from Russia for those years was: 42,145 for 1891; 35,626 for 1893; 36,725 for 1894, and 33,332 for 1895. The cause of it was men-

[1] See article "Migration" in the *Jewish Encyclopedia*, where the figures are interesting but the sources do not justify complete reliability.

tioned in a former chapter—that the largest part of the Jewish immigration now consisted of families or near relatives brought over by those who have established themselves here. The condition of those remaining there was becoming continually worse, while those who were here could, with a little exertion and self-denial, save enough, even in slack times, to save their immediate relatives from the conditions which were becoming unendurable in Russia.

For this large and increasing mass of Russians, the relations between the United States and Russia were a matter of grave concern. And to them, in conjunction with the Galician Jews and the Roumanian Jews, who were, roughly estimated, nearly half as strong numerically as the Russians, the question of the restriction of immigration, which was then being discussed in Congress and in the country generally, was of most vital interest. The fear that the oppressed Jews who were left home could not come in now, and that there might be difficulty even in bringing over members of the family, sufficed to make this question overshadow all others in the mind of the Jewish immigrant; to make it not only the most important, but with many, the sole Jewish problem.

A minor problem which had also become more acute under the changed conditions was the Sunday Laws of the various states. While the laws themselves date further back, some of them from the eighteenth century, and they were not enforced with any more severity than before, the opportunities for conflict with them were now much more frequent. The Jewish immigrants of the former periods, who were mostly traders doing business with their Gentile neighbors, and were also inclined toward Reform Judaism, usually rested Sunday, for economic reasons as well as on account of their religious views. But now there were in many large cities, and especially in New York, large Jewish neighborhoods where brisk trading was done among Jews themselves. There were Jewish shops and factories in which the owners, the managers and foremen, as well as the workers, were

Jews. And not only was the proportion of Orthodox Jews among them very large, but even the unbelievers and the radicals among them thought the Sunday laws oppressive and incongruous. It was certainly not what most of them expected to find in the Land of Liberty: to be hampered and interfered with for practices which were then practically permissible in countries like Russia and Austria, where the Churches rule supreme and where Jews are harassed on every imaginable pretext.

Two incidents in the relations with Russia aroused the interest of the Russian Jews in America at that time. The first related to the Treaty of Extradition which was negotiated between the two governments during the first administration of President Cleveland, but was not pressed for ratification, owing to protests which were made against it by Russian Jews and which were seconded by many liberal Americans and by a considerable portion of the press. But the document itself, signed by the representatives of the two governments seven or eight years before. remained in the State Department, and was again presented to the Senate by John W. Foster, a former American Minister to Russia, who held the office of Secretary of State in the last months of the administration of President Benjamin Harrison (1833-1901). It was ratified by the Senate in February, 1893, and the report of its ratification and exchange with Russia was a painful surprise for the Jews of the country, especially for the natives of Russia. Happily the fears about the possible effects of the treaty proved absolutely groundless. Every extradition case under this treaty which was fought in the United States courts was won, and, as far as it is known, not one Russian refugee who made the plea against extradition, claiming that he was wanted for political offences, was ever delivered to Russia.

The second occurrence pertained to a difficulty of long standing: to the general treaty between the United States and Russia which was concluded in 1832. The number of Jews in the United States at that time was comparatively small, and very few of them came from Russia. The intercourse between the two countries was insignificant, and probably no Jew of that time thought of going from America to Russia for any purpose. It could therefore not have occurred to the representatives of our Government in negotiating the treaty that Russia would discriminate against American Jews who might come there. As a matter of fact, the language of the treaty implied equal treatment for all American citizens alike, and is much less objectionable than was the treaty with Switzerland, which was concluded later (see above Chapter XXIII), in which discrimination against Jews was knowingly accepted. And while a case of discrimination against an American-Jewish citizen in Switzerland was under consideration by the State Department in Washington at the very time when the treaty of 1855, with the highly objectionable clause, was adopted, more than forty years passed after the adoption of the Russian treaty of 1832 before the question of Russia's disloyalty to the terms of the treaty attracted the attention of the American Government, although there seems to have been some correspondence about it as early as 1866.[1] The name of a naturalized Jewish citizen, Theodore Rosenstrauss, appears frequently in the diplomatic correspondence of the State Department from 1873 to 1879, and his case was the cause of the following Joint Resolution being introduced in the House of Representatives of the 46th Congress in June, 1879, by Mr. Samuel S. Cox of New York, a member of the Committee on Foreign Affairs:

JOINT RESOLUTION IN RELATION TO TREATY NEGOTIATIONS WITH RUSSIA AS TO AMERICAN CITIZENS.

Whereas, It is alleged that by the laws of the Russian Government, no Hebrew can hold real estate, which unjust discrimination is enforced against Hebrew citizens of the United States resident in Russia; and

Whereas, The Russian Government has discriminated against one T. Rosenstrauss, a naturalized citizen of the United States, by pro-

[1] See *The American Passport in Russia* in the American Jewish Year Book for 5665; also *The Passport Question in Congress,* ibid. for 5670.

hibiting him from holding real estate after his purchasing and paying for the same, because of his being an Israelite; and

Whereas, Such disabilities are antagonistic to the enlightened spirit of our institutions and age, which demand free exercise of religious belief, and no disabilities therefrom; and

Whereas, The Secretary of State, under date of April 29, 1879, expresses doubt of his ability to grant the relief required under existing treaty stipulations; therefore

Resolved, By the Senate and the House of Representatives of the United States of America in Congress Assembled, that the rights of the citizens of the United States should not be impaired at home or abroad because of religious belief; and that if existing treaties between the United States and Russia be found, as is alleged, to discriminate in this or any other particular, as to any other classes of our citizens, the President is requested to take immediate action, to have the treaties so amended as to remedy this grievance.

After a debate, in which the fact that English Jews were permitted to own land in Russia, was brought out, this Resolution passed the House of Representatives June 10, 1879, and as far as known was not heard of again.

In the diplomatic correspondence which followed, the American Government insisted on its rights under the treaty and urged its minister to claim absolutely equal treatment for all American citizens alike, Jews as well as others. The arguments and the mode of procedure which are now familiar to every one who is interested in the question, were all used thirty years ago, though the only effective remedy, suggested by the first resolution, "to take immediate steps to have the treaties amended," had not been resorted to. But the question of former Russian subjects who return to Russia as American citizens, in which the principle of expatriation and right of naturalization is involved, is not touched upon in these early disputes. There is even a clear intimation that the Russian Government's chief objection was against naturalized Jews from Germany. Mr. Foster, who was then our representative in St. Petersburg, in a dispatch dated December 30, 1880, reports an interview which he had with M. de Giers, the Russian Minister of Foreign Affairs, and says:

So far as concerned Jews who are bona fide American citizens (not disguised German Jews), he would assure me of the most liberal treatment, as he knew it was the desire of the Emperor to show all possible consideration to American citizens. If such came to St. Petersburg and encountered any trouble, if I would merely send him an unofficial note, he would give them all the time I might ask for them to remain here to attend to their business. . .

The same dispatch reports also a conversation with the Minister of Worship, who "listened with much interest to my presentation of the subject. He said that a commission was now engaged in studying the question of reform in these laws," and "frankly recognized that the laws were not fully in accordance with the spirit of the age." But in the end of this document Mr. Foster acknowledges his failure to obtain what he wanted and says that "the Russian Government was disposed to grant what we desired only as a favor when my government asked it as a right" (quoting Loris Melikov).

In a dispatch sent by Secretary of State James G. Blaine to Mr. Foster, dated July 29, 1881, the entire subject is historically reviewed and the principles involved are restated in strong and lucid terms. Two passages from this dispatch are worth quoting. One reads: "From the time when the treaty of 1832 was signed down to within a very recent period, there had been nothing in our relations with Russia to lead to the supposition that our flag did not carry with it equal protection to every American within the dominions of the empire." The second is the last sentence of the dispatch and reads: "I cannot but feel assured that this earnest presentation of the views of this government will accord with the sense of justice and equity of that of Russia, and that the questions at issue will soon find their natural solution in harmony with the spirit of tolerance which pervaded the ukase of the Empress Catherine a century ago, and with the statesmanlike declaration of the principle of reciprocity found in the later decree of the Czar Alexander II. in 1860." Actual dealings with Russia were a novel experience for American diplomatists, and even so eminent a statesman as Mr. Blaine could believe—after the pogroms of the spring of that year—that the question would be solved in the same manner as in Switzerland—by the final emancipation of the Jews of that country.

In the meantime new cases had arisen, and the question was again brought before Congress. Representative Samuel S. Cox of New York introduced a second resolution in the House of Representatives on January 26, 1882, which was passed four days later, requesting the President, if it was not incompatible with the public service, to communicate to the House all correspondence between the Department of State and the United States minister at St. Petersburg, relative to the expulsion of American Israelites from Russia, and the persecution of the Jews in the Russian Empire. Another resolution, asking for further correspondence on the subject, was introduced by Mr. Cox on July 31 of the same year and referred to the Committee on Foreign Affairs. He submitted the same resolution again in February, 1883, when it was passed. There was another resolution in 1884, and more correspondence in 1886 between Secretary of State Thomas F Bayard and the American representative in Russia, with no better results than before.

The subject was taken up more earnestly than before in the following decade. Congressman S. Logan Chipman of Michigan introduced in the House, in February, 1892, a resolution "To inquire into the operation of the Anti-Jewish Laws of Russia on American Citizens." It was referred to the Committee on Foreign Affairs and reported on April 6, 1892, in a much amplified form, but its passage is not recorded. Mr. Irvine Dungan, of Ohio, introduced, on June 10, 1892, a joint resolution "directing the severance of diplomatic relations with Russia," which seems not to have gone any further than the Committee on Foreign Affairs. There was new correspondence, too, as the result of new cases, and probably also as an indirect result of the resolutions which were introduced in the House. A letter written from the State Department in 1893 to Mr. Andrew D. White (b. 1832), the educator and historian, the greatest man who ever represented the United States in Russia, contained the "surmise that some strange misapprehension exists in this regard in the mind of His Majesty's Government, which your accustomed ability and tact may explain and perhaps remove." The events proved that he could do neither.

In 1894 the subject was again brought before the House, for the first time by a representative of Jewish extraction. Isidor Rayner (b. in Baltimore, 1850), who was successively a member of the Maryland Legislature, a State Senator, a representative in Congress for three terms, the Attorney-General of the State of Maryland, and is now serving his second term as United States Senator from that State (beginning March 4, 1911), was then serving his third term in the House and was recognized as one of the ablest orators and leaders of his party (the Democratic) in the popular branch of Congress. But his resolution, which was introduced May 28, 1894, in which the President was "directed to call the attention of the Government of Russia to its continued violation of the treaty rights," met with no better fate than the preceding ones which were introduced by non-Jews. The disposition of the resolutions made, however, little difference, for the Government was urging a settlement of the difficulties as strongly as if it was commanded by Congress to do so.

Minister Breckinridge, who was in St. Petersburg in 1895, writing to the Russian Minister of Foreign Affairs in that year, states "that it has long been a matter of deep regret and concern to the United States that any of its citizens should be discriminated against for religious reasons while peacefully sojourning in this country." The subject was apparently taken up more seriously now than before, and there was justification for the belief that it would have to be settled soon. Mr. H. H. D. Peirce, Secretary of Legation, writing in June, 1895, of an interview which he had with a high Russian official, declares that the latter admitted the force of the argument and "expressed himself as hopeful that it would be possible to bring about a satisfactory revision of Russian practice as regards the admission of American Jews into the Empire." In the following month Assistant Secretary of State A. A. Adee wrote to the Legation at St. Petersburg:

> Your conclusion that it is inexpedient to press the complaint to a formal answer at present appears to be discreet, but the Department must express its deep regret that you have encountered in the foreign office a reluctance to consider the matter in the light in which this Government has presented it. The Russian Government can not expect that its course in asserting inquisitorial authority in the United States over citizens of the United States as to their religious or civil status can ever be acceptable or even tolerable to such a Government as ours, and continuance in such a course after our views have been clearly but considerately made known may trench upon the just limits of consideration.

There were three more dispatches of considerable length sent about this subject in the same year, 1895; one from Mr. Breckinridge to Secretary of State Richard Olney, dated July 4; the second from Mr. Adee to Mr. Breckinridge, dated August 22, and a third, dated October 23, from Washington to the Russian capital, beginning with the acknowledgment of the receipt of a set of regulations relating to the Jews in Russia and commenting on it that: "If anything, it presents the subject in a still more unfavorable light, for it seems that those Russian agents in a foreign territory may in their discretion inquire into the business standing of the principal of the commercial house employing a Hebrew agent, and act favorably or unfavorably, according to their own judgment of its importance." It continues that even "assuming for the arguments's sake but not by way of admission, that such a right may technically exist, the question remains whether the assumption to exercise it in face of the temperate but earnest remonstrances of this Government against foreign interference with the private concerns of its citizens, is in accordance with those courteous principles of comity which this Government is so anxious to observe in its relations with all foreign states."

All this was of no avail, and the question was again brought before Congress. Representative John F. Fitzgerald (b. in Boston, 1863; now Mayor of Boston) of Massachusetts introduced the following resolution in the House of Representatives, March 31, 1897, which was referred to the Committee on Foreign Affairs:

Resolved, That the Secretary of State be requested to demand from the Russian Government that the same rights be given to Hebrew-American citizens in the matter of passports as now are accorded to all other classes of American citizens, and also inform the House of Representatives whether any American citizens have been ordered to be expelled from Russia or forbidden the exercise of the ordinary privileges enjoyed by the inhabitants, because of their religion.

The same resolution was re-introduced by Mr. Fitzgerald in December, 1899, with no better results. In the meantime, a Jewish banker from California, Mr. Adolf Kutner, was refused admission to Russia in 1897, and this caused Senator J. C. Perkins of that State to introduce a lengthy resolution about this question in the United States Senate (May 25, 1897), which was followed by a shorter one presented in the House by Representative Curtice H. Castle of the same State in December of that year.

In 1902 the question was again brought to the attention of the House by a Representative who not only is himself a Jew, but represents a district most of whose inhabitants are immigrant Jews who are interested in the passport question. Henry Mayer Goldfogle (b. in New York City, 1856), who was twice elected Judge of the Municipal Court in an East Side district, was in 1900 elected, as a Democrat, to represent the Ninth Congress District of New York, which includes the most thickly populated part of the East Side, and has been re-elected at every Congressional election since, serving now (1911) his sixth term. It was during his first term that he introduced what became well known as the "Goldfogle Resolution" and has been before Congress in one form or another for nearly a decade. Its original form as it was introduced, March 28, 1902, was as follows:

Resolved, By the House of Representatives of the United States, that the Secretary of State be, and he is hereby, respectfully requested to inform the House whether American citizens of the Jewish religious faith, holding passports issued by this Government, are barred or excluded from entering the territory of the Empire of Russia, and whether the Russian Government has made, or is making, any discrimination between citizens of the United States of different religious faiths or persuasions, visiting or attempting to visit Russia, provided with American passports; and whether the Russian Government has made regulations restricting or specially applying to American citizens, whether native or naturalized, of the Jewish religious denomination, holding United States passports, and if so, to report the facts in relation thereto, and what action concerning such exclusion, discrimination or restriction, if any, has been taken by any department of the Government of the United States.

This resolution was amended by adding the words "if not incompatible with the public interest" after the word "House" in the third line. It was passed by the House April 30, 1902. Shortly afterwards (June 27) Senator E. W. Pettus of Alabama introduced a resolution in the Senate requesting the President, "if not incompatible with the public interest, to inform the Senate as to the attitude of the Russian Government toward American citizens attempting to enter its territory with American passports." This was also passed by the Senate, but the reply was given to the House before the Senate Resolution was introduced. The essence of the letter to the House, written by Secretary of State John Hay (1838-1905), dated May 2, 1902, that American Jews are not at a greater disadvantage before that Government than are the Jews of other countries; that the exclusion of naturalized citizens of Russian origin was explained by Secretary Olney in his report to the President in 1896 as due to circumstances under which a "conflict between national laws, each absolute within its domestic sphere and inoperative beyond it, is hardly to be averted"; that the effort to secure uniform treatment for American citizens in Russia, begun many years ago, had continued, although it had not been attended with encouraging success; and that the Department of State send to all persons of Russian birth who received passports an unofficial notice showing what were the provisions of Russian law liable to affect them, in order that they might not incur danger through ignorance.

The subject has been treated officially and semi-officially in various manners since that time, but practically without results. It came up several times in Congress, and was ably discussed by Jewish representatives and their friendly colleagues, hardly a voice ever being raised in defence of the Russian Government. There were new resolutions by Judge Goldfogle, who was now recognized as the Jewish Representative in Congress; new correspondence between the State Department and the American Ambassador in St. Petersburg; a personal letter from President Theodore Roosevelt to Count Witte (who came to the United States to negotiate a treaty of peace with Japan in 1905), in which that Muscovite statesman was begged "to consider the question of granting passports to reputable American citizens of the Jewish faith," and a letter from Secretary of State Elihu Root (b. 1845; now a Senator from New York) to Mr. Jacob H. Schiff in October, 1908, telling him that the Administration "has urged the making of a new treaty for the purpose of regulating the subject." It was the subject of a notable address delivered by the well known attorney and communal worker, Louis Marshall (b. in Syracuse, N. Y., 1856), at the convention of the Union of American Hebrew Congregations which was held in New York in January, 1911, and was afterward brought before President William H. Taft (b. 1857) by a delegation which was appointed by that convention. Public men in various parts of the country became interested in the question. They were encouraged by an almost unanimous public press to stand up for the rights of American Citizenship, regardless of creed, and the movement became well-nigh irresistible. Numerous State Legislatures adopted resolutions favoring the abrogation of the treaty unless the American passport be fully recognized as conferring the right of domicile in all parts of the Russian Empire. Congress was flooded with resolutions which were adopted by Jewish organizations all over the country, and many meetings were held to express the public indignation, as well as the dissatisfaction with the Government's dilatoriness in obtaining justice for its Jewish citizens. The most imposing meetings were held under the auspices of the National Citizens' League, a newly formed organization, composed mostly of prominent non-Jews, of which Andrew D. White became the chairman.

In December, 1911, the resolution for the abrogating of the treaty, which was introduced in the House of Representatives by William Sulzer, of New York, was adopted with practical unanimity. But President Taft had anticipated this action by the instructions which he gave several days before to the American Ambassador in St. Petersburg, to serve formal notice on Russia that the Treaty of 1832 would be abrogated on December 31, 1912, i. e., after one full year shall have elapsed after the notice of abrogation, as it is provided by the terms of the agreement itself. Both houses of Congress soon afterwards approved the President's act without a dissenting vote, and the battle was won, as far as the American side of it was concerned. But the work of negotiating and concluding a new treaty was perforce left to the slow procedure of diplomacy, which is doubly slow when a government, like the Russian, which is so unwilling to recognize the rights of Jews, is one of the contracting parties.

CHAPTER XXXIV.

LEGISLATION ABOUT IMMIGRATION. SUNDAY LAWS AND THEIR ENFORCEMENT.

Jewish interest in immigration—The first legislation on the subject—The Nativists or "Know Nothings"—A Congressional investigation in 1838—President Taylor's invitation to foreigners to come and settle here—A law to encourage immigration passed on Lincoln's recommendation in 1864—The General Immigration Law of 1882—The "Ford Committee"—Permanent Immigration Committees in Congress—Continued agitation and legislation on the subject—A bill containing the requirement of an educational test is vetoed by President Grover Cleveland in 1897—The last Immigration Law of 1907—The Immigration Commission of 1907 and its report in 1910—Sunday Laws and their significance for the Orthodox Jew—Laws of various States and Territories—Their effect on movements for municipal reform—Status of the problems.

The question of immigration, or rather of its restriction, was always of great interest to the Jews, not only because they are great wanderers and many of them are looking for a home, but also because to the many who came from countries where they were persecuted or from which they were exiled, exclusion meant a much more serious matter than to those who had a home to go back to. The immigrants of the second period, from 1815 to 1880, were more fortunate in this respect than those who came very early and were harrassed by frank discrimination against them as Jews, as was related in earlier parts of this work; and also more than the later arrivals, many of whom were excluded as undesirable, along with the defective and helpless of other races and nationalities. From the time of the establishment of the Government of the United States until about 1835, immigration was taken as a matter of course; the only legislation enacted, and practically all that was proposed, was the law of 1819 for the regulation of the carriage of steerage passengers at sea, which law also for the first time provided that statistics relative to immigration to the United States be recorded.

The second period, from 1835 to 1860, is sharply defined by the so-called "Native American" and "Know Nothing" movements, which, as is well known, were largely based on the opposition to the immigration of Catholics.[1] The hostility early took the form of a political movement, and in 1835 there was a Nativist candidate for Congress in New York City, where that party nominated a candidate for mayor in the following year. It spread over various states, and in 1845, when it held its first national convention in Philadelphia, it had six Representatives in Congress from New York and two from Pennsylvania. The chief demands of this convention were a repeal of the naturalization laws and the appointments of native Americans only to office.

While these societies were stronger in local politics than in national, their few Representatives in Congress attempted to make Nativism a national question. As a result of their efforts, the United States Senate in 1836 agreed to a resolution directing the Secretary of State to collect certain information respecting the immigration of foreign paupers and criminals. In the House of Representatives on February 19, 1838, a resolution was agreed to which provided that the Committee on Judiciary be instructed to consider the expediency of revising the naturalization laws so as to require a longer term of residence in the United States, and also to consider the propriety and expediency of providing by law against the introduction into the United States of vagabonds and paupers deported from foreign countries. This resolution was referred to a select committee of seven members, and

[1] See *Abstract of the Report on Federal Immigration Legislation* by the Immigration Commission, issued by the Government, Washington, 1911.

its report (House Report No. 1040, 25th Congress, 2d session) was the first resulting from a Congressional investigation of any question bearing upon immigration. It proposed a system of consular inspection, and there was even talk of a tax of $20 to be paid by the immigrant upon his receipt of a passport from the consul. The bill presented on recommendation of the committee provided heavy penalties for any master taking on board his vessel with the intention of transporting to the United States any alien passenger who was an idiot, lunatic, maniac or one afflicted with any incurable disease, or any one convicted of an infamous crime; it was further provided that the master should forfeit $1,000 for any alien brought in who had not the ability to maintain himself.

Congress did not even consider this bill, and during the next ten years little attempt was made to secure legislation against the foreigner.

In a message to Congress on June 1, 1841, President John Tyler (1813-62) referred to immigration, in part, as follows:

> We hold out to the people of other countries an invitation to come and settle among us as members of our rapidly growing family; and for the blessing which we offer them, we require of them to look upon our country as their country, and unite with us in the great task of preserving our institutions and thereby perpetuating our liberties.

As a consequence of the increase of immigration about the middle of the nineteenth century, the old dread of the foreigner was revived, and in the early fifties the Nativist politicians again became active. The new, like the earlier movement, was closely associated with the anti-Catholic propaganda. The new organization assumed the form of a secret society. It was organized probably, in 1850, in New York City, and in 1852 it was increased in membership by drawing largely from the old established Order of United Americans. Its meetings were secret, its indorsements were never made openly, and even its name and purpose were said to be known only to those who reached the highest degree. Consequently the rank and file, when questioned about their party, were obliged to answer: "I don't know"; so they came to be called "Know Nothings." They participated in local, State and even in national elections, and claimed as many as forty-three Representatives and five Senators in the Thirty-fourth Congress. But in the end they disappeared without having accomplished anything against immigration, adopted citizens, or Catholics, and, as a matter of fact, some legislation favorable to foreigners was passed during these periods of agitation. The passenger law of 1819 was amended in 1847, and again in 1848, in order to improve the condition of the steerage of immigrant ships. The act organizing the Territories of Nebraska and Kansas, passed in 1854, was also favorable to foreigners, it being provided that the right of suffrage in such Territories should be exercised by those declaring their intentions to become citizens and taking an oath to support the Constitution of the United States and the provisions of the act. During the discussion of the homestead act in 1854, which act, however, was not finally passed until 1862, there was considerable reference to immigrants and to whether they should be allowed to enjoy the advantages of the act. The "Know Nothings" proposed to strike out the section of the bill permitting the granting of land to foreigners who had filed their intention of becoming citizens; but the attempt failed.

Although the National Government did not assume control of immigration until 1882, Congress in 1864, on the recommendation of President Lincoln, passed a law to encourage immigration. It provided for a Commissioner of Immigration, to be under the direction of the Department of State, and that all contracts that should be made in foreign countries by emigrants to the United States, whereby emigrants pledged the wages of their labor for a term not exceeding twelve months to repay the expense of emigration, should be held to be valid in law and might be enforced in the courts of the United States or by the several States and Territories, and that no such contract could in any way be considered as creating a condition of slavery or servitude. Following the enactment of the law several companies were established to deal in contract labor, but they were not satisfied with the law and wanted its scope enlarged. This indirectly led to the abolition of the entire law in 1868, and the brief period of national encouragement of immigration was over. A campaign against contracting for foreign labor began soon afterward, though no legislation to forbid it was enacted until many years later. A law, enacted in 1875, which provided for the exclusion of prostitutes, was chiefly designated to regulate Chinese immigration, and thus early touched two subjects with reference to which the most stringent exclusion laws were to be enacted in the period of national control over immigration, which was now approaching.

In 1876 the Supreme Court of the United States declared laws enacted by several States to regulate and tax immigration to be unconstitutional, and expressly recommended that Congress should exercise full authority over immigration. This ultimately led to the enactment of the first general immigration law, which was approved by President Chester A. Arthur (1830-86) August 3, 1882. It provided for a head tax of 50 cents on all aliens landed at United States ports, the money thus collected to be used to defray the expenses of regulating immigration and for the care of immigrants after landing. It also provided that foreign convicts, except those convicted for political offences, lunatics, idiots and persons likely to become public charges, should not be permitted to land. Aside from a law forbidding the importation of contract laborers, adopted in 1885 and strengthened by supplementary laws in 1887 and 1888, and aside from the laws about Chinese immigration which do not concern us here, there was no legislation affecting general immigration for nearly a decade, though the question was now widely discussed in the press and there was considerable agitation for further restriction.

In 1888 the House of Representatives authorized, by resolution, the appointment of a select committee to investigate the charges which were made that the immigration laws were being extensively evaded. The committee, known as the "Ford Committee," in its report more than sustained the charges; it praised the immigrants of the past and deprecated those who were then coming; and proposed a new bill which added polygamists, anarchists and persons afflicted with a loathsome or dangerous contagious disease to the excluded classes. Congress, however, did not act upon the recommendations of that committee.

In 1889 a Standing Committee on Immigration in the Senate and a Select Committee on Immigration and Naturalization in the House were established. In 1890 these committees were authorized jointly to make an inquiry relative to immigration. Various reports were submitted, and the conclusion was that a radical change was not advisable, although it had been found that throughout the country there existed a demand for a stricter enforcement of the immigration laws. During 1890 one or more political parties in twenty-three States had demanded additional regulation of immigration. Consequently a law strengthening the existing law in several important details, but making no radical departure from the former policy, was adopted in 1891.

But the question continued to receive the attention of Congress. There was another investigation by a joint committee in 1892, which reported in July of that year, and still another investigation ordered by the Senate. Two new bills were proposed—one establishing additional regulations, the other entirely prohibiting immigration for one year, on account of the epidemic of cholera then prevailing in Europe. But neither this measure, nor the educational test which was then for the first time recommended by a Congressional committee, was adopted, and the revised immigration law, which was approved by President Harrison March 3, 1893, was by no means radical. The head tax on immigrants was raised from fifty cents to one dollar by an amendment to an appropriation act in 1894.

The agitation of the subject in Congress continued, however, and finally both houses adopted a bill for an educational test, excluding persons physically capable and over sixteen years of age who could not read and write the English language or some other language, parents, grandparents, wives and minor children of admissible immigrants being excepted. President Grover Cleveland (1837-1908) returned the bill with his veto on March 2, 1897. He objected to the radical departure from the previous national policy relating to immigration, which welcomed all who came, the success of which policy was attested by the last century's great growth. In referring to the claim that the quality of recent immigration was undesirable, he said: "The time is quite within recent memory when the same thing was said of immigrants who, with their descendants, are now numbered among our best citizens." In referring to "the best reason that could be given for this radical restriction," the "protecting of our population against degeneration and saving our national peace and quiet from imported turbulence and disorder," President Cleveland said that he did not think that the nation would be protected against these evils by limiting immigration to those who could read and write, for, in his mind, it was safer "to admit a hundred thousand immigrants, who, though unable to read and write, seek among us only a home and an opportunity to work, than to admit one of those unruly agitators who can not only read and write, but delight in arousing by inflammatory speech the illiterate and peacefully inclined to discontent." Those classes which we ought to exclude, he claimed, should be legislated against directly. Some sections of the bill against aliens who come regularly into the United States from neighboring countries for the purpose of obtaining work, he declared to be "illiberal, narrow and un-American."

On March 3, 1897, the House passed the bill over the President's veto by a vote of 193 to 37, but no action was taken in the Senate, and the veto was thus sustained. The same bill was introduced in the following Congress (fifty-fifth) and passed by the Senate, but the House, by a vote of 103 to 101 refused to consider it.

By an act of June 18, 1898, Congress created an Industrial

Commission "to investigate questions pertaining to immigration, and to report to Congress and to suggest such legislation as it may deem best upon these subjects." The final report of this commission was submitted to Congress in February, 1902, and shortly afterwards a bill was introduced in the House which was substantially in accord with the recommendations made. The House added a literary test to this bill, but it was eliminated by the Senate, which raised the head tax from one dollar to two. This was accepted by the House, and the bill, as it was approved by the President March 3, 1903, made no radical change in the existing laws. The same may be said of the present immigration law, which was approved February 20, 1907, which, besides raising the head tax from two to four dollars and somewhat strengthening the provisions against the defective or undesirable classes, made no innovation or departure from the policy of admitting all who may be expected to be able to provide for themselves and to become good citizens. The number as well as the percentage of those excluded is now considerably larger than in former years; but the tide of immigration is not stemmed, and after the quick recovery from the hard times which began with the panic of 1907, there is now again a very large influx of immigrants, among whom the proportion of Jews is by no means smaller than in former years.

The act of 1907 also created an Immigration Commission to "make full inquiry, examination, and investigation, by sub-committee or otherwise, into the subject of immigration." This commission submitted its report, in forty volumes, in 1910, and recommended some strong restrictions, with the view that "a sufficient number may be debarred to produce a marked effect upon the present supply of unskilled labor." It also advised that "as far as possible the aliens excluded should be those who come to this country with no intention to become American citizens or even to maintain a permanent residence here; but merely to save enough, by the adoption, if necessary, of low standards of living, to return permanently to their home country. . . . A majority of the Commission favor the reading and writing test as the most feasible single method of restricting undesirable immigration." Congress has not acted on these recommendations at the time of this writing (1911).

* * * * *

The question of enforced rest on Sunday is much older than the question of regulating immigration. Several States have Sunday laws which were in their original form enacted in the eighteenth century. In the Carolinas these laws have been but little changed since Colonial times. But the reviews of these laws in the various States and Territories, their effect on the Jews, and the leading cases under them in various times and places, give no adequate idea of their significance for the Orthodox immigrant of the later period. What our best authority on the subject, Albert M. Friedenberg,[1] could collect and collate, contains only a record of such cases which originated in, or were carried up to, higher courts of record. These are usually lawsuits which affected men of means, who could hire attorneys and fight the question as a matter of principle. But these recorded cases give no indication of the tens of thousands of arrests which were made in the large cities, especially in New York City, in the last years, where the cases never went higher than the first instance, because the poor man, if he was not discharged in the Police Court, had to pay his fine or be imprisoned. Appeals to higher courts and insistence upon constitutional or statutory rights are out of the question, not only on account of poverty or ignorance, but also because of familiarity with such procedure in the Old World. The Sunday laws are not constantly enforced in the same manner, there being periods of severity and periods of lenience even under the same local administration, and often a complete change

[1] See his *The Jews and the American Sunday Laws* in "Publications," XI, pp. 101-15 (also note ibid., XII, pp. 171-73), and his *Sunday Laws in the United States and Leading Judicial Decisions Having Special Reference to the Jews* in The American Jewish Year Book for 5669, pp. 152-89.

of policy under a new administration, though the statute or State law remains the same. The Jew of Russia or Roumania has been too well accustomed to intermittent police tyranny for the purpose of extortion at home, to be able to interpret the frequent changes in administrative policy or in police regulations here in any other way, and this also tends to discourage appeals to higher courts. The question ought to be investigated not juristically but statistically; the number of arrests made, the loss of time and money sustained by those who are charged with transgressing these laws, and the contrast in the enforcement of them at various periods: if such facts and figures were placed before the American people and before legislators, the attitude of many in regard to Sunday laws would probably be changed. But the figures are not available in a form to be used in a work like the present, and only the hope can be expressed here that they will be collected in the near future by one of the agencies which gather data of that kind relating to Jewish subjects.

There is no Federal Sunday Law, although the distillation of spirituous liquors on the first day of the week is prohibited. California only prohibits labor by any employee on more than six days out of every seven, but not specifying any compulsory day of rest. In Colorado only trafficking in liquors and barbering are prohibited on Sunday and in Montana there is a law against barbering only.

In most of the other States, as well as in the Territories and in the District of Columbia (which is also counted as a Territory), there are more or less stringent laws, most of them forbidding not only manual labor but also the carrying on of trade or business. There are eleven States—Arkansas, Illinois, Kansas, Minnesota, Missouri, Nebraska, New Jersey, New York, South Dakota, Texas and Virginia—where servile or manual labor is permitted on Sunday to those who observe Saturday as their day of rest. In thirteen more—Connecticut,: Indiana, Iowa, Kentucky, Maine, Massachusetts, Michigan, North Dakota, Ohio, Oklahoma, Rhode Island, West Virginia and Wisconsin—the exceptions in favor of Seventh-Day Sabbatarians affect both manual labor and trade or business. But the statute is not always a criterion of the observance or enforcement of Sunday laws in a certain locality. Some of the laws, like that of New York, decree that "it is a sufficient defense to a prosecution for work on the first day of the week, that the defendant uniformly keeps another day of the week as holy time, and does not labor on that day, and that the labor complained of was done in such manner as not to interrupt or disturb other persons in observing the first day of the week as holy time." In many localities, especially in large cities, the Sunday laws are simply obsolete, and are usually revived in the name of Reform after the success of a Reform Party at the polls, only to become obsolete again when that party is voted out of office at the succeeding election. The defeat usually comes for no other reason than the dissatisfaction of a large number of citizens with the strict enforcement of the Sunday laws. Jews are by no means the only element of the population which resents stringency in these matters. It may be said that the coupling together of strict enforcement of the Sunday laws with the good government movements in the large cities has been a greater drawback to municipal reform in the United States than any other single cause.

Of all these three problems which are of special interest to the Jews of the United States, the first, or the passport question, seems at the present moment to be nearest to solution. The immigration question is certain to remain open for many years to come, as neither side of the conflicting interests who work against each other is likely to yield in the near future. The trade unions, which see in the immigrant a menace to the highly-paid laborer, and the so-called patriotic societies, which fear a deterioration of the American race or stock by the admixture of people from nationalities and races which they consider to be inferior, keep up a constant agitation for more restrictive measures against the influx of strangers. On the other hand, there is a constantly increasing demand for workmen in the expanding industries, for farm laborers and for domestic servants, and the million or more immigrants who now arrive in a year of ordinary business activity are so easily absorbed that their usefulness cannot be denied. While the adoption of some restrictive legislation may be forced on Congress by the pressure of those who agitate for it, real restriction seems to be out of the question before the country is filled up and built up; and this will take so long a time that all speculations as to what may happen afterwards are at present premature.

There is hardly any agitation for or against the Sunday laws, as such. New and mostly restrictive measures are adopted, either against the liquor business as a concession to the Prohibition element, which is backed by the churches; or against single trades, like those of butchers or barbers, as a concession to the sentiment in favor of overworked laborers. The time for abolishing the Sunday laws or for adopting explicit exemptions in favor of Jews, making the observance of Saturday not a defense against prosecution but a security against molestation, has not yet arrived; but the sense of justice and righteousness is unmistakably growing, and there is no doubt of the ultimate triumph of liberal tendencies over this heritage of intolerant ages, when nobody considered himself bound to respect the rights, especially the religious rights, of helpless minorities.

CHAPTER XXXV.

END OF THE CENTURY. THE SPANISH-AMERICAN WAR. THE DREYFUS AFFAIR. ZIONISM.

Jews in the Spanish-American war—Commissioned and non-commissioned officers, privates and "Rough Riders"—Jews in the Navy: Simon Cook, Joseph Strauss and Edward David Taussig—The career of Rear-Admiral Adolph Marix—His part in the Inquiry about the "Maine" and in the war—The significance of the Dreyfus Affair—Its influence on the spread of Zionism—The American press almost as pro-Dreyfus as the Jewish—The Zionist movement in America—The rank and file consists of immigrants from Slavic countries, under the leadership of Americans.

In the short war between the United States and Spain in 1898, in which the most progressive and liberal of modern nations was pitted against a nation whose greatness began to wane soon after it expelled the Jews in the year of the discovery of America, a large number of Jews enlisted as volunteers, besides the number who were in the regular service of the Army and the Navy. It is roughly estimated that about four thousand Jews were found in the military and naval forces which operated against Spain[1] most of them immigrants of the last period, of whom a considerable proportion had served in the armies of Russia, Austria and Roumania before their arrival here. The Jewish army officers of the highest rank were four Majors, who were officers in the army before the outbreak of the war. They were: Major

[1] See *Preliminary list of Jewish Soldiers and Sailors who served in the Spanish-American War* in The American Jewish Year Book for 5661, pp. 525-622.

Surgeon Daniel M. Appel (b. in Pennsylvania, 1854) and Major Surgeon Aaron H. Appel (b. 1856), both of whom are now colonels in the Medical Corps of the regular army; the third was Major (of volunteers) George W Moses, a native of Ohio, who graduated from the Military Academy of West Point in 1892, and was a Lieutenant in the 3rd Cavalry Regiment when he was assigned to duty as a major of volunteers and returned to the regular service in 1899; the fourth was Major Felix Rosenberg of Cleveland, O., who was stationed at Fort Thomas. There were also in the army about a half dozen Captains, one of whom, Moses G. Zalinski (b. in New York, 1863), a graduate of the Artillery School (1894), is now a Lieutenant-Colonel in the regular army. There were also about a dozen Lieutenants, most of whom graduated from the Military Academy of West Point.

Several hundred Jews served as non-commissioned officers and privates in the regular army, or enlisted as United States Volunteers. The bulk of the Jewish soldiers, however, served in the regiments of State Volunteers, and were represented among the soldiers of every State of the Union, having among them a goodly proportion of non-commissioned officers, and also a number who held commissions from the State organizations. They were naturally represented in largest numbers in the regiments or companies which were organized in the large cities; some companies in New York regiments containing between twenty-five and thirty Jewish recruits. At least a half dozen Jews are known to have served in the First United States Volunteer Cavalry Regiment (known as the regiment of "Rough Riders"), which was organized by Theodore Roosevelt (b. in New York City, 1858), who later served as President of the United States, from September 14, 1901, to March 4, 1905, as the successor of President William McKinley (1843-1901), and then served a full term (March 4, 1905, to March 4, 1909), until he was succeeded by the present incumbent, William Howard Taft (b. in Cincinnati, O., 1857).

There were about twenty Jewish officers of various ranks in the Navy during this war, and almost all of them were graduates from the United States Naval Academy of Annapolis, Md. One of them, Simon Cook (b. in Illinois, 1856; d. in St. Louis, Mo., 1907), who was appointed to Annapolis from the old Third Congressional District of Missouri in 1873 and graduated in 1877, served with distinction in the Philippines; and a disease which he contracted there forced his retirement, with the rank of Commander, before he reached the age limit of retirement. Another Jewish officer of the Navy during the war, Lieutenant Joseph Strauss, is still in the active service with the rank of Commander (which is equivalent to the rank of Lieutenant-Colonel in the Army). A third officer of Jewish descent attained to a higher rank. Edward David Taussig (b. in St. Louis, 1847) entered the Naval Academy in 1863 and graduated in 1867, and was a Lieutenant-Commander (since 1892) at the time of the outbreak of the war. He served on the Pacific and European Stations and in the coast survey until 1893, when he was made commander of the "Bennington." He took possession of Wake Island (Oceanica) for the United States, and was placed in charge of Guam when that island was ceded by Spain on February 1, 1899. In 1902 he became a Captain (which is equal to the rank of Colonel in the Army); in 1903 he was appointed commander of the Navy Yard at Pensacola, Fla. He was retired with the rank of Rear-Admiral (the equivalent of Brigadier-General) in 1909.

The most conspicuous part played by a Jew in the events which led to the war with Spain, if not in the war itself, fell to the lot of Lieutenant-Commander (now Rear-Admiral, retired) Adolph Marix (b. in Germany, probably of Russian parents, 1848), who came to America in his boyhood, and entered the Naval Academy in 1864, graduating four years later. He advanced step by step, becoming an ensign in 1869, a master in 1870, a lieutenant in 1872, after which he was assigned to special service in the Judge Advocate-General's office, where he gained valuable experience and became an expert in naval and maritime law. In 1893 he was promoted to the rank of Lieutenant-Commander, and in September, 1895, he was transferred from the command of the receiving ship "Minnesota" to be the first commander of the ill-fated battleship "Maine," which was then put in commission. He was transferred to the "Scorpion" in January, 1898, several weeks before the "Maine" arrived in the harbor of Havana, where she was destroyed by an explosion on February 15 of the same year.

Lieutenant-Commander Marix was chosen secretary or recorder of the Court of Inquiry which investigated the blowing up of the "Maine," and he prepared the report, which was one of the contributing causes of the war. He himself laid the ominous document before President McKinley on March 26, 1898, and soon returned to engage in the war which was to terminate Spanish dominion in the New World. In the same month he was advanced to the rank of Commander and was later advanced, by act of Congress, two numbers for "eminent and conspicuous conduct in battle in two engagements at Manzanillo (Cuba), July 1 and July 18, 1898. When President Taft was Governor-General of the Philippines, Commander Marix was a naval attaché in the islands. He later rose to the rank of Rear-Admiral, and having attained the age-limit (62), he was retired in April, 1910, after forty-six years of service. He now resides in New York City.

* * * * *

By the time the Spanish War was over and Spain was stripped of the last vestige of advantage which she gained by the discovery of America, the attention of the civilized world was concentrated on the celebrated Dreyfus Case. The last desperate effort of the forces of reaction to foist an anti-Jewish policy on a great progressive nation served only to prove in the end that the world has advanced beyond such tactics, and that the voice of Justice cannot be stifled in a civilized community, where the people ultimately decide all-important questions. Not only was France shaken to its foundations and the existence of the Government itself endangered on account of the grievous wrong which was done to the Jewish army officer, but the entire civilized world was aroused by the incident as it probably never was before by the fate of one insignificant individual. It was the first and only attempt of a real "Judenhetze" in a modern free country, and so much depended on the outcome, that not only the Jews everywhere were intensely interested, but also their friends and their enemies felt the full importance of the "affaire" and the bearing which the issue must have on Jewish conditions everywhere. Had anti-Semitism triumphed in France, it would mean that even political liberty, universal suffrage and government by the people could not solve the Jewish problem; that Western Culture could not effect the true emancipation which was expected of it, and that other means than those suggested by the principles of the great liberal movement of the last century—adjustment to surroundings, adoption of the speech and mode of life of the nations among whom they live—must be sought to deliver Israel from his ancient suffering even in the most highly civilized countries.

Fortunately for France, for civilization and for the Jews, anti-Semitism was utterly defeated in the open political combat for the first time in modern history. The barrier erected by Liberty proved sufficiently strong to stem the tide of raging injustice; the very excitement caused by the wrong was the best warning against the danger which the revival of medieval bigotry brings to an enlightened country. Persecution and discrimination were again forced back and confined to the more shady corners of the earth, to the countries where the masses of the people are still oppressed by tyranny and handicapped by ignorance. It was in these countries that the Dreyfus agitation was seized upon by the enemies of the Jews and exploited to the umost extent, and it was there that many Jews began to despair. If France could become anti-Semitic at the end of the nineteenth century, what hope was there for the Jew in the backward countries, in political progress and cultural development? The full force of the victory over the French reactionaries was known and felt only in the free countries; elsewhere the impression remained that the Jews of France remained in a lamentable position, and that the future looked as gloomy to them as is usually the case in Russia after a new outbreak of anti-Jewish riots.

The result of this new hopeless view of the Jewish situation was the sudden spread of the new Zionist movement, which was inaugurated about that time on the Continent by Dr. Theodore Herzl (1860-1904). He and his first supporters were Austrians, they obtained their largest following in Russia and Galicia, and in the large cities in other countries where there were numbers of Jewish Immigrants from slavic countries. When the movement began to show signs of life in the English speaking countries, native or assimilated Jews joined it and became its leaders. And so it came to pass that although the American press, with few and unimportant exceptions, was as strongly pro-Dreyfus as the Jewish press itself, and the victory of Justice and liberalism was as much emphasized here as in Paris, a limited field was prepared here for the Zionist movement, as well as in Russia, Austria and Roumania. The old "Chowewe Zion," or believers in the colonization of Palestine, joined the new political movement here, as they did abroad, and the "Maskilim," or Germanized Hebrew scholars, who were forced to the background by the advent of the popular radical leaders of the new period of immigration, were also attracted by the new movement which helped to restore the equilibrium among the intellectual Jewish classes. The first Zionist societies of New York consisted almost entirely of immigrants. But when the "Federation of Zionist Societies of Greater New York and Vicinity" (organized 1897) expanded by absorbing societies outside of New York, and became, at a convention held in New York in July, 1898, the "Federation of American Zionists," American Jews were placed at the head of the movement.

Professor Richard J. H. Gottheil was elected President of the Federation, and held the position for six years, when he was succeeded, in 1904, by Dr. Harry Friedenwald (b. in Baltimore, 1864), whose father, Dr. Aaron Friedenwald (b. in Baltimore, 1836; d. there 1902), was one of the first Vice-Presidents of the Federation. The first Secretary was Rev. Stephen S. Wise (b. in Budapest, Hungary, 1872), who was brought to this country in his childhood, and is now the minister of the Free Synagogue in New York. His successors were Isidore D. Morrison, Jacob de Haas, Rev. Dr. Judah L. Magnes (b. in San Francisco, Cal., 1877) and Miss Henrietta Szold. The Federation consisted of about twenty-five societies, having a membership of about one thousand when it was first organized. At the Thirteenth Annual Convention, which was held in Pittsburg in July, 1910, it was reported that the number of societies was 215, and of Shekel payers 14,000.

The Order Knights of Zion, which has its headquarters in Chicago, is considered as an independent Western Federation of Zionists.

PART VII.

THE TWENTIETH CENTURY. PRESENT CONDITIONS.

CHAPTER XXXVI.

SYNAGOGUES AND INSTITUTIONS. THE ENCYCLOPEDIA. ROUMANIA AND THE ROUMANIAN NOTE.

Synagogues and other Jewish Institutions—General improvement and moderation—The Jewish Encyclopedia—Its editors and contributors—The Roumanian situation and the American Government's interest in it since 1867—Benjamin F. Peixotto, United States Consul-General in Bucharest—Diplomatic correspondence between Kasson and Evarts—New negotiations with Roumania in 1902—The Roumanian Note to the signatories of the Berlin Treaty—The question still in abeyance.

More than six hundred thousand Jews arrived in the United States from the beginning of the new exodus in 1881 until the end of the nineteenth century, and the total number in the country was now considerably more than one million. There were Jews in more than five hundred places, and there were 791 congregations, 415 educational and nearly five hundred charitable institutions of a distinctly Jewish character, according to an enumeration made in the beginning of the new century.[1] But the number of congregations or synagogues was very much larger, probably more than double than the figures gathered by the enum-

[1] American-Jewish Year Book for 5661 (1900-1901).

erators. For the American, even the American Jew, had then not yet learned to take seriously those small and exceedingly unchurchlike synagogues of the small congregations, of which five or six, or even a larger number, can sometimes be found in one block in a thickly settled Jewish neighborhood in the great cities. A second and more thorough enumeration made in 1907 gave to New York City alone a number of synagogues almost as large as the one given by the statistics of 1900 to the entire country; but the actual increase was very far from such proportions. Probably four-fifths of the congregations of New York and of the other great Jewish centers in the East and the Middle West were more than ten years old, and they simply escaped the notice of former enumerators. The organizing of small synagogues is now out of fashion; the tendency is to consolidate the smaller ones and to erect more fashionable and spacious buildings in the newest neighborhoods, to which the immigrants usually move after they leave their earliest abode in the tenement house districts. In the fields of charity and education the predilection for new organizations is disappearing, and there is a desire to build on more solid foundations, and to improve and strengthen rather than form anew. New synagogues are now built usually in new communities or in new Jewish neighborhoods, or by old congregations who need a larger edifice.

America now had the largest community of free Jews in the world, *i. e.*, of Jews who labored under no special disadvantages and who had no special difficulties, like those which are making life a burden to the Jews of Russia or Galicia. The great masses which arrived in the last twenty years progressed rapidly and were becoming Americanized in every respect. There arose new intellectual needs; the extremists had to yield to the influence of those who were more acclimatized, and even the most radical periodicals began to respect the susceptibilities, if not the opinions, of the other classes. The number of the educated and the well-to-do was fast increasing, and the community was now well prepared for "the capital event in the history of Jewish learning in America"—the publication of the *Jewish Encyclopedia*.

This monumental work, the greatest Jewish work of reference in any language, was projected by Dr. Isidore Singer (b. in Weisskirchen, Moravia, 1859; a. 1895) and edited by a board of well-known scholars, of whom Dr. Isaac Funk (b. in Clinton, O., 1839; d. 1912; of the firm of Funk and Wagnalls, which published the work) was chairman, and Frank H. Vizitelly (b. in London, Eng., 1864) secretary. The original editors were: Cyrus Adler, Gotthard Deutsch (b. in Kanitz, Austria, 1859; a. 1891), Professor of History at the Hebrew Union College; Louis Ginzberg (b. in Kovno, Russia, 1873; a. 1899), now Professor of Talmud at the Jewish Theological Seminary of America in New York; Richard Gottheil; Joseph Jacobs (b. in Sydney, N. S. W., 1854; a. 1900), the folklorist and statistician; Marcus Jastrow; Morris Jastrow, Jr.; Kaufman Kohler; Frederick de Sola Mendes (b. in Jamaica, W. I., 1850; a. 1873), rabbi of the West End Synagogue of New York; Isidor Singer, and Crawford H. Toy (b. in Norfolk, Va., 1836), Professor (now "emeritus") of Hebrew and Oriental Languages at Harvard University. This editorial board was given on the title page of the first volume which appeared in May, 1901; but several changes were made during the five years of its publication. From the beginning of the second volume Herman Rosenthal became editor of the new Department of the Jews of Russia and Poland, and it is due to his efforts that the Jews of the Slavic countries are more extensively treated in the historical and biographical parts of the Encyclopedia than was ever the case in works of Jewish science which appeared outside of Russia. Dr. Emil G. Hirsch of Chicago succeeded Morris Jastrow as editor of the Department of the Bible, with the beginning of the third volume. From the fourth till the seventh volume the name of Solomon Schechter (b. in Fokshan, Roumania, 1847; a. 1902), the President of the Jewish Theological Seminary, appears as editor of the Department of the Talmud; and from the eighth volume to the end the name of Wilhelm Bacher of Budapest (b. in Hungary 1850) appears as editor of the Department of the Talmud and Rabbinical Literature, succeeding both Schechter and Ginzberg. The editorial board

Prof. Gotthard Deutsch.

was assisted by boards of American and foreign consulting editors, which included many of the best known Jewish scholars and Orientalists, and many other scholars from various countries were among the four hundred contributors who participated in the preparation of the work, in which the vast "Record of the History, Religion, Literature and Customs of the Jewish People from the earliest times to the present day" was for the first time systematized, classified and made available in a modern scientific manner.

* * * * *

The situation of the Jews in Roumania had been growing worse since the financial crisis of 1899, and in the last year of the century there was a stampede of Jews from that country, some of them walking hundreds of miles before they could find a place to rest or until they reached a port from which they could embark for England or America. Still, neither the Jewish immigration in general nor the immigration from Roumania could give the slightest cause for uneasiness to the government of the United States, the tide of immigration was now again rising from the lowest ebb it had reached since 1879—229,295 in 1898—and neither the 5,613 Roumanian Jews who arrived at the port of New York in 1901 nor the 6,395 who came in 1902, when the general immigration was 487,918 and 648,743, respectively, could be taken seriously as a cause for interference or protest. There would have been much more cause for protests of that nature after the great massacres in Russia several years later, when the number of Jews who arrived in one year (1906) exceeded 150,000. The interest that the Government of the United States took in the Roumanian situation is therefore believed to have been due principally to the friendly attitude of President Theodore Roosevelt and Secretary of State John Hay towards Jews in general.

It was, however, nothing new for the American Government to use its good offices in behalf of the persecuted Jews of Roumania. As early as 1867, Secretary of State Seward corresponded with Mr. Morris, the American Minister to Constantinople, about the persecutions of that year; and the latter reported having told Mr. Golesco, the agent of the Danubian principalities, that the sufferings of the Jews there "has all the appearance of religious persecution, and that the confidence of the Government of the United States would be impaired in the Government of Bucharest, unless the proscriptive measures against the Jews discontinued."[1]

In 1870 official—or it would perhaps be more correct to call it semi-official—relations with Roumania were established temporarily, by the appointment of a consul-general of the United States in Roumania. The man chosen by President Grant for this position was a prominent Jewish attorney-at-law, Benjamin Franklin Peixotto (b. in New York, 1834; d. there 1890), who later served as United States Consul at Lyons, France (1877-85), and when he returned to New York founded (1886) the "Menorah," a monthly Jewish magazine which existed for more than two decades. The Jewish official became an intimate friend of Prince (now King) Charles, but Roumania continued on its old way, and the riots of Ismail and Bessarabia occurred during Peixotto's stay in Bucharest. "His reports to the United States Government resulted in that government addressing letters to its ministers at the various European courts inviting co-operation in the humane endeavor to stop Jewish persecution in Roumania. Peixotto's reports were also the cause of a great meeting at the Mansion House in London, which called forth Lord Shaftesbury's message of sympathy. Peixotto was instrumental, too, in founding the Society of Zion in Roumania, an organization with similar aims to the B'nai B'rith; and it was his influence as a United States official, his intimacy with the European philanthropists and the force of his own personal magnetism that finally caused the calling of the conference of Brussels, to which he was a delegate, and which culminated in the action taken by the Berlin

[1] See Adler, *Jews in American Diplomatic Correspondence*, "Publications" XV, pp. 48-73.

Congress of 1878, when Roumania acquired the status of a sovereign kingdom only upon the express condition that the civil and political rights of the Jews should be recognized." (E. A. Cardozo, in *Encyclopedia* IX, p. 582, s. v. Peixotto.)

Peixotto remained in Roumania six years, and about two years after he left Bucharest, Mr. John A. Kasson, the American Minister to Austria, wrote to Secretary of State Evarts (under date of June 5, 1878) that in anticipation of Roumanian independence, which was soon to be granted by the Congress of Berlin, Germany, had begun negotiations with the Roumanian Government for a commercial treaty. But Germany finally dropped the negotiations because, "according to information received here, the hostility of Roumania to the recognition of equal rights for Jews of a foreign nationality with other citizens or subjects of the same nationality would have practically proscribed a portion of the German subjects." Yet Mr. Kasson proposes in the same letter that: "It would be to the honor of the United States Government if it could initiate a plan by which at once the condition of American Hebrews resident or travelling in Roumania and the condition of natives of the same race could be ameliorated and their equality before the law at least partially assured." In the following year Mr. Kasson reports about the attempt to enter into diplomatic relations with Roumania, and about a conversation he had with Mr. Balatshano, the envoy and minister of Roumania to Austria, in the course of which allusion was made to the preliminary requirements of the Berlin treaty in respect to the Jews. According to the letter (dated February 16, 1879), the representative of Roumania replied "that the necessary changes would be made in their laws to give satisfaction on this point, and to establish for the Jews the basis of absolute equality with other races." On November 28, 1879, Secretary Evarts writes to Mr. Kasson:

"In connection with the subject of Roumanian recognition, I inclose for your consideration the copy of a letter under date of the 30th ultimo from Mr. Myer S. Isaacs, president, and other officers of tne board of delegates on civil and religious rights of the Hebrews, asking that the Government of the United States may exert its influence towards securing for its Hebrew subjects and residents in Roumania the equality of civil and religious rights stipulated in Article XLIV of the treaty of Berlin.

"As you are aware, this government has ever felt a deep interest in the welfare of the Hebrew race in foreign countries, and has viewed with abhorrence the wrongs to which they have at various periods been subjected by the followers of other creeds in the East. This Department is therefore disposed to give favorable consideration to the appeal made by the representatives of a prominent Hebrew organization in this country in behalf of their brethren in Roumania, and while I should not be warranted in making a compliance with their wishes a *sine qua non* in the establishment of official relations with that country, yet any terms favorable to the interest of this much-injured people which you may be able to secure in the negotiations now pending with the Government of Roumania would be agreeable and gratifying to this Department.

"I am, etc.,

"WM. M. EVARTS."

It was therefore only a continuance of its old policy when the Government of the United States, which has—as Mr. Evarts expressed it in 1879—"ever felt a deep interest in the welfare of the Hebrew race in foreign countries," again began, in 1902, to pay attention to the pitiable condition of the Roumanian Jews. There still existed no treaty or diplomatic relations between the United States and Roumania, and a new attempt was made by our Department of State to negotiate a naturalization convention, and perhaps by these means influence that country to treat its Jews more favorably. The negotiations were carried on through the American legation at Athens, Greece, and Secretary Hay sent, on July 17, 1902, a long confidential dispatch to Mr. Charles L. Wilson, the *Charge d'Affaires ad interim* in Athens, which contained the largest part of the famous "Roumanian Note" to the signatories of the Treaty of Berlin, which was issued in the following month. Wilson's reply, dated August 8, states that "since the draft of the treaty approved by the Department was submitted to the Roumanian minister for foreign affairs nothing further has been accomplished, as the Roumanian Government refused to consider the project favorably." The Roumanian Minister to Greece frankly admitted to the American representative that the King was against the proposed treaty, because, "according to His Majesty's opinion, a naturalization treaty would be most injurious to Roumania, for the reason that it would complicate the already troublesome Jewish question in that country."

Three days after the date of that dispatch, John Hay issued, on August 11, 1902, the Roumanian Note, which was sent to the representatives of the United States to France, Germany, Great Britain, Italy, Russia and Turkey. The full text of this unique circular note, which made a profound impression in the entire civilized world, is as follows:

"Department of State.
"Washington, August 11, 1902.

"EXCELLENCY:—In the course of an instruction recently sent to the Minister accredited to the Government of Roumania in regard to the base of negotiations begun with that government looking to a convention of naturalization between the United States and Roumania, certain considerations were set forth for the Minister's guidance concerning the character of the immigration from that country, the causes which constrain it, and the consequences so far as they adversely affect the United States.

"It has seemed to the President appropriate that these considerations, relating as they do to the obligations entered into by the signatories of the Treaty of Berlin of July 13, 1878, should be brought to the attention of the Governments concerned, and commended to their consideration in the hope that, if they are so fortunate as to meet the approval of the several Powers, such measures as to them may seem wise may be taken to persuade the Government of Roumania to reconsider the subject of the grievances in question.

"The United States welcomes now, as it has welcomed from the foundation of its Government, the voluntary immigration of all aliens coming hither under conditions fitting them to become merged in the body politic of this land. Our laws provide the means for them to become incorporated indistinguishably in the mass of citizens, and prescribe their absolute equality with the native horn, guaranteeing to them equal civil rights at home and equal protection abroad. The conditions are few, looking to their coming as free agents, so circumstanced physically and morally as to supply the healthful and intelligent material for free citizenhood. The pauper, the criminal, the contagiously or incurably diseased are excluded from the benefit of immigration only when they are likely to become a source of danger or a burden upon the community. The voluntary character of their coming is essential; hence we shut out all immigration assisted or constrained by foreign agencies. The purpose of our generous treatment of the alien immigrant is to benefit us and him alike—not to afford to another state a field upon which to cast its own objectionable elements. The alien, coming hither voluntarily and prepared to take upon himself the preparatory and in due course the definite obligations of citizenship, retains hereafter, in domestic and international relations, the initial character of free agency, in the full enjoyment of which it is incumbent upon his adoptive State to protect him.

"The foregoing considerations, whilst pertinent to the examination of the purpose and scope of a naturalization treaty, have a larger aim. It behooves the State to scrutinize most jealously the character of the immigration from a foreign land, and, if it be obnoxious to objection, to examine the causes which render it so. Should those causes originate in the act of another sovereign State, to the detriment of its neighbors, it is the prerogative of an injured State to point out the evil and to make remonstrance; for with nations, as with individuals, the social law holds good that the right of each is bounded by the right of the neighbor.

"The condition of a large class of the inhabitants of Roumania has for many years been a source of grave concern to the United States. I refer to the Roumanian Jews, numbering some 400,000. Long ago, while the Danubian principalities labored under oppressive conditions which only war and a general action of the European powers sufficed to end, the persecution of the indigenous Jews under Turkish rule called forth in 1872 the strong remonstrance of the United States. The Treaty of Berlin was hailed as a cure for the wrong, in view of the express provisions of its forty-fourth article, prescribing that in Roumania the difference of religious creed and confessions shall not be alleged against any person as a ground for exclusion or incapacity in matters relating to the enjoyment of civil and political rights, admission to public employments, functions, and honors, or the exercise of the various professions and industries in any locality whatsoever, and stipulating freedom in the exercise of all forms of worship to Roumanian dependents and foreigners alike, as well as guaranteeing that all foreigners in Roumania shall be treated without distinction of creed, on a footing of perfect equality.

"With the lapse of time these just prescriptions have been rendered nugatory in great part, as regards the native Jews, by the legislation and municipal regulations of Roumania. Starting from the arbitrary and controvertible premises that the native Jews of Roumania domiciled there for centuries are 'aliens not subject to foreign protection,' the ability of the Jew to earn even the scanty means of existence that suffice for a frugal race has been constricted by degrees, until every opportunity to win a livelihood is denied; and until the helpless poverty of the Jew has constrained an exodus of such proportions as to cause general concern.

"The political disabilities of the Jews of Roumania, their exclusion from the public service and the learned professions, the limitation of their civil rights and the imposition upon them of exceptional taxes, involving as they do, wrongs repugnant to the moral sense of liberal modern peoples, are not so directly in point for my present purpose as the public acts which attack the inherent right of man as a breadwinner in the ways of agriculture and trade. The Jews are prohibited from owning land, or even from cultivating it as common laborers. They are debarred from residing in the rural districts. Many branches of petty trade and manual production are closed to them in the overcrowded cities where they are forced to dwell and engage, against fearful odds, in the desperate struggle for existence. Even as ordinary artizans or hired laborers they may only find employment in the proportion of one 'unprotected alien' to two 'Roumanians' under any one employer. In short, in the cumulative effects of successive restrictions, the Jews of Roumania have become reduced to a state of wretched misery. Shut out from nearly every avenue of self-support which is open to the poor of other lands, and ground down by poverty as the natural result of their discriminatory treatment, they are rendered incapable of lifting themselves from the enforced degradation they endure. Even were the fields of education, of civil employment and of commerce open to them as to 'Roumanian citizens,' their penury would prevent their rising by individual effort. Human beings so circumstanced have virtually no alternative but submissive suffering or flight to some land less unfavorable to them. Removal under such conditions is not and cannot be the healthy, intelligent emigration of a free and self-reliant being. It must be, in most cases, the mere transplantation of an artificially produced diseased growth to a new place.

"Granting that, in better and more healthful surroundings, the morbid condition will eventually change for good, such emigration is necessarily for a time a burden to the community upon which the fugitives may be cast. Self-reliance and the knowledge and ability that evolve the power of self-support must be developed, and, at the same time, avenues of employment must be opened in quarters where competition is already keen and opportunities scarce. The teachings of history and the experience of our own nation show that the Jews possess in a high degree the mental and moral qualifications of conscientious citizenhood. No class of immigrants is more welcome to our shore, when coming equipped in mind and body for entrance upon the struggle for bread, and inspired with the high purpose to give the best service of heart and brain to the land they adopt of their own free will. But when they come as outcasts, made doubly paupers by physical and moral oppression in their native land, and thrown upon the long suffering generosity of a more favored community, their immigration lacks the essential conditions which make alien immigration either acceptable or beneficial. So well is this appreciated on the Continent that, even in the countries where anti-Semitism has no foothold, it is difficult for these fleeing Jews to obtain any lodgment. America is their only goal.

"The United States offers asylum to the oppressed of all lands. But its sympathy with them in no wise impairs its just liberty and right to weigh the acts of the oppressor in the light of their effects upon this country and to judge accordingly.

"Putting together the facts now painfully brought home to this Government during the past few years, that many of the inhabitants of Roumania are being forced, by artificially adverse discriminations, to quit their native country; that the hospitable asylum offered by this country is almost the only refuge left to them; that they come hither unfitted, by the conditions of their exile, to take part in the new life of this land under circumstances either profitable to themselves or beneficial to the community; and that they are objects of charity from the outset and for a long time—the right of remonstrance against the acts of the Roumanian Government is clearly established in favor of this Government. Whether consciously and of purpose or not, these helpless people, burdened and spurned by their native land, are forced by the sovereign power of Roumania upon the charity of the United States. This Government cannot be a tacit party to such an international wrong. It is constrained to protest against the treatment to which the Jews of Roumania are subjected, not alone because it has unimpeachable right to remonstrate against the resultant injury to itself, but in the name of humanity. The United States may not authoritatively appeal to the stipulations of the Treaty of Berlin, to which it was not and cannot become a signatory, but it does earnestly appeal to the principles consigned therein, because they are the principles of international law and eternal justice, advocating the broad toleration which that solemn compact enjoins and standing ready to lend its moral support to the fulfilment thereof by its co-signatories, for the act of Roumania itself has effectively joined the United States to them as an interested party in this regard.

"You will take an early occasion to read this instruction to the Minister for Foreign Affairs and, should he request it, leave with him a copy.

"I have the honor to be

"Your obedient servant,

"JOHN HAY."

The note made a great impression on the entire civilized world, but was followed by no practical results. The only government which took any notice of it was—as could have been expected—the British. Mr. John B. Jackson, who had in the meantime been appointed minister of the United States to Greece and was also accredited to Roumania, wrote from Athens (March 31, 1903) that, having been in charge of the American embassy at Berlin at the time when the note was received, he "understood that immediately after the same instruction has been communicated to the foreign office at London, the British Government, without in any way making known its own views contained therein, had addressed a communication to the other Governments which were parties to the Berlin treaty of 1878, inquiring what they proposed doing in the matter. So far as I am aware, however, no action was taken by any of these Governments, and the contents of the circular was never formally brought to the attention of the Roumanian Government. . ."

This letter, and another dated Athens, April 18, and still another dated September 7, 1903, contain statements made by Roumanian statesmen explaining the situation from their point of view, and observations made by Mr. Jackson himself during his travels through Roumania. The last letter, which closes the correspondence, ends with the remark that "the general feeling (in Roumania) is that the naturalization of Jews must be a gradual matter, as they become educated up to being Roumanians"—a feeling much more likely to be found in America than in Roumania.

There is still no treaty with Roumania, but there is an American Envoy Extraordinary and Minister Plenipotentiary (the usual designation of an ordinary minister) sent to Roumania and accredited also to Servia and Bulgaria, who resides at the Roumanian capital, Bucharest, where there is also an American consul-general. The representation is, as was the case in the time of Peixotto, one-sided, the Roumanian Government having no representative in the United States. The Roumanian question may therefore be considered neither as solved nor as abandoned, but to be in abeyance until a favorable opportunity shall present itself for further negotiations, which may ultimately lead to the only adjustment which can be acceptable to the United States as well as to the Jews.

CHAPTER XXXVII.

HELP FOR THE VICTIMS OF THE RUSSIAN MASSACRES IN 1903 AND 1905. OTHER PROOFS OF SYMPATHY.

The Kishinev massacre—Official solicitude and general sympathy—Protest meetings and collections—The "Kishinev Petition" and its fate—Less publicity given to the later pogroms, whose victims were helped by "landsleut" from this country—The influence of pogroms on immigration—The frightful massacres in Russia in the fall of 1905, and the assistance rendered by this country—A Resolution of sympathy adopted in Congress—The 250th Anniversary of the Settlement of the Jews in the United States—Relief for Moroccan Jews proposed by the United States—Oscar S. Straus in the Cabinet.

While the correspondence about the Jews of Roumania was still carried on by our State Department, the civilized world was shocked by the reports of the brutal massacre of Jews in Kishinev in the three days of April 19-21, 1903. This massacre which is still within every one's memory, aroused the press and the people of the United States more than the riots of 1881. "Almost from the first, the world's indignation centered in the United States. Served by a vigorous press, whose liberal spirit voices the prevailing attitude; animated by a humanitarianism which lies at the foundation of all our public institutions; realizing also that America was the chief refuge of all victims of persecution; the people of the United States became, again, the world's logical leaders in a campaign of humanity."[1] President Roosevelt's opening remark in his speech to the Executive Committee of the Independent Order of B'nai B'rith on June 15, 1903, when he said:

[1] Rabbi Maximilian Heller in *American Jewish Year Book* for 5664, p. 21.

"I have never in my experience in this country known of a more immediate or a deeper expression of sympathy for the victims and of horror over the appalling calamity that has occurred," was fully justified.

The news filtered very slowly through the usual channels, and more than a week passed before the enormity of the Russian crime became fully known. On the 29th of April the following dispatch was sent by our Department of State:

McCormick, Ambassador, St. Petersburg:

It is persistently reported upon what appears to be adequate authority that there is great want and suffering among Jews in Kishinev. Friends in this country would like to know if financial aid and supplies would be permitted to reach the sufferers.

Please ascertain this without discussing political phase of the action.

HAY.

Ambassador McCormick replied, ten days later, that it is "authoritatively denied that there is any want or suffering among Jews in Southwestern Russia and aid of any kind is unnecessary." But the people here understood that the Ambassador reflected the official view of the Russian Government, and efforts to raise money for the thousands of families which were left destitute by pillage, and for the hundreds of widows and orphans of the martyrs, were soon made, and large sums were collected in New York, as well as in many other places. More than seventy-five meetings of protest and indignation were held in fifty localities in twenty-seven States (and the District of Columbia) during the months of May and June, the most notable of which was the one held in New York, May 27, where Mayor Seth Low presided and ex-President Grover Cleveland was the principal orator. Among the largest meetings of the other places were those of Baltimore (May 17), of Philadelphia (June 3) and of New Orleans (June 13). In the most cases the prominent non-Jewish citizens, including high officials and ministers of religion, delivered addresses or expressed their sentiments in letters. Numerous sermons against Russia were preached in various churches and hundreds of editorial articles appeared in all sorts of periodicals. Public opinion was again, as it was twenty-two years before, practically unanimous in condemning Russia, and in encouraging every enterprise for the assistance of the sufferers from its barbarity.

The response to the appeals for material help was quick and generous. The contributions were sent either directly to the central office of the "Alliance Israelite Universelle" at Paris or to one of three agencies in New York—to the Relief Committee of which Emanuel Lehman was chairman and Daniel Guggenheim, treasurer, and which was in communication with the "Alliance"; to the Relief Committee of which K. H. Sarasohn was chairman and Arnold Kohn, treasurer, and which was in communication with the Central Relief Committee at Kishinev; or to Mr. William Randolph Hearst, whose newspapers, in New York, Chicago and San Francisco, did much to arouse the public to the gravity of the situation, and who forwarded the money collected by them to Treasurer Arnold Kohn. The sum sent to Kishinev from the United States through all these agencies was set down in a report made on June 7, 1903, by the Central Relief Committee at Kishinev to the "Hilfsverein der deutschen Juden" at Berlin, at 192,443 roubles (somewhat less than $100,000). It is about half of the sum which was collected in Russia itself, and a fourth of what was contributed by all the countries of the world.

It was generally understood that little could be accomplished by representations or remonstrances to Russia, but the desire to do something more than collect alms was very strong, and the sentiment naturally crystallized itself in an effort to ask the Government of the United States to use its good offices in behalf of the Jews of Russia. A petition was framed by the Executive Committee of the Independent Order of B'nai B'rith and submitted to the President of the United States with the request that it be transmitted to the Emperor of Russia. The President received the Committee cordially, and said at the conclusion of his remarks: "I will consider most carefully the suggestion that you have submitted to me, and whether the now existing conditions are such that any further official expression would be of advantage to the unfortunate survivors, with whom we sympathize so deeply."

The petition was couched in courteous terms, extolling the Czar personally and pleading that "he who led his own people and all others to the shrine of peace, will add new luster to his reign and fame by leading a new movement that shall commit the whole world in opposition to religious persecution." The petition was circulated in thirty-six States and Territories, and 12,544 signatures were obtained. Among the signers were Senators, Members of the House of Representatives, Governors (22), high judicial officers, State Legislators, Mayors of cities (150), clergymen of all denominations, including three Archbishops and seven Bishops, a large number of other officials, and many prominent men in the professional and the business world. President Roosevelt consented to transmit the petition, but the Russian Government declined to receive it, and the matter was thus ended. By permission of the President, the separate sheets of the petition bearing all the signatures, suitably bound and enclosed in a case provided for the purpose, have been placed in the archives of the Department of State.[1]

It was impossible to arouse the general public and even the general Jewish public at the recurrent pogroms and massacres at near intervals after Kishinev. But as is always the case with Russian or Galician or Roumanian cities when they suffer from fires, it became now the custom for all natives of an afflicted city to form some sort of organization in the rather rare occasion when there existed no synagogue or benevolent society of the

[1] See Adler, *The Voice of America on Kishineff*, Philadelphia, 1904. Among the books which appeared in the United States on this subject are also *Russia at the Bar of the American People*, by Isidore Singer, New York, 1904, and *Within the Pale*, New York, 1903, by the Irish patriot, Michael Davitt, who was sent to Russia soon after the massacre as a representative of Mr. Hearst's papers.

"landsleut," and to collect funds for the succor of the unfortunate families of the victims at home. Each of the riots and massacres between Kishinev and the terrible October days, the largest of which occurred at Homel (September 10-14, 1903), when eight Jews were killed and nearly one hundred injured; at Bender (May 1, 1904), and at Zhitomir (May 6, 1905), where twenty-nine were killed—each of these riots was a miniature Kishinev among the natives of the stricken place or its vicinity in this country. America became for the suffering Jews of Russia the Egypt of the time of the Patriarch Jacob, and the Russian immigrant who settled here before was the prosperous brother Joseph whom God sent to the New World before them to preserve life. To the emissaries from Palestine and from religious institutions in Russia, especially the Talmudical Academies or Yeshibot, who were coming regularly to the United States for many years to make collections among the conservative immigrants who prospered here, were now added emissaries from the radical or revolutionary parties from Russia, who were enthusiastically received by the working classes and the radical element in general, and their appeals for funds were seldom in vain.

The most substantial and most beneficial form of assistance sent from here to Russia was, however, not in response to appeals through Jewish newspapers or through personal representatives of causes, of parties or of institutions, but to requests made by members of families, by relatives or by friends to be taken out of Russia as soon as possible. While public appeals were made for charity of various kinds and for defense funds and similar objects, private correspondents solicited only one thing—steamship tickets. And the private responses, while they attracted less attention, were more generous, and in many instances verged on self-sacrifice. This can be deduced from the results, i. e., from the increased Jewish immigration, which was easily absorbed and little burdensome to the general Jewish public or to the larger charities, because most of the new arrivals had near relatives or friends who took care of them in the short time which elapsed until they could find employment. The increase of Jewish immigration on account of the pogroms can best be seen by a comparison of the number of Jewish arrivals at the Port of New York, where nearly nine-tenths of them arrive, with the general immigration for the five years 1903-07 (each ending June 30). The figures for 1903 are: Jews 58,079, total immigration, 857,046; for 1904: Jews 80,885, total 812,870; for 1905: Jews 103,941, total 1,027,421; for 1906: Jews 133,764, total 1,100,735; for 1907: Jews 117,486, total 1,285,349. It is seen that while general immigration in 1904 was about 45,000 less than in 1903, Jewish immigration was about 22,000 more. On the other hand, while general immigration rose to an unprecedented height in 1907, and was larger than the preceding year by 185,000, the number of Jews arriving in New York was about 16,000 less. The Jewish immigrant is not the man who fails at home or the adventurer who cares for no home; he could get along very well where he is if he were not molested, and Jewish immigration from Russia would become as insignificant as Jewish immigration from Germany if the former country could rise to the political and social conditions of the latter.

* * * * * *

The small pogroms which were designated above as miniature Kishinevs, and even Kishinev itself, were soon forgotten or began to look very small in comparison with the frightful massacres of the last day of October and the first days of November, 1905, with which the Russians inaugurated their quasi-constitutional regime. This time there were about a thousand Jews killed, the wounded numbered many thousands, the losses by destruction of property amounted to hundreds of millions. America again responded nobly, and a committee, of which Oscar S. Straus was chairman and Jacob H. Schiff, treasurer, collected considerably more than a million dollars, from Jews and non-Jews, mainly through the same agencies and by the same methods as the funds for the sufferers from Kishinev were collected. There were again mass-meetings at which prominent non-Jews spoke words of

Photo by Dupont, N. Y.

Hon. Jacob H. Schiff.

sympathy for the martyrs and their families and condemned the government which permitted such carnage. The general press was as friendly and sympathetic to the Jews as on former occasions. When the great march of Jewish mourners after the martyrs took place through the streets of New York, in which nearly one hundred thousand participated (December 4, 1905), several Christian churches tolled their bells in expression of sympathy with the weeping masses which passed by.

There was also an official expression of sympathy from Congress. Representatives Henry M. Goldfogle and William Sulzer introduced into the House resolutions to that effect, and a third one as a substitute was introduced by Representative Charles A. Towne, who, like the former two, represented a New York City District. The House Committee on Foreign Affairs granted a hearing, on February 8, 1906, to those interested in the passage of the resolutions. In its final form the joint resolution was introduced into the Senate by the late Anselm J. McLaurin of Mississippi, and in the House by Robert G. Cousins of Iowa, and read as follows:

> *Resolved by the Senate and House of Representatives of the United States of America in Congress assembled*, That the people of the United States are horrified by the reports of the massacre of Hebrews in Russia, on account of their race and religion, and that those bereaved thereby have the hearty sympathy of the people of this country.

This resolution was adopted without debate, and unanimously, by both houses on June 22, and approved by the President on June 26, 1906.

On two other occasions about the same time the friendly disposition of the people and the Government of the United States towards the Jews was manifested to the world. The first occasion was only semi-official, when the Jews of the country celebrated the Two Hundred and Fiftieth Anniversary of the Settlement of the Jews in the United States, on Thanksgiving Day (November 30), 1905. Meetings and special services were held in more than seventy localities between November 24 and December 10, but the principal celebration was in New York on the above mentioned date, in Carnegie Hall, where notable addresses were delivered by former President Grover Cleveland, Governor Francis W. Higgins of the State of New York, Mayor George B. McClellan of New York City, and Bishop David Greer. Cordial letters were received from President Roosevelt and Vice-President Charles W. Fairbanks. The principal oration at that memorable meeting was delivered by Judge Mayer Sulzberger of Philadelphia. Our present Ambassador to Russia, Curtis Guild, Jr., who was at that time Lieutenant-Governor of Massachusetts, was one of the speakers at the celebration meeting which was held in Boston, a day before the New York meeting.[1]

The second occasion attracted less attention, but was strictly official. The International Conference about Morocco, which was held in Algeciras, Spain, from January 6 to April 7, 1906, was participated in by the United States, and its first delegate, Henry White (Ambassador to Italy), received instruction by a special letter from Secretary of State (now Senator) Elihu Root to work for the protection of the Jews of Morocco. These instructions were accompanied by a letter received by Secretary Root from Mr. Jacob H. Schiff, setting forth the pitiable condition of the Jews of that country and enumerating the legal restrictions to which they were subject. Through the exertion of Mr. White, a provision was inserted, on April 2, in the treaty, with which the Conference was concluded, according to which the signatory nations guarantee the security and equal privileges of the Jews in Morocco, both those living in the ports and those living in the interior. (See "American-Jewish Year Book" for 5667, pp. 92-98.) The chief value of this provision, however, consists only in its indication of the good will of the Government of the United States. Its practical value for the Jews of

[1] Volume XIV of the *Publications* is devoted to the proceedings and the addresses of this celebration. It also appeared in a separate volume entitled *The Two Hundred and Fiftieth Anniversary of the Settlement of the Jews in the United States.* New York, 1906.

Oscar S. Straus.

Hon. Oscar S. Straus.

Morocco, as far as protection from riots and massacres are concerned, is hardly more than that of the well known "Article 44" of the Treaty of Berlin regarding the Jews of Roumania. The Jews of Morocco probably never heard of that provision, and the credit of ameliorating their condition rightfully belongs to France, which has, according to the latest agreement among European Powers, become the protector, or ruler of the Shereefian Empire.

Near the end of the same year (1906) President Roosevelt appointed Oscar S. Straus, the author and diplomatist, Secretary of Commerce and Labor. The first Jew to be thus honored with a seat in the Cabinet has served twice as minister plenipotentiary (and since he left the Cabinet, again as Ambassador) to Turkey, and also succeeded the late Benjamin Harrison, former president of the United States, as a member of the Permanent Court of Arbitration at The Hague. His oldest brother, Isidor Straus (b. in Bavaria, 1845; a. 1854; drowned with the "Titanic" April 15, 1912), was a well known merchant and philanthropist in New York, who was a member of the Fifty-third Congress, and has been for many years President of the Educational Alliance. Another brother, Nathan Straus (b. in Bavaria, 1848: a. 1854), who is also known as a philanthropist and served as Park Commissioner, and, for several months, as President of the Board of Health of New York, is two years older than the former Cabinet Minister.

CHAPTER XXXVIII.

THE AMERICAN-JEWISH COMMITTEE. EDUCATIONAL INSTITUTIONS AND FEDERATIONS.

Formation of the American Jewish Committee—Its first fifteen members and its membership in 1911—The experimental Kehillah organizations—The re-organized Jewish Theological Seminary—Faculty of the Hebrew Union College—The Dropsie College of Hebrew and Cognate Learning—The Rabbi Joseph Jacob School—Other Orthodox "Yeshibot"—Talmud Torahs and "Chedarim"—Hebrew Institutes—They become more Jewish because other agencies now do the work of Americanizing the immigrant—Technical Schools—Young Men's and Young Women's Hebrew Associations—Federations of various kinds.

The massacres of 1905 aroused and united the Jews of the civilized world, and the necessity of an organization to cope with the situation and with similar situations in the future began to be generally felt. The time when the Alliance Israelite Universelle, with its preponderance of French Jews and French methods, could act for the Jewry of all countries was now past, and only a new organization in which each country was independently represented could answer the purpose. The same was also true, in a more restricted sense, in the United States itself. None of the national Jewish bodies, not even the Order B'nai B'rith, with its Board of Delegates, could now assume to speak with undisputed authority in the name of American Jewry as it is now constituted. An attempt to form a representative international Committee of Jews was made at the General Jewish Conference which was convened at Brussels, Belgium, in the last days of January,

Photo by Gutekunst, Phila.

Judge Mayer Sulzberger.

1906, where a resolution to that effect was adopted. But the plan was not carried out.

Within a week after the Brussels Conference (February 3-4), a conference was held in New York City "to consider the formation of a General Jewish Committee or other representative body of the Jews in the United States."[1] A committee which was appointed by the chairman, Judge Mayer Sulzberger of Philadelphia, submitted its report to the conference at a subsequent meeting (May 19), which was referred to a Committee of Five, with instructions to select another Committee of Fifteen, representative of all Jewish societies of the United States, to be increased to fifty members, if considered desirable. About a month later, the chairman announced the following Committee as the nucleus of the American Jewish Committee, which was ultimately increased to sixty: Cyrus Adler, Washington, D. C.; Nathan Bijur, New York; Joseph H. Cohen, New York; Emil G. Hirsch, Chicago, Ill.; D. H. Lieberman, New York; Julian W. Mack, Chicago, Ill.; J. L. Magnes, New York; Louis Marshall, New York; Isidor Newman, New Orleans, La.; Simon W. Rosendale, Albany, N. Y.; Max Senior, Cincinnati, O.; Jacob H. Schiff, New York; Oscar S. Straus, New York; M. C. Sloss, San Francisco, Cal., and Simon Wolf, Washington, D. C.

The American-Jewish Committee was organized with sixty members, and adopted a constitution (November 11, 1906), which begins: "The purpose of this committee is to prevent infringement of the civil and religious rights of the Jews, and to alleviate the consequences of persecution. In the event of a threatened or actual denial or invasion of such rights, or when conditions calling for relief from calamities affecting Jews exist anywhere, correspondence may be entered into with those familiar with the situation, and if the persons on the spot feel themselves able to cope with the situation, no action need be taken; if, on the other hand, they request aid, steps shall be taken to furnish it." The Committee was later again increased on account of the en-

[1] See *American-Jewish Year Book* for 5667, pp. 230, 233, 234.

largement of the representation from New York City, owing to the organization of the "Kehillah," and last year consisted of the following, representing the thirteen districts into which the country was divided for that purpose:

Dist. I: Florida, Georgia, North Carolina, South Carolina, 2 members: Ceasar Cone, Greensboro, N. C.; Montague Triest, Charleston, S. C.

Dist. II: Alabama, Mississippi, Tennessee, 2 members: Jacques Loeb, Montgomery, Ala.; Nathan Cohn, Nashville, Tenn.

Dist. III: Arizona, Louisiana, New Mexico, Texas, 2 members: Maurice Stern, New Orleans, La.; Isaac H. Kempner, Galveston, Tex.

Dist. IV: Arkansas, Colorado, Kansas, Missouri, 3 members: Morris M. Cohen, Little Rock, Ark.; David S. Lehman, Denver, Col.; Elias Michael, St. Louis, Mo.

Dist. V: California, Idaho, Nevada, Oregon, Utah, Washington, 3 members: Max C. Sloss, San Francisco, Cal.; Harris Weinstock, Sacramento, Cal.; Ben. Selling, Portland, Ore.

Dist. VI: Iowa, Michigan, Minnesota, Montana, Nebraska, North Dakota, South Dakota, Wisconsin, Wyoming, 4 members: Henry M. Butzel, Detroit, Mich.; Emanuel Cohen, Minneapolis, Minn.; Victor Rosewater, Omaha, Neb.; Max Landauer, Milwaukee, Wis.

Dist. VII: Illinois, 7 members: Edwin G. Foreman, M. E. Greenebaum, B. Horwich, Julian W. Mack, Julius Rosenwald, Joseph Stolz, all of Chicago, Ill.; Samuel Woolner (deceased), Peoria, Ill.

Dist. VIII: Indiana, Kentucky, Ohio, West Virginia, 5 members: Louis Newberger, Indianapolis, Ind.; Isaac W. Bernheim, Louisville, Ky.; David Philipson, Cincinnati, O.; J. Walter Freiberg, Cincinnati, O.; E. M. Baker, Cleveland, O.

Dist. IX: New Jersey, Pennsylvania, 9 members: Cyrus Adler, Philadelphia, Pa.; Isaac W. Frank, Pittsburg, Pa.; Wm. B. Hackenburg, B. L. Levinthal, M. Rosenbaum, all of Philadelphia, Pa.; Isadore Sobel, Erie, Pa.; Mayer Sulzberger, Philadel-

Photo by Trover-Weigel, Salem, Oregon.

Hon. Benjamin Selling.

phia, Pa.; A. Leo Weil, Pittsburg, Pa.; Benjamin Wolf, Philadelphia, Pa.

Dist. X: Delaware, District of Columbia, Maryland, Virginia, 2 members: Harry Friedenwald, Baltimore, Md.; Jacob H. Hollander, Baltimore, Md.

Dist. XI: Connecticut, Maine, Massachusetts, New Hampshire, Rhode Island, Vermont, 3 members: Isaac M. Ullman, New Haven, Conn.; Lee M. Friedman, Boston, Mass.; Harry Cutler, Providence, R. I.

Dist. XII: New York: Joseph Baroudess, Samuel Dorf, Bernard Drachman, Harry Fischel, William Fishman, Israel Friedlaender, Samuel B. Hamburger, Maurice H. Harris, Samuel I. Hyman, S. Jarmulowsky, Leon Kamaiky, Philip Klein, Nathan Lamport, Adolph Lewisohn, J. L. Magnes, M. Z. Margolies, Louis Marshall, H. Pereire Mendes, Solomon Neumann, Jacob H. Schiff, Bernard Semel, P. A. Siegelstein, Joseph Silverman, Cyrus L. Sulzberger, Felix M. Warburg; 25 members.

Dist. XIII: New York (exclusive of the city), 2 members: Abram J. Katz, Rochester; Simon W. Rosendale, Albany.

Members-at-large: Nathan Bijur, New York City; Isidor Straus, New York City.

The officers are: Mayer Sulzberger, President; Julian W. Mack and Jacob H. Hollander, Vice-Presidents; Isaac W. Bernheim, Treasurer; Herbert Friedenwald, Secretary. The Executive Committee consists of Cyrus Adler, Harry Cutler, Samuel Dorf, J. L. Magnes, Louis Marshall, Julius Rosenwald, Jacob H. Schiff, Isadore Sobel, Cyrus L. Sulzberger and A. Leo Weil.

The strength of the committee consists mainly in its personnel, as it comprises the most influential as well as the most active Jewish communal leaders of the country. The membership from the large centers of population, like New York, Philadelphia and Chicago, includes also representatives of the immigrants of the last period, and the plan of the Jewish Alliance of twenty years ago[1] to bring together the older and the younger portions

[1] See above, Chapter XXXI.

of the community is, to some extent, consummated in this Committee. It has made some valuable efforts on behalf of the suffering Jews in other countries, and also in the interest of a speedy solution of the vexed Russian passport question, and it is becoming recognized as the representative Jewish body in the United States.

When the Jewish community or "Kehillah" was formed in New York in 1909, consisting of the representatives of congregations, fraternal and educational organizations, the plans of those who wanted to have the American Jewish Committee re-organized on a more democratic basis, and to make it the elected and authorized representative of the Jewish masses, was partially carried out. The twenty-five members of the Executive Committee of the New York "Kehillah" are the New York members of the American-Jewish Committee. The Jews of Philadelphia have now also formed a "Kehillah" on the same basis of representation. But these new forms of amalgamating the large communities and forming authoritative Jewish central bodies is yet in the experimental stage, and several years, perhaps several decades, will have to pass before their permanent existence will be assured and justified. The great difference between the Committee and the "Kehillahs" is, that in the first men of power and authority who worked effectively for Jewish interests before, individually or as leaders of communal bodies, have united to work together in the same direction. The "Kehillahs" on the other hand, have yet to create the forces which are to sustain them and make them formidable. Their chief value consists of their being symptoms of the times, indicating the approach of the end of the period of chaos in general Jewish affairs, and an inclination to submit to representative authority in communal matters. The most conspicuous act of the New York "Kehillah" was its foundation of a Bureau of Education under the direction of the well-known Jewish educator, Dr. Samson Benderly (b. in Safed, Palestine, 1876), who conducted Jewish schools in Baltimore with marked success and is now working out his original plans

Prof. Solomon Schechter.

in educating Jewish teachers who should be capable of suitably performing their duties to the coming generation. But the soundness and the practicability of his plans are as problematical as that of the "Kehillah" itself.

Much other valuable work was done in the cause of Jewish education in the last ten years. The Jewish Theological Seminary, which was reorganized in 1902, when the presidency was assumed by the famous Roumanian Jewish scholar, Solomon Schechter, now has on its faculty as professors: President and Professor of Jewish Theology, Solomon Schechter; Biblical Literature and Exegesis, Israel Friedlaender; Talmud, Louis Ginzberg; History, Alexander Marx; Homiletics, Mordecai M. Kaplan; Instructor in the Talmud, Joshua A. Joffe; Instructor in Hebrew and Rabbinics, Israel Davidson; English Literature and Rhetoric, Joseph Jacobs. There is also now a Teachers' Institute connected with the Seminary, of which Prof. Mordecai M. Kaplan is the principal.

The Hebrew Union College of Cincinnati, which is maintained by the Union of American Hebrew Congregations, has also been considerably strengthened in the last few years. Its faculty consists of the following professors: Homiletics, Theology and Hellenistic Literature (President), Kaufman Kohler; Jewish History and Literature, Gotthard Deutsch; Ethics and Pedagogy, Louis Grossman; Jewish Philosophy, David Neumark; Biblical Exegesis (Associate), Moses Buttenwieser; Biblical Literature, Henry Englander; Instructor in Bible and Semitic Languages, Julian Morgenstern.

The youngest of the Jewish higher institutions of learning in the United States is The Dropsie College of Hebrew and Cognate Learning of Philadelphia, which was incorporated in 1907. Moses Aaron Dropsie (b. in Philadelphia, 1821; d. there 1905), an attorney and street railway owner of Dutch descent, bequeathed the bulk of his fortune, amounting to nearly one million dollars, to the foundation of that college, which was opened in 1909. The faculty consists of: President, Cyrus Adler; Max

L. Margolis, in charge of the Biblical Department; Henry Malter, in charge of the Rabbinical Department; Jacob Hoschander, Instructor Department of Cognate Languages; Hon. Mayer Sulzberger, Resident Lecturer in Jewish Jurisprudence and Institutes of Government.

An institution of an entirely different kind is the Rabbi Joseph Jacob School, or Yeshibah, of New York, which was organized in 1901, whose founder, Samuel S. Andron, still retains the presidency. It is the only considerable Jewish school on the denominational or parochial plan, where English and general studies according to the curriculum of the public schools are pursued together with the study of the Hebrew language, Bible, Talmud and Rabbinical literature. It is the first attempt to combine a strictly Orthodox and a thorough American education, and, if possible, to educate American rabbis who should be acceptable to the old style pious immigrant as well as to the generation which is growing up here. There are other Yeshibot in all of the large cities in the United States, but most of them simply follow their prototype, the Talmudical Academy of the Slavic countries, where there is no other official subject of study except the Talmud and Rabbinical literature, and secular studies are pursued clandestinely or not at all. In some of the Yeshibot here, like in the Rabbi Isaac Elchanan Theological Seminary of New York, some concessions were made to secular studies, but there was no attempt, and perhaps no desire, to harmonize the systems and to supply a good American education.

The original forms of the elementary Jewish school, the private "Cheder" and the public or semi-public Talmud Torah, is represented among the Jews of the Slavic countries in all its varieties, from the old-fashioned Russian school, where the Hebrew text is translated in a traditional Yiddish, which the pupil who is born or brought up here understands but imperfectly, to the Americanized place, where the translations are made in the English, and the modernized Russian school, in which Hebrew is used in interpreting the Scripture and the text books prepared for the purpose. Naturally the oldest and largest Talmud Torah of New York, the "Machzike Talmud Torah" of East Broadway (organized 1882), of which Moses H. Phillips is president and I. A. Kaplan superintendent, is looked upon as a model institution of its kind. There are nearly two score Talmud Torahs in New York City, some of them attached to synagogues, but most of them separate institutions with buildings of their own, several of which, like the Up-Town Talmud Torah and the one in Brownsville (Brooklyn), are magnificent establishments, with incomes which prove the material well-being of the immigrant classes, as well as their willingness to pay for Jewish education.

There are large Talmud Torahs in every city where there is a considerable Jewish population, and, as in many other respects, New York conditions are duplicated in Chicago, Philadelphia and other great centers. In the smaller towns a Talmud Torah is now established soon after the foundation of a synagogue, and the private teacher, who is often also the Shochet and Chazzan or Mohel, usually antedates them both. There is one important difference, however, between the Talmud Torah of the Old World, especially Russia, and the same institutions here. There the Talmud Torah is mainly for the children of the very poor, for destitute orphans, foundlings and the like. Here the scarcity of good private teachers, the high compensation which they require, and the limited time which could be given to Jewish studies, makes the organized school preferable also for the children of parents who are willing and able to pay for tuition. Some Talmud Torahs which are maintained by single synagogues for their members, especially in small communities, partake of the nature, and even of the exclusiveness, of the Sabbath School which is an adjunct to almost every well conducted Reform Temple. *Volks-Schulen*, or Hebrew schools for girls, have lately been established in several sections of New York, and also in other cities.

There are also in every large community and in some sections of large cities educational institutions whose chief object is to facilitate the Americanization of the immigrants. The model institution of that sort is the Educational Alliance (formerly the Hebrew Institute) of New York. Some of them bear the name Educational Society, and a large number, among which the Chicago institution, of which Julius Rosenwald (b. in Springfield, Ill., 1862) is the chief patron, prefer the old name of Hebrew Institute. This class of institutions have been undergoing material changes for the last ten or fifteen years, and those founded lately are entirely unlike those which belonged to the earlier period. All fear that the newcomers will not become Americanized sufficiently fast has now disappeared; and, besides, the work of Americanization which was formerly done by private charity, like the maintenance of evening classes and even of day classes for adult immigrants, to instruct them in English and elementary knowledge, is now done by the cities themselves. Private efforts are now made more in the direction of Jewish education and religious or semi-religious activities, and some of the Hebrew Institutes, notably the youngest and those established and maintained by immigrants themselves, are almost Talmud Torahs, often combined with synagogues, in which the religious element predominates, and in some of them rabbis occupy the leading positions.

Lastly, there is a class of splendid educational establishments, founded and endowed by Jewish philanthropists, for the technical development of the young Jewish immigrants. The most important of these in New York are the Baron de Hirsch Trade School, the Hebrew Technical Institute (organized 1883), and the Hebrew Technical School for Girls. Chicago has the Jewish (formerly the Manual) Training School (incorporated 1887); Baltimore its Maccabean House (incorporated 1900); Boston its Hebrew Industrial School (organized 1889), and the Jewish Educational Alliance of St. Louis, Mo., has a large industrial school; Cincinnati has a Boys' Industrial School; while Philadelphia has the B'nai B'rith Manual Training School and the Industrial Home for Jewish Girls. The Young Men's Hebrew Associations, the Young Women's Hebrew Associations and other Jewish organizations of a like character in numerous places, maintain various classes—religious, technical, etc.—offering educational opportunities to new arrivals and to young working people who cannoot utilize the regular institutions of public education.

The efforts to organize and to federate, which resulted in the formation of the American-Jewish Committee, produced several other communal federations of variegated character. The oldest and most substantial of these is the Federation of Galician and Bukowinian Jews in America (organized 1904), which founded and maintains the Har Moriah Hospital in New York. There have also lately been organized a Federation of Roumanian Jews and one of Russian-Polish Jews. There is also in New York a Federation of Contributors to Jewish Communal Institutions and a Federation of Jewish Organizations, both of which were organized in 1906.

CHAPTER XXXIX.

THE JEWS IN THE DOMINION OF CANADA.

The legend about the Jewish origin of Chevalier de Levis—Aaron Hart, the English Commissary, and Abraham Gradis, the French banker—Early settlers in Montreal—Its first Congregation—Troubles of Ezekiel Hart, the first Jew to be elected to the Legislature—Final Emancipation in 1832—Jews fight on the Loyalist side against Popineau's rebellion—Prominent Jews in various fields of activity—Congregation "Shaar ha-Shomaim"—Toronto—First synagogue in Victoria, B. C., in 1862—Hamilton and Winnipeg—Other communities—Agricultural Colonies—Jewish Newspapers.

The beginning of the history of the Jews in Canada goes back to legend. There is a tradition that the founder of the house of Levis, from whom descended Henri de Levis, Duke de Vontadur, Viceroy of Canada for some time after 1626, and his more distinguished relative, Chevalier de Levis, who was Montcalm's successor as commander of the French forces in Canada (1759) and later became a marshal of France, were descendants of the patriarch Levi Ben Jacob, and a cousin of Mary of Nazareth.[1]

The earliest authentic records of the Jews of Canada go back to the period when England and France were engaged in their final contest for the mastery of the northern part of the continent. Aaron Hart (b. in London, 1724) was Commissary in General Amherst's army, which invaded Canada from the south, and there were in the same army three more Jewish officers:

[1] See Kohler in Publications IV, p. 87. See also for the sources of this chapter "Publications" I, pp. 117-120, and the article "Canada" in the *Jewish Encyclopedia.*

Emanuel de Cordova, Hananiel Garcia and Isaac Miranda. Hart was later attached to General Haldimond's command at Three Rivers, and at the close of the war settled in that city and became seignior of Bécancour.

There were, of course, no Jews on the other side of the struggle, for France at that time suffered no Jewish inhabitants in her colonies, nor Jewish soldiers in her armies. But it was a Jew, Abraham Gradis (d. 1780), the head of the great French banking house founded by his father, David Gradis (naturalized in Bordeaux, 1731; d. 1751), who furnished money and supplies to the French King to carry on the unsuccessful war with England. Abraham Gradis had founded (in 1748) the Society of Canada, a commercial organization, under the auspices of the French government, and erected magazines in Quebec. Exceptional privileges were later granted to him and his family in the French colonies, and full civil rights were accorded him in Martinique in 1779. But the house of "the Rothschilds of the 18th century" was finally ruined by the insurrections in Santo Domingo and Martinique, combined with the losses which were occasioned at home by the French Revolution. (See Wolf, *"The American Jew . . ."* pp. 476-82.)

About the time of the Canadian conquest by England (*circa* 1760), a number of Jewish settlers took up their residence in Montreal, including Lazarus David (b. 1734), Uriel Moresco, Samuel Jacobs, Simon Levy, Fernandez da Fonseca, Abraham Franks, Andrew Hays, Jacob de Maurera, Joseph Bindona, Levy Solomons and Uriah Judah. Lazarus David was a large land owner and was noted as a public spirited citizen. Several of the others held offices in the English army; there were also among them some extensive traders, who did much for the development of the newly acquired colony. After they had been reinforced by other settlers, a congregation, called "Shearit Israel," was organized in 1768, which for nearly a century remained the only Jewish congregation in Canada. Most of the members were Sephardim, and they stood in close communion with the Spanish and Portuguese Jews of London, who presented them with two scrolls of the Law for the newly founded congregation. At first the congregation met for worship in a hall on St. James Street; but in 1777 the members built the first synagogue, at the junction of Notre Dame and St. James Streets, close to the present court house, on a lot belonging to the David family, whose founder, the above mentioned Lazarus David, died one year previously, and was the first to be interred in the cemetery which the congregation acquired in 1775. His son, David David (1764-1824), was one of the founders of the Bank of Montreal in 1808.

The Rev. Jacob Raphael Cohen was the first regular minister of the Montreal congregation of whom there remains any record. He came there in 1778 and remained until 1782, when he went to Philadelphia, where he became rabbi of Congregation Mickveh Israel. The president or parnas of the Montreal congregation in 1775 was Jacob Salesby (or Salisbury) Franks, a member of the family whose other branch played an important part in Philadelphia in the period of the Revolution. Abraham Franks (1721-97) supported the British in repelling the American invasion, while his son-in-law, Levy Solomons, who later became parnas of the Montreal congregation, was commanded by the invading American general, Montgomery, to act as purveyor to the hospitals for the American troops. But after the death of General Montgomery and the retreat of the American forces from Canada, Solomons, who was never paid for the services he rendered to the invaders, was exposed to the resentment of the British, as one suspected of sympathy for the revolting colonists. He and his family were expelled from Montreal by General Burgoyne, but eventually was permitted to return.

In 1807 Ezekiel Hart, one of the four sons of Commissary Aaron Hart, was elected to represent Three Rivers in the Legislature. He declined to be sworn in according to the usual form, "on the true faith of a Christian," but took the oath according to the Jewish custom, on the Pentateuch, and with his head covered. At once a storm of opposition arose, due, it is said, not to religious prejudice or intolerance, but to the fact that his political opponents saw in this an opportunity of making a party gain by depriving an antagonist of his seat. After heated discussions and the formality of a trial, he was expelled, and when his constituents re-elected him, the House proposed passing a bill to put his disqualification as a Jew beyond doubt. But the governor, Sir John Craig, dissolved the Chamber before the bill could pass. After a bill, in conformity with a petition by the Jews, was passed in 1829, and sanctioned by royal proclamation in January 1831, authorizing the Jews to keep a register of births, marriages and deaths, they felt encouraged and made another attempt to secure recognition of their civil rights. When a new bill extending the same political rights to Jews as to Christians was introduced in the Legislative Assembly in March, 1831, it met with no opposition. It rapidly passed both the Assembly and the Council, and received the royal assent June 5, 1832. The Jews of Canada were thus emancipated about a quarter century before their co-religionists in the mother country. Mr. Nathan of British Columbia was the first Jewish member of the Canadian Parliament.

When Canada was convulsed in 1837-38 by the rebellion led by Papineau and others, a number of Jews fought on the Loyalist side. Two members of the David family held cavalry commands under Wetherell at the action at St. Charles, and took a distinguished part in the battle of St. Eustache. Aaron Philip Hart, grandson of the commissary, temporarily abandoned his large law practice to raise a company of militia, which rendered valuable service. Jacob Henry Joseph and his brother Jesse were with the troops on the Richelieu and at Chambly. Several Canadian Jews won distinction in various capacities in the first half of the last century. Dr. Aaron Hart David (b. in Montreal, 1812; d. there 1882), a grandson of Lazarus David, was dean of the faculty of medicine of Bishop's College; Samuel Benjamin was the first Jew elected to the Montreal City Council; and Jesse Joseph (b. in Berthier, Canada, 1817; d. in Montreal,

1904), one of a family of merchant princes, established the first direct line of ships between Antwerp and Montreal, and was appointed Belgian Consul in the latter city. His brother Jacob was connected with the promotion of early Canadian railways and telegraph lines, and another brother, Gershom, was the first Jewish lawyer to be appointed a queen's counsel in Canada. All these men were officers of the synagogue, at the time when its rabbi, Rev. Abraham de Sola (b. in London, 1825; d. in New York, 1882), was professor of Semitic languages and literature at the McGill University.

The Congregation Shearit Israel passed through a crisis when the old synagogue building had to be demolished, when the land on which it stood reverted to the heirs of David David, after his death in 1824. It was again forced to worship in a hall, until the new synagogue on Chenneville Street was dedicated in 1838. It had no regular minister after the retirement of Rabbi Cohen, until nearly 60 years later, when Rabbi David Piza was appointed in 1840 and was, six years later, succeeded by Rabbi Abraham de Sola, who was in turn succeeded by his son, Dr. Meldola de Sola (b. 1853), who is still one of the ministers of the congregation, his associate being Rev. Isaac de la Penyha.

A second congregation, of Polish and German, or Ashkenazic Jews, was organized in Montreal in 1846, but existed only for a short time. Another effort was made about twelve years later with more success, and the result was the congregation "Shaar Hashomaim," which was established in 1858, Abraham Hofnung, M. A. Ollendorf and Samuel Silverman were among the most active of its charter members, and the Rev. Samuel Hofnung was its earliest minister, who was soon succeeded by Rev. M. Fass. The first building of this congregation was in St. Constant Street, and was dedicated in 1860. In 1886 it removed to its present edifice in McGill College avenue. It has now two rabbis, Rev. Dr. Herman Abramowitz and S. Goldstein. In 1863 was founded the Young Men's Hebrew Benevolent Society (now called the Baron de Hirsch Institute and Hebrew Benevolent Society), through which Baron de Hirsch and his executors did much for the education and colonization of the Russian immigrants who began to come to Canada in considerable numbers after 1881. The present Jewish population of Montreal is probably about 40,000, and it has ten synagogues, besides the two mentioned above. Of these, the Bet David Congregation (established 1888) is designated as Roumanian; the Bet Israel Congregation, of which Rev. Hirschel Cohen is rabbi, is surnamed "Chevra Shaas"; the B'nai Jacob Synagogue (founded 1885) is mainly Russian. There is also an Austro-Hungarian Congregation, a Galician ("Chevra Kadisha Jeshurun") and a Reform Temple (Emanuel, founded 1882). There is also the usual complement of charitable, educational, fraternal and social organizations, including Talmud Torah, a branch of the Jewish Theological Seminary of New York, and a Jewish Lads' Brigade. The Jewish community in Montreal and in Canada generally is in many respects like the communities of the United States of a similar size. But owing to the dissensions between religious denominations, and especially the complicated school question, there is more open partisan hostility to Jews, both on the part of the press and in public life, than in the United States, where the government is strictly secular.

About 1845 a sufficient number of Jews had settled in Toronto, Ont., to begin to think about the organization of a synagogue; but little was accomplished until 1852, when a cemetery was purchased and the Holy Blossom congregation was established. Mark Samuel, Lewis Samuel and Alexander Miller did much to sustain the congregation in its early struggles. It grew in strength and numbers under the presidency of Alfred D. Benjamin during the closing years of the nineteenth century, and it became necessary to remove from its first building in Richmond Street to the present commodious edifice in Bon Street (1902). Toronto, which had 1425 Jews in 1891 and 3,038 in 1901, now has considerably over 10,000, with about ten congregations and several charitable and fraternal organizations.

The discovery of gold in British Columbia in 1857 led to the settlement there of a number of Jews, who built a synagogue in Victoria in 1862. In 1882 a synagogue was erected in Hamilton, and several years later the Jews of Winnipeg(who numbered 645 in 1891) organized two congregations. There are now seven congregations in Winnipeg, with a Jewish population of about 8,000. It also has among the various communal organizations a Hebrew Liberal Club and a Hebrew Conservative Club. North Winnipeg is now represented in the Provincial Parliament of Manitoba by S. Hart Green (b. ab. 1885), the honorary secretary of the Congregation Shaare Shomayim and the president of the local B'nai B'rith Lodge.

There are now Jewish communities in more than twenty-five separate localities in Canada, and the total number of Jews is about 70,000 and growing very fast (it was only 16,060 in 1901). Besides the towns mentioned, there are Jews in Berlin (Ont.), Belleville, Brandford, Calgary (Alberta), Chatham, N. B.; Dawson (Yukon Territory), Glace Bay, C. B.; Halifax, London, Magnetowan, Ont.; Ottowa, Quebec, Regina (Saskatchewan), St. Catherine's, St. John, Sydney, Sherbrooke, Vancouver, Woodstock and Salt River, N. B.; Yarmouth and Yorkton.

There are in Canada about a dozen Jewish agricultural colonies, most of which were founded or promoted by the Baron de Hirsch Fund. The most important of them are Bender, Hirsch, Ox Bow and Qu'appelle. There are altogether about 700 Jewish farms occupying more than 110,000 acres, and sustaining a farming population of about 3,000.

Montreal has a Yiddish daily newspaper, the "Canadian Eagle," and an English Jewish weekly, "The Jewish Times," and there is a Yiddish weekly in Winnipeg called the "Canadian Jew."

CHAPTER XL.

JEWS IN SOUTH AMERICA, MEXICO AND CUBA.

The first "minyan" in Buenos Ayres, Argentine, in 1861—Estimate of the Jewish population in Argentine—Occupations and economic condition of the various groups—Kosher meat and temporary synagogues as indications of the religious conditions—Communities in twenty-six other cities—The Agricultural Colonies—Brazil—The rumor that General Floriano Peixotto, the second president of the new Republic, was of Jewish origin—Communities in several cities—The Colony Philippson—Jews in Montevido, Uruguay—Other South American Republics—Isidor Borowski, who fought under Bolivar—Panama—Moroccan Jews are liked by Peru Indians—About ten thousand Jews in Mexico—Slowly increasing number in Cuba, where Jews help to spread the American influence.

The immigration statistics of the modern Argentine Republic, which began to be collected in 1854, did not count the Jews, as such, and there is practically no records of the first settlement of Jews there, which took place in the second half of the nineteenth century. It is related that there was a "minyan" in Buenos Ayres on Yom Kippur, 1861, which was kept up irregularly for ten years, and was composed of English, French and German Jews. During the yellow fever epidemic of 1871 almost all of them, who were agents or representatives of business houses, fled the capital, and the "minyan" in that year was held in a little town where most of them met. This little community organized a "Congregacion Israelita" and built the first synagogue, before Jews from Russia began to go there in considerable numbers. A congregation of Moroccan Jews, "Congregacion Israelita Latina," was organized in 1891.

The report of the Jewish Colonization Association for 1909, which contains a study of the Jewish population of Argentine, estimates the number of Jews living in Buenos Ayres at 40,000, and that of the interior towns—outside of the colonies—at 15,000 more. If we add to it the number of about 20,000 living in the colonies Moiseville (Santa Fé), Clara, San Antonio, Santa Isabel, Lucienville (Entre Rios), Mauricio, Baron de Hirsch (Buenos Ayres) and Berriasconi (Pampa), in addition to the Jewish immigration for the last three years, which averages about 9,000 or 10,000, it seems certain that there are now in the Republic of Argentine over 100,000 Jews, which means a larger number than in any country of the New World outside of the United States.

About eight-tenths of the Jewish population of Buenos Ayres are from Russia. The earliest settlers among them, who are now also the wealthiest, are former colonists of the I. C. A. (as the Jewish Colonization Association of Paris is designated). The remainder is divided into about 3,000 Turkish, Arabian and Greek Jews; 1,000 Moroccans and Italians; 1,500 French, German, English and Dutch, etc. The first two groups contain many wealthy merchants, but the great majority consists of dealers in second-hand goods and of peddlers. The last group, which is the oldest, consists of merchants of the higher grades. Among the Russians there are also a large number of business people, but a very large number are artisans in various trades. As to their date of arrival, the English, French and German are the oldest, as stated above. Some Moroccan and Italian families have lived there about thirty years, but the majority of that group came in the last decade. The earliest Turkish Jews came there less than fifteen years ago, but the great majority of them came about 1905. The Russians began to come in considerable numbers about the time of the establishment of the first colonies, and they still keep on coming in increasing numbers.

There are in Buenos Ayres about one hundred Jews engaged in the liberal professions, two-thirds of whom are natives of

Russia. The communal institutions leave much to be desired, but there has been some improvement lately, and it is reported that a large Jewish hospital will be erected there in the near future. The religious conditions are indicated by the fact that about 7,000 kilograms of "Kosher" meat was sold there daily in 1909, and that on Yom Kippur of that year services were held in not less than twenty-four different places, including the temple. M. Samuel Halphen, a former religious teacher, was lately chosen rabbi of Buenos Ayres, while Dr. Herbert Ashkenazi, who studied at Berlin, and was chosen by the I. C. A. as chief rabbi of the colonies, also resides in that city.

The Jews are now scattered all over Argentine, and some can be found in almost any locality, especially in the provinces of Buenos Ayres, Santa Fé, Entre Rios and Cordoba. The above-mentioned inquiry[1] deals with the Jewish population of twenty-six cities besides the capital, beginning with Rosario, Santa Fé, which has among its 173,000 inhabitants more than 3,000 Jews, 2,500 are Russians, 359 Orientals and Moroccans and about 100 French and Germans. The cemetery was acquired in 1905 and the congregation was organized in 1907. In Santa Fé, which has less than 600 Jews, the Moroccans bought a cemetery as early as 1895. Parona has a small community of less than 300, with a *Sociedad Israelita Argentina de Beneficencia*, which was founded in 1897. But most of the communal institutions and the communities themselves are less than ten years old, which means that Jews are just beginning to spread over the country. A majority of the Jews in the interior towns of Argentine are former colonists, and most of them are doing tolerably well. Their presence in a free and progressive country, where they can be useful to themselves and to their neighbors, must therefore be credited to the I. C. A. which has thus accomplished some

[1] *Enquete sur la Population Israelite en Argentine*, in the "Rapport de l'Administration Centrale . . ." of the I. C. A. for 1909. Paris, 1910, pp. 251-308.

good, even for those whom it could not, for various reasons, turn into successful farmers.

The largest share of attention was, however, paid in the last two decades to that part of the Jewish population of Argentine which has settled in the agricultural colonies established by the I. C. A. As early as 1889 independent attempts had been made by Jewish immigrants from Russia to establish colonies in Argentine, but it was not done on a well-ordered plan, and later these colonies and colonists were absorbed by the Jewish Colonization Association. The oldest and most successful colony, Moiseville, founded by Russian immigrants in 1890, before the establishment of the I. C. A. was re-organized by that association in 1891. Mauricio, in the province of Buenos Ayres, was established about the same time, and the large group of colonies in the province of Entre Rios, which is collectively called Clara (after the Baroness de Hirsch), was founded in 1894. Despite the friction which caused many colonists at considerable expense, to leave the places where they were settled, and despite the prejudice which was aroused against the entire colonization scheme by these seemingly interminable quarrels, the agricultural colonies in Argentine, as a whole, are succsssful and their future is bright. The colonists are fast paying off their debts to the association which assisted them to settle there, and many of them are even chafing under the limitations which prevent them from paying off more rapidly. The centers of Jewish population, both agricultural and—indirectly—urban, which were thus artificially created by the munificence of Baron de Hirsch, have become healthy and natural, and are now attracting independent immigration. There are now, as stated above, nearly 20,000 souls in the colonies, but more than a fourth are described as non-colonists. There are 44 schools with more than 3,000 pupils in the colonies, and the statistical tables from year to year show a slow and solid progress, which augurs well for the future of the Jews in Argentine.

* * * * *

There were, as far as known, but very few Jews in modern

Brazil, even under the humane and scholarly Emperor Dom Pedro II. (1825-91), who was well versed in Hebrew, and maintained friendly relations with several Jewish scholars in Europe. The immense country attracted but few Jews after the Emperor was deposed and a republican form of government instituted in 1889. There were some rumors at that time that General Floriano Peixotto, one of the leaders of the revolution, who was the first Vice-President and the second President (1891-94) of the new republic, was of Jewish origin. But like the statements about the Jewish ancestry of Christopher Columbus and many other notables, they could never be verified, and there is not available sufficient genealogical material in either case to prove or disprove assertions of that nature.

In 1900 a number of Roumanian Jews went to Brazil, but effected no permanent settlement. A list of the leading merchants of the various cities in Brazil, which was published by the Bureau of American Republics about 1901, discloses a large number of names unmistakably Jewish, most of them apparently of German origin (*Jewish Encyclopedia,* s. v. Brazil). The formation of a Jewish community in Rio de Janeiro, the capital of Brazil, was reported in January, 1905 (in the *South American Journal* of London), and a report in the *Jewish Emigrant* of St. Petersburg, the Russian organ of the I. C. A., five years later (1910, No. 20), tells of Jewish merchants in many large cities of Brazil, including Rio Grande, Pelatas, Sao Gabriel, etc., and of Porto Alegra, Rio Grande do Sul, where a community was then about to be organized. The existence of a synagogue in Para, "where they worship on the festivals," was reported in 1910. (*Jewish Chronicle,* Oct. 21, 1910.)

The chief interest of the Jewish world in the Jews of Brazil is, however, concentrated on the agricultural colony, Philippson, in the state of Rio Grande, where there are now settled about 400 Russian Jews, mostly from Bessarabia. It was founded by the I. C. A. about six years ago, and is now under the direction of M. Leibowitz, one of its former oldest employees in Argentine. The colony is in a flourishing condition, and it is being constantly enlarged, while new settlements are projected in the same part of the country. Here, too, like in Argentine, the colony attracts some Jewish immigration, and it was also the cause of the establishment of small Jewish settlements in the nearby towns of Pinhal, Santa Maria, Cruz Alta, etc. The number of Jews in Brazil is now estimated at 3,000.

There are, according to the report mentioned at the beginning of this chapter, about 150 Jews in Montevido, the capital of Uruguay, South America, most of whom came there from Buenos Ayres. About half of them are from Russia, the remainder hail from Greece, France and Alsace, and Roumania. They are engaged in various occupations and their material condition is not bad. Ten young Russian Jews joined the army and three of them attained the rank of sergeant. There is hardly any religious activity, except for a "minyan" held on Yom Kippur. Matzoth for the Passover are brought from Buenos Ayres, and a "Mohel" is also usually brought from there when the occasion arises.

There are several thousand Jews scattered over the other republics of South America, but they are mostly recent arrivals and unorganized, and very little is known about them. It is probable that the Polish-Jewish military adventurer, Isidor Borowski (b. in Warsaw, 1803; killed at the siege of Herat, Afghanistan, 1837), who fought under the great hero of South American independence, Simon Bolivar (1783-1830) in many battles,[1] was then the only Jew in that part of the world. Even at present, the number of Jews in the countries liberated by Bolivar is insignificant. There are about 500 Jews in Venezuela, mostly in the capital, Caracas, where the first Jewish congregation was founded in 1899. (American-Jewish Year Book 5660, p. 289). According to the writers of the American chapter in *Outlines of Jewish History* by Lady Magnus, for which—as stated in the preface—"Lady Magnus is in no wise responsible,"

[1]See *Jew. Encyclopedia,* Vol. III, p. 326-27.

Jewish congregations were formed in Caracas and Coro, Venezuela, in the middle of the nineteenth century, presumably by Jews who lived there formerly as Maranos. But if these congregations existed at all, they must have been short-lived, and it is not certain that even the latest "first congregation" of 1899 is still in existence.

Hardly anything is known of Jews in Bolivia or Colombia, but it is certain that a considerable number are now to be found in the diminutive Republic of Panama, through which the great isthmian canal is now being cut by the United States. There were enough Jews in the city of Panama before that time to acquire a cemetery about 1905. The Alliance Israelite Universelle of Paris assisted a number of Moroccan Jews to settle in Peru, where they were reported as doing well and being better liked by the Indians than either Europeans or Chinese. But the climate does not agree with them, and many of them leave Peru as soon as they save a sufficient amount of money. About 100 Jewish residents, Moroccan, French and English, who own the largest stores and rubber plantations, are found in Iquitos, Peru, which was at one time an Indian village. There is a small community of Russian Jews in Lima. A number of prosperous Jewish merchants are located in Santiago, Chile, and in other cities of that republic, but there is no record of religious organization or of communal activities.

The number of Jews in Mexico is estimated to be not far from 10,000, mostly Syrians, Moroccans and French Alsatians. But as far as it is known, there is among them no organization and no religious life except an occasional "minyan" on the high holidays.

There is also a slowly increasing number of Jews in Cuba, mostly at Havana, where Moroccan and Syrian or Turkish Jews came to trade long ago; but since it was liberated from the Spanish yoke by the United States, Jewish immigrants from Europe, who formerly lived in the United States, settle there and help to spread the American influence.

CHAPTER XLI.

MEN OF EMINENCE IN THE ARTS, SCIENCES AND THE PROFESSIONS.

Jews who attained eminence in the world of art and of science—Moses J. Ezekiel—Ephraim Keyser—Isidor Konti—Victor D. Brenner—Butensky and Davidson—Painters: Henry Mosler, Constant Mayer, H. N. Hyneman and George D. M. Peixotto—Max Rosenthal and his son, Albert—Max Weyl, Toby E. Rosenthal, Louis Loeb and Katherine M. Cohen—Some cartoonists and caricaturists—Musicians, composers and musical directors—The Damrosch family, Gabrilowitsch, Hoffman and Ellman—Operatic and theatrical managers and impressarios—Playwrights and actors—Scientists: A. A. Michelson, Morris Bloomfield, Jacob H. Hollander, Charles Waldstein and his family—Charles Gross—Edwin R. A. Seligman, Adolph Cohn, Jaques Loeb, Simon Flexner and Abraham Jacobi—Fabian Franklin—Engineers: Sutro, Gottlieb and Jacobs—Some eminent physicians and lawyers—Merchants and financiers.

While the social and political success of the Jews in a country are usually taken as an indication of its liberalism and the equality of its citizens, regardless of their creed, the contribution of Jews to its intellectual and artistic achievements is the best proof that this equality brings its own reward for the general good. We have seen in the preceding chapters how the Jews of the United States assisted in the material development of the country, how they participated in the battles for its independence and for its preservation, and how they are now doing their share of the country's useful work as working men, as business men, as professional men, etc., some of them having occupied before, and others occupying now, prominent positions in various walks of life. It remains now to cite several instances of Jews who attained distinction in the noble callings of the artist and the scientist, reflecting glory on their professions, as well as on the country of their birth or adoption.

Moses Jacob Ezekiel (b. in Richmond, Va., 1844), the sculptor, now residing at Rome, is probably the greatest Jewish artist that this country has produced. He was educated at the Virginia Military Institute, from which, after serving as a Confederate soldier in the Civil War, he graduated in 1866. He then studied anatomy at the Medical College of Virginia, and in 1868 removed to Cincinnati, going from there a year later to Berlin, where he studied at the Royal Academy of Art. He was admitted to membership in the Berlin Society of Artists for his colossal bust of Washington, which is now in the Cincinnati Art Museum, and he was the first foreigner to win the Michael Beer prize. During a visit to America in 1874 he executed in marble the group representing "Religious Liberty"—the tribute of the Independent Order of B'nai B'rith to the centennial celebration of American independence. The statue was unveiled in 1876 in Fairmount Park, Philadelphia (see the frontispiece). Upon his return to Rome Ezekiel leased a portion of the ruins of the Baths of Diocletian (Emperor of Rome, 284-305) and transformed them into one of the most beautiful studios in Europe. He has been elected a member of various academies and received other distinctions. Among his best known productions are: busts of Eve, Homer, David, Judith and Liszt; the Fountain of Neptune, for the town of Neptune, Italy; the Jefferson Monument, for Louisville, Ky.; Virginia Mourning Her Dead, at Lexington, Va., and a dozen heroic statues (of Phidias, Raphael, Michelangelo, Titian, Rembrandt, etc.), which are placed in the niches of the Corcoran Art Gallery at Washington.

Ephraim Keyser (b. in Baltimore, Md., 1850) is another prominent Jewish-American sculptor. He was educated at the public schools and the City College of Baltimore, and later studied at the Royal Academies of Fine Art in Munich and Berlin. He maintained a studio in Rome from 1880 to 1886, lived in New York from 1887 to 1893, when he settled in his native city as instructor in modelling at the Maryland Institute Art School, and also (since 1902) at the Rhinehart School for Sculpture. Among his best known works are the statue of Major-General Baron De Kalb, erected by the United States Government at Annapolis, Md., the tomb of President Chester A. Arthur at the Rural Cemetery, Albany, N. Y., and portrait busts of well known men.

Isidore Konti (b. in Vienna, 1862; a. 1890) executed the most important of his works after he came to the United States. He did much decorative, monumental and ideal work for the Chicago Exposition in 1893, for the Dewey Arch, the Buffalo Exposition of 1901 and the St. Louis Exposition of 1904, having made for the latter more than twenty different groups. Among his other works are a marble fountain at Yonkers, N. Y., where he resides, and a group representing South America for the building of the International Bureau of American Republics in Washington. Konti received numerous medals for his work here and abroad, and is a member of various societies of artists, numismatists, etc.

Victor David Brenner (b. in Shavly, Russia, 1871; a. 1890), the medallist and sculptor, is now best known to the general public as the designer of the "Lincoln penny." He received awards from the Exposition and the Salon in Paris, 1900; from the Buffalo Exposition of 1901 and the World's Fair of St. Louis in 1904. He has works in the Paris Mint, Munich Glyptothek, Vienna Numismatic Society, Metropolitan Museum of Art of New York and the Boston Museum of Fine Arts.

Julius Butensky (b. in Novogrudek, Russia; a. 1905) is another sculptor and medallist of the younger generation who did his best work since he came to this country, of which the best known is the statue at the Metropolitan Museum of Art of New York representing "The Beating of Swords Into Plowshares"; and a medal presented to Henry Rice (b. in Germany, 1835) on his retiring from the presidency of the United Hebrew

Charities of New York. Joseph Davidson, also a native of Russia, who came here as a child and developed his talent in New York, is one of the youngest sculptors whose work has attracted favorable attention.

Henry Mosler (b. in New York, 1841), the *genre* painter, occupies a prominent position among American artists. He was taken to Cincinnati when a child, and began to study art there at the age of ten. In 1863 he went to Europe, where he continued his study of art, first in Dueseldorf and later in Paris. He came back to Cincinnati in 1866, but returned to Europe in 1874, and spent the following twenty years in Munich and Paris. A picture which he exhibited in the latter city in 1879 was afterwards purchased by the French government for the Luxemburg gallery, being the first work so purchased from an American artist.

Constant Mayer (b. in Besancon, France, 1832), the French painter, who arrived in the United States in 1857 and lived here more than a generation before he returned to his native country, was among the best known artists of his time here. Herman Naphtali Hyneman (b. in Philadelphia, 1849), who studied for eight years in Germany and France, and George D. M. Peixotto (b. in Cleveland, O., 1857), eldest son of Benjamin F. Peixotto, are recognized as masters among American portrait painters, the latter also having done notable work as a mural decorator. Other well-known Jewish artists are: Max Rosenthal (b. in Turek, Russian-Poland, 1833; a. 1849), who was artist for the Government during the Civil War, making illustrations for reports of the United States Military Commission, and who afterwards etched many historical portraits and painted a considerable number of pictures; Albert Rosenthal (b. in Philadelphia, 1863), widely known as etcher and painter of portraits of famous Americans, his son and pupil; Max Weyl (b. in Germany, 1837; a. 1855), best known as a landscape painter, and Toby Edward Rosenthal (b. in New Haven, Conn., 1848), who won medals in Europe and America, a *genre* and portrait painter, who resides in Munich, Bavaria; Louis Loeb (b. in Cleveland, O., 1866; d. in New York, 1909), a painter and illustrator; Miss Katherine M. Cohen (b. in Philadelphia, 1859), a well-known sculptor and painter.

Among the caricaturists or cartoonists of the day deserve to be mentioned Frederick Burr Opper (b. in Madison, O., 1857); Henry (Hy) Mayer (b. in Worms, Germany, 1868; a. 1886) and Reuben Lucius Goldberg (b. in San Francisco, 1883).

The number of Jews who achieved distinction as musicians, composers of music, musical directors, etc., is very large, and only a few of them can be mentioned here. Dr. Leopold Damrosch (b. in Prussia, 1832; d. in New York, 1885) came to New York in 1871 as conductor of the Arion Society, and soon became very successful, both as a violinist and as conductor of his own compositions. He was successively director of the Philharmonic Society, of the Symphony Society and of the Metropolitan Opera House of New York. His older son, Frank H. (b. in Breslau, Germany, 1859), who was director of music of the New York public schools for eight years, is (since 1905) at the head of the Institute of Musical Art in that city, which was founded by a bequest made for that purpose by the late Solomon Loeb. A second son, Walter Johannes Damrosch (b. in Breslau), the composer and director, married Margaret J. Blaine, the daughter of the great American statesman, James G. Blaine, who was a candidate for the presidency in 1884. A daughter of Dr. Damrosch is married to David Mannes, the director of the New York Music School Settlement.

Among the eminent Jewish musicians who frequently visit the United States are the pianist, Joseph Gabrilowitsch, a native of Russia, who married the only surviving daughter of the great American humorist, Samuel L. Clemens (1835-1910, better known as "Mark Twain"), Joseph Hoffman, and Mischa Ellman, the violinist, likewise a native of Russia.

In the operatic and theatrical world Jews are predominant as managers and impressarios. The best known among them are David Belasco (b. in San Francisco, Cal., 1859), who is also a dramatic author; Abraham Lincoln Erlanger (b. in Buffalo, N. Y., 1860), whose brother, Mitchell Louis, was elected a justice of the Supreme Court of New York County in 1906; Daniel Frohman (b. in Sandusky, O., 1853), and his brother, Charles (b. there 1860).

Charles Klein (b. in London, Eng., 1867) is a well-known playwright, two of whose most successful plays, "The Auctioneer" and "The Music Master," were especially written for David Warfield (b. in San Francisco, 1866), also a Jew, who is in the front rank of the theatrical profession in this country. These plays were produced under the management of David Belasco, and it presents only one of many such instances on the American stage in which the author, the actor or actress playing the leading part and the manager, or impressario, are all Jews. Oscar Hammerstein (b. in Berlin, 1847; a. 1863) is an inventor, playwright, builder and manager of theatres and opera houses, who has rendered valuable service in the development of operatic productions in the United States. Sydney Rosenfeld (b. in Richmond, Va., 1855) is the author of dramas, operettas and musical plays which have found much favor with the public.

In the world of science many Jews have attained eminence as original investigators and as university professors. Professor Albert Abraham Michelson (b. in Strelno, Germany, 1852) was brought as a child to San Francisco, and was from there appointed to the U. S. Naval Academy at Annapolis, Md., graduating in 1873. He was an instructor in physics and chemistry at the Naval Academy in 1875-9, and was in the office of the Nautical Almanac in Washington until 1880, when he resigned from the United States Navy. After spending several years studying in Germany and France he became professor of physics at the Case School of Applied Science in Cleveland, O. (1883-9). For the following three years he occupied a similar position at Clark University, in Worcester, Mass. Since 1892 he has been professor and head of the department of physics in the University of Chicago. He is a member of various learned societies here and abroad, including a corresponding membership in the Academy des Sciences of the Institute de France. He won numerous prizes and medals for his great scientific achievements, some of which, like the Copley Medal, awarded by the Royal Society of London, and the Nobel Prize for physics (both in 1907), indicate that he is recognized as one of the greatest scientists of the age. He is best known as the discoverer of a new method for determining the velocity of light. His younger brother, Charles Michelson (b. in Virginia City, Nev., 1869), is editor of the "Chicago American," and their sister, Miss Miriam (b. in Calaveras, Cal., 1870), is a dramatic critic and has also written numerous short stories and several novels.

Maurice Bloomfield (b. in Bielitz, Austria, 1855), who was brought here at the age of twelve, is a prominent Sanskrit scholar and is recognized as the chief living authority on the Atharva Veda. He has written several important works on his special subjects, and has been professor of Sanskrit and Comparative philology at Johns Hopkins University in Baltimore, Md., since 1881, Jacob H. Hollander (b. in Baltimore, 1871), who was appointed by President McKinley special commissioner to Porto Rico and later treasurer of that island colony, is professor of political emonomy at the same university. Professor Hollander was appointed by President Roosevelt United States special agent on taxation in Indian Territory (1904), and was in the following year sent as special commissioner to the Republic of San Domingo to investigate its public debt, and was the confidential agent of the Department of State with respect to Dominican affairs. Since 1908 he has been the financial adviser of the Dominican Republic. Professor Hollander takes an active interest in Jewish affairs, and has contributed valuable papers on Jewish history to the publications of the American-Jewish Historical Society, of which he is an officer.

Professor Charles Waldstein (b. in New York, 1856), the

great authority on Greek art and archeology of Cambridge University, England, is another American-Jewish scholar of the highest type, who is interested in Jewish matters. Among many other books, he wrote *The Jewish Question and the Mission of the Jews* (1899). Louis Waldstein, the pathologist and author (b. in New York, 1853), and Martin Waldstein (b. 1854), the chemist, are his older brothers. Lewis Einstein (b. in New York, 1877), formerly secretary of the American Embassy in Constantinople, and later secretary of legation in Peking, who has recently been appointed by President Taft as United States Minister to the Republic of Costa Rico, is a brother-in-law of Professor Waldstein.

Charles Gross (b. in Troy, N. Y., 1857; d. 1909), professor of history and political science at Harvard University, who was at the time of his death considered the chief authority in the world on English mediæval and economic history, was one of the vice-presidents of the American-Jewish Historical Society, and contributed to our historical literature a profound study on *The Exchequer of the Jews in the Mediaeval Judiciary of England,* and an English translation of Dr. Kayserling's notable work on the participation of the Jews in the discovery of the New World.

Professor Edwin R. A. Seligman (b. in New York, 1862), a member of the well known family of financiers and philanthropists, who began to lecture on economics in Columbia University, New York, in 1885, and has been professor of political economy there since 1891, is a recognized authority on the question of taxation and the author of standard works on the subect. Adolphe Cohn (b. in Paris, France, 1851; a. 1875), a son of the French-Jewish philanthropist, Albert Cohn (1814-77), has been professor of romance, languages and literatures at Columbia since 1891. Jaques Loeb (b. in Germany, 1859), the eminent biologist, who taught at American universities for about twenty years, is now at the head of the department of experimental biology in the Rockefeller Institute for Medical Research in New York. The head of that institute is likewise a Jew, Dr. Simon Flexner (b. in Louisville, Ky., 1863), formerly professor of pathology and anatomy at Johns Hopkins University (1891-99) and at the University of Pennsylvania (1899-1904). His serum for the cure of cerebro-spinal meningitis is one of the great medical achievements of the age.

Dr. Abraham Jacobi (b. in Westphalia, 1830; a. 1853), who came to New York after his participation in the revolutionary movement in Germany in 1848, was for more than fifty years professor of the diseases of children at the University of New York (Columbia, 1870-1902). He was highly honored on the occasion of the eightieth anniversary of his birth in 1910, and was in the following year elected president of the American Medical Association.

Fabian Franklin (b. in Eger, Hungary, 1853), a nephew of Michael Heilprin, came here as a child and was educated in Washington. He was a civil engineer and surveyor from 1869 to 1877, and a professor of mathematics at Johns Hopkins University, 1879-95. For the following thirteen years he was editor of the "Baltimore News," and is now (since Oct., 1909) associate editor of the "New York Evening Post."

Adolph Heinrich Joseph Sutro (b. at Aix-la-Chapelle, Rhenish Prussia, 1830; a. 1850; d. in San Francisco, 1898) was educated at the polytechnic schools of his native country, and when he came to America he was soon attracted by the discovery of gold in California, and from there went to Nevada. He projected and later (1869-79) built the Sutro tunnel under the Comstock lode, and when it was finished he settled in San Francisco, of which city he was elected Mayor in 1894. It was said that he owned about one-tenth of the area of San Francisco, including Sutro Heights, which he turned into a beautiful public park and which became the property of the municipality after his death. His library, which consisted of over 200,000 volumes, contained over 100 rare Hebrew manuscripts.

Abraham Gottlieb (b. in Bohemia, 1837; a. 1866; d. in Chicago, 1894) graduated from the University of Prague, and was engaged as an engineer in the construction of an Austrian railroad when he went to America and settled in Chicago. When he was elected president of the Keystone Bridge Company, he removed to Pittsburg (1877). In that capacity he constructed many bridges in various parts of the country, including the Madison Avenue bridge in New York City, He returned to Chicago in 1884 and was for a time connected (as consulting engineer and as chief engineer of the construction department) with the World's Columbian Exposition. He also took an active interest in Jewish affairs, and was for a time president of the Rodeph Shalom congregation in Pittsburg, and later of Zion congregation, Chicago.

Charles M. Jacobs (b. in Hull, England, 1850), who designed the tunnels which connect the Pennsylvania Railroad and the Long Island Railroad with the center of New York, is an English Jew, who is considered to be the greatest authority on tunnel building, both here and abroad.

Jews are well represented in the front ranks of the medical and the legal professions. Among the eminent physicians, besides those mentioned formerly, are men like Dr. Isaac Adler (b. in Alzey, Germany, 1849; a. 1857), Dr. Max Einhorn (b. in Grodno, Russia, 1862; a. 1884), both of New York; Dr. Jacob da Silva Solis-Cohen (b. in New York, 1838) and his brother, Solomon (b. in Philadelphia, 1857), who reside in Philadelphia, and Dr. Nathan Jacobson (b. in Syracuse, N. Y., 1857) of the Syracuse University. Samuel Untermyer (b. in Lynchburg, Va., 1858) of New York, Louis D. Brandeis (b. in Louisville, Ky., 1856) of Boston, Levy Mayer (b. in Richmond, Va., 1858) of Chicago, and Judge Max C. Sloss (b. in New York, 1869, recently re-elected Justice of the Supreme Court of California) of San Francisco, are but a few of the Jewish lawyers who have attained eminence in their profession.

While the number of Jews who are prominent in commerce, finance and industry is considerable, and some families, like the Guggenheims, Lewisohns, Schiffs or Strauses of New York, and men like Julius Rosenwald and Edward Morris (b. 1866) of Chicago, stand high in the world of large affairs, none of them is classed among the small number of immensely wealthy Americans. It is rather in the diffusion of wealth, in the large number and large proportion of well-to-do and affluent, than in the preeminence of the Jew as the greatest of capitalists, that the condition of the Jews in America is seen to the best advantage.

CHAPTER XLII.

LITERATURE: HEBREW AND ENGLISH. PERIODICALS.

Curiosities of early American Jewish literature which belong to the domain of bibliography—Rabbinical works: Responses, commentaries and Homiletics—Hebrew works of a modern character—Ehrlich's Mikra Ki-Peshuto and Eisenstein's Ozar Israel—Neo-Hebrew Poets and literati—Jewish writers in the vernacular—"Ghetto Stories"—Writers on non-Jewish subjects—Scientific works—Writers on Jewish subjects and contributors to the "Jewish Encyclopedia"—A. S. Freidus—Non-Jewish writers about Jews—Daly—Frederic, Davitt and Hapgood—Journalists, editors and publishers—The Ochs brothers; the Rosewaters—Pulitzer and de Young of Jewish descent—The Jewish denominational press in English—The "Sanatorium."

Jewish literature in the New World, as in almost all countries of the Old World, begins with Hebrew works of a religious nature, and branches out on one side into the special dialect which is spoken by the Jews among themselves, and on the other—into the vernacular. The strictly religious work is not the only one written in Hebrew for any length of time, for there is always a movement towards secular knowledge, which usually begins with a tendency to study Hebrew for its scientific value rather than for its sacredness. In modern times this process of development can be traced clearly in Germany, Holland, Poland and Russia, as well as in America, although here we are yet at the very beginning of our literary activity, and what has been accomplished until the present time may in the future be of more interest to the bibliographer than to the historian of literature. All that was written here by Jews for Jews in Hebrew, Judeo-Spanish and English until about the middle of the nineteenth century, including the works and periodicals that have been mentioned in the preceding chapters, while the authors or editors were under consideration, mostly belongs to the domain of curiosities.[1] It was only in the second half of the last century, when the number of Orthodox Jews and of those able to read modern Hebrew was fast increasing, that a serious attempt to write books for them was made in this country.

The strictly rabbinical works, like "responses" on disputed points of religious law or practice, commentaries on parts of the Talmud, and homiletic works, represent the continuation of the most ancient form of Jewish literature, and deserve to be treated first. According to Mr. Eisenstein, the honor of being the author of the first book of American "responsa" belongs to Rabbi Josep Moses Aronson (d. in New York, 1874), author of *Matai Moshe*, a work which, like numerous others by orthodox rabbis of this country, was printed in Jerusalem. Other rabbinical works, of which there were written in this country a larger number than is generally supposed, include *Heker Halakah* (New York, 1886), by Rabbi Aaron Spivak, formerly of Omsk, Russia; *Sefer Har-El* on tractate Bikkurim of the Jerusalem Talmud by Rabbi Abraham Eliezer Alperstein (Chicago, 1886); *Shoel Ke-Inyan* (Jerusalem, 1895), by Rabbi Shalom Elhanan Joffe (b. in Russia, 1845); *ha-poteah, we-hahotem,* by Rabbi Benjamin Gitelson of Cleveland (New York, 1898); *Torat Meir* on Rashi's Talmudical commentary, by Meir Freiman (New York, 1904); *Yegiot Mordecai* on the Talmud by Mordecai Garfil (Piotrkow, 1907); *Bet Abraham,* by Rabbi Abraham Eber Hirshowitz (Jerusalem, 1908). The venerable Rabbi A. J. G. Lesser is the author of Bet ha-Midrash (Chicago, 1897), which

[1] Those who want to follow up the subject, which is by no means uninteresting, are referred to *Early Jewish Literature in America*, by Geo. A. Kohut, in "Publications" III, pp. 103-47, and to J. D. Eisenstein's *The Development of Jewish Casuistic Literature in America*, ibid XII, pp. 139-47.

contains homiletics and halaka, and Rabbi Moses Simon Sivitz of Pittsburg (b. 1855) is the author of four books on various rabbinical subjects, all printed in Jerusalem. The number of works on "derush" or homiletics is still larger, and includes ha-Emet ha-Ibriah (Chicago, 1877) and *Or Haye Lebabot* (New York, 1885), by Jehiel Judah Levinsohn (d. in New York, 1895); *Ateret Zebi,* by Rabbi Zebi Lass (New York, 1902); *Nehmad le-Mare,* by Zeeb Dob Wittenstein (Cleveland, 1903); *Shebil ha-Zohab,* by Rabbi Baruch Kohen (New York, 1903); *Maaseh Hosheb,* by Rabbi H. S. Brodsky of Newark (New York, 1907). *Teome Zebiah* (Chicago, 1891), by Baruch Ettelson (1815-91), on some difficult passages in Agadah, and *Shaare Deah* (New York, 1899), by Rabbi Shabbetai Sofer, belong to the same class, though of a somewhat different nature.

The first substantial Hebrew book printed in America, *Abne Joshua* (New York, 1860), by Joshua Falk ben Mordecai ha-Kohen, though nominally a rabbinical book, actually belongs to the more secular class of literature, which borders on *Haskalah.* The same can also be said of Holzman's *Emek Rephaim* (New York, 1865), and perhaps also of *Tub Taam* in defense of the Jewish method of slaughtering cattle for Kosher food, by Aaron Zebi Friedman of Stavisk (1822-66), which is said to have been translated into English, German and French.[1] *Ha-Mahnaim* (New York, 1888), by Mayer Rabinowitz, and Wolf Schur's *Nezah Israel* come nearer to the spirit of modernity or "enlightenment," while works like *ha-Dat we-ha-Torah* (New York, 1887) and *Meziat ha-Shem we-ha-Olam* (ibid, 1893), by Shalom Joseph Silberstein (b. in Kovno, 1846; a. 1881), go far in the direction of free thinking. Valuable contributions to the Science of Judaism were made by Nehemiah Samuel Libowitz (b. in Kalna, 1862; a. 1881), author of a biography of Leon Modena (New York, 1901) and other works; by Benzion Eisenstadt, au-

[1] See Dr. B. Drachman, *Neo-Hebraic Literature in America*, appended to the Seventh Biennial Report of the Jewish Theological Seminary Ass'n (New York, 1900).

thor of *Hakme Israel be-America* (ibid, 1903); by Arnold B. Ehrlich (b. in Wlodowka, Russia, 1848), author of a remarkable commentary on the Bible which he calls *Mikra Ki-Peshuto* (Berlin); by Abraham H. Rosenberg (b. in Pinsk, 1838; a. 1891), of whose *Ozar he-Shemot,* a Cyclopedia of Biblical literature, four volumes were issued in New York; and by Judah David Eisenstein, a prolific writer in Hebrew and English, who is now editing the *Ozar Israel,* a Hebrew Encyclopedia, of which seven volumes have appeared, and to which the editor is himself the principal contributor of articles. Rabbi Mordecai Zeeb (Max) Raisin (b. 1879) is the author of a short "History of the Jews in America" in Hebrew, which appeared in Warsaw, Poland, in 1902.

Of literature in the restricted sense, or fiction, hardly anything worth mentioning was written in Hebrew in America. But the study and writing of neo-Hebrew cannot be thought of without the production of poetry, and some collection of Hebrew songs possessing considerable merit were published in this country, mostly by authors who acquired their reputation abroad before arriving in this country. The poetical works of Naphtali Hirz Imber, Menahem Mendel Dolitzki and Isaac Rabinowitz ("Ish Kovno," d. in New York, 1900, aged 54) belong to that class, and the same can be said of the quasi-scientific works of Joseph Loeb Sossnitz (1837-1910) and Ephraim Deinard (b. 1846), who has recently compiled a list containing about six hundred names of works in Hebrew and Yiddish which appeared in the United States. There were also some earlier writers of Hebrew poetry in America, notably Moses Aaron Schreiber, who composed the Centennial poem *Minhat Yehudah* in 1876, and the hazzan Hayyim Weinshel (1834-1900), author of *Nitei Naamonim* (New York, 1891). Gerson Rosenzweig, the epigramatist and author of the excellent Talmudical parody, *Maseket America,* who has also translated the American national songs into Hebrew, came here a young man, and his talent is more distinctively American.

The Hebrew periodical literature, which begins with Hirsch Bernstein's *ha-Zofah be-Erez ha-Hadashah* (1870-76), which was mentioned in a former chapter, was never securely established in this country up to the present time. Most of the Hebrew Journals or magazines, like Deinard's weekly *ha-Leomi* and Rosenzweig's monthly *Kadimah,* existed for less than a year. The *Hekal ha-Ibriyah,* edited by N. B. Ettelsohn and S. L. Marcus in Chicago, appeared from 1877 to 1879 as a supplement to their Judeo-German *Israelitische Presse.* Michael Levi Rodkinson (Frumkin, d. in New York, 1904, aged 59), who later prepared a translation of parts of the Babylonian Talmud into English, edited his weekly *ha-Kol* in New York for about two years (1889-90). Wolf Schur's *he-Pisgah,* which was later called *ha-Tehiyah,* appeared irregularly in New York, later in Baltimore, and still later in Chicago, during the last decade of the nineteenth century. The monthly *Ner ha-Maarabi,* edited by Abraham H. Rosenberg and later by Samuel Schwarzberg, existed less than three years (1895-97), and another monthly, *ha-Modia la-Hadashim,* edited by Herman Rosenthal and Abraham H. Rosenberg (1900-1), had a still shorter life. The weekly *ha-Ibri,* which was founded by K. H. Sarasohn and edited by Gerson Rosenzweig, appeared regularly from 1892 to 1898. Moses Goldman (b. 1863; a. 1890) began the publication of his *ha-Leom* as a monthly in 1901; it later appeared for several years as a weekly and afterwards for a short time as a daily. Since its suspension America had no other Hebrew periodical until the neo-Hebrew litterateur, Reuben Brainin, began to publish in New York (1911) his weekly *ha-Deror,* of which fifteen numbers appeared. Rosenzweig's monthly *ha-Deborah* and Rabbi T. Isaacson's *ha-Rabbani,* also a monthly, are now the Hebrew periodicals appearing in the United States.

* * * * *

The contribution of Jews to American literature consists mostly of descriptions of Jewish life, and of what has lately became known as "ghetto stories." Emma Lazarus, whose work was described in a preceding chapter, did not confine herself to Jewish themes, and was followed in this respect by other Jewish writers of her sex, like Mary Moss, the critic; Martha Morton, the playwright, and Emily Gerson Goldsmith, the author of Juvenile stories. Annie Nathan Meyer, the founder of Barnard College (Columbia University, New York), also belongs to this class of writers; while Martha Wolfenstein (1869-1906) of Cleveland, O., belongs to the front rank of the other class of writers who attempted to depict Jewish life in this country or abroad. To the latter class belong Herman Bernstein (b. 1876; a. 1893), who writes on Russian as well as on Jewish subjects; Rudolph Block (b. in New York, 1870), the journalist, who writes of Jewish life under the pen-name "Bruno Lessing"; Ezra S. Brudno (b. 1877); Abraham Cahan, the labor leader and Yiddish journalist; Isaac K. Friedman (b. in Chicago, 1870), and James Oppenheim (b. in St. Paul, Minn., 1882), who has also written on other than Jewish subjects. To the same class may be added Rabbi Henry Iliowizi (b. in Russia, 1850; d. in London, Eng., 1911), who has lived in the United States more than twenty years and has written poetical and prose works, mostly on Jewish and Oriental subjects. Bret Harte, the poet and novelist, was of Jewish descent, but he cannot be considered a Jewish author.

The works written on scientific subjects by Jews who have attained eminence in various branches of knowledge, some of whom were mentioned in the preceding chapter, are of a comparatively high standard of value. To these may be added the works of the art critic, Bernhard Berenson (b. in Wilna, Russia, 1865), who now resides in Italy; of the anthropologist, Franz Boas (b. in Germany, 1858), of Columbia University, and of the statistician, Isaac A. Hourwich (b. in Wilna, 1860; a. 1891), who is also an occasional contributor to the Jewish press. Morris Hillquit (b. in Riga, Russia, 1869; a. 1886), the Socialist leader and historian of Socialism in the United States, has likewise often written for various radical periodicals. Arnold W. Brunner (b. in New York, 1857), the architect, has written works on "Cottages" and on "Interior Decorations."

A considerable number of works on a variety of Jewish subjects were written by American-Jewish scholars. David Werner

Photo by Elton, Cleveland, O.

Martha Wolfenstein.

Amram (b. in Philadelphia, 1866) wrote *The Jewish Law of Divorce* (1896); Maurice Fishberg (b. in Russia, 1872; a. 1890) is the author of *The Jews: a study of Race and Environment* (1911); Julius H. Greenstone (b. in Russia, 1873) wrote on *The Messiah Idea in Jewish History* (1906); while Max J. Kohler, Geo. A. Kohut, Henry S. Morais and numerous others wrote on American-Jewish history in separate works, in the "Publications" and in the *Jewish Encyclopedia*. Isaac Markens (b. in New York, 1846) is the author of *The Hebrews in America* (1888), whose valuable material, like that contained in the works of the others mentioned here and in the notes, was utilized in the preparation of the present work. Abraham Solomon Freidus (b. in Riga, Russia, 1867; a. 1889), the eminent Jewish bibliographer at the head of the Jewish department in the New York Public Library, which contains one of the most valuable collections of Hebraica and Judaica in the world (donated by Mr. Jacob H. Schiff), is the author of bibliographical lists of Jewish subjects and of "A Scheme of Classification for Jewish Literature," which is of great value to Jewish bibliophiles and librarians. Alois Kaiser (1840-1908) and William Sparger are authors of *A Collection of the Principal Melodies of the Synagogue* (Chicago, 1893), and Platon G. Brounoff (b. in Russia, 1863), the composer, has published, among other works, a volume of Jewish folk-songs.

The most notable of the books on Jewish subjects written by Gentiles in the United States is *The Settlement of the Jews in North America*, by Charles P. Daly (1816-99), which was one of the sources of the present work. Dr. Madison C. Peters has written several popular and sympathetic works about the Jews; while Harold Frederic's *The New Exodus* (New York, 1892) gives a vivid description of the conditions in Russia at the time of the renewed expulsions from Moscow and other places in 1891. Hutchins Hapgood, author of *The Spirit of the Ghetto*, and Myra Kelly (Mrs. Allan Macnaughton; d. 1910) are among those who attempted to describe the Jewish immigrant in his new surroundings in the thickly settled quarters in the first period after his arrival, when he was in many respects unintelligible to himself, as well as to others.

As journalists, editors and publishers of newspapers, a number of Jews have occupied, and still occupy, prominent positions. Mordecai Manuel Noah was one of the influential newspaper men of New York in his time (see above p. 162). Edwin de Leon, who has also been mentioned in a former chapter, was the editor of the *Southern Press* of Washington, which was at that time considered the representative organ of the southern people at the national capital. Barnet Phillips (b. in Philadelphia, 1828; d. 1905) was for more than thirty years connected with the *New York Times,* which is now published by Adolph S. Ochs (b. in Cincinnati, 1858), who married a daughter of Rabbi Isaac M. Wise. A younger brother, George Washington Ochs (b. in Cincinnati, 1861), is now at the head of the *Public Ledger* of Philadelphia, and still another brother, Milton Barlow Ochs (b. in Cincinnati, 1864) was managing editor of the *Chattanooga Times* and is now the publisher of the *Nashville American.* Morris Phillips (1834-1904) was the chief editor and proprietor of *The New York Home Journal* for a generation. Edward Rosewater (b. in Bohemia, 1841; a. 1854; died in Omoha, Neb., 1906) was for many years the editor of the *Omaha Bee,* which became under him one of the great newspapers of the Middle West, and is now edited by his son, Victor Rosewater (b. in Omaha, 1871), who was a member of the Republican National Committee for the State of Nebraska. Philip Rapoport (b. in Germany, 1845) was for nearly twenty years editor of the *Indianapolis Tribune.* Samuel Strauss, of Des Moines, Ia., owned the *Register and Leader* there, and was later publisher of the *New York Globe.* Joseph Pulitzer (b. in Hungary, 1847; a. 1864; d. 1911) of the *New York World* was of Jewish descent, and so is Michael Harry de Young (b. in St. Louis, 1848), who owns and edits the *San Francisco Chronicle.* Solomon Solis Carvalho (b. in Baltimore, 1856), the son of the artist, Solomon

Mordecai Manuel Noah.

N. Carvalho, is the general manager of W. R. Hearst's newspapers. A large number of Jews hold various positions on the staffs of newspapers and magazines all over the country, from editors, literary, dramatic and musical critics down to reporters. Many are also engaged in the business parts of the work, as publishers, advertising managers, etc.

The most important of the older Jewish periodicals in the vernacular were mentioned in former chapters. The *Menorah Monthly*, which was for many years edited by Moritz Ellinger (b. in Bavaria, 1830; d. in New York, 1907), was the best Jewish magazine in America, as well as the one which existed for the longest time. *The New Era Illustrated Mabazine*, which was published for several years by Isidor Lewi (b. in Albany, N. Y., 1850), of the editorial staff of the *New York Tribune*, was an other valuable periodical. The Zionist *Maccabean* is now the only Jewish monthly magazine published in America. There is one semi-monthly, the *B'nai B'rith Messenger*, of Los Angeles, Cal. (established 1897), and over twenty weeklies, most of which are of only local interest. The more important are: The *American Hebrew* of New York, established 1879, by Philip Cowen (b. in New York, 1853); the *American Israelite* and its Chicago edition, founded by Isaac M. Wise in 1854; The *Emanuel* of San Francisco, Cal., which was founded in 1895 by Rabbi Jacob Voorsanger (b. in Amsterdam Holland, 1852; d. 1908); *The Hebrew Standard* of New York, established 1883 by Jacob P. Solomon (b. in Manchester, Eng., 1838; d. in New York, 1909); *The Jewish Comment* of Baltimore, established 1895, of which Louis H. Levin (b. in Baltimore, 1866) is the editor; *The Jewish Exponent* of Philadelphia, established 1886; *The Jewish Voice* of St. Louis, established, in 1884, and still edited by Rabbi Moritz Spitz (b. in Hungary, 1848); the *Reform Advocate* of Chicago, established, in 1891, and still edited by Dr. Emil G. Hirsch. One bi-monthly which deserves to be mentioned is the *Sanatorium*, edited since 1907 by Dr. C. D. Spivak (b. in Kremenchug, Russia, 1861) and published as the organ of the Jewish Consumptives' Relief Society of Denver, Colorado.

CHAPTER XLIII.

YIDDISH LITERATURE, DRAMA AND THE PRESS.

Yiddish poets of the United States equal, if they do not excell, the poets of the same tongue in other countries—Morris Rosenfeld—"Yehoash" and Sharkansky—Bovshoer and other radicals—Zunser—Old fashioned novelists—The sketch writers who are under the influence of the Russian realistic writers—Abner Tannenbaum—Alexander Harkavy—"Krantz," Hermalin, Zevin and others—Abraham Goldfaden and the playwrights who followed him—Jacob Gordin and the realists—Yiddish actors and actresses—The Yiddish Press—The high position attained by the dailies—Weekly and monthly publications.

Judeo-German or Yiddish literature has attained in this country a respectable state of development, and some of the better work done here compares favorably with the same kind of work in Russia. This is especially true of poetry and of the drama, though the first consists mostly of ballads or short lyrical songs, and the last rarely goes beyond adaptation. Morris Rosenfeld (b. in Russian-Poland, 1862; a. 1886) is considered the best Yiddish poet in the New World, and some of his works have been translated into English and several other European languages. Solomon Bloomgarden ("Yehoash," b. in Wirballen, Russia, 1870; a. 1892) is hardly less gifted, and the songs of Abraham M. Sharkansky (1867-1907) rank with the best in the language. The late David Edelstadt, Morris Winchevsky (b. in Russia, 1856; a. 1893) and I. Bovshoer (b. in Russia, 1874; incapacitated by sickness 1899) are the radical poets, in whose songs the tendency often overshadows the art. The old, popular bard, Eliakim Zunser (b. in Wilna, Russia, about 1840; a. 1889), has written some excellent songs since he came to this country. The most Jewish, and in some respect the greatest, of all Yiddish song writers, Abraham Goldfaden (b. in Russia, 1840; d. in New York, 1908), belongs as a poet, even more than as a playwright, to the Old World.

Of the old-fashioned novelists Nahum Meyer Schaikewitz ("Shomer," b. in Russia, 1849; d. in New York, 1905); Moses Seifert (b. in Wilkomir, Russia, about 1850; a. 1887) and the Hebrew poet, Dolitzki, are the best known representatives. Those who follow new methods are mostly sketch writers under the influence of the Russian realists, and they include, among others: Jacob Gordin (b. in Russia, 1853; a. 1890; d. in New York, 1909), Bernhard Gorin ("Goido," b. in Lida, Russia, 1868; a. 1893), Leon Kobrin (b. in Russia, 1872; a. 1892), Z. Libin (b. in Russia, 1872; a. 1893), and David Pinski, all of whom have also written for the stage and for various periodicals. Of the numerous writers, or rather translators and adapters, of long sensational stories which appeared serially in *Heften* or in newspapers, and later in bulky volumes, only one, the originator, deserves to be mentioned.

This one is Abner Tannenbaum (b. in Shirwint, Russia, 1848; a. 1887), the most useful Yiddish writer in America. His easy style made his writings intelligible to people who were not used to read at all, and he has thus helped to create the large audience whom he has been instructing for more than twenty years by his translations of stories containing much information about the physical and technical world, like those of Jules Verne, and by his innumerable articles on popular scientific and historical subjects.

Alexander Harkavy (b. in Novogrudek, Russia, 1863; a. 1882) has done much useful work for the Jewish immigrant from the Slavic countries in another direction, by writing a number of manuals of the English language, Yiddish-English, Russian-English, Hebrew-English, dictionaries, vocabularies, phrase-books, conversation books, letter writers, etc. He has also contributed much to Yiddish periodicals and edited several of them, including *The Hebrew-American Weekly* (New York, 1894), in which the Yiddish text was translated into English line by line.

"Philip Krantz" (pen-name for Jacob Rombro, b. in Podolia, 1858; a. 1890) is the author of several instructive works, including a *History of Culture* and an *English Teacher for Jews.* David M. Hermalin (b. in Vaslin, Roumania, 1865; a. 1886) has written and translated a number of works of a variegated character, from treatises on methaphysical subjects to extremely realistic stories. Israel J. Zevin ("Tashrak," b. in Russia, 1872; a. 1889), who has developed a typically American-Jewish humor, has published a collection of his humorous stories and descriptions of life among the semi-Americanized Jewish immigrants. Similar collections by other humorists, like A. D. Ogus and D. Apotheker (d. 1911), have also appeared in the last few years. Benjamin Feigenbaum, Dr. Abraham Kaspe and other radical propagandists have written many books and pamphlets of a quasi-scientific nature, mostly with the object of expounding their theories to the masses. B. R. Robbins was the publisher of a "History of the Jews" in Yiddish, the only work of that nature compiled in America.

The popular orator, Hirsch Masliansky (b. in Sluzk, Russia, 1856; a. 1895), is in a class by himself as the author of a book of *Yiddish Sermons* (1908).

The Yiddish drama, which grew less independently than any other part of its literature, attained its freest and highest development here. The melodramas and operettas of Abraham Goldfaden, several of which were written in this country, still remain the best pieces in the entire Yiddish repertoire, and bid fair to survive the more serious works of the later period. A large majority of the plays written or translated or adapted for the Yiddish stage in the United States belong to the same class as the Goldfaden plays, and in many of them his influence is clearly discernible. The most productive and successful playwrights of this class are, in order of their priority in this country: Joseph Lateiner (b. in Roumania about 1855; a. 1883), Moses Horwitz (b. in Stanislau, Galicia, 1844; a. 1884; d. in New York, 1910), and N. M. Schaikewitch and recently his son, Abraham S. Schomer. Rudolph Marks (Rodkinson), Feinman and Thomashefsky, the actors; Seifert, Sharkansky, Hermalin, Solaterevsky, Anshel Shor and others have written occasionally, with more or less success.

Jacob Gordin was at the head of a more serious school of Jewish dramatists in America, whose effort to introduce—also by translations and adaptations—the problem-play, the psychological play and the realistic play, on the Yiddish stage, began a new epoch, which is now practically ended. His good style and technique insured for some of his pieces a considerable popularity for a time, and they are now much played in the revived Yiddish theater of Russia. Z. Libin and L. Kobrin were for a time his most consistent followers, and several other literary men have attempted to follow in his footsteps. But aside from the temporary popularity of some plays, the school itself, which was founded on Russian ideals and conceptions, could not take root here. Bernhard Gorin and David Pinski have also written plays that possess literary merit, and so have several others who cannot be classed as followers of the new school.

The most talented actors and actresses of the original troupes which the founder of the Yiddish theater, Goldfaden, organized in Roumania, Russia and later in Austria, came to this country at various periods during the last three decades. They, together with other able players and managers who learned much from their American colleagues, have brought the Yiddish stage here to a higher state of development than it has reached in other countries. The most prominent among them are Jacob P. Adler (b. in Odessa, 1855; a. 1886) and his wife, Sarah; Sigmund Mogulesco (b. in Bessarabia, 1858), who arrived about the same time; Mrs. K. Lipzin; Mrs. Bertha Kalich, who has left the Yiddish for the American stage; Boris Thomashefsky (b. in Kiev, 1866; a. 1881) and his wife, Bessie; David Kessler, Regina Prager

Mme. Lobel, Bernhard Bernstein, Moskovich, Thornberg (d. 1911), Mrs. Epstein, Mrs. Abramowich, Blank, Glickman, Fishkind, Graf, Gold, Mr. and Mrs. Tobias, Mr. and Mrs. Tanzman, and others. Moritz Morrison, the German actor, occasionally appears on the Yiddish stage, and lately Rudolph Schildkraut, a native of Roumania, who was for some years prominent on the German stage in Europe, has settled as a Yiddish actor in New York.

Almost all the authors of Yiddish works mentioned above, and many of the playwrights, have written, or are still writing, for the Yiddish press, which has attained here its highest development. Influenced by the example of the American newspapers, the Yiddish press has in the last two decades, by the directness of its appeal, by the attention it pays to news and questions in which its readers may be interested, and by keeping in touch with the current of life, reached a height far above the level of Yiddish newspapers in countries where their potential audience is much larger. The *Jewish Gazette* of New York is now the oldest periodical in the world which is printed in Hebrew characters, and the younger popular weekly, *Der Amerikaner* (established 1904), has probably outdistanced all Jewish magazines of the past and the present. The Yiddish daily papers occupy the front rank among the foreign language newspapers in the United States in regard to circulation, probably because the sufferings of the Jews in the Slavic countries causes the immigrant Jew to remain interested in periodicals which bring the news and discuss the questions of his old home country, longer than is the case with non-Jewish immigrants. The oldest of the Yiddish dailies is the *Jewish Daily News,* now edited by Leon Zolotkoff, founder and for many years editor of the *Jewish Courier* of Chicago (established as a weekly 1887; daily since 1891). The next in age is the *Volksadvokat,* which was established as a weekly in 1887, from which grew the *Daily Jewish Herald* (1894), which in 1905 became the *Warheit,* edited by Louis Miller. The socialistic *Forward,* of which Abraham Cahan is the editor, was established in 1897, and, like the other two, appears in the afternoon. The *Jewish Morning Journal,* the fourth New York Yiddish daily, was founded in 1901 by Jacob Saphirstein (b. in Byelostok, Russia, 1853; a. 1887), its present managing editor; and it has also a Philadelphia namesake, under the direction of Jacob Ginsburg.

The *Jewish Press* of Chicago, the *Jewish Daily Press* of Cleveland, O., and the *Jewish Daily Eagle* of Montreal, Canada, of which Reuben Brainin is the editor, complete the list of Yiddish daily papers in America. Of the weeklies, the *Freie Arbeiter Stimme* (est. 1899) is mildly anarchistic; the Jewish *Labor World* (est. 1909) is the organ of the Chicago radicals; *Der Kibetzer* is the oldest of the humorous illustrated periodicals appearing in New York. There are also several trade papers, like the *Neue Post* of the garment workers and *Der Yiddishe Backer* of the bakers' union, etc.

The conservative *Volksfreund,* edited by Josephr Selig Glick, has appeared in Pittsburgh since 1889; *Das Yiddishe Folk* is the Zionist organ, established in New York 1909 and now edited by Ab. Goldberg; and *Der Yiddisher Record* of Chicago began to appear in 1910. The monthly *Zukunft* has had a checkered career since 1892, while Ch. J. Minikes' *Yom Tob Blätter* has appeared several times each year since 1897.

A class of professional writers and editors, some of them specialists of marked ability, grew up to supply the needs of the Yiddish publications, especially of the daily newspapers. Besides those mentioned above it includes among others: Gedaliah Bublik, J. L. Dalidansky, William Edlin, L. Elbe, J. Entin, Jacob Fishman, Dr. Fornberg, Jos. Friedkin, Israel Friedman, J. Gonikman, Dr. B. Hoffman, S. Janowski, E. and N. Kaplan, Z. Kornblith, A. Liesin (Wald), Jacob Magidoff, Ch. Malitz, Abraham Reisen, Bernhard Shelvin, Joel Slonim, Nathan Sovrin, J. M. Wolfson, Dr. Ch. Zhitlovsky and Israel Ziony. Of those who departed this life, M. Bukansky (1841-1904) and John Paley (1871-1907) deserve to be mentioned among those who contributed to the advancement of Yiddish newspaperdom in America.

CHAPTER XLIV.

PRESENT CONDITIONS. THE NUMBER AND THE DISPERSION OF JEWS IN AMERICA. CONCLUSION.

Dispersion of the Jews over the country and its colonial possessions—The number of Jews in the United States about three millions—The number of communities in various States—The number of Jews in the large cities—The number of the congregations is far in excess of the recorded figures—The process of disintegration and the counteracting forces—The building of synagogues—Charity work is not overshadowing other communal activities as in the former period, and more attention is paid to affairs of Judaism—The conciliatory spirit and the tendency to federate—Self-criticism and dissatisfaction which are an incentive to improvement—Our great opportunity here—Our hope in the higher civilization in which the injustices of the older order of things may never reappear.

Jews are living at present (1911) in every State and Territory of the United States, and there are small communities in Hawaii, Porto Rico and the Philippine Islands. There are some forms of Jewish organizations, synagogues, lodges or cemetery associations in more than 750 separate localities, from places where there is only a "minyan" on the High Holidays at the beginning of the Jewish year, to the immense Jewish community of New York City, which is estimated to consist of nearly 1,000,000 souls. Wherever actual figures as to the number of Jewish inhabitants in smaller places and the number of synagogues in larger cities are obtained, they are usually far in excess of the published figures and estimates, and there seems to be justification for placing the number of Jews in the country at not far below

3,000,000, if not actually at that number. While the largest communities, as well as the largest number of communities, remain in the East and the Middle West, the dispersion is much more extensive than is generally supposed.

There are, for instance, nearly forty cities and towns in Texas which have Jewish communities; other Southern States, like Alabama, Louisiana, Mississippi and Virginia, have each about, or nearly, half that number, and Arkansas, Georgia, North Carolina, South Carolina and Tennessee about ten each. Each of the new States of Arizona and New Mexico have three or four Jewish communities, Oklahoma has five; Florida, in the extreme South, and Maine, the furthest North, each have about a half dozen; California has more than both of them together; Washington has three, and Oregon one. Of the other far Western States Utah has two communities, Montana two, Nevada one, Idaho one, Wyoming one and Colorado nine.

Coming to the nearer Western States and toward the border States, we find four communities in Nebraska, eight in Kansas, twelve in Missouri, thirteen in Iowa, eight in Kentucky and five in West Virginia. North Dakota has five, Minnesota eight, while Wisconsin, with nineteen, and Michigan, with twenty-four, show the result of proximity to the great Central States where Jews have been settled in considerable numbers for the last two generations. Among those States Illinois has the largest number of Jews, owing to the great community of Chicago, while the number of cities containing Jewish communities—twenty-three—is somewhat smaller than that of Indiana, which has twenty-six, and of Ohio, with its twenty-seven. We notice the same in the two greatest States in the East, where, if we consider Greater New York City as one community, the number of places containing Jewish organizations is slightly less than in Pennsylvania, which has sixty-two such places. New Jersey has more than forty, and of the New England States Massachusetts leads with thirty-five, and Connecticut is second, having twenty. Rhode Island has seven; Vermont and New Hampshire four each. The list is completed with one community in the District of Columbia, five in Maryland and one in Delaware.[1]

Philadelphia and Chicago are, besides New York, the only two cities which contain about 100,000 or more Jews each. Boston has about three-fourths of that number, Baltimore, Cleveland and St. Louis about 50,000 each, and after them come in the order named: Newark, San Francisco, Pittsburg and Cincinnati (with about 30,000 each); Detroit, Buffalo, Providence and Jersey City, each having about half of that number, while Rochester, Syracuse, New Haven, Milwaukee, Louisville, New Orleans and Kansas City belong to the class which have 10,000 or more. The twin cities of Minneapolis and St. Paul would belong to that class if they were considered as one, which they really are. Washington, the national capital, belong to the class of cities having between 5 and 10,000 Jews, which includes Albany, N. Y.; Columbus, Ohio; Dallas, Tex.; Denver, Colo.; Fall River, Mass.; Hartford, Conn.; Indianapolis, Ind.; Los Angeles, Cal.; Memphis, Tenn.; Omaha, Neb.; Paterson, N. J.; Portland, Ore.; Scranton, Pa.; Seattle, Wash., and Trenton, N. J. There are some old and important settlements containing less than 5,000, but the number which would have to be included in a class of communities of that size is too large to be mentioned.

Congregations are continually being organized and synagogues built in localities where none existed before, thus showing a gradual dispersion of Jews to all parts of the country, while new houses of worship in the large cities usually owe their erection to consolidation or to the settlement in new neighborhoods. But only the buildings which are entirely devoted to religious services are apt to be noticed by those making records or gathering statistical material, while the small congregation which worships in a

[1] The figures are based on the exhaustive though necessarily incomplete *Directory of Jewish Local Organizations in the United States*, which appeared in the "American-Jewish Year Book" for 5668 (published in 1907), and allowance must be made for some omissions, as well as for increases in the last five years.

private dwelling is usually overlooked. The statistics about Jewish congregations in the United States are for this reason more defective than the figures about any other phase of Jewish activity, and the total given by the above mentioned Year Book (for 5669, p. 65), *i. e.*, 1745, for the entire country, should be doubled to be nearer the truth, even if the lowest estimate of the number of Jews in the country is accepted as the most probable one.

If it must be admitted that a process of disintegration is going on, in which the pessimist sees something worse than a transformation or re-adjustment to new conditions in a new world, it is, on the other hand, obvious that a strong effort is made to counteract the forces of dissolution. The various elements of the community, representing many countries and different strata of immigration, are coming together in a conciliatory spirit, as if instinctively impelled to co-operate. The widespread activity in the building of synagogues, in which many whose attitude was formerly indifferent, and even hostile, now participate, is only one phase of the attempt to preserve Judaism in this country. Much is done for charity and for Jewish education, the latter receiving more attention than ever before. The public school systems of most of the larger cities, following New York's example, have taken over the largest part of the work which was done before in Jewish institutions to Americanize the immigrant. Not only the proporton, but the actual number, of the dependents on charity is decreasing, and while the needs of Jewish charitable institutions are still great, more attention can now be paid to specifically Jewish matters than at the time when the problem of the material wants of the immigrants was overshadowing every other communal activity.

The attempts to organize on a more general scale, and to consolidate or federate existing organizations, which are frequently made and are more often successful than in the preceding periods, are the clearest manifestation of the spirit of the times in American Jewry. In most of the large cities outside of New York the important local Jewish charities are now federated, and the plan of federation is continually gaining in favor. The federations, of which there are now more than a dozen, and many other benevolent institutions of large and of smaller communities, are represented in the National Conference of Jewish Charities of the United States (organized 1899).

There is also noticeable in our communal life, as in American public life in general, that tendency to self-criticism which often degenerates into slander—that eternal dissatisfaction with things accomplished and with present conditions, which implies a sincere desire to achieve still better results. While this discontent and the poor opinion which many of us have of the spiritual condition of the Jews in America are of immense value as incentives to improvement, it dims the eye of the foreign observer, especially if he comes from a country where complacency and self-praise are the rule. It may still be too early to summarize the communal activities of the Jews in America, or to attempt to indicate how far we have approached the solution of the most pressing problems. But signs of throbbing life are visible everywhere, and the interest of the individual Jew in Jewish affairs is increasing. There is, therefore, every reason to believe and to hope that the opportunity which is afforded here to set the Jewisht house in order—the best, and perhaps the first, in the diaspora—will be utilized to its full extent by the future generations of native American Jews.

We are happy to have no Jewish problem here, in the sense in which the term is understood in the backward countries of the Old World. We need not waste a part of our best energies in repelling attacks from an anti-Semitic press or a Judophobe party, and our usefulness to ourselves as well as to our neighbors is thereby enhanced. Members of strange and hostile races and nationalities get along together in this country much better than anywhere else in the past or the present time, and their native children emerge from the "melting pot" united by a patriotism and a desire for improved conditions and improved relations which characterizes the American. The secularity of the Government and the diversity of religious beliefs preclude the spread of the denominational bigotry which is the real cause of the persecution of the Jews in other countries; while the liberty and equality which are vouchsafed to every citizen must themselves be lost before the unfavorable conditions which prevail elsewhere can confront us here. The Jew can become an American and at the same time preserve his religious distinctiveness, which he can lose only by his own negligence or disloyalty. Let us hope that those who now earnestly work to strengthen and build up Judaism in America will be successful, and that the fate or Divine Providence which has preserved us for thousands of years brought us here to participate under new circumstances in the advancement to a higher civilization in which the injustices of the older one may never reappear.

INDEX.

B

D

G

M

O

P

S

T